MICROECONOMICS:

RESOURCE ALLOCATION AND PRICE THEORY

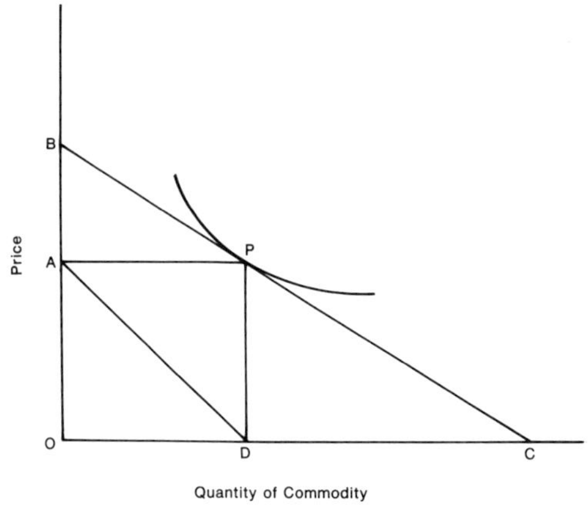
B
A
P
Price
O
D
C
Quantity of Commodity

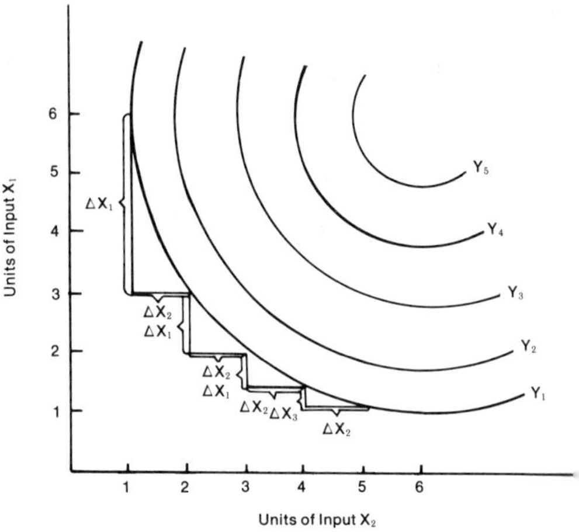
Units of Input X_1
ΔX_1
ΔX_2
ΔX_1
ΔX_2
ΔX_1
ΔX_2 ΔX_3
ΔX_2
Y_5
Y_4
Y_3
Y_2
Y_1
1
2
3
4
5
6
Units of Input X_2

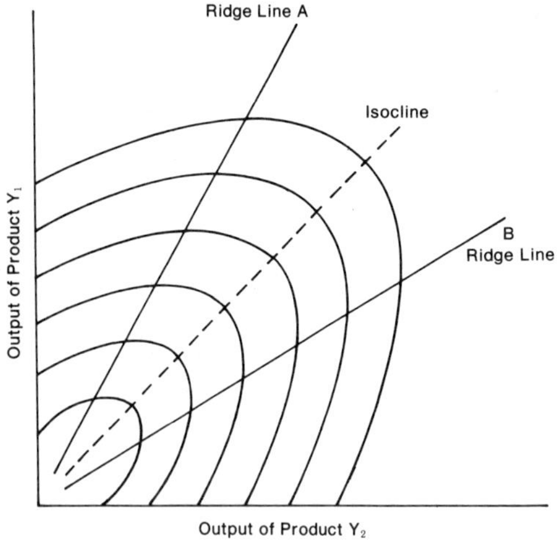
Ridge Line A
Isocline
B
Ridge Line
Output of Product Y_1
Output of Product Y_2

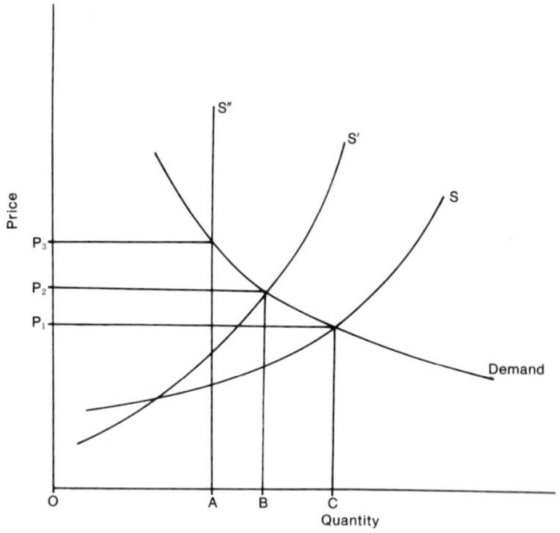
S″
S′
S
Price
P_3
P_2
P_1
Demand
O
A
B
C
Quantity

MICROECONOMICS:

RESOURCE ALLOCATION AND PRICE THEORY

Barbara J. Redman, Ph.D.

University of Georgia
Athens, Georgia

John C. Redman, Ph.D.

University of Kentucky
Lexington, Kentucky

AVI PUBLISHING COMPANY
Westport, Connecticut

Library of Congress Cataloging in Publication Data

Redman, Barbara J
Microeconomics, resource allocation and price theory.

Includes index.
1. Microeconomics. 2. Production (Economic theory. 3. Consumption (Economics) I. Redman, John C., 1921- joint author. II. Title.
HB172.R38 338.5 80-24922
ISBN 0-87055-367-4

Printed in the United States of America by
Eastern Graphics, Inc., Old Saybrook, Conn.

Preface

In this book we have tried to emphasize some of the principles of economics which we consider essential to begin serious study of problems in the business world. The book is selective rather than encyclopedic in nature with a belief that a student can best start serious study if he or she has a good grasp of microstatic economics from which to depart. Thus, most of the macroeconomic analysis which also is extremely important in a student's training is omitted from this volume.

We do not propose to present anything new in economic theory. Most concepts discussed in static economics nowadays are not new, as they have been handed down through the ages with some recasting from time to time. However, we have made several innovations in their presentation. First, we have stressed the unity of microeconomic theory, especially across production and consumption decisions. Regardless of context, the same economic principles operate. Second, we have made extensive use of geometry in providing examples for theories presented. It has been our experience that although the mathematical level of economics has steadily increased, students can visualize economic relationships more easily through graphs than through mathematical equations. This book was designed for a course where calculus is not a prerequisite. Third, the market structure section departs considerably from traditional treatment. Monopolistic competition and oligopolistic models are standard fare in most textbooks, but practically useless in actual application. We have dropped these models and substituted a continuum of market characteristics between perfect competition and monopoly.

In recent years, much progress has been made in adapting and using these economic concepts in examining problems associated with business and agriculture. We have provided several such illustrations throughout the text and especially at the end of its major subsections. A large number of examples can be cited, but we have tried to avoid an excessive number so the instructor can use his or her own favorite collection to illustrate the economic concepts.

We have found from experience that students majoring in economics, business and agricultural economics as undergraduates need to consider economic principles on a more advanced level than commonly taught in the introductory survey courses in principles of economics and in the more applied courses, such as marketing, introductory management, land economics, taxation and finance. We have also found that many beginning graduate students who either transferred from other fields of study such as agriculture, mathematics, psychology, sociology, etc., or did not have the opportunity to pursue economics to the level usually expected of beginning graduate students need a beginning course on an intermediate level covering some of the basic principles of economics necessary to analyze problems which are economic in nature. For such courses, we hope that this volume will lessen the burden for both the instructor and the students.

Much credit is due many teachers and writers who have tried to implant in us basic economic ideas. Their influence is obvious. Particular credit is due to our associates at the University of Kentucky, Iowa State University and the University of Georgia who in numerous ways contributed concept after concept to this collection. Also, the staff members of the Department of Economics at the University of Chicago contributed greatly to clarification of many concepts while the junior author was a postdoctoral fellow of the Social Science Research Council. We cannot begin to recognize with whom or where each idea had its origin, but the impact through either writings or personal contact with such economists as Friedman, Stigler, Knight, Boulding, Hicks, Harberger, Kaldor, etc., is obvious. Glenn Johnson, a former teacher and colleague, certainly contributed in guiding the junior author's thinking in economics. Our own graduate students have served as a constant source of inspiration and encouragement to develop a volume of this nature. Following Adam Smith's dictum that division of labor leads to increased productivity, the junior author was largely responsible for chapters on production and consumption, cost, and supply and demand, and the senior author entirely responsible for the chapters on market structure, capital, and general equilibrium in addition to revision of the other chapters and general editing of the total text. We alone assume the responsibility for the inaccuracies, inconsistencies and any shortcoming this volume may have.

These authors would also like to express their gratitude to Dr. N. W. Desrosier, Ms. Lisa E. Melilli, and Barbara J. Flouton of the AVI Publishing Company for their assistance and encouragement in bringing this book into being.

BARBARA J. REDMAN, Ph.D.
Athens, Georgia

JOHN C. REDMAN, Ph.D.
Lexington, Kentucky

May 1980

Contributors

BARCLAY, THOMAS N. Graduate Student. Department of Agricultural Economics, University of Georgia, Athens.

HASSAN, ZUHAIR A. Economist. Research Division, Economics Branch, Agriculture Canada, Ottawa.

JOHNSON, S.R. Professor. Department of Economics and Agricultural Economics, University of Missouri, Columbia.

OLSON, RUSSELL O. 2334 Millenium Lane, Reston, Virginia 22091

Contents

1

The Nature and Scope of Economics

DEFINITION OF ECONOMICS

Each person is involved in and has some idea of the meaning of "economics." However, definitions tend to vary. A particular difficulty in defining this discipline, as with any other, lies in trying to be general enough to cover all aspects of what is generally regarded as economics and yet be sufficiently specific to have a clear-cut meaning. Such definitions of economics as "a study of mankind in making a living," or "a science of wealth," or "economics is what economists do," are of such a general nature that one may still wonder what economics is about.

Considering a somewhat narrower scope of economics, a more informative working definition of economics is *the study of principles governing the allocation of scarce means among competing ends when the objectives of the allocation are to maximize the attainment of those ends.* Whether or not this is an adequate definition would depend partly upon what is to be emphasized. However, in activities where the emphasis is largely on production and consumption by individual units, this definition would be quite appropriate.

There are three parts of this definition worthy of a second thought. First, the *ends* are the objectives which motivate activity, whether they be profits of firms or wants of human beings. These ends may be more or less intermediate ends such as profit, prestige, power, leisure, etc., which finally reduce down to a common denominator: Satisfaction. Second, the *scarce means* can be considered as the resources which are versatile and capable of satisfying several different uses; yet, because they are limited, all uses cannot be satisfied at the same time. Third, there is a notion of *a maximum*. With this, it is assumed that a maximum fulfillment of what is sought is a logical aim of human activity.

SUBJECT MATTER OF ECONOMICS

Economics, which may thus be regarded as *the science of the satisfaction of human wants*, has assisted us in distinguishing the various functions which are exercised in satisfying those wants. It has enabled us to distinguish the services of the resources—land, labor and capital—which are coordinated by the entrepreneur to produce various goods which may be consumed directly or used for further production. It has set out a number of principles which, under certain circumstances, govern the production of goods and satisfaction of the wants of a society striving constantly to raise its standard of living.

All lines of endeavor are essentially parts of an integrated system organized to provide a living for all. The business person may not be keenly aware of being a member of a huge team each of whom is guided by pursuit of individual gain. Everyone has a vital interest in how well the economy performs and in the relationships therein. The farmer, for example, being human, has a special interest in the welfare of self, family and how the farm business fits into the complex economy. The farmer wishes to know, among other things, what determines his or her performance, how well he or she performs and the explanation of these performances in order to predict future events and to devise plans which will improve performance.

Economics goes far in providing such an explanation. The nature of economic activity is influenced greatly by the political and institutional framework of the area in which it occurs. In the United States, the economy is largely capitalistic, with a large measure of economic power residing with individuals. Because of this, the various resources, which are scarce relative to the demands for them, are utilized via the workings of the marketplace to satisfy the wants of humankind. Socialistic systems aim to attain the same results, yet the present wants of individuals are often foregone in favor of major nationalized endeavors. This is simply because the concentration of economic power in the government allows the setting of different economic goals, which are expected (by the planners) in the long run to benefit the individual more directly and fully. The planners in a socialist system usually have a distinct time preference for future (over present) consumption for the economy. This preference for the future cannot be directly enforced in a capitalistic economy.

FUNCTION OF ECONOMIC ANALYSIS

An analysis of economic problems goes beyond mere identification and description, although these are important segments of economic analysis.

Economic analysis consists essentially of construction of models which have relevance to the problems of explanation and correlation although these often are considered as a part of analysis. The use of a model which is a simplified system of fewer variables than found in real life, tested for internal logic and consistency, increases a person's ability to predict or understand why a prediction failed. One cannot isolate and understand the effects of single variables without holding other variables constant for the duration of analysis.

The primary function of economic analysis is to obtain and define knowledge of the basic forces which control the operation of the economic system and to show why the profit seeking motive impels the private producer to put the resources to uses which bring the largest yields. This is desirable for the following reasons:

(1) It is as important for an individual to accomplish some understanding of the economic system in which he or she lives and operates as it is to understand other aspects of daily life, even if only for the sake of knowledge itself.
(2) Knowledge of the principles explaining the many relationships within the economic system will enable more accurate predictions to be made of future events. For example, if it is known that the aggregate supply and demand of a certain product are relatively inelastic, a drastic change in prices can be predicted if a sudden shift in supply occurs unaccompanied by a comparable shift in demand.
(3) A knowledge of the principles of economic relationships would be necessary if the entrepreneur expects to exercise some control over his or her activities to his or her own advantage and to that of the economy.
(4) A knowledge of the principles of economic relationships would provide a basis for establishing a set of criteria for judging the efficiency of entrepreneurial or managerial activities, as well as that of the economic system, in achieving some desired ends or objectives.

FUNCTIONS OF THE ECONOMIC SYSTEM

The general purpose of an economic system is to organize resources in ways which will result in higher standards of living or greater satisfaction. Where division and differentiation of labor and effort are practiced, it is necessary to have a coordination of efforts. Any social group must have a mechanism to perform at least five tasks,[1] the performance of which constitutes the general task of an economic system.

(1) *The ends must be determined.* The determination of the quantities of the various goods and services that are to be produced can be considered from two viewpoints: the individual's and the society's. The individual demands those goods and services which he or she thinks will most satisfactorily meet his or her personal wants. However, the wants may be influenced consciously and deliberately or unconsciously and indirectly by the society in which an individual resides. The determination of what goods and services to produce is essential in the study of economic efficiency. The explanation and solution of economic problems related to this task lies largely in the theory of demand.

(2) *Resources must be allocated.* In order to provide the goods and services to satisfy the ends or desires as fully as possible, the resources must be allocated at three levels:
   (a) *The firm level*—Resources must be allocated within each producing unit (firm) in order to produce the desired goods and services.
   (b) *The industry level*—Some means must exist to allocate resources within each industry. For instance, which firms are to secure what resources and in what quantities is an important question.
   (c) *The economy level*—The allocation of the resources to the industries which produce the goods and services desired must be made. Depending upon the type of economy, the resources will be allocated either in a free market or through some governmental directive.

(3) *The product must be distributed.* The distribution of income plays a large part in the distribution of the product among the members of the economy. Money incomes depend upon the distribution and the productivity of the ownership of resources and the price paid for their use. The price system seeks to apportion the product to those who are productive at the expense of those engaged in unproductive activities.

(4) *Consumption must be adjusted in relation to the fixed supplies of goods and services.* In a short-run time span, the quantity of goods and services available for immediate use is relatively fixed. How-

[1] This section follows closely that of Knight, F. H. 1933. Social economic organization. *In* Syllabus for the Second Year Course in the Social Sciences, 2nd Edition. Univ. of Chicago Press, Chicago.

ever, given sufficient time to allocate or organize resources, it is possible to increase greatly the production of most goods and services to meet increased need. In the meantime, society must ration among users the temporary short supply of goods and services during the period prior to the increased production.

(5) *Expansion of the economic system must be provided.* One of the most important functions of the system of prices is to adapt the organization of economic activities to the ever-changing world. Population growth and improvement of its skills, discovery of new resources, accumulation of capital equipment, development of new production techniques and new forms of business organization must be provided for the satisfaction of the ever-changing wants of the citizens. These wants in turn are influenced by technological developments and by deliberate economic activities such as advertising. Thus, the institutional setting has an important impact on the decisions which determine the rate of change or amount of progress made. Such decisions are particularly important for resources fixed in supply since the more that is allocated to the future the less there will be available for immediate use. Thus, society must decide the rate and direction of expansion, the organization of resources to secure this end and the distribution of costs among its members.

RELEVANCE OF ECONOMIC INSTITUTIONS TO RESOURCE ALLOCATION

Economic principles which can be considered valid for all types of economic systems are generally those which make few assumptions as to the economic institutions which prevail in national economies. Many of these principles can be more relevantly ascribed to technical and human aspects than to purely economic or monetary ones. It will be found that economic principles which assume openly or tacitly the existence of the economic institutions of capitalism are valid only under capitalism or where some degree of freedom of enterprise occurs. Thus, a few principles, especially in the fields of value and distribution, depend directly upon the existence of such freedom and can claim little significance in situations where these institutions are not present. However, it could well be argued that basic economic principles are to some extent similar in different types of economies, and that efficient operation of any particular type of economic system depends upon the degree of application of these principles. This is already a possibility since all economic institutions provide the framework within which decision-making principles operate. Therefore, basic economic principles can be used to a large extent to evaluate the efficiency of an economic system, given certain criteria and objectives.

BASES OF ECONOMIC ACTIVITY

The basis of all economic activity originates from the desire to satisfy human wants which may be varied and many. Wants express the aims, ends or purposes of individuals. Within the elastic bounds of law and convention, the individual person is accorded discretion to formulate and pursue his or her own wants. Some people want as much leisure as possible, while others want an abundance of material goods ranging from the ordinary to the esoteric and extravagant purposes. There is virtually an infinite variety of personal conceptions of a "good life." Some seek intellectual attainment and/or power or prestige, while others are content with ordinary comforts habitually enjoyed. These ends or aims, whatever they may be, guide and motivate the individual in economic activity. These human wants or aims are governed to a large degree by custom or convention, habit and the desire to be alike or to be different from others. The charge that convention, habit, emulation and ostentation are irrational elements in the determination of wants presupposes that the critic has established canons of rationality. Such canons, in turn, may appear irrational to others.

BASIC PROBLEM AREAS OF ECONOMICS

From the preceding, the student may have realized that the study of economics is a complex and difficult science in all its ramifications. The task of a science is

(1) to describe
(2) to analyze
(3) to explain and
(4) to correlate the relationships

In order to better achieve the task, the basic problem areas of economics have been more or less arbitrarily placed into special phases.

There are many classifications of economic problem areas. A useful one is to divide first the whole field of economics into *macroeconomics* and *microeconomics*. Macroeconomics is that part of the study of economics which deals with the great aggregates and averages of the system rather than particular items within it, and attempts to define these aggregates in a useful manner and to examine their relationships.

In studying economic policy on the national or regional basis, macroeconomics is extremely important. Economic policies of the government are concerned with large groups and aggregates of individual economic units and not with the particular individual units. The national economy may be viewed as an aggregate of individual units, but the size of the national economy is not simply their summation since interrelationships between individual units prevent this. Thus, the business person must appraise ultimately the prospective action of the mass of other business people and consumers if he or she is to anticipate with some accuracy the best use to be made of his or her productive resources.

Microeconomics is the study of particular firms, particular households and related prices, wages, incomes, etc. The theory of the individual firm and industry and its important tool of marginal analysis are particularly useful in studying the many relationships found in business activity.

Another important classification of problem areas revolves around the organization of production or consumption. The organization of production, or *resource allocation*, involves questions of the optimum or best allocations of resources among different products at a given point in time and at different periods of time. These must be solved within the individual business firm.

The organization of consumption, or *income allocation*, is concerned with the allocation of the income or product among different consumption possibilities at a given point in time and over time. In beginning the study of basic economic principles or relationships, it is desirable to recognize this division of major problem areas in economics. However, as will be pointed out in subsequent sections, this rigid distinction becomes unrealistic. A knowledge of a few basic concepts provides enough tools for handling a wide range of problems. This fortunate situation arises from the fact that most problems involve making a choice of alternatives.

Additional problem areas have been added by some economists to supplement, but often they overlap the problems of resource and income allocation. The *economics of distribution* involves the study of the principles which govern what each contributing factor of production receives from the total product. If one accepts the idea that each factor should receive a share of the total product according to its contribution, then the principles of resource allocation would be a useful body of theory. The *economics of exchange*, which is concerned with problems related to the ratios at which goods are exchanged for one another, or their value in terms of money, is really the surface part or a continuation of the more basic study of principles of resource and income (consumption) allocation. *Economic dynamics* deals with problems of economic adjustments over time, including economic growth.

BOUNDARIES AND LIMITS OF ECONOMICS

Sciences are usually referred to as *disciplines*, which means they are systematic bodies of knowledge that contain statements of laws and principles universally accepted as being correct. Accepted economic principle provides a common logic whereby scientific objectivity and interpersonal validity of conclusions can be attained even in the absence of empirical data and analysis.

Most economic knowledge takes the form of establishing relationships. Economics has a high value in that it applies a technique of thinking and represents a distinct type of training of the mind. What a student of economics may obtain from such study is not so much in black and white but provides him or her with the tools for tackling a problem. Often the study of economics does not lead to tangible results until after a long period of study, practice and development of skill.

The modern theory of knowledge leaves no doubt that it is impossible to grasp reality without construction of theoretical formulae. In the broad fields of business and agriculture, research conducted in the various agricultural experiment stations and research institutes has made available an unlimited quantity of facts and figures. No single human mind can possibly comprehend and retain all of the possible facts related to a given subject. Through a process of classifying these facts, the finite mind can understand and encompass the basic laws and principles which relate to a particular field of science. Thus, an understanding of the relationships among the various classes of facts can be made which then can be applied to particular situations.[2] Goethe was reported to have said that the greatest thing would be to realize that everything factual implies a statement of theory.

Economics does not judge the goodness or the badness of the ends or wants of the society. This is a moral judgment and the responsibility for selecting the ends rests upon each person in the society. The definition of social ends must be left to the philosopher, the theologian, the statesman and to the public. The determination of what the people want in the way of goods and services and why they differ falls in the field of psychology (study of mental behavior), sociology (study of group behavior), anthropology (study of human race and culture) and perhaps physiology (the biological study of how organisms function).[3] It is not the task of eco-

[2] For a philosophical discussion of the nature and possibility of economic theory, *see* Redman, B. J. 1976. On economic theory and explanation. J. Behav. Econ. *5* (1) 161–176.

[3] For a complete discussion of the contributions of and the relationships among economics, psychology and sociology, *see* Redman, B. J. 1979. Consumer Behavior: Theory and Applications. AVI Publishing Co., Westport, Conn.

nomics to establish and explain precise technological laws that determine how inputs of resources are transformed into outputs of goods and services. Such questions need the help of such noneconomic studies as the physical sciences and engineering. Economics cannot and should not cover every fact of the universe. It must take certain things as given, or for granted, as having been established by workers in other scientific fields. Such factors as the institutional framework of society, tastes of individuals and technology are often taken as given in order to study certain problems and then relaxed in order to study others.

CHAPTER 1: REVIEW QUESTIONS

(1) What is economic theory?

(2) Many people have advocated abolition of research in agriculture because we already have the capacity of producing several times greater than the rate of consumption. How do you answer such people?

(3) In order to reduce the complexity of the "real" world to a more simple and manageable basis for analysis, economists resort to the concepts of static economics. What is meant by static economics and what assumptions are used to make an economy static?

(4) "It is not an exaggeration to say that, at the present day, one of the main dangers to civilization arises from the inability of the mind trained in the natural sciences to perceive the difference between the economical and the technical." Provide a framework within which this statement can be evaluated.

(5) Discuss the functions or tasks of an economic system.

(6) It has been noted that economic theory has, for the most part, been developed by Western economists and in reference to the relatively advanced economies; further, there is little economic theory designed uniquely for low-income countries. Accordingly, it has been suggested that the existing literature on economic theory has little relevance for today's low-income countries in Latin America, Asia and Africa.

Do you agree with the above paragraph? Explain carefully. (In your answer, indicate the nature and role of economic theory.)

2

Elementary Theory of Resource Allocation I

THE PRODUCTION PROCESS

Production is of central interest in the study of economics because it deals with so many problems. The firm buys or obtains control of goods and services which are often referred to as resources and transforms them into a product which is available for sale. Thus, production can be defined as *the creation of utility*. The firm which operates in a free enterprise economy is faced with many decisions and the purpose of the principles of resource allocation is to give the entrepreneur tools which may assist in decision-making.

Production results only when a number of factors or resources are combined. As shall be indicated subsequently, the productivity of one resource depends upon the level at which other resources are used. Thus, interrelationships exist among the resources employed. Among the forces which influence the entrepreneur in decisions on how to produce, what combination of resources to use, how much output to produce and what combination of products to produce is the technical knowledge of different combinations which are possible for producing the output of goods or services from available resources.

The principles involved in the production relationships provide not only the foundation for an analysis of costs and supplies of goods, but the basis for analysis of resource pricing and employment and the distribution of products.

ASSUMPTIONS OF STATIC ECONOMICS

Scholars who observe phenomena in order to isolate certain fundamental relations face the problem of not being able to observe an infinitely large number of complex facts since their minds are finite. Thus, it is important to note that almost any problem must be reduced to manageable proportions by classifying the observations and eliminating temporarily, or assuming "away" for the time being, those influences not deemed pertinent to the problem under study. The simple cases and simple relationships can be modified to approach reality more closely by relaxing the simplifying assumptions. The value of a theory depends upon its degree of closeness to reality, i.e., the ease with which the transition to real problems can be made without essential readjustments of the theoretical structure.

When the problem is abstracted from the influence of time, a static approach is achieved. Thus, the static situation may be likened to snapshots of the variables as they exist at a moment in time, i.e., the variables studied are not considered to change their values with time. When one instant of time is studied and compared with another instant of time, we have comparative statics. In order to facilitate analysis of problems in an ever-changing economy, several assumptions are usually made.

First, the production function is assumed to be fixed, which means that the state of arts or technology is fixed and that the total quantity of resources is fixed but the distribution between the firms is not fixed.

Second, the utility functions are assumed to be fixed which means that tastes, habits, customs and nonfirm institutions such as schools and churches do not change and, also, the population is considered constant or stable.

Third, assumptions are made with respect to motivation which include the assumption of maximization of satisfaction by consumers, of profits by firms and of incomes by owners of resources.

Fourth, assumptions are made with respect to the structure of institutions which include the conditions of a given governmental framework and an economy which permits free choice by economic agents.

Additional assumptions frequently made include rationality of human beings in the decision-making process and perfect knowledge and foresight. All of these assumptions may be fairly realistic in the short run with the exception of that pertaining to perfect knowledge and foresight. Of course, it can be argued that many decisions are made "against my better judgment" or on some emotional basis, but it can also be argued that they were rational according to their standards at that time. When the assumption of perfect knowledge and foresight is relaxed, an approach to the study of dynamic economics is being made. In a sense, when this assumption is relaxed, all assumptions are relaxed because we have incomplete knowledge about the economic phenomena which were previously assumed to be fixed at some level. However, the relationships to be described will hold for given states of the decision-maker's knowledge; the person will maximize utility, etc., on the basis of available information.

THE PRODUCTION FUNCTION

The physical relationship between the rates of inputs of productive services and the rate of output of the product is known as the *production function.* It is essentially a summary of the technological knowledge underlying the economic analysis of production. The production function changes as innovations are introduced since it is concerned with the physical aspect of production. Thus, it is external to economics and lies in the realm of production engineering. The technician should be able to tell us that given kinds and quantities of resources would result in a specific output of a given output. Thus, the output which a firm can produce is a function of (or depends upon) the quantities of resources used. This dependence can be expressed in a functional notation:

$$Y = f(X_1, X_2, X_3, \ldots, X_n)$$

When Y is the product or output, $X_1, X_2, X_3, \ldots, X_n$ represent the various resources or inputs involved in the production process; the letter "f" refers to "the function of." The nature or shape of the production function is influenced by the peculiarities of the factors used which must be accepted as given. These peculiarities may make the function flexible or rigid. In most cases, however, the technical conditions are such that the factors can be combined in varying proportions to produce a given output. Economics deals largely with the functional relationships existing among the variables.

Actually, when the output is a function of several inputs, $Y = f(X_1, X_2, X_3, \ldots, X_n)$, this does not express the amount of output "Y" that will change as the quantities of several inputs, $X_1, X_2, X_3, \ldots, X_n$, change. To express the quantitative relationship among the variables, the function must be expressed in some algebraic form, such as

$$Y = aX_1^bX_2^c$$

Mathematically, a variable "Y" is said to be a function of a second variable "X" if a relationship exists between them such that to each of a given set of values of "X" there corresponds one or more values of "Y." If only one value exists, it is said to be single valued. The variable to which values are assigned is known as the *independent* variable and the value obtained from these is known as the *dependent* variable; i.e., the value of the dependent variable is dependent upon the value of the independent variable.

In ultimate, long-run situations or in the planning stage when no resources are committed, all inputs are variable. However, the farmer in most cases faces the fact that for any particular period some of the inputs are fixed, such as barns and mechanical equipment, while others are considered variable, such as fertilizer, feed or hired labor. Those inputs which are variable and those which are fixed depend upon the conditions encountered; no hard and fast classification of fixed and variable inputs can be made for all situations. The symbol commonly used for separating the variable inputs from the fixed inputs in a functional notation is the vertical bar which is illustrated in the notation:

$$Y = f\ (X_1 \mid X_2, X_3, \ldots, X_n)$$

This means that the output Y depends upon the variable input X_1 with the other inputs $X_2, X_3, \ldots, X_n$ fixed at some level. As will be explained subsequently, when the level of any one or more of the fixed inputs is changed to a different level, the relationship between the output and the variable inputs is also changed.

THE FACTOR-PRODUCT RELATIONSHIPS

Many decisions fall within the framework of the factor-product relationships which are often referred to as input-output relationships. The question arises as to the quantity of an input required to produce a given output. More precisely, the most profitable level of the variable input to use with the fixed inputs is one of fundamental importance in production. For example, how much fertilizer should be applied to 0.4 ha (an acre) of crops, how much grain should be fed to a dairy cow or how much labor should be applied to 0.4 ha (an acre) of tobacco are typical questions faced by farm managers. To answer such questions, the entrepreneur must have some idea of (1) the relationship between the output Y and the input X_1 of the function:

$$Y = f\ (X_1 \mid X_2, X_3, \ldots, X_n)$$

and (2) the relative prices of output Y and input X_1.

Nature of Returns

The quantitative relationships between a single variable input and the variable output must be considered within the assumption that all other inputs are held constant at some level. The relationship of the function $Y = f\ (X_1 \mid X_2, X_3, \ldots, X_n)$ can take the form of any one of any combination of three possible forms:

(1) constant returns
(2) increasing returns and
(3) decreasing returns.

Constant Returns.—The relationship between the variable input factor X_1 and product output Y is linear; therefore, constant returns exist if all units of X_1 which are applied to the fixed input factors $X_2, X_3, \ldots, X_n$, result in additions to the total output of product Y which are equal over all values of X_1. When a function of this nature is graphed (Fig. 2.1) with the product output Y on the vertical axis and factor input X_1 on the horizontal axis, the resulting product curve would be a straight line. Thus, the function is said to be linear when the total product curve which relates the total output of product Y to the factor input X_1 is a straight line. This means that each additional unit of X_1 would yield exactly the same quantity of product Y as the preceding unit, and so a marginal physical product curve, which denotes the change in Y occasioned by a change in X_1, would be a horizontal line.

In farming, many recommendations are made based upon linear relationships, such as to apply a given amount of nitrogen per 35.4 liters (1 bu) of corn or a given quantity of total digestible nutrients per 0.45 kg (1 lb) of a given quality of milk. For example, the usual feeding recommendations for feeding for milk production imply a linear function of concentrates and roughage up to a limit, beyond which no additional milk is produced. According to the tables which appear in several publications, each 0.45 kg (1 lb) of grain will produce 1.04 kg (2.3 lb) of 4% fat-corrected milk, or each 2.27 kg (5 lb) input of grain will produce 5.2 kg (11.5 lb) of milk. When each of the 5.2 kg (11.5 lb) increments in output is graphed against the inputs, a horizontal curve results. This indicates a constant marginal physical product of grain.[1]

Much of the budgetary data used in research and recommendations also imply constant returns to the variable input. The assumption of linear relationships in data when nonlinear relationships are more appropriate makes users of the data very skeptical of the validity of the conclusions. However, linear relationships may be present within ranges, particularly in some engineering relationships, although not so frequently in biological activities. In industries where production is organized around a given producing unit, such as a cigarette machine, the output of products produced may be a linear function of the number of producing units used to their capacities.

Increasing Returns.—When successive units of the variable input X_1 are applied to the group of fixed inputs $X_2, X_3, \ldots, X_n$, if the resulting additions to the total output of product Y are increasing in quantity, then the nature of the relationship is one of increasing returns. Graph-

[1] *See* Redman, J. C. 1952. Economic aspects of feeding for milk production. J. Farm Econ. *34* (3).

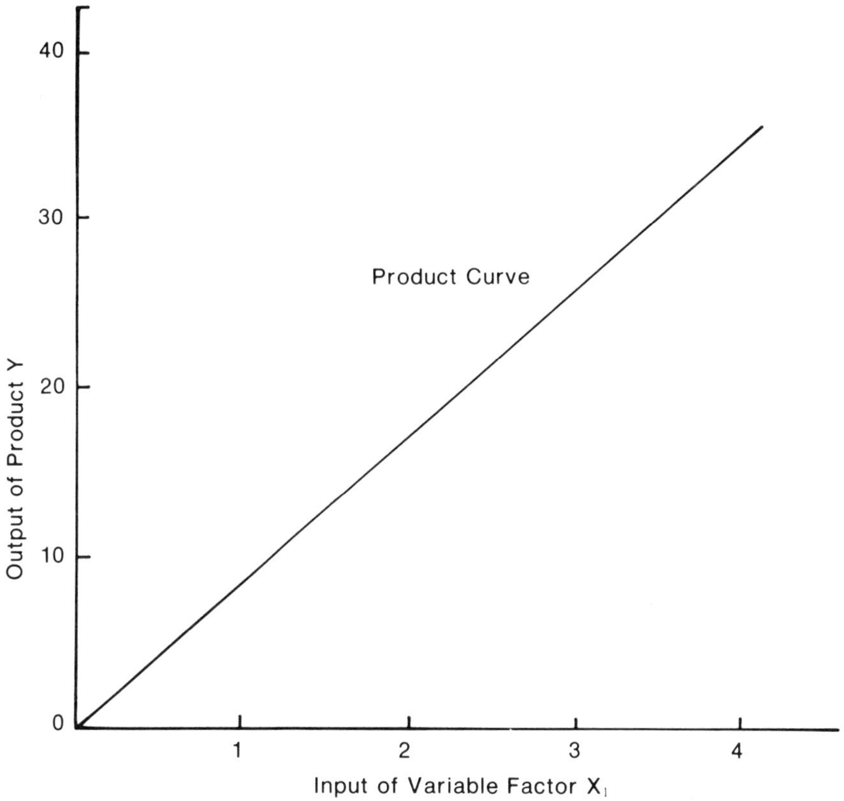

FIG. 2.1. PRODUCTION FUNCTION EXPRESSING CONSTANT RETURNS TO A SINGLE VARIABLE FACTOR

ically, the total physical product curve expressing this relationship would be rising at an increasing rate (Fig. 2.2). This relationship is likely to be found when relatively small quantities of a single variable input, say operating capital, are combined with relatively large quantities of fixed factors, such as land and other resources. However, it cannot be expected that increasing returns to operating capital will prevail indefinitely since larger and larger quantities of the variable input will be used. Optimum proportions of the variable input and the fixed inputs would soon be reached; if surpassed, there would be decreasing incremental returns to the variable input.

Decreasing Returns.—Decreasing returns to a single input factor X_1 exist when each additional unit of input adds less to the total output of product Y than the previous unit. In this situation, the relationship of Y and X_1 is not linear since the total physical product increases at a decreasing rate (Fig. 2.3). Decreasing returns, often referred to as di-

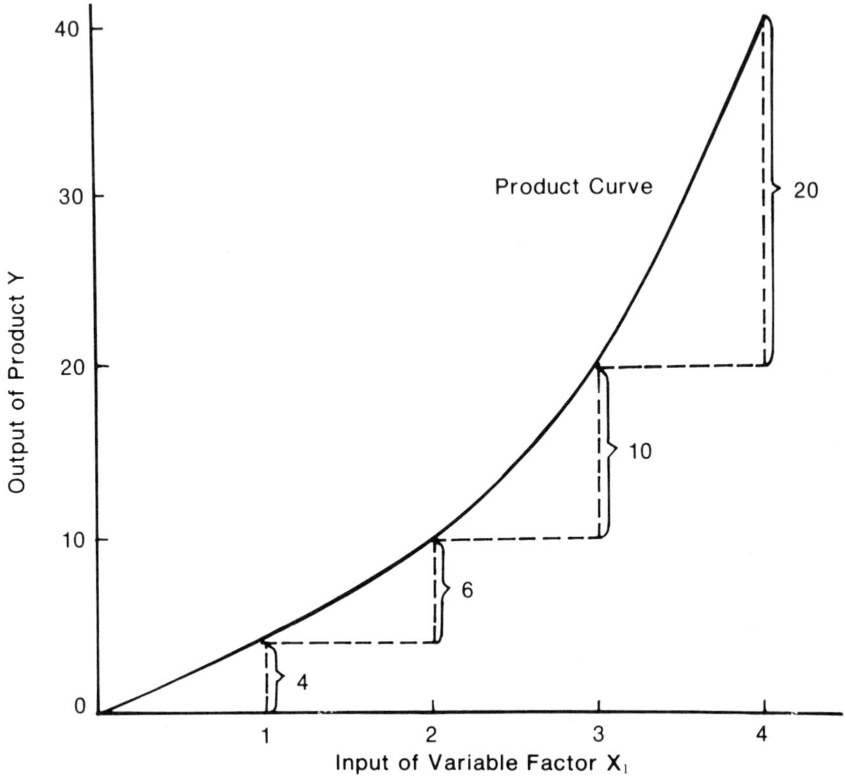

FIG. 2.2. PRODUCTION FUNCTION EXPRESSING INCREASING RETURNS TO A SINGLE VARIABLE FACTOR

minishing returns, may or may not occur in actual situations for the first few units of the variable input.

The classical law of diminishing returns combines the phase of increasing returns and the phase of decreasing returns, but most texts perhaps tend to overemphasize the importance of the phase of increasing returns. It has academic interest, but from a practical viewpoint it constitutes a phase of irrational production. The classical principle states that if the input of one resource is increased by equal increments per unit of time while the inputs of other resources are held constant, the total product will increase first at an increasing rate and then beyond some point of use the total product will increase at a decreasing rate. Consider the production of learning as a function of study time. The first few half-hours of studying greatly increase a student's knowledge of a particular subject. As time passes, however, an extra half-hour of studying is less and less beneficial for learning the given material. If enough of the input of the variable resource (study time) is added to the fixed factors

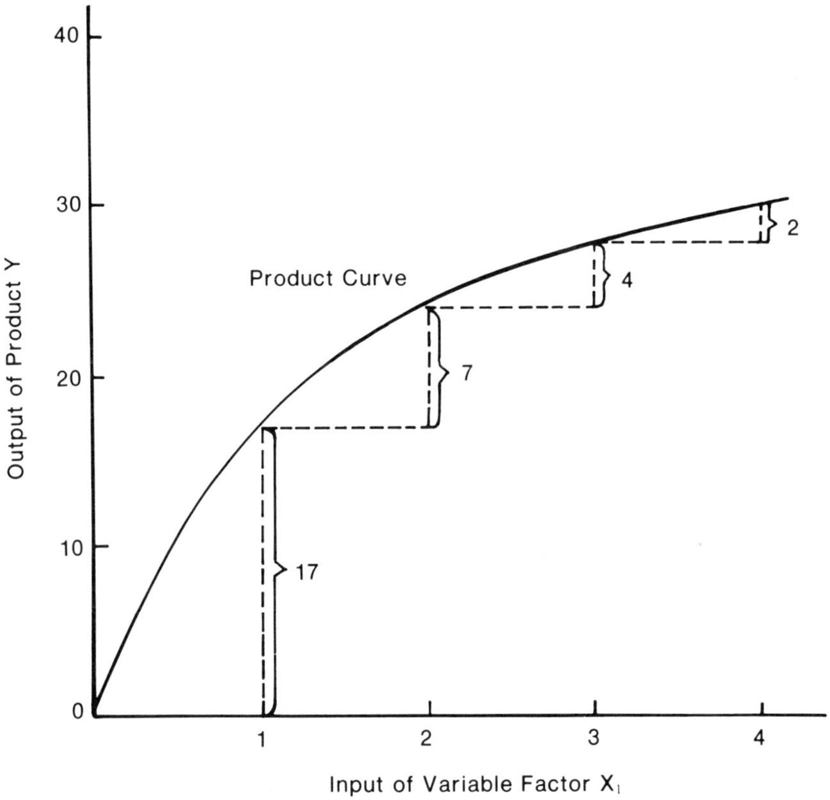

FIG. 2.3. PRODUCTION FUNCTION EXPRESSING DECREASING RETURNS TO A SINGLE VARIABLE FACTOR

(i.e., the textbook), the total product will eventually reach a maximum and then may decline (in this case, perhaps through overfamiliarity with the text or simple exhaustion).

The concept of diminishing returns, which is fundamentally a law of technology, was perhaps first lucidly expressed by Turgot, a distinguished French physiocrat, and has become increasingly important in the thinking of all people, particularly scientists. No one has ever discovered or proved any important exceptions to this important principle. Several reasons have been advanced why variations in rate of return are observed. One reason stresses the indivisibility of the fixed factor. This argument, which carries much weight, rests on the belief that if the fixed factor were finely divisible there would not exist varying rates of returns to each unit of variable factor used. There exists a strong appeal in this explanation of perfect divisibility and, thus, constant returns to the variable input. This reason, if accepted, renders the second reason superfluous which rests on the idea that superior efficiency or a more effective organization of resources is obtained when a large quantity of resources is used. It is argued that one resource aids another. How much aid can exist depends upon the quantity of the resource. If the fixed factor is large in relation to the units of variable factor, the variable units receive much aid. As the number of units of the variable factor increase, they receive less and less aid from the fixed factor. This reason is essentially the same as the other.

The Product Curves

Curves are useful in depicting the relationships found in studying variables. They are easy to use and are adequate for economic work on an intermediate level. The curves can be almost of any nature and there is no one graphical illustration that will represent all possibilities of all firms since obviously situations vary greatly. However, a graphical illustration has been generally accepted to represent the general relationships (Fig. 2.4) of a factor-product function.

The Total Product Curve.—The fundamental curve involved in analysis is the total physical product curve (TPP) which represents the relationship between the product Y and the variable input X when other inputs are fixed at some level (Fig. 2.4). When the TPP curve is drawn to be continuous, it is assumed that the units of the variable input are perfectly divisible. The total product in liters (bu) of corn of a given number of units of the variable input of nitrogen is obviously the amount secured by the assistance of that quantity of nitrogen. When the dollar value is assigned to the total physical product, a total value product (TVP) is obtained. Sometimes this curve is also known as the total revenue curve. Thus, the total product curve (Fig. 2.4) can be referred to as total physical product (TPP) or total value product (TVP) depending upon whether the physical relationships or value relationships are being considered.

The Average Product Curve.—The average physical product (APP) of a given number of units of the variable input results when the total physical product is divided by the number of units of the variable input required. The average physical product reaches its maximum at the point where a straight line drawn from the origin is tangent to the total physical product curve (Fig. 2.4). In other words, a line from the point of tangency with the TPP curve to the origin will give the largest angle obtainable from any point on the TPP curve. If the angle increases as more inputs are added, the APP is increasing; if the angle decreases as more inputs are added, the APP is decreasing. A different straight line

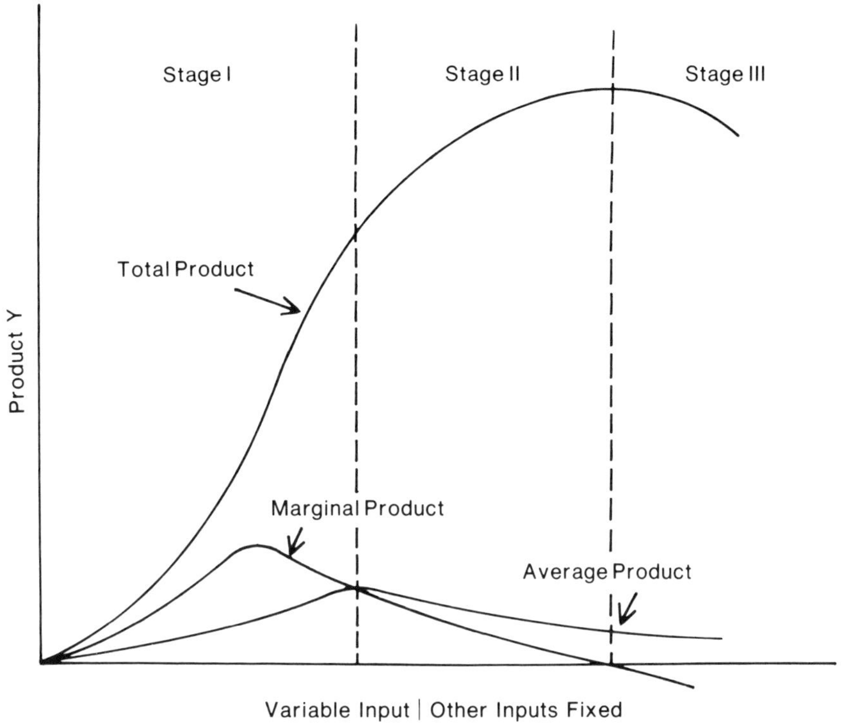

FIG. 2.4. VARIOUS PRODUCT RELATIONSHIPS

from the origin exists for each point on the total product curve and only one can have a maximum slope. When the average physical product is assigned a dollar value, an average value product is obtained. The average product curve illustrates the value or physical output per unit of input, such as output of corn per man-hour, output of corn per kg (lb) of nitrogen, or output of milk per 45.4 kg (100 lb) of feed. Often research projects in agriculture are designed to determine the maximum output per unit of input which forms a recommendation to farmers. As will be seen subsequently, this type of recommendation has very little value from an economic viewpoint.

The Marginal Product Curve.—The most significant and useful curve involved in studying the productivity of a unit of resources is the marginal physical product curve (Fig. 2.4). This curve is the first derivative of the total physical product curve. This means that the marginal physical product curve expresses the rate of change in the total physical product, e.g., the amount added to the total physical product by the addition of another unit of the resource.

The slope of the total physical product curve is equal to the marginal physical product. However, in many practical situations, the average marginal physical product would be appropriate in making decisions because there is little need to have the resource in infinitely small units, such as grams (0.4 oz) of nitrogen or feed, as would be required in the exact or instantaneous rate of change. The difference between the marginal product and the average marginal product becomes clear when one examines the derivation of the marginal curves more fully.

In a function in which the product Y increases as the input X increases (Fig. 2.5) one may ask at what rate the product Y is increasing with respect to the input X at any point P (x, y). To answer this, first let the

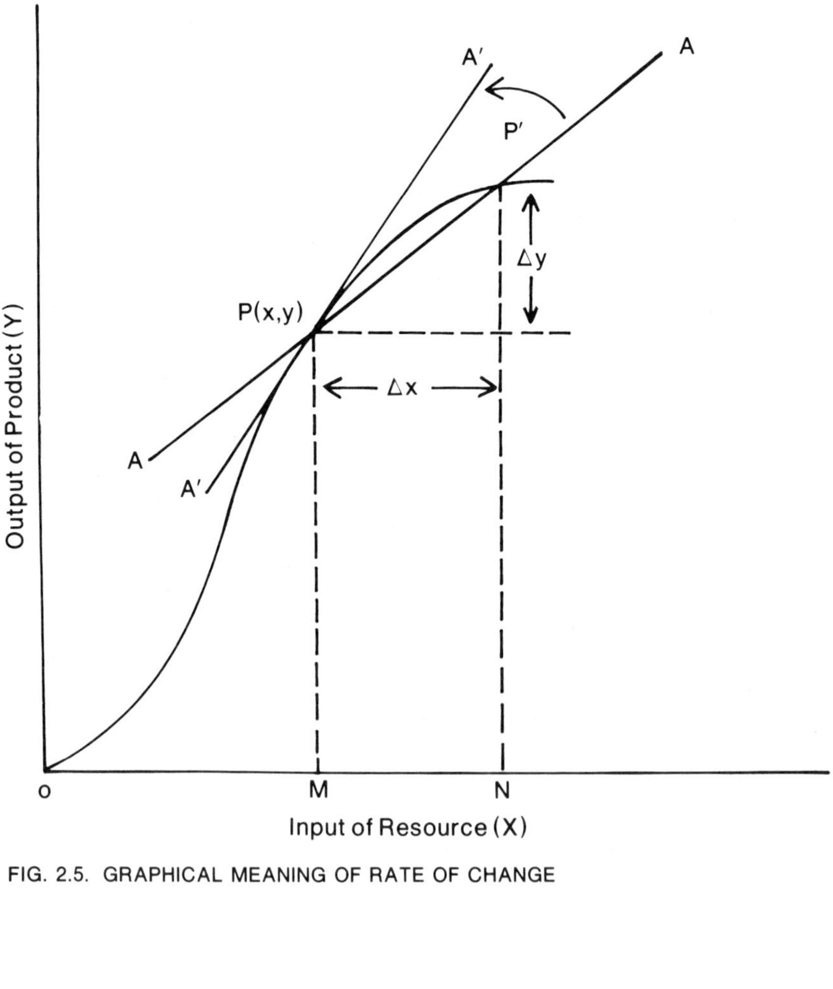

FIG. 2.5. GRAPHICAL MEANING OF RATE OF CHANGE

input X increase by an amount Δx and determine the amount by which the product Y increases[2] which is denoted by Δy. Second, the quotient obtained by dividing the increase in product Δy by the increase in the input Δx gives the average rate of increase (average marginal physical product) in product Y with respect to the input X over the interval by which the input is increased (size of the change in input). This is indicated by the slope of the line AA (Fig. 2.5). For example, if an extra 13.6 kg (30 lb) unit of nitrogen produces an increase of 637 liters (18 bu) of grain, each 0.45 kg (1 lb) of nitrogen would produce 21.4 liters (3/5 bu) of grain on an average within this interval. Third, if one reduces the size of the change in input X (Δx) to smaller and smaller values, the corresponding set of values or quotients of $\Delta y/\Delta x$ will still represent the average rate of change in product Y with respect to the input X but over smaller and smaller input intervals beginning at point P. Thus, as the change in size of the input Δx becomes infinitely small, i.e., as Δx approaches zero, the limit of the quotient $\Delta y/\Delta x$ defines the instantaneous rate of change in product Y at point P and is denoted by the slope of line A'A' (Fig. 2.5). This is the marginal physical productivity of an infinitely small quantity of the input X at M quantity. The quotient of $\Delta y/\Delta x$ gives the slope of the secant line AA, and as Δx approaches zero ($\Delta X \rightarrow 0$) and point P′ approaches point P, the secant line AA turns about point P and approaches a position of tangency to the total product curve at point P, which is designated as line A'A' (Fig. 2.5). Thus, although an extra 13.6 kg (30 lb) of nitrogen may produce an extra 637 liters (18 bu) of grain, perhaps an extra 6.8 kg (15 lb) of nitrogen (from the original level) would produce an extra 354 liters (10 bu) of corn and result in an average marginal physical product of two-thirds. In the limit, the marginal physical product of nitrogen (at the original level) may be three-fourths, which would correspond to the slope of line A'A' (Fig. 2.5).

The slope of a straight line tangent to the total physical product curve is equal to the marginal productivity of the input at that particular point in the factor-product relationship. This is an important concept since, as will be explained subsequently, a straight line can be used to denote the unit factor price-product value ratio. When this line expressing the price ratio is equal in slope or coincides with the line tangent to the total physical product curve which equals marginal physical product, the optimum level of production of Y and the optimum amount of input X to use are defined.

[2] Cases may exist where the value of the function is decreasing, in which case an increase in the input X produces a decrease in product Y. In these cases, Δy and Δx will have opposite signs.

Stages of Production

The productivity curves of the nature described (Fig. 2.4) show that an input may be used economically in certain quantities while in other quantities it would not be profitable regardless of price relationships. There are three distinct phases or stages of which only one constitutes the rational zone of production.

Stage I.—The first stage of the production relationship is characterized by the increasing average productivity of the input (Fig. 2.4). The marginal physical product is always greater than the average physical product of the input in this stage which is an irrational stage of production. If it is profitable to use the input to produce any quantity of the product, it is profitable to use the input until the average return is the highest. This is the point of separation between Stage I and Stage II. This is also the point reached when entrepreneurs obtain the highest physical output per unit of input which does not necessarily indicate the most profitable level of production.

Stage II.—The second stage of production is characterized by both a decreasing average physical product and a decreasing marginal physical product of the input (Fig. 2.4). In this stage, the marginal physical product is always less than the average physical product and is always positive since the total physical product continues to increase. This stage of production which is the rational zone is extremely important as here the physical relationships are not sufficient to specify the optimum level of production. Thus, some choice indicator, such as price relationships, must be involved. It is in this zone that the factor-product price relationship must be considered along with the physical relationships to determine the most profitable level of production. Also, this is the zone which provides the basis for discussions on the nature and characteristics of the demand and supply relationships as well as the cost relationships.

Stage III.—The third stage is characterized by a declining total physical product and consequently a negative marginal physical product (Fig. 2.4). Like Stage I, this stage constitutes an irrational zone of production. Regardless of the price relationships, it is not profitable or logical to use enough of the input to push production into this stage.

Choice Indicators

The physical relationships of the nature just discussed provide the necessary conditions to define the optimum level of production but they are not sufficient. The sufficient condition results when some choice indicator is employed. The problem in production is one of deciding which one of the many levels of input use will maximize the objective desired. This maximum condition can be defined only by a choice indicator.

Price Ratios.—In defining the economic optima among production relationships, the price ratio becomes the criterion by which choices are made. It is recognized, however, that there is room for consideration of other criteria as choice indicators which may be subjective in nature, since monetary price merely serves as a convenient proxy for cost and/or benefit to a person. These other criteria will be discussed briefly in a subsequent section.

The problem is to find the level at which the variable input should be combined with the quantity of fixed inputs to maximize profits. The factor-product price ratio is the choice indicator when the various physical factor-product relationships are known. The factor-product price ratio must equal the marginal physical productivity of the input. This necessary condition for maximization of profit can be stated as

$$\frac{P_x}{P_y} = \frac{\Delta Y}{\Delta X}$$

where P_x refers to price of the input X, P_y refers to price of the product Y and $\Delta Y/\Delta X$, as was pointed out previously, refers to the marginal physical productivity of the input X. This necessary condition can also be stated in other forms, depending upon what is being presented, as

$$MPP_x\,(y) = \frac{P_x}{P_y}$$

$$MVP_x\,(y) = P_x \text{ or } MVP_x(y) = MFC_x$$

$$\frac{MVP_x\,(y)}{P_x} = 1$$

where MPP_x (y) refers to marginal physical product of input X in the production of Y (equivalent to $\Delta Y/\Delta X$), MVP_x (y) refers to marginal value productivity of input X in the production of Y and is found by multiplying MPP_x (y) by the price of Y (P_y, constant for all levels of Y under conditions of perfect competition), and MFC_x refers to the marginal factor cost of input X and is equivalent to P_x under conditions of perfect competition which will be discussed in Chapter 12 and which are assumed in this volume to exist in the factor markets unless otherwise noted. By simple algebraic treatment these relationships can be placed in the form desired.

These relationships can also be presented graphically. Graphs add to the precision of discussion and are useful tools in analysis. Maximum profit conditions can be specified for a factor-product physical relationship by the tangency of a given factor-product (n-corn) price ratio (Fig. 2.6) to the total physical product curve. The slope of the total physical product at any point, as previously indicated, denotes the marginal physical product of the factor (nitrogen). The factor-price ratio (nitrogen-corn) is denoted by the slope of a straight line. The point of tangency indicates the optimum level of production and input required to produce it. The point of tangency also denotes the condition specified previously where MPP of the 117th lb (0.45 kg) of nitrogen in the production of corn is equal to the price of nitrogen/price of corn ratio, that is,

$$MPP_n(c) = P_n/P_c$$

Converting this equality to value terms, the $MVP_n(c) = P_n$ or $MVP_n(c) = MFC_n$ with $P_n = MFC_n$ because both represent the cost of a unit of nitrogen at least for small increments of nitrogen.[3] These equalities indicate that the value added to the product must be equal to the cost of a unit used in production.

The equality

$$\frac{MVP_x(y)}{P_x} = 1$$

is a useful expression when the factor X has many uses and is unlimited in supply. A farmer would logically apply the factor among the many uses until its marginal value productivities in the various uses are equal and then apply the factor in such quantities in all uses that the value of the added return would equal the cost of a unit of the factor. This condition can be expressed as

$$\frac{MVP_x(y_1)}{P_x} = \frac{MVP_x(y_2)}{P_x} = \ldots, = \frac{MVP_x(y_n)}{P_x} = 1$$

If the supply of the factor is limited, the farmer can maximize the return from the scarce resource merely by equating the ratios, which will not be equal to 1.

---

[3] The MPP_n curve is, strictly speaking, the average marginal product and is so plotted, using 13.6 kg (30 lb) units of N. The point of input use necessary to give $MVP_n = MFC_n$ is the same as the point of tangency would require. In graphic analysis the optimum point may be obtained somewhat more easily by finding the point of tangency.

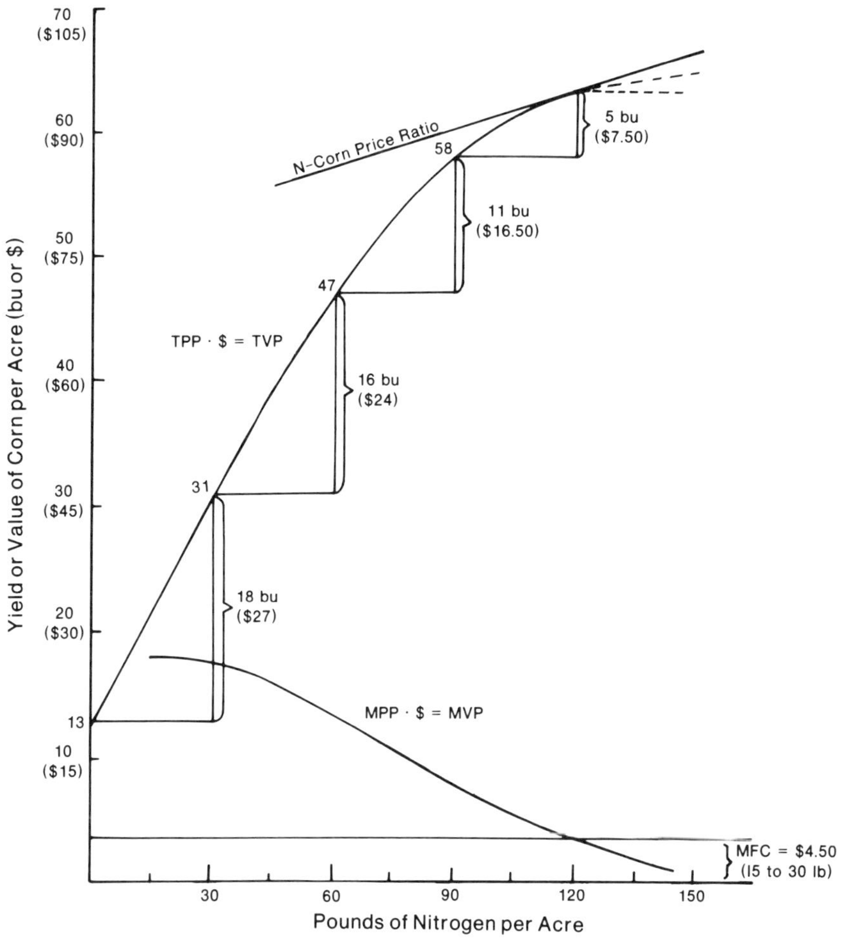

From Cope (1955). Fertilizing corn in Alabama. Chilean Nitrate Farm Forum 53.

FIG. 2.6. RELATION OF YIELD OF CORN TO VARIOUS LEVELS OF NITROGEN WITH ABOUT 25 LB OF PHOSPHORIC ACID AND POTASH PER ACRE IN ALABAMA, AVG. OF 309 EXPERIMENTS, 1925–1952

1 acre = 0.4 ha. 1 bu/acre = 88 liters/ha. 1 lb/acre = 1.125 kg/ha.

It is obvious that as the factor-product price ratio varies, given the technical factor-product relationship, the optimum level of input use and production will vary. When the factor cost becomes higher relative to the value of the product it will, of course, require a reduction in the level of production if the maximum profit condition is maintained. All industries

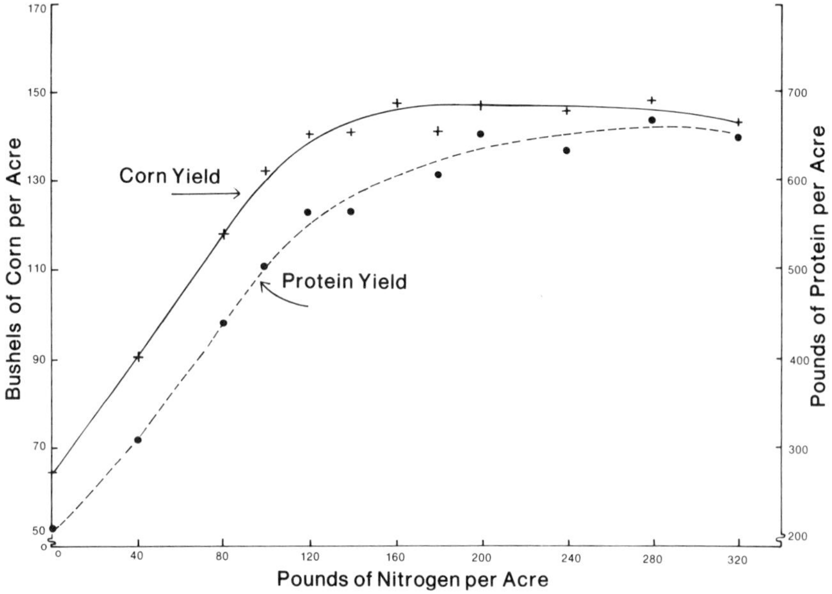

FIG. 2.7. RELATIONSHIP OF THE YIELD OF CORN AND PROTEIN TO DIFFERENT QUANTITIES OF NITROGEN PER ACRE

1 bu/acre = 88 liters/ha. 1 lb/acre = 1.125 kg/ha.

TABLE 2.1. EFFECT OF INCREASING QUANTITIES OF NITROGEN FERTILIZER UPON THE YIELD, EAR WEIGHT, TOTAL PROTEIN OF CORN, GRAIN AND THE PERCENTAGE OF APPLIED N RECOVERED IN THE GRAIN

N (lb/Acre)	Yield (bu/Acre)	Ear Weight (lb/Ear)	Protein (%)	Protein (lb/Acre)	N Recovered in Grain (%)
0	64.6	0.25	6.92	211	—
40	90.4	0.35	7.27	310	39.6
80	118.2	0.45	7.86	439	45.5
100	132.4	0.49	8.06	504	46.7
120	140.7	0.53	8.45	562	46.6
140	141.0	0.52	8.46	564	40.0
160	146.8	0.56	8.74	606	39.4
180	141.2	0.57	9.00	602	34.8
200	147.1	0.53	9.30	647	34.7
240	145.8	0.55	9.17	632	28.0
280	147.8	0.54	9.55	665	25.8
320	143.6	0.54	9.58	650	21.9

Source: Hunter, A.S. and Yugen, J.A. 1955. Soil Sci. Soc. Am. Proc. *19*, 214–218.

possess numerous physical input-output relationships that can be used to illustrate this principle but the agricultural industry, through its extensive research program, has a wealth of excellent empirical data useful for realistic illustrations.

For linear input-output relationships it is easily seen that the optimum level of production is not determinable short of unlimited production. In other words, if anything is produced, it will be profitable to produce to the capacity of the firm. When there is very little difference in the slope of the factor-product price ratio and the slope of the total physical product curve, a very little shift in the price ratio can cause the volume of production to fluctuate from the extremes of no production to maximum production.

Subjective Considerations.—For some entrepreneurs, price considerations may not be the only choice indicator involved in making decisions. Personal preferences, wants, goals, etc., which cannot be handled in dollar terms can modify the importance of the price ratio as a choice indicator. In large industrial firms, personal preferences may play a lesser role than in small family size firms as many of the personal preferences of an individual may be dissipated when a board of directors sets the major policies.

In farming, the subjective considerations play a very important role. These, no doubt, change with the life cycle of the farm family as well as with the financial position of the business. The nature of these subjective values is also conditioned by the education, experiences and cultural atmosphere in which the entrepreneur operates. For instance, one farmer who follows one plan of conservation of resources may adopt a system which permits little or no land to be devoted to grain production while another who places little emphasis on a long-term conservation program may devote larger quantities of resources to grain production and may realize a greater net farm income from this program within the time period under consideration. Both farmers, according to their own values, may be following a rational program of farming.

Personal values play an important role in determining an optimum situation for a given entrepreneur. They are more likely to play an important role if the entrepreneur has low managerial ability. Such enterpreneurs are more likely to rely on existing practices followed by those whose technical knowledge does not vary radically from their own because they apparently place a high value on technical uncertainty. Entrepreneurs with low managerial ability face increasingly subjective uncertainty in making adjustments because their knowledge of technical relationships diminishes rapidly as they move outside the range of what is customarily performed.

CHAPTER 2: REVIEW QUESTIONS

(1) Suppose it has been determined experimentally at an experiment station that $y = 30 + 0.578x - 0.000578x^2$ where y is bushels (35.4 liters) of corn and x is pounds (0.45 kg) of 10-10-10 fertilizer. What can be done with this information?

(2) Assume three different single variable input production functions:

(a) increasing marginal productivity
(b) decreasing marginal productivity and
(c) constant marginal productivity.

Draw diagrams to illustrate each of these relationships. Show and/or explain for each the zone of relevance, maximum profit point and how much of the input the operator should use in each case.

(3) Prove by illustrations and discussion that the most profitable output of corn per 0.4 ha (1 acre) must be less than the maximum yield which can be obtained from it.

(4) The yield of crops per 0.4 ha (1 acre) is considerably higher in Europe than in the United States, although the soil is inherently no more fertile. Can you explain why this is true and link this with the world food problem?

(5) Prove that constant returns to scale require that marginal and average products be equal.

(6) The concept of efficiency used in many studies and recommendations, such as highest output per hour of labor or lowest amount of labor per unit of output that comes from many engineering or work simplification studies, can, if followed, lead to economic disequilibrium in the use of resources and, consequently, loss of profits. Use appropriate tools which we have developed in this chapter to analyze this statement and tell whether it is true or false.

(7) An administrator of an agricultural extension education program comes to you for advice on how he/she might allocate scarce resources over the state in which he/she is located. Assume there are three general areas over which his/her employees and materials can be spread:

Area I is rough and mountainous where people have difficulty in acquiring subsistence levels of income.
Area II is rolling land with small towns and few urban centers. Relative to Area I the people are well off, but Area II is not as prosperous and endowed with agricultural resources as Area III.
Area III is abundant with agricultural resources and relative to the rest of the state has high income.

In each area, resources can be grouped into *land, labor, capital* and *management*. The extension service can affect mainly the supply curve of management. Set up three production functions where management is an input and income (in general) is the output. Make your assumptions explicit with respect to

(a) levels of other resources
(b) substitution between management and other resources and
(c) the choice indicator.

Provide a framework within which you can advise the extension administrator as to optimum allocation of his/her resources.

3

Elementary Theory of Resource Allocation II

FACTOR-FACTOR RELATIONSHIPS

In the preceding chapter, the discussion was centered around the relationship of the product to one of the inputs, or a group of inputs considered as one, with the other inputs fixed at some level of use. In this chapter, the discussion will be concerned with functions where two inputs are variable along with the product, such as

$$Y = f(X_1, X_2 \mid X_3, \ldots X_n).$$

Special attention will be centered around the relationships of X_1 and X_2 and how changes in either or both inputs affect the product Y with all other inputs, $X_3, \ldots X_n$, fixed at some level.

A powerful concept in allocating resources is that of substitution. It is common knowledge that when producing a product there are often many ways of achieving the same result. Since one way can be substituted for another, the central problem is to find an optimum or least-cost combination of the factors involved in producing a given output. In this way, the manager is concerned with the rate of substitution.

The Product Contours

A factor-factor type of relationship can be presented easily by means of a contour map. Following the usual interpretation, every point on a given contour is of equal value, from this comes the term *isoproduct*[1] *curve, isoquant,* or simply, *product contour.*[2] Every point on a given product contour represents a particular combination of the two factors, X_1 and X_2, used in production. Successive levels of input usage will provide a family of product contours (Fig. 3.1).

[1] The word "iso" is derived from the Greek "isos" meaning equal.
[2] Contour line connects points on a surface that have the same elevation or value.

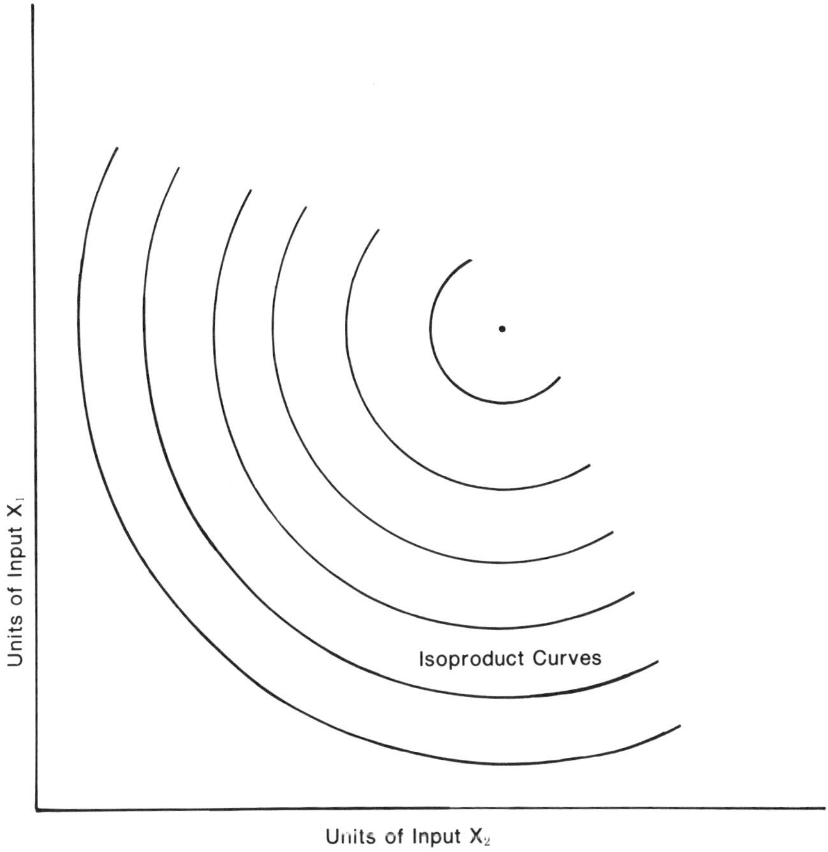

FIG. 3.1. A FAMILY OF ISOPRODUCT CURVES SHOWING FACTOR-FACTOR RELATIONSHIPS

Properties of Product Contour Curves.—A system of product contour curves shows some definite characteristics of general interest. In the rational area of production which is of concern to the entrepreneur, the product contours slope down to the right (Fig. 3.1). This means that they are negatively sloped curves. Occasionally, they may be horizontal or vertical within ranges which would take the producer into the irrational zone since more of one resource is used without a reduction in the other resource.

The product contour is generally convex to the origin in a graphic presentation (Fig. 3.1). However, in certain relationships it may be a straight line. The product contour indicates also the nature or degree of substitution of one factor or another, that is, the slope of the product contour defines the marginal rate of substitution. The marginal rate of substitution refers to the amount by which one resource is decreased as the input of another resource is increased by one unit to give the same output.[3] This means that the convexity of a product contour depends upon the degree of technical substitutability of the resources.

Generally, the product contours are characterized as a nonintersecting family of curves. If they should appear to intersect on a contour map, obviously the highest contour for a given combination of resources would be selected following the assumptions of profit maximization.

Constant Rate of Substitution.—When the amount by which one resource is decreased remains the same while the input of another resource is increased by one unit, with output held constant, then a constant rate of substitution of inputs exists for the function. The quantity of X_1 (ΔX_1) being replaced by a unit of X_2 (ΔX_2) will always remain the same regardless of the initial amount of X_1, and the product contour representing the rate of substitution will be a negatively sloping straight line (Fig. 3.2).

The marginal rate of substitution of X_2 for X_1 can be denoted specifically as $\Delta X_1/\Delta X_2$ as $\Delta X_2 \rightarrow 0$, which will always be negative and constant at all points in the case of constant rates of substitution. Often, inputs with a constant rate of substitution are referred to as perfect substitutes. This relationship represents one extreme in resource relationships; in this case, the resources actually may be considered as the same or equivalent to each other.

Complementarity.—The other extreme in resource relationships occurs when the resources must be combined in a fixed way to produce a given output. This means that resources cannot be substituted in any manner and the product contours would be of the nature of right angles (Fig. 3.3). The classic example taken from chemistry is water produced from the ratio of two units of hydrogen and one unit of oxygen, with no possibility of substituting one for the other.

Diminishing Rate of Substitution.—Most of the decisions involving resource substitution center around the factors which substitute for each other at diminishing rates. Diminishing rates exist when the amount changes by which one resource is decreased as the input of another resource is increased by one unit. For example (Fig. 3.4), an increase of X_2 from one to two units will result in a decrease of three units of X_1, an

[3] Like the concept of average marginal physical product, the average marginal rate of substitution can be used advantageously in many situations. For example, *see* Redman, J. C. and Olson, R. O. 1956. Economic problems in feeding dairy cows. Kentucky Agric. Exp. Stn. Bull. *648*. This study made extensive use of production economic concepts.

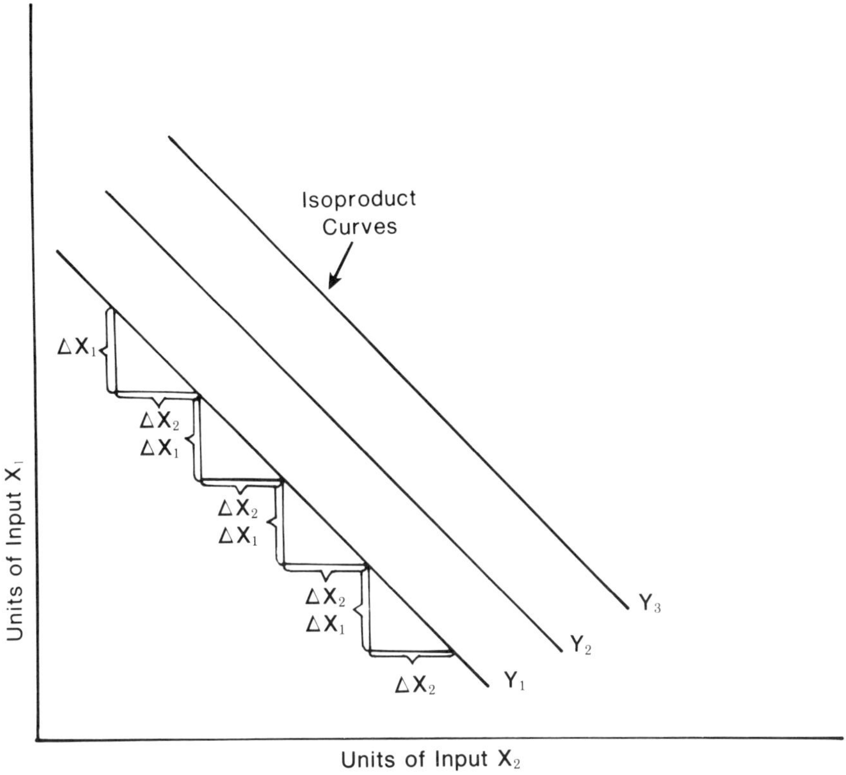

FIG. 3.2. A FUNCTION SHOWING THE CONSTANT RATE OF SUBSTITUTION BETWEEN TWO INPUTS

increase from two to three units of X_2 will result in a decrease of one unit of X_1 and an increase from three to four units and four to five units of X_2 will result in the decrease of 0.6 and 0.3 units of X_1, respectively. The decreasing amount of X_1 replaced by a unit of X_2 reflects a diminishing rate of substitution. This means that resources are less than the perfect substitutes or the perfect complements referred to as the extremes in the preceding sections. The degree of substitutability or complementarity of the inputs is reflected in the curvature or degree of convexity to the origin of the product contour. Estimates of the rates of substitution of inputs used in production have occupied the interests of many economists in recent years, especially agricultural economists.

Level of Input Use.—It may be desirable now to point out more fully the logic of why the productivity of an input depends upon the level at

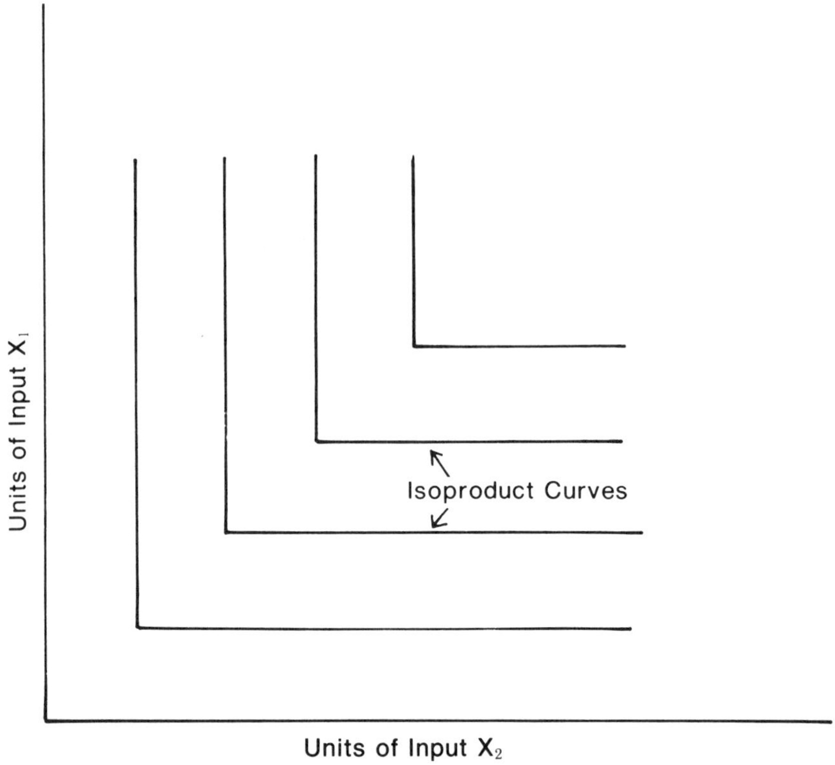

FIG. 3.3. A FUNCTION SHOWING PERFECT COMPLEMENTARITY BETWEEN TWO INPUTS

which other inputs are used. Recommendations are often made by agricultural specialists on the optimum use of an input without consideration of the level of other inputs present. The shortcoming of such recommendations can be illustrated simply by the tools thus far introduced. When one of the inputs X_1 is fixed at levels "a," "b" and "c" (Fig. 3.5), a slice of the surface at those levels will give total physical product curves at corresponding levels (Fig. 3.6). At a given level of input use of X_2, a total physical product curve of X_2 with X_1 = c will have a slope as reflected by the slope of line cc′ greater than the slope of the total physical product curve with X_1 = b as reflected by the slope of line bb′. Likewise, the slope of these curves will be greater than the slope of the total physical product curve with X_1 = a at the same level of input use of X_2. As discussed in the previous chapter, the slope of the total physical product curve at any point gives the marginal physical productivity of that input; the greater the slope, the greater the productivity. Therefore, an explanation can be obtained for the idea that the productivity (marginal) of an input (X_2) depends upon the level at which other inputs (X_1 and others at designated levels) are fixed.

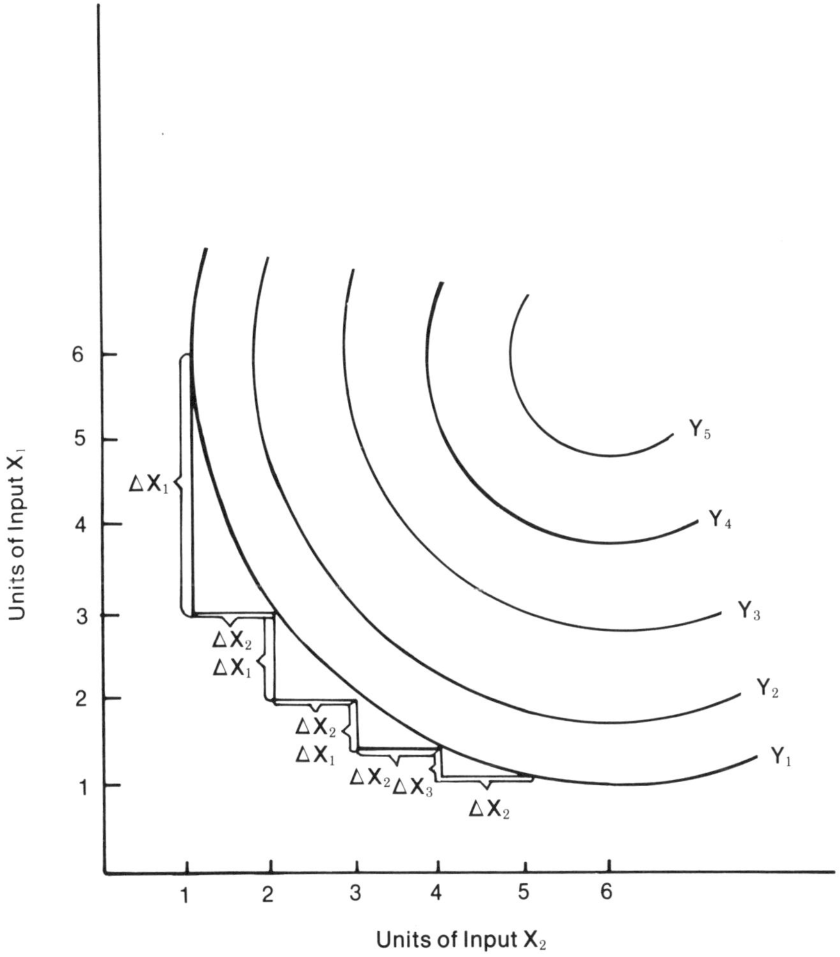

FIG. 3.4. A FUNCTION SHOWING DIMINISHING RATE OF SUBSTITUTION BETWEEN TWO INPUTS

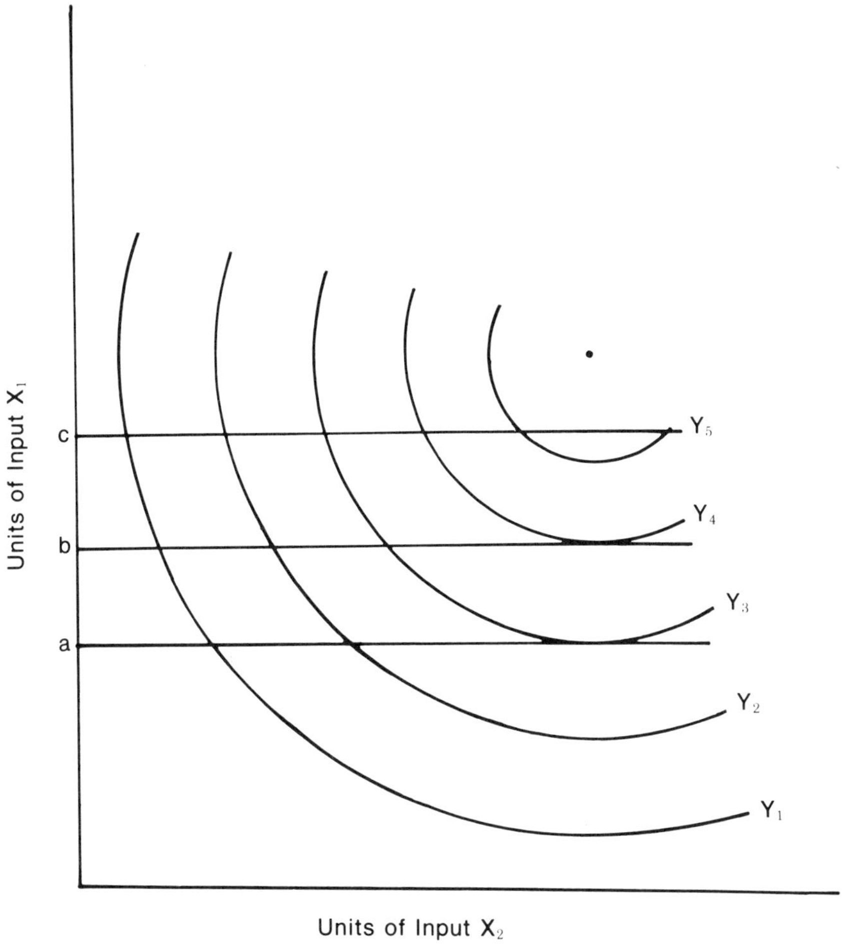

FIG. 3.5. PRODUCTION SURFACE OF A FUNCTION WITH ONE INPUT AT VARIOUS LEVELS

Choice Indicator

The physical relationships provide the necessary conditions for determining the optimum combination but they are not sufficient since some choice indicator is needed. The optimum combination will result when the cost of the combined resources is at the minimum. The factor price ratio serves as the choice indicator if the dollar returns are to be maximized.

The factor price ratio can be indicated graphically by the slope of an isocost curve.[4] An isocost curve shows all the possible combinations of the two factors which can be purchased with a given outlay of funds at a given price per unit of each resource (Fig. 3.7). For example, assuming that two resources, X_1 and X_2, are in question and the unit prices are P_{x_1} and P_{x_2}, respectively, let TC represent total cost outlay. Then if only resource X_1 is used, $\frac{TC}{P_{x_1}}$ units of X_1 can be purchased. If only resource X_2 is used, $\frac{TC}{P_{x_2}}$ units of X_2 can be purchased. A straight line joining these two points shows all combinations of X_1 and X_2 which can be purchased with

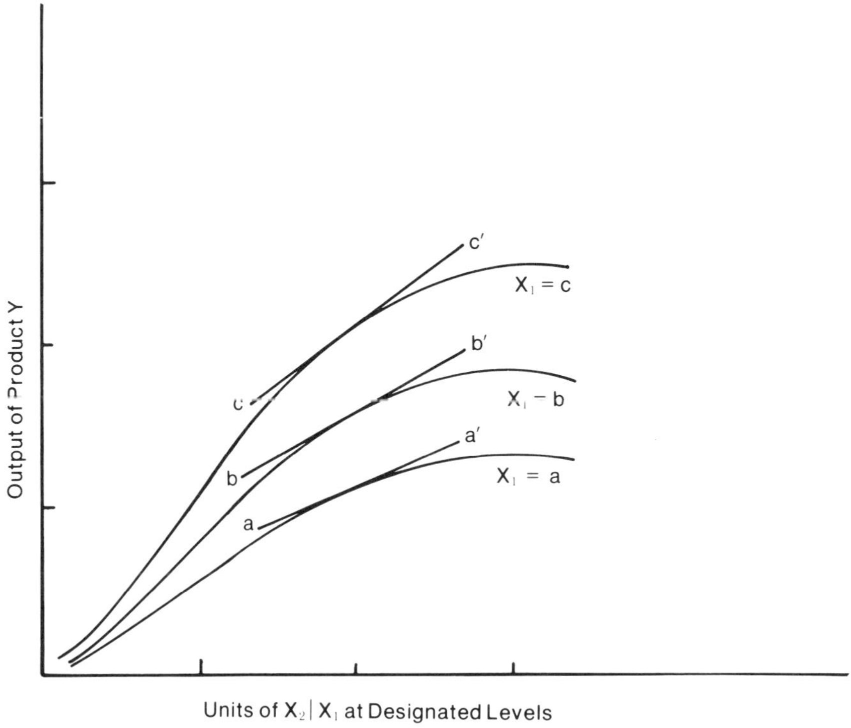

FIG. 3.6. THE PRODUCTIVITY OF A SINGLE INPUT AS RELATED TO LEVEL OF OTHER INPUTS

[4] Used interchangeably with the terms constant outlay curve, price line, budget line or possibility curve.

the given total outlay (Fig. 3.7). The slope of this isocost curve at all points is

$$\frac{\frac{TC}{P_{x_1}}}{\frac{TC}{P_{x_2}}} = \frac{TC}{P_{x_1}} \cdot \frac{P_{x_2}}{TC} = \frac{P_{x_2}}{P_{x_1}}$$

Optimum Combination

The problem by a firm is either to get on the highest product contour the isocost curve will permit or to produce a given quantity of product at the least cost. Both of these objectives can be reached when the marginal rate of substitution of the input factors is equal inversely to the factor price ratio. It has been noted previously that the marginal rate of substitution of X_1 for X_2 is denoted by the slope of the product contour at a point $\Delta X_1/\Delta X_2$ as $\Delta X_2 \rightarrow 0$. Also, it was discussed in an earlier chapter

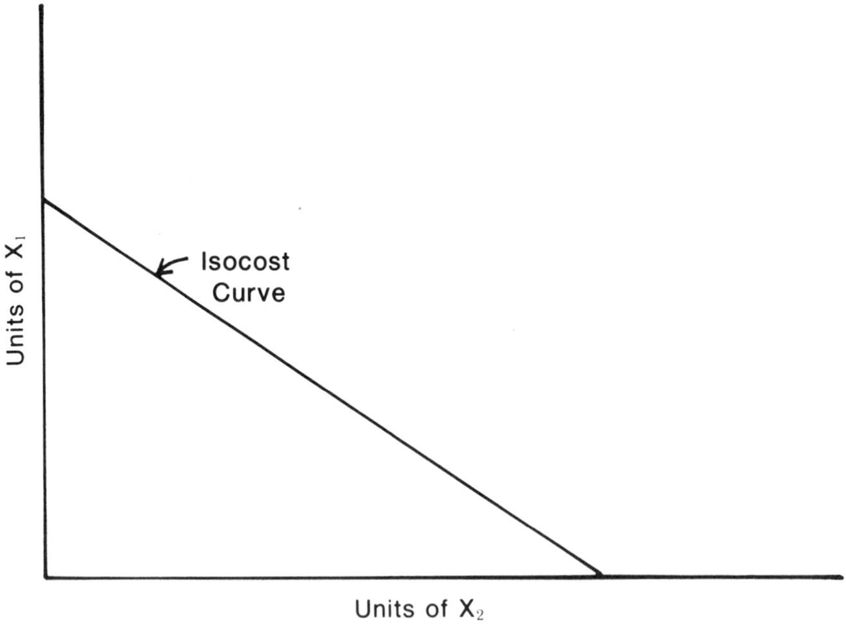

FIG. 3.7. ISOCOST CURVE SHOWING POSSIBLE COMBINATIONS OF TWO RESOURCES TO A CONSTANT OUTLAY OF FUNDS

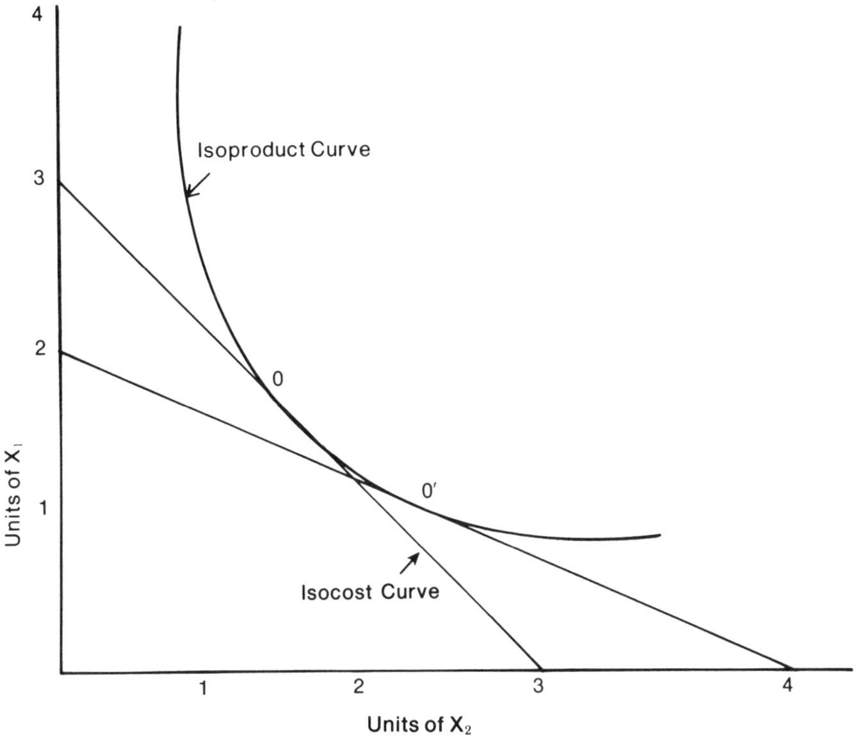

FIG. 3.8. OPTIMUM COMBINATION OF RESOURCES SHOWN BY THE TANGENCY OF THE TWO CURVES

that the slope of a curve at a point is equal to the slope of a straight line tangent to the product contour curve at that point. When the tangent of the product contour at a point, which may be shown graphically by a straight line, is equal to the isocost curve which is also shown graphically by a straight line, the firm has found an optimum combination of resources for a given level of production which will give maximum net returns (Fig. 3.8, point 0). In short, the tangency of the isocost curve to the product contour indicates that their slopes are equal, and thus the marginal rate of substitution is equal to the price ratio at this point. Any other point on the isocost curve will produce on a lower product contour, or any other point on the product contour will require more outlay. Thus, only at this point of tangency can the firm have maximum net returns.

The point of tangency shifts as the factor price ratio shifts (Fig. 3.8, point 0′).

At any point on the isoproduct curve (Fig. 3.8), the marginal rate of substitution of X_2 for X_1 is also equal to MPP_{x_2}/MPP_{x_1}. Since the slope of the isocost curve is P_{x_2}/P_{x_1}, the least-cost combination in producing the given level of production is

$$\frac{MPP_{x_2}}{MPP_{x_1}} = \frac{P_{x_2}}{P_{x_1}}$$

Through manipulation,[5] this ratio can be written as

$$\frac{MPP_{x_2}}{P_{x_2}} = \frac{MPP_{x_1}}{P_{x_1}}$$

Only when these ratios are exactly equal is it impossible to expand output from a given outlay of expenditure by transferring the outlay between the two inputs.

Ridge Lines and Isoclines

After determining the optimum combination of resources, the next task is to isolate some relationships which are needed to determine the optimum level of production. By successive applications of X_1 and X_2 to the group of fixed inputs, a system or a family of product contours is obtained which indicates higher and higher levels of production as these inputs are increased (Fig. 3.9). These contours are not necessarily concentric since they depend upon the nature of the physical relationships found in the function. Several significant and useful relationships may be noted as the level of production is moved from one contour to another.

It has been noted that in the relevant area of production the product contours are negatively sloped and convex to the origin. The lines defining the relevant or rational area of the production surface are known as *ridge lines* (AB and CB in Fig. 3.9). Factor combinations outside these confines are irrational and uneconomic since there would be a positive substitution ratio. It would require an increase in both X_1 and X_2 to remain at the same level of production. At each point on the ridge line, tangents to each particular product contour are parallel to either the X_1 or the X_2 axis. When the tangent to the product contour is vertical, the

[5] Students may review the techniques in manipulation of ratios by consulting any good algebra text.

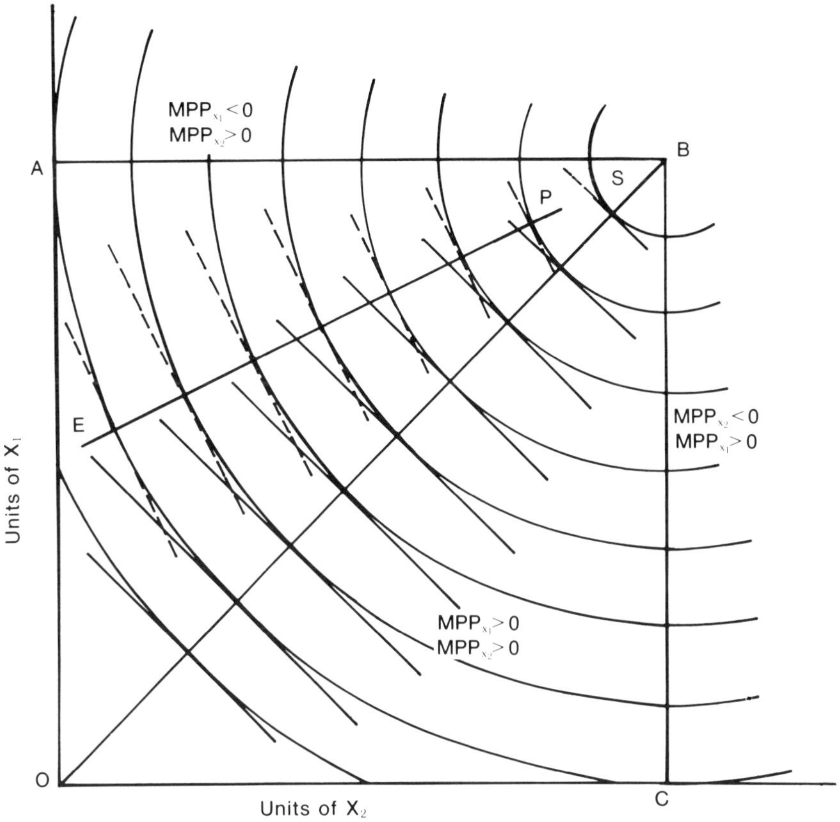

FIG. 3.9. FAMILY OF PRODUCT CONTOURS

marginal rate of substitution of X_2 for X_1 is infinite or the marginal physical product of X_1 is zero along the ridge line AB. If larger quantities of X_1 were used, the $MPP_{x_1} < 0$. When the tangent to the product curve is horizontal, the marginal rate of substitution of X_2 for X_1 is zero or the marginal product of X_2 is zero along the line CB. Larger quantities of X_2 would have a $MPP_{x_2} < 0$. The ridge line AB which connects points of equal MRS (infinity) of X_2 for X_1 indicates the minimum amount of X_2, and ridge line CB which connects points of equal MRS (zero) of X_2 for X_1 indicates the minimum amount of X_1, necessary to produce different quantities of the product.

Within the ridge lines, other points of equal marginal rate of substitution can be isolated and connected which form lines of similar nature as ridge lines known as *isoclines*.[6] Along each isocline the MRS from one product contour to another is constant. Thus, ridge lines are a special type of isocline.

When the function is such that the product can be expanded only by a unique simultaneous increase in both factors which form a family of product contours reflecting perfect complementarity (such as in Fig. 3.3), the usually divergent ridge lines would coincide and form a straight line through the origin. The other extreme results when the two factors are substitutable at a constant rate (such as in Fig. 3.2). In such cases the ridge lines coincide with the X_1 and X_2 axes and the isoclines are thus indeterminate.

Expansion Paths and Scale Lines

As indicated in a previous section, the factor combination selected from the many ways of producing the same output depends upon the factor price ratio. The firm is interested in the least-cost combination of resources at each level of output. If a given isocost curve is made tangent to the product contour which gives the least-cost combination and if the outlay is increased in quantity to make the successive isocost curves tangent to successive levels of product contours, the *expansion path* will result from a locus of all points of least-cost combinations (EP in Fig. 3.9). When the factor prices are constant, the isocost curves are parallel to each other, and the expansion path follows the course of an isocline since by definition an isocline is a locus of all points of equal MRS. Under competetive conditions, the factor price ratio determines which isocline becomes the expansion path since $P_{x_2}/P_{x_1} = MRS$.

If the expansion path is linear and passes through the origin of a three-dimension graph (OS in Fig. 3.9) a special type of expansion path known as a *scale line* results which shows a proportionate simultaneous increase in all factors as the level of output is expanded. Scale relationships are indicated by the intersection of line OS with the product contours. As the inputs are increased in equal proportions, the output may vary at either a constant rate, at an increasing rate or at a decreasing rate in the sense of a factor-product type of relationship, depending upon the possibilities of increasing the inputs in the same proportion. The inputs can be increased proportionately if all the inputs are perfectly divisible which, logically, would return a product at the constant rate, i.e.,

[6] For an example, where isoclines found a practical use see Heady, E.O., Pesek, J.T. and Brown, W.G. 1955. Crop response surfaces and economic optima in fertilizer use. Iowa Agric. Exp. Stn. Bull. *424*.

it would be a linear homogeneous production function.[7]

The optimum level for production expansion depends upon the price of the product (P_y) and the cost of the combined factors of production. The tools set forth in the preceding chapter on factor-product relationships are useful in determining the optimum output. A slice of the production surface along the expansion path or along the scale line would reveal in a two-dimension relationship whether or not constant, increasing or decreasing returns to the factors are present. The optimum level results when the marginal value product of the inputs combined in scale line proportions or according to the expansion path is equal to the cost of the combined inputs, i.e.,

$$MVP_{x_1 \text{ and } x_2} = MFC_{x_1 \text{ and } x_2}$$

Sometimes it may become practical to convert the physical quantities of the inputs X_1 and X_2 to a common denominator, such as dollars worth of inputs, to obtain homogeneous units of inputs.

Elasticity of Substitution

The concept of elasticity with respect to substitution is used to denote a particular property. When applied to a factor-product type of relationship, the elasticity of production (E_p) refers to the relation of the percentage change in output to the percentage change in input. Similarly, elasticity of substitution (E_s) refers to the relation of the percentage change in input combinations to the percentage change in the marginal rate of substitution of inputs in producing a constant output.[8] For example, if relative factor prices change, and thus the equilibrating marginal rate of substitution changes, factor combinations will change; the elasticity of substitution measures by how much they will change. It can be calculated roughly by dividing the percentage change in the input ratio ($\Delta(X_1/X_2)$ / (X_1/X_2)) by the percentage change in the marginal rate of substitution [(ΔMRS)/MRS]. This rough calculation, which extends over a portion of the contour rather than at a specific point, indicates how quickly the slope of the contour changes, i.e., the speed of the decline of the MRS. When extended over a portion of the contour, it is known as the "arc" method and indicates an *average*, rather than an *exact* elasticity.

[7] This view of production phenomena has been contested because there is a law of "size." *See* Chamberlain, E. Proportionality, divisibility and economics of scale. Q. J. Econ. *Feb.* 1948.

[8] *See* Weintraub, S. 1949. Price Theory. Pitman Publishing Co., New York.

Multiple Input Relationships

Most of the production processes involve the use of many inputs. This makes geometric representation an impossibility since only three planes can be graphically represented or conceived. Thus, algebraic representation is the only practical alternative. Both mathematics and economic logic indicate that the many inputs are combined in an optimum manner when

$$\frac{MPP_{x_1}}{P_{x_1}} = \frac{MPP_{x_2}}{P_{x_2}} = \frac{MPP_{x_3}}{P_{x_3}} =, \ldots, = \frac{MPP_{x_n}}{P_{x_n}}$$

with n referring to the last variable input used within the planning span under consideration. The law of diminishing returns is relied upon to make this equation hold. The manager who finds that this relationship does not exist in producing a good can increase net returns by shifting limited funds from one resource to another in order to make the equation hold. Suppose, for example, the preceding equation has the following values:

$$\frac{11}{6} = \frac{8}{2} = \frac{10}{5}, \ldots, = \frac{6}{3}$$

The manager would be able to increase profits by shifting expenditure from resource X_1 to resource X_2 or until the following equilibrium is obtained:

$$\frac{12}{6} = \frac{4}{2} = \frac{10}{5} =, \ldots, = \frac{6}{3}$$

By using less of X_1, the MPP_{x_1} is increased (from 11 to 12) and by using more of X_2 the MPP_{x_2} is decreased (from 8 to 4). Thus, through diminishing returns and shifting of resources, the equilibrium is attained which is essential for maximum profits.

In the same illustration, it is noted that under conditions of equilibrium and where $P_y = 1$ [since $MVP_x = (MPP_x)(P_y)$], each dollar spent would return two. A manager with unlimited funds would expand the use of each input as long as its marginal value product is greater than its cost. The above algebraic relationship would become:

$$\frac{MVP_{x_1}}{P_{x_1}} = \frac{MVP_{x_2}}{P_{x_2}} = \frac{MVP_{x_3}}{P_{x_3}} =, \ldots, = \frac{MVP_{x_n}}{P_{x_n}} = 1$$

Using the price of inputs used in the preceding example, the entrepreneur would expand the use of the inputs to produce the following value relationship:

$$\frac{6}{6} = \frac{2}{2} = \frac{5}{5} = , \ldots , = \frac{3}{3} = 1$$

Again, it is through diminishing returns when prices are constant that the marginal value product declines in order to equal the input price.

CHAPTER 3: REVIEW QUESTIONS

(1) The following terms commonly are used in production economics theory:
  (a) Isoclines
  (b) Least cost combinations
  (c) Ridge lines
  (d) Expansion path
  (e) Scale lines

  Briefly, what is the meaning of each term and what are the similarities (if any) between any two of them?

(2) Discuss elasticity of production *vs* returns to scale.

(3) "It is impossible for the marginal rate of substitution between two inputs to be positive." True or false?

(4) "The ridge lines enclose the area of rational operation." Explain.

(5) "An 18 percent protein ration should be fed to feeder calves *regardless* of the price ratio of protein and carbohydrate feed materials." *Evaluate.*

(6) "It is false economy to hire the least expensive productive factor." Appraise this statement.

(7) What information must a person have to determine the optimum point on an expansion path? What would be the effect of a rise in price of one input (land) on the optimum combination of resources?

(8) Discuss the effects of placing an absolute limit on the amount of one of a pair of factors being used to produce a product. If you were interested in restricting the output of the product to a given level by restricting the input of one of the two factors, what are the appropriate criteria to use in deciding which factor to restrict and in setting a limit on its amount? How would this choice be affected by the form of the production function?

(9) Assume that 100 units of output can be produced when 30 units of factor Y and five units of factor X are employed, and that: (1) the MRS of X for Y is −2/1 until 16Y are employed, (2) thereafter the MRS falls to −1/1 until 6Y and 22X are employed, (3) after which it falls to −1/2.

(a) Compute in the table provided below the factor combinations which yield the constant amount of output.

(b) Plot diagrammatically the constant product curve indicated by your computations.

(c) Assuming that a 10% increase in factors increases output by 10% without altering the MRS ratios, compute and plot the new factor combinations.

(d) Draw in the isoclines indicated.

(e) How would you describe the isoquants drawn?

TABLE OF CONSTANT PRODUCT CURVES

Factor Combinations Output 100	MRS Ratios	Factor Combinations Output 100

(10) The data following were taken from the results of an experiment designed to determine the influence of varying fertilizers, varieties and plant stand on yield of corn in bushels per acre on Norfolk Loamy Sand. Potash and phosphorus were determined and held constant at 80 lb per acre. (1 acre = 0.4 ha; 1 bu = 35.2 liters; 1 lb/acre = 1.125 kg/ha.)

No. of Plants per Acre	Pounds of Nitrogen per Acre 20	70	120	170
		Bushels		
4,000	39	52	59	57
7,000	39	58	67	65
10,000	41	65	69	72
13,000	36	59	73	73
16,000	35	54	74	73

Source: Krantz, B.A. 1947. Research points the way for higher corn yields in N.C. Better Crops with Plant Food *31* (2).

Develop the appropriate production notation.

Select the appropriate concepts to analyze and describe graphically, using the preceding data, the following (use graph paper):

(1) Various product contours
(2) Optimum combination of nitrogen and plants (use current or a reasonable set of prices)
(3) Expansion path
(4) Optimum level of nitrogen and plants to use
(5) Optimum amount of nitrogen to use on 4000 plants, 7000 plants, 9000 plants and 11,000 plants

What general recommendations can you make using the preceding data and analysis?

4

Elementary Theory of Resource Allocation III

PRODUCT-PRODUCT RELATIONSHIPS

In the preceding chapters, the single enterprise theory of the firm has been discussed. In the present day, firms are commonly engaged in many lines of production. In some instances, resources are specialized and can be used only in production of a single commodity. In most instances, however, resources can be used in the production of any one or a combination of several commodities. Thus, managers must select the most profitable commodities and produce an optimum combination of commodities from some given quantity of resources which are available during the planning period under consideration. These enterprises must be selected with some idea of the coefficients of the factor-product and factor-factor relationships.

The Function

The functional relationship of the various alternative uses of a given quantity of resources parallels very closely the factor-factor relationship discussed in the preceding chapter. Instead of holding the product constant and varying the resources as discussed previously, this chapter will be concerned with the relationships among the products while the quantity of resources is held constant.

When a given quantity of resources can be used in conjunction with a given quantity of fixed resources to produce several products, such as

$$Y_1 = f_1 (X_1, X_2, X_3 \mid X_4, \ldots, X_n)$$

$$Y_2 = f_2 (X_1, X_2, X_3 \mid X_4, \ldots, X_n)$$

then the output when resources are devoted to producing one product is a function of the output when they are devoted to producing another product. Algebraically, when two dependent variables are the function of the same independent variables, then the two dependent variables are functions of each other. Thus, $Y_1 = f(Y_2)$ or $Y_2 = f(Y_1)$. For example, in farming, for a given quantity of resources over a given time, the amount of corn and other grain crops produced depends upon the amount of hay and other forage crops, and vice versa. This relationship is known as a *transformation function*[1] which indicates the amount of one product sacrificed or "transformed" into another product as the given quantity of resources that can be varied are shifted to the production of one product from the other.[2] The complex problem of selecting an optimum enterprise program involves the consideration of availability of resources, production coefficients and choice indicators such as prices and personal preferences of farmers.

Usually, an entrepreneur will not have available all the technical information or complete knowledge of the future relevant to the firm. Yet, in spite of this, he or she must make many decisions concerning the combination of enterprises. These decisions are more likely to result in greater profit if the entrepreneur acts on the basis of proven economic logic rather than on some traditional basis. Thus, it is the purpose here to give the general framework within which such decisions may be made.

Basic Enterprise Relationships

The technical relationships that can exist in the functional notation noted in the preceding section are many, varied and often complex. These relationships must be understood, however, if a farmer desires to make the most efficient use of limited resources. A farmer who does not know the exact nature of the various relationships existing under his or her own peculiar conditions must make estimates even though they may be somewhat crude. However, the more accurate the estimates made are the more likely there will be a reward in the form of net returns.

These enterprise relationships may vary from one extreme to another. First, they may have a range of various degrees of *complementary* relationships in which an increase (decrease) in output of one enterprise results in an increase (decrease) of the other enterprise as a result of shifting a given quantity of resources (Fig. 4.1, segments db and eh).

[1] The terms *transformation curve, opportunity curve, production possibility curve, iso-resource curve* and *isofactor curve* are generally used and will be used in this volume synonymously when expressing physical output. They also have the same general meaning as *isocost curve* and *iso-outlay* when expressing monetary value of output.

[2] This concept has the same meaning as the concept of *opportunity cost*. As will be shown later, this permits a graphical illustration of the valuable opportunity cost concept.

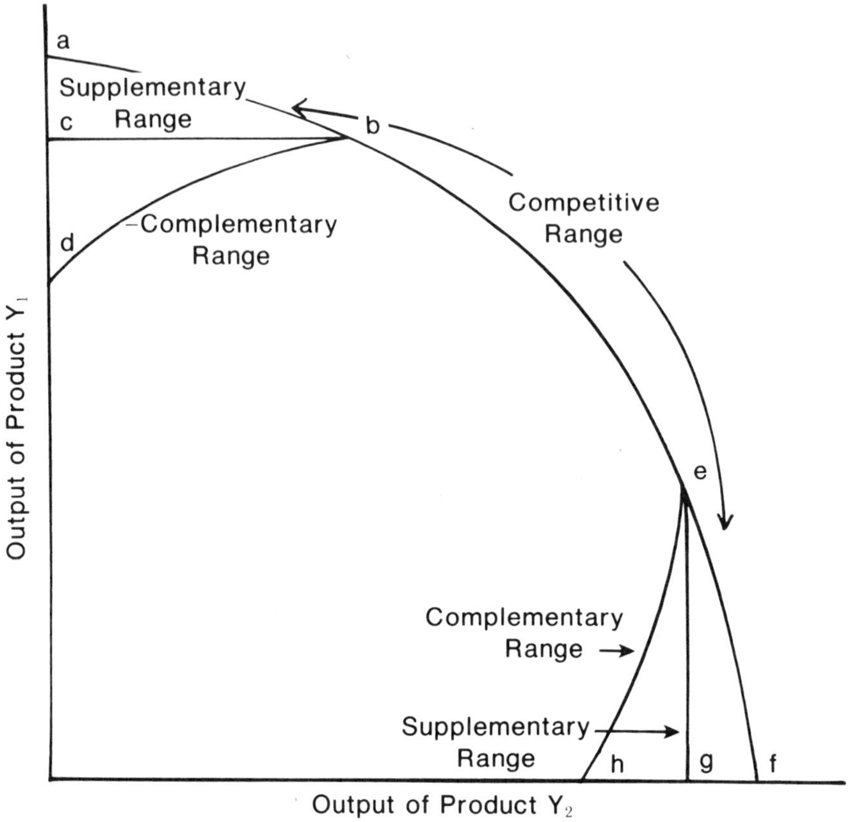

FIG. 4.1. TRANSFORMATION CURVE SHOWING VARIOUS PRODUCT RELATIONSHIPS

Second, the relationships may be of a *supplementary* nature for a range of production possibilities in which an increase in output of one product does not affect the output of the other product (Fig. 4.1, segments cb and eg). Third, they may have a rather wide range of various degrees of *competitive* relationships which means that as the output of one enterprise is expanded from a given quantity of resources, the output of the other enterprise must be reduced (Fig. 4.1, segment abef). Fourth, they may be of a *joint product* relationship which refers to a situation in which two or more products must be produced in a fixed proportion (Fig. 4.2). Finally, they may be of such a nature as to permit a convex production possibilities curve for a given quantity of resources which indicates that as one product Y_2 is substituted for another product Y_1, decreasing sacrifices are made in Y_1 for each unit of Y_2 obtained (Fig. 4.3). All of these relationships may or may not be present in enterprise relationships on a given farm. In addition, the production possibilities curves may be kinky, wavy, linear, discontinuous or any possible combination of situations.

Joint Products.—One of the extreme relationships found in agriculture is that of two or more products which must be produced in fixed proportions (Fig. 4.2). These joint products result from a single production process, i.e., one product cannot be produced without producing another, such as mutton and wool, corn and stover, etc. In a very short period of time these proportions appear to be fairly well fixed because the farmer has committed his or her resources according to a given production technique and cannot shift their use readily. However, even then, there may still be some possibility of making readjustments in the planned techniques and achieving a different product combination. For example, the farmer may be able to change from combination A_3 (Fig. 4.2) of Y_1

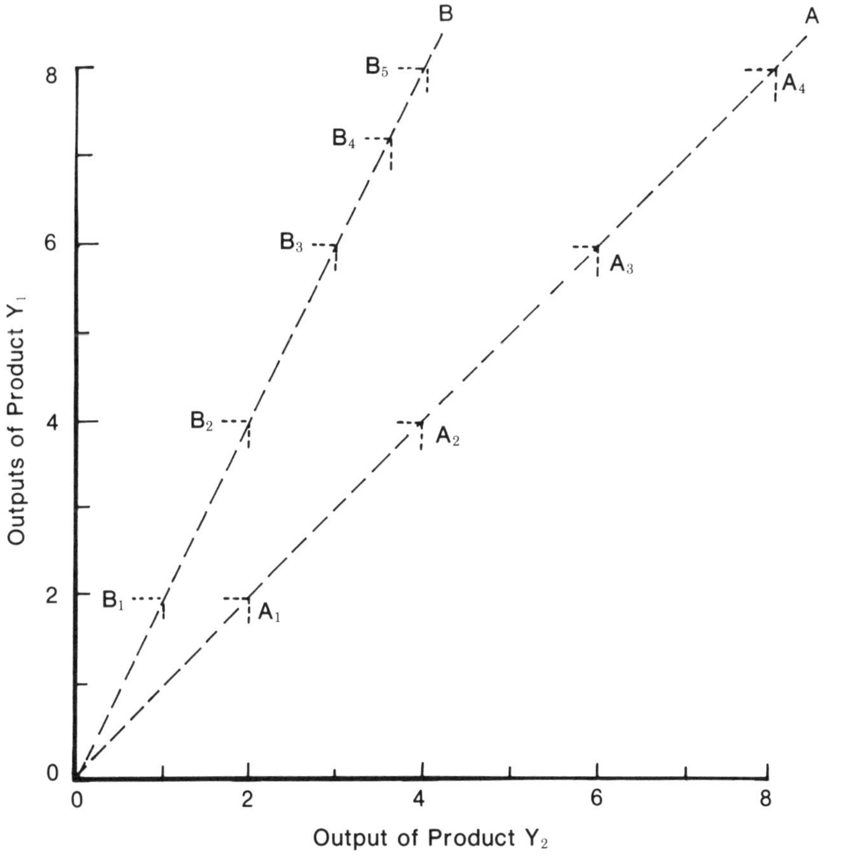

FIG. 4.2. JOINT PRODUCTS PRODUCED IN FIXED PROPORTIONS WITH INCREASED LEVELS OF RESOURCE USE

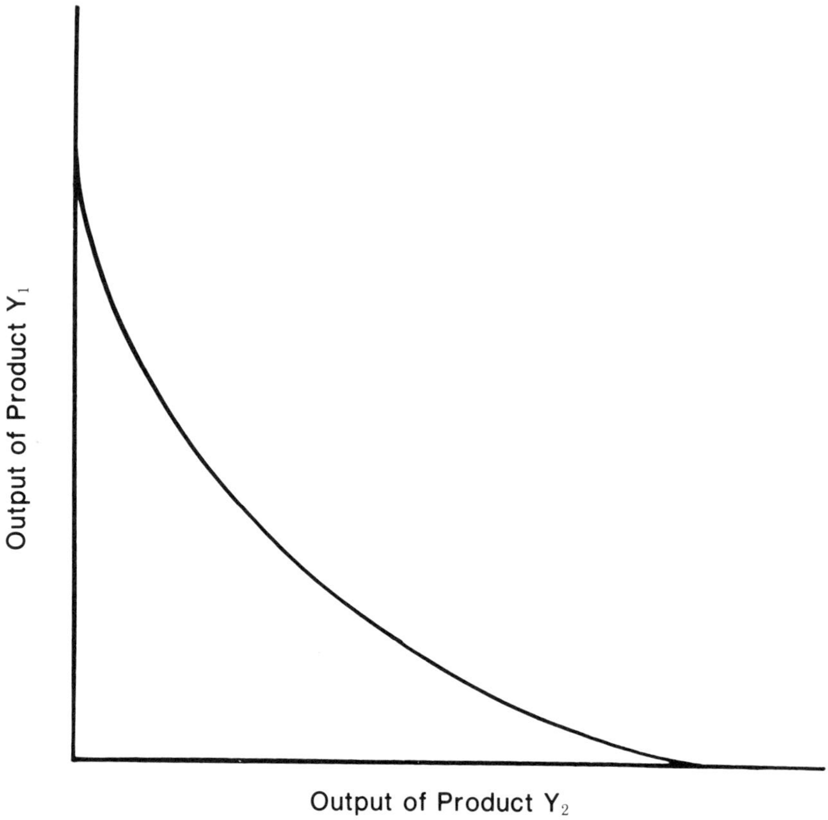

FIG. 4.3. A CONVEX PRODUCTION POSSIBILITIES CURVE INDICATING DECREASING RATE OF SUBSTITUTION

and Y_2 to combination B_4 of Y_1 and Y_2 using a given amount of resources by taking advantage of the small amount of flexibility left in the production process, such as selling hogs early primarily for bacon purposes rather than feeding out primarily for lard. The proportion after the shift is constant whether B_1, B_2, B_3, B_4 or B_5 level of resources is used. With joint products there is little or no degree of flexibility.

Complementary Enterprises.—Two or more enterprises are said to be technical complements when an increase in the output of one makes it possible to increase the output of the other from a given quantity of resources. Complementary enterprises are common in agriculture. It must be noted, however, that while enterprises are generally complementary when all resources are used together they may be highly competitive, as we shall see later, in the use of specific resources. For example, forage and grain are generally regarded as complementary enterprises but they often compete for the use of the labor resource.

An extreme case of complementary relationships may approach that of joint products (Fig. 4.2). However, the usual complementary relationships are less extreme and relationships can vary in degree up to the point where the increased output of one enterprise from a given quantity of resources does not affect (increase or decrease) the output of the other enterprise (Fig. 4.4.) In this situation, all the production possibility curves representing the various degrees of complementarity reach a point of maximum output (Fig. 4.4, point B) common to both enterprises and there exists no possibility of product substitution. However, when the time period is sufficient to permit a portion of the resources to be varied and used in conjunction with the fixed resources, and long enough to

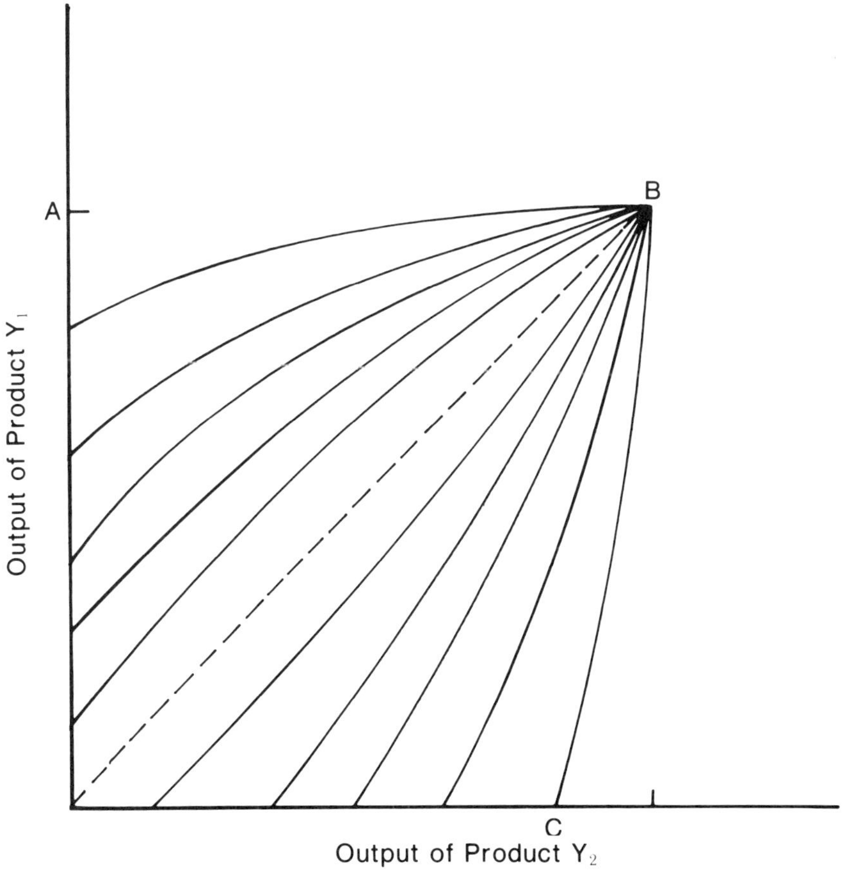

FIG. 4.4. PRODUCTION POSSIBILITIES CURVES SHOWING VARIOUS DEGREES OF COMPLEMENTARITY OF PRODUCTS

permit the full complementary effects to be realized, then only a portion (or portions) of the production possibilities curve is in the complementary range (Fig. 4.1, segments db and eh) after which the product relationships enter into the competitive range (Fig. 4.1, segment eb).

There are three ways in which complementarity of enterprises can be said to occur. First, a joint product provided by one enterprise can contribute to the production of the second enterprise. In farming, for example, the nitrogen, organic matter, improved soil structure and other products produced jointly with forage contribute to the total production of grain. Similarly, grain production may contribute to the production of forage by killing weeds or acting as a nurse crop. To achieve complementary relationships of this kind requires sufficient time for the complementary effects in the product to occur. In a time span of 1 year forage and corn would nearly always compete with each other for resources while over a longer period they can be regarded as complementary. The relationship may be illustrated also in tabular form (Table 4.1).

Second, complementarity may result from withdrawal of some surplus resources which have pushed the production of one product into Stage III, the stage of negative marginal returns, and the diversion of those surplus resources to the production of another product which is still in Stage I or Stage II. This action would increase production of both products (Fig. 4.5). Suppose M quantity of variable resources X_1, X_2, X_3, when combined with a given quantity of $X_4, \ldots X_n$ produces OA output of Y_1 and none of Y_2, or when devoted to Y_2 produces OC output of Y_2 and none of Y_1. The factors $X_4, \ldots X_n$, are common to the production of both products. By reducing the quantity of X_1, X_2, X_3 allocated to the production of Y_1 by NM amount, the production of Y_1 can increase by AB amount (Fig. 4.5A). In addition, if the NM quantity of X_1, X_2, X_3 is devoted to production of Y_2, then OE amount of that product will be produced also (Fig. 4.5C). Similarly, if the same quantity of variable inputs, X_1, X_2, X_3 were allocated with the fixed factors, $X_4, \ldots X_n$, for the production of Y_2, then OC amount could be produced (Fig. 4.5B) and none of Y_1. By reducing the quantity of X_1, X_2, X_3 allocated to the production of Y_1 by N′M′ amount (Fig. 4.5B) the output of Y_2 can be increased by CD amount. In addition, if the N′M′ quantity of X_1, X_2, X_3 is devoted to production of Y_1 along with $X_4, \ldots X_n$ factors, then OF quantity of Y_1 can be produced also (Fig. 4.5D). The preceding can be simply illustrated with a single production possibility function (Fig. 4.5E) which indicates that Y_1 and Y_2 are complementary (segments AB and CD, Fig. 4.5E).

The third way in which complementary relationships may occur involves the changing proportion of joint products while output is increasing. For example, the proportion of fat and lean in pork production changes as the hog grows. In the early period of growth apparently both

TABLE 4.1. ENTERPRISE RELATIONSHIPS ON WOOSTER AND CANFIELD SILT LOAMS, OHIO, 1937–1943

Cropping System[1]	Acres of Land		Out of Total Production		Rate of Substitution of Hay for Grain[2]
	Hay	Grain	Grain	Hay	
C	0	100	217,840	—	+ 10.9 (Complementary)
C–C–C–W–A	20	80	229,776	128,800	– 0.19 (Competitive)
C–W–A	33	67	215,480	203,200	– 0.22 (Competitive)
C–C–W–A–A	40	60	190,672	316,000	– 0.53 (Competitive)
C–W–A–A	50	50	165,928	363,000	

Source: Heady, E.O. and Jensen, H.R. 1952. Economics of crop rotations. Iowa Agric. Exp. Stn. Bull. *383*.
[1] C = Corn, W = Wheat, A = Alfalfa.
[2] Pounds of grain sacrificed for each pound of hay gained.
1 acre = 0.4 ha.
1 lb = 0.45 kg.

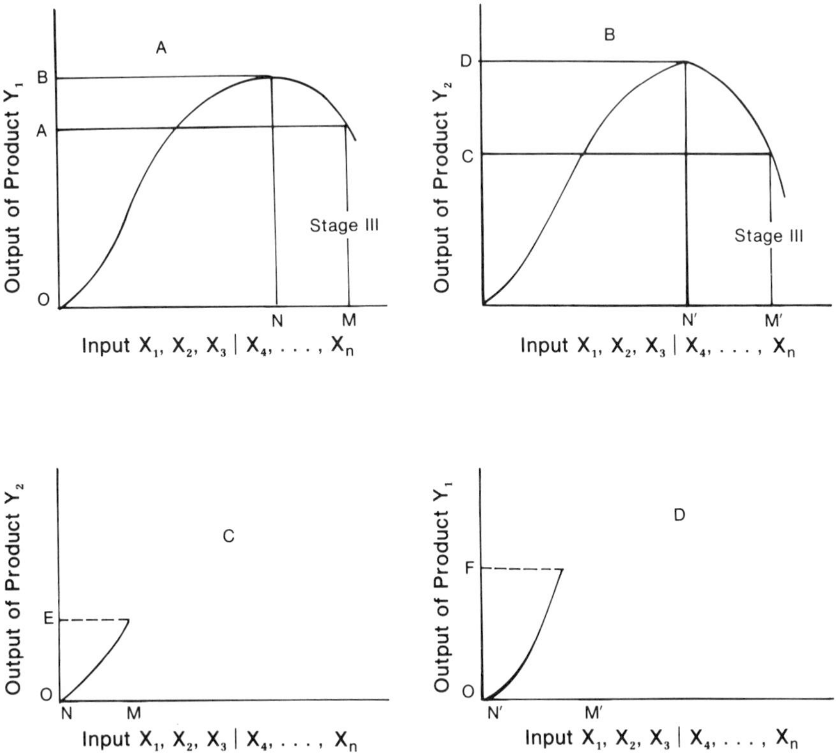

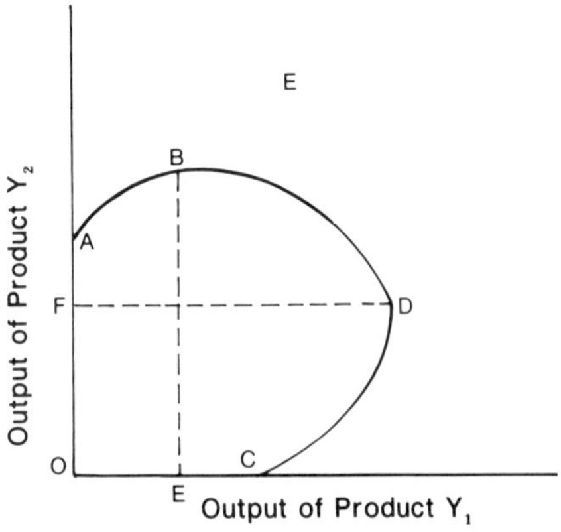

FIG. 4.5. PRODUCTION FUNCTIONS AND RESULTANT PRODUCTION POSSIBILITIES CURVE SHOWING COMPLEMENTARY RELATIONSHIPS OF PRODUCTS Y_1 AND Y_2

fat and lean proportions increase, but at heavier weights there is an increasing proportion of fat.

From the study of the complementary relationships between products, it is clear that a farmer would not produce rationally in the complementary ranges. It is also clear that in order to maximize profits some of both products must be produced regardless of the relative prices of the products and even if the price of one product is zero.

Supplementary Enterprises.—When the output of one product can be increased from a given quantity of resources without a change in the output of another product, then the two enterprises are said to be supplementary. This relationship arises from the nature of the fixed resources. These give off a continued flow of services which often are used in the production of one product Y_1 yet at the same time may be used occasionally in the production of another product Y_2. The production of Y_2 will not affect the output of Y_1, or vice versa. In the supplementary relationship, resources cannot be withdrawn physically from producing one product and used for another product.

With graphic examples, the supplementary range is noted by horizontal segment AB and vertical segment CD of the production possibility curve (Fig. 4.6). Supplementary relationships are very common in all industries. They exist wherever a stock or flow of resource services is available but cannot be utilized entirely by one enterprise. However, it should be noted that supplementarity may exist with respect to one resource and not for others. Actually, in many firms most enterprises are only partially supplementary in that many resources may be used in other enterprises but some one or important resource group would not be utilized fully in other enterprises. For example, labor may be used in many enterprises, and in the off-season (for agricultural products) agricultural labor may be used in nonagricultural production. However, if the nonagricultural production requires skilled labor and the agricultural laborers are unskilled, they cannot be fully utilized. Thus, supplementarity may be said to result.

Competitive Enterprises.—A competitive relationship exists between two enterprises when as the output of one product expands from a given quantity of resources, the output of the other enterprise must be reduced, i.e., one enterprise will be produced at the expense of the other. What part of one enterprise must be sacrificed to gain one unit of another depends upon the peculiarity of the production functions underlying the enterprises. The degree by which one product substitutes for another can vary from the one extreme of a constant rate of substitution (curve ABC, Fig. 4.7) to the other extreme where no possibility of product substitution exists (curve AEC, Fig. 4.7). The latter extreme is a case of perfect sup-

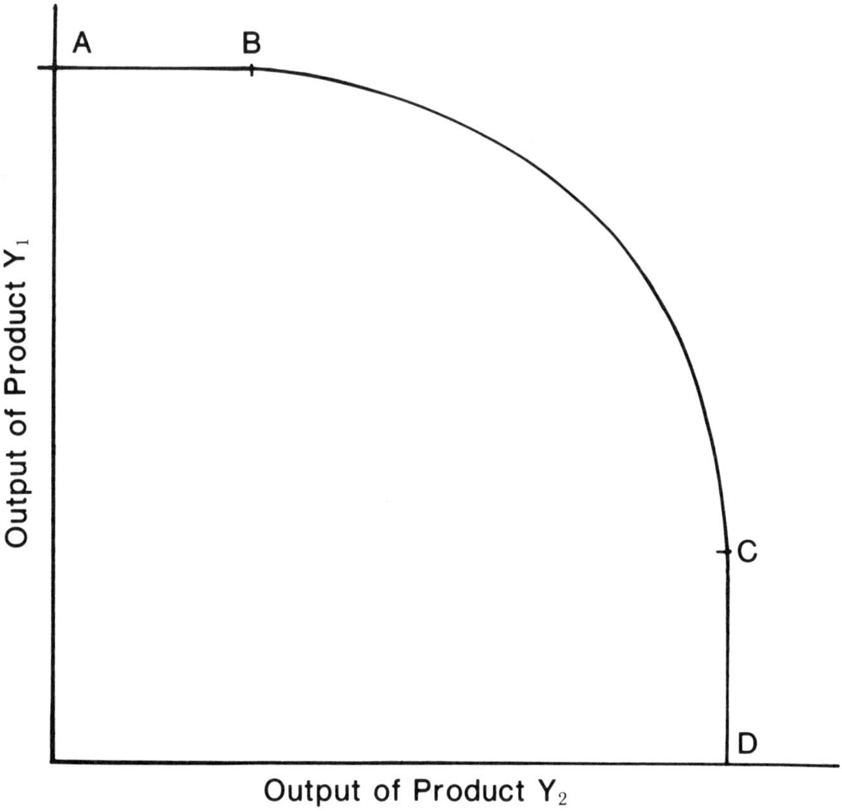

FIG. 4.6. PRODUCTION POSSIBILITIES CURVE SHOWING SEGMENTS OF SUPPLEMENTARY RELATIONSHIPS

plements through the entire range of production possibilities and represents a completely inflexible situation. However, less extreme situations are much more common in production (curve ADC, Fig. 4.7).

The concept of marginal rate of substitution with respect to the product-product relationships has the same meaning as in the factor-factor relationships. It refers to the amount of change in one product associated with a change in one unit of a competing enterprise and is measured by the ratio, $\Delta Y_1/\Delta Y_2$.

A linear production possibilities curve indicates a constant rate of production substitution. For each unit of one product gained, a constant amount of another product must be sacrificed when the quantity of resources is held constant. To have a linear production possibilities curve, the underlying production functions must be linear also. In addition, the resources must be homogeneous, otherwise there would be an increasing rate of product substitution. If one or both of the underlying production functions are discontinuous with linear segments (Fig. 4.8A and B), the maximum production possibilities curve will be of the general nature approaching the one of increasing rate of substitution (Fig. 4.8C).[3]

A curved production possibilities curve indicates an increasing rate of product substitution. This means that increasing sacrifices in the production of one product must be made for each unit increase in the output of the other product when the quantity of resources is held constant. This curve is always concave to the origin (line ADC, Fig. 4.7; segment BC, Fig. 4.6). An increasing rate of product substitution will always result when one or both the underlying production functions possesses a diminishing rate of return to the resources employed (Stage II) and the other function possesses at least a constant rate of returns. Another contribut-

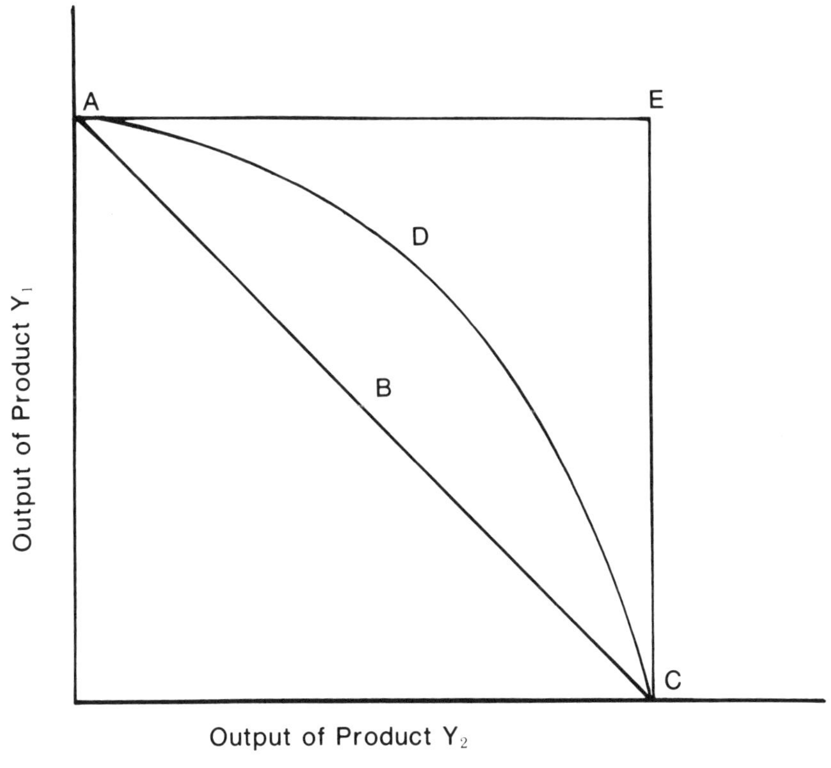

FIG. 4.7. PRODUCTION POSSIBILITIES CURVES INDICATING LINEAR, INCREASING AND ZERO RATES OF SUBSTITUTION

[3] For the student who wishes to calculate this hypothetical example, the following conditions were assumed: Only 30 units of X_1 and 20 units of X_2 were used to produce products Y_1 and Y_2 with the production functions, $X_1 + X_2 = Y_2$ and $2X_1 + X_2 = Y_1$.

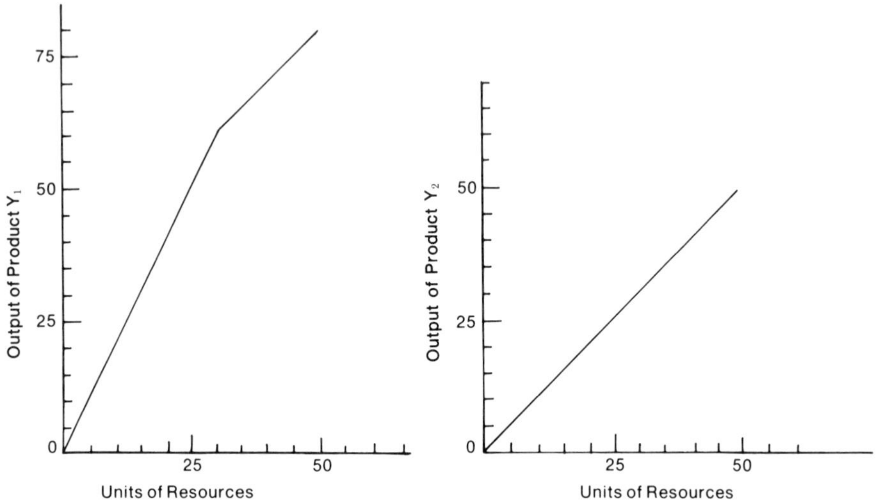

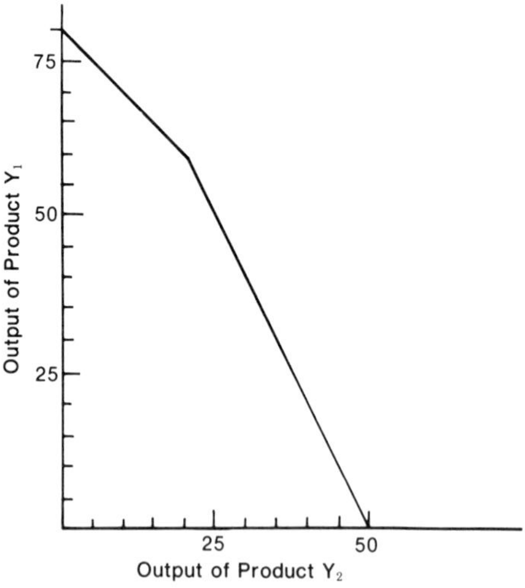

FIG. 4.8. PRODUCTION POSSIBILITIES CURVE WITH UNDERLYING PRODUCTION FUNCTIONS SHOWING THE EFFECT OF A DISCONTINUITY

ing influence to the increasing rate of substitution is the nonhomogeneity of resources, such as soil, labor, etc. As pointed out previously, homogeneity of inputs is essential for constant rates of substitution. As the combination of resources becomes less homogeneous, particularly with respect to time, supplementary conditions gradually become prevalent. The degree of curvature of the production possibilities curve reflects the marginal rate of substitution of one product for another and is measured by the ratio $\Delta Y_1/\Delta Y_2$. It can be observed readily that this ratio increases as one moves along various points on the curve from the Y_1 axis to the Y_2 axis.

Antagonistic Enterprises.—Approaching the extreme of competition between two enterprises is a situation described by a production possibilities curve which is convex to the origin (Fig. 4.3). The curvature of this curve reflects a decreasing rate of product substitution as indicated by the ratio $\Delta Y_1/\Delta Y_2$, which means that as enterprise Y_2 expands, with the quantity of resources held constant, decreasing amounts of enterprise Y_1 are sacrificed. This situation occurs when the underlying production functions possess the nature of increasing returns to the resources used (Stage I). The increasing returns stage may not be widespread but it is generally believed to be found in firms with very little capital. The classical example in agriculture is one where turkeys and chickens grown on the same farm tend to create a disease problem. In such situations, regardless of the relative prices of the two products, the entrepreneur will grow either one enterprise or the other but seldom both.

The ranges of product competition can be isolated from the complementary or supplementary ranges by use of the *ridge lines* as was done in the preceding chapter. By permitting for the moment the quantity of resources to increase, a series of curves representing production possibilities can be drawn (Fig. 4.9). Ridge lines A and B intersect each production possibility curve where the complementary or supplementary range gives way to the competitive range. It will be remembered that the slopes of production possibility curves are equal at the points of intersection. Ridge line A, for example, intersects each possibility curve where it is tangent to a horizontal line, while ridge line B intersects each possibility curve where it is tangent to a vertical line. Each ridge line represents all points where the marginal rates of substitution of product Y_2 for product Y_1 are equal, but also the lines set the boundaries within which product substitution is possible at an increasing rate. Between the two ridge lines, any number of lines, which are called *isoclines*, can be drawn, each representing equal MRS of products for each possibility curve.

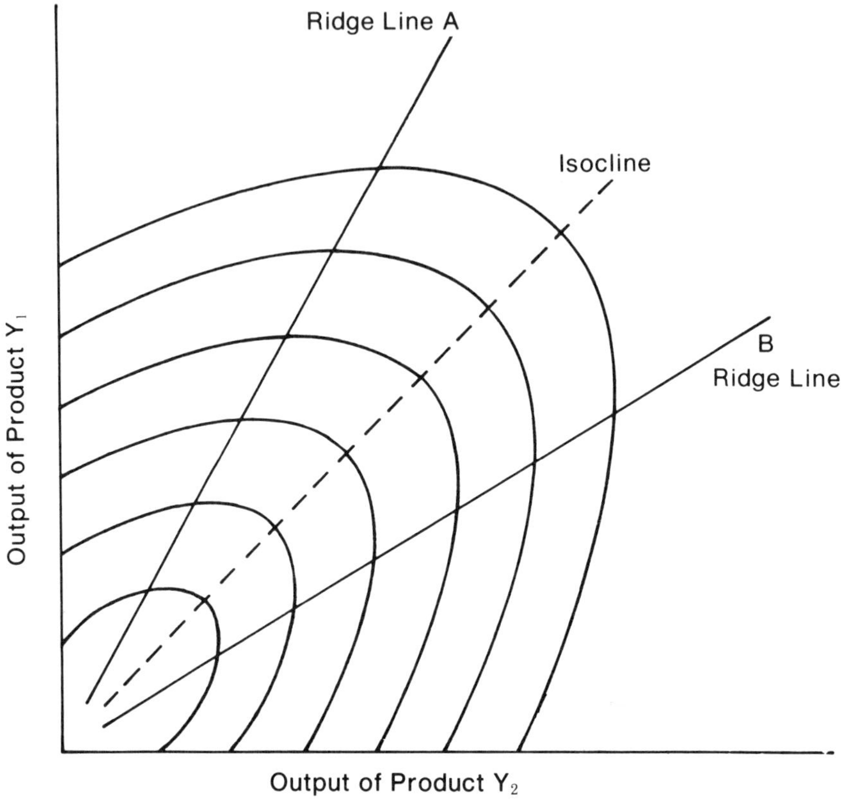

FIG. 4.9. A SERIES OF PRODUCTION POSSIBILITY CURVES WITH RIDGE LINES

Choice Indicators

This chapter has been concerned with the relationships underlying the objective of a maximum return from a given quantity of resources. The question of determining the optimum proportions of the products to produce when these products compete for the use of resources has not yet been completely answered. As the preceding functional relationships point out, there are many production possibilities open to the entrepreneur. The one which is chosen will depend upon the criteria employed.

There exist in these relationships many possibilities where no particular set of criteria is needed save the presumption that the entrepreneur prefers more of the product that has positive value to less of it. These possibilities include all of those found in complementary ranges, supplementary ranges, the antagonistic ranges and, in most instances, those possibilities which lie within the production possibilities curve. An entrepreneur who operates within any of these "irrational" areas can increase output, hence income, from a given quantity of resources, or reduce the quantity of resources required to produce some given output, hence costs, without the knowledge of prices.

The entrepreneur must have some criterion to specify the choice of the possibilities that exist along the production possibilities curve falling in the competitive range. The choice indicator as pointed out in preceding chapters may be one that is largely subjective in nature or one that is largely economic. In this volume, the principal concern will be with price ratios as choice indicators. However, before the subjective considerations are dismissed it should be noted that the policy followed by an entrepreneur is largely an expression of not only economic values but also subjective values, i.e., wants, preferences, goals and capacities which cannot be handled in dollar terms. These values may change with the life cycle of the family as well as the financial position of the business. They are also conditioned by education, experiences and the cultural atmosphere in which the entrepreneur operates. Personal values are likely to play a more important role if the entrepreneur possess low managerial ability, since it is probable that such an entrepreneur with little knowledge of technical relationships will rely on usual existing organization and practices found in the local community.

For a firm with a goal of maximum profits, the choice indicator involves the price ratio of its products. This ratio defines the slope of a line called an *isorevenue curve* which is a locus of all points representing all possible combinations of two products that will bring in equal revenue. There can be any number of isorevenue curves but the objective is to attain the greatest possible revenue from a given quantity of resources. Thus, to determine the optimum combination of products to produce requires a knowledge of choice indicators such as price relationships as well as the technical relationships between the products.

Optimum Combinations of Enterprises

Optimum combination of enterprises results when there is no possibility of increasing income by shifting the fixed quantity of resources between the products. Thus, maximum revenue (hence maximum profits) occurs, with the resources fixed in quantity (hence costs), when the marginal rate of product substitution (MRS) is equal inversely to the price ratio. The marginal rate of product substitution is the ratio of the decrement in product Y_1 required to compensate for a unit increase in Y_2 along the production possibility curve. Thus, MRS $= -\Delta Y_1/\Delta Y_2$.

The price ratio of Y_1 and Y_2 written as P_{Y_2}/P_{Y_1} indicates the slope of the isorevenue line (Fig. 4.10). The slope of an isorevenue curve is also de-

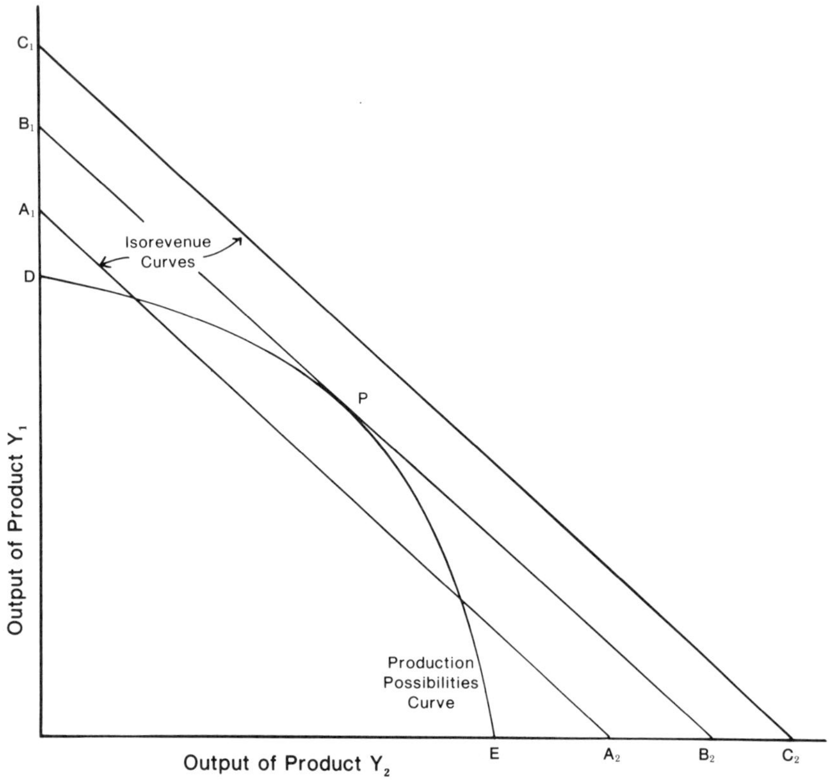

FIG. 4.10. PRODUCTION POSSIBILITIES CURVE WITH ISOREVENUE CURVE DEFINING OPTIMUM COMBINATION

fined by the ratio, $-\Delta Y_1/\Delta Y_2$. Both the slope of the production possibility curve and the slope of the isorevenue curve are measured by the ratio, $-\Delta Y_1/\Delta Y_2$, but their values are not always the same. When referring to the isorevenue line, $-\Delta Y_1/\Delta Y_2 = P_{Y_2}/P_{Y_1}$ and when referring to the production possibilities curve $-\Delta Y_1/\Delta Y_2$ = MRS.[4] The MRS $= P_{Y_2}/P_{Y_1}$ only when the value of $-\Delta Y_1/\Delta Y_2$ is the same for both curves. This still does not define maximum revenue, as the slope of the isorevenue curve

[4] The student may desire further exploration of these relationships. The revenue equation may be written as $P_{Y_1} \Delta Y_1 + P_{Y_2} \Delta Y_2 = \Delta R$. With the revenue and prices constant, if more is obtained from sale of a unit of Y_2, in the amount $P_{Y_2} \Delta Y_2$, the amount sold of Y_1 must be reduced in the amount $-P_{Y_1} \Delta Y_1$. Thus, $P_{Y_2} \Delta Y_2 = -P_{Y_1} \Delta Y_1$, or $-\Delta Y_1/\Delta Y_2 = P_{Y_2}/P_{Y_1}$.

for the same value can intersect the production possibilities curve (A_1A_2, Fig. 4.10) or lie beyond the production possibilities curve (C_1C_2, Fig. 4.10). It is obvious that neither A_1A_2 nor C_1C_2 will define the maximum revenue possible. C_1C_2 is unattainable, and in the case of A_1A_2 a higher revenue can be attained through a more efficient use of resources. Only when the isorevenue curve is tangent to the production possibilities curve will the maximum isorevenue curve be attained (B_1B_2, Fig. 4.10). This is the curve referred to when the condition for maximum revenue is stated. At the point of tangency (point P, Fig. 4.10), the optimum combination of enterprises Y_1 and Y_2 is defined by the coordinates of the point.

The movement of MRS can be traced by drawing a line tangent to each point on the production possibility curve, for the value of the tangent which measures the slope or the rate of change of the curve is equal to $-\Delta Y_1/\Delta Y_2$. In the competitive range, the MRS has its roots in diminishing productivity of the underlying production functions. At the point of tangency of these two curves, the condition

$$\frac{MPP_{Y_2}}{MPP_{Y_1}} = \frac{P_{Y_2}}{P_{Y_1}}$$

is true.[5] Since the condition, $-\Delta Y_1/\Delta Y_2 = P_{Y_2}/P_{Y_1}$, also holds true for

[5] More detailed explanation of this may be desired. The equation for the production possibility curve or isofactor curve may be written as $MPP_{Y_1}\,\Delta\,Y_1 + MPP_{Y_2}\,\Delta\,Y_2 = \Delta P$. The term MPP_{Y_1} refers to the productivity of the unit of resources withdrawn from production of Y_1 and devoted to production of Y_2. Thus, the productivity of the unit of resources devoted to the production of product Y_1 becomes an input in the production of product Y_2. Likewise, the term MPP_{Y_2} refers to the productivity of the unit of resources withdrawn from the production of product Y_2 and devoted to the production of Y_1. The productivity of this unit of resources devoted to Y_2 becomes an input in the production of Y_1. The term P refers to the total production of output, fixed in quantity, that can be produced from a given quantity of resources. With resources constant, if any of these resources are shifted to produce a unit of Y_2, in the amount $MPP_{Y_2}\,\Delta\,Y_2$, there must be a reduction in resources to produce Y_1, in the amount $-MPP_{Y_1}\,\Delta\,Y_1$. Thus, $MPP_{Y_2}\,\Delta\,Y_2 = -MPP_{Y_1}\,\Delta\,Y_1$,

or

$$\frac{MPP_{Y_2}}{MPP_{Y_1}} = \frac{\Delta Y_1}{-\Delta Y_2}.$$

It has been demonstrated that

$$-\frac{\Delta Y_1}{\Delta Y_2} = \frac{P_{Y_1}}{P_{Y_2}}.$$

Therefore,

$$\frac{MPP_{Y_2}}{MPP_{Y_1}} = \frac{P_{Y_2}}{P_{Y_1}}$$

maximum revenue, it becomes profitable to produce more of Y_2 and less of Y_1 as long as $-\Delta Y_1/\Delta Y_2 < P_{Y_2}/P_{Y_1}$. This means that an increase in production of Y_2, and a reduction of product Y_1, is always profitable so long as the slope of the production possibility curve is less than the slope of the isorevenue (segment DP, Fig. 4.10). Similarly, it is profitable to produce more of Y_1 and less of Y_2 as long as $-\Delta Y_1/\Delta Y_2 > P_{Y_2}/P_{Y_1}$, that is, as long as the slope of the production possibilities curve is greater than the slope of the isorevenue curve (segment EP, Fig. 4.10).

A change in the optimum combination of enterprises, as defined by the coordinates of the point of tangency and the underlying resource use, will occur without a change in price ratio when there is a change in the MRS of the products through changes in the techniques of production of either product. In other words, the new production possibility curve's tangency with the isorevenue curve will define a new optimum combination of enterprises.

The effect of a changing product price ratio on the optimum combination of enterprises can be seen readily through graphs. In a situation where a linear production possibilities curve exists, a slight change in the product price ratio can cause a shift entirely from one product to another (Fig. 4.11). When the possibilities curve is AB and the isorevenue curve is CB, the entrepreneur would produce all of Y_2 and none of Y_1. If the isorevenue curve should shift to AD, which may be a very small change, the producer would produce all of Y_1 and none of Y_2. Of course, shifts in isorevenue curves can take place without affecting the product combination.

When the production possibilities curve is such that an increasing rate of substitution prevails throughout the entire range, there is a range where a relatively large shift in the product price ratio can cause a relatively small change in the enterprise combination (Fig. 4.12). Given the production possibility curve (ACDB, Fig. 4.12), a change in slope of isorevenue curve from EJ to GF, which is a relatively large shift, will cause a shift from point C to point D. This is a relatively small change in enterprise combination as compared with what could take place under a linear production possibilities curve. Only when the value of product Y_2 is zero, as indicated by horizontal isorevenue curve AI, would a person produce all of the product Y_1. When the value of product Y_1 is zero, as indicated by vertical isorevenue curve BH, only then would a person produce all of product Y_2. A clearer situation is that of a perfectly inflexible position such as exists with joint and complementary products (Fig. 4.2 and Fig. 4.4), and at the extremes of perfect supplementarity. In these cases, the effect of a given shift of the product price ratio on the optimum combination of enterprises is zero.

When two products are complementary to each other, profit can be maximized only when some of both products are produced (Fig. 4.13). This situation will remain true even if the price of product Y_2 is zero as indicated by the horizontal isorevenue curve FI, or if the price of product Y_1 is zero as indicated by the vertical isorevenue curve KH. Between these two extremes, the competitive range is present. Points C and E set the limits of the complementary effects. In the case of range AC, for example, Y_2 will be produced because there will be greater outputs of Y_1 up to point C. In farming, it has been found that forages are complementary to grain. When this is true, profits can be increased as the forage hectarage is increased within the complementary range irrespective of the price of forage. Thus, forage production poses no particular utilization problem so long as it is complementary to grain. No direct return need be made on forage within this range but, of course, any return that can be realized from forage is a net addition to profits.

In the supplementary ranges of enterprise combination, prices again play no role (Fig. 4.14). As long as the supplementary enterprise has any value at all, it is profitable to produce to the extent of the supplementarity. If product Y_2 has a zero price as indicated by the horizontal isorevenue line AH, the production of Y_2 would be indeterminate and may or may not be zero. Likewise, if the product Y_1 has a zero price as indicated by the vertical isorevenue line BG, the production of Y_1 would also be indeterminate. Because of this, it is clear that if either the product Y_1 or product Y_2 has any value, there certainly would be some of both products produced. For example, if the price ratio of Y_1 and Y_2 results in an isorevenue line FI, which indicates that Y_2 has relatively little value, some of both products would be produced which would be indicated by the coordinates of point D. This would give a higher return than the combination defined by point C at the limit of the supplementary range. Supplementary relationships are widespread and important since they explain why certain farm products are produced at very low prices and why certain resources remain in use when their value productivity seems to be lower than would be if they were used for other products.

In a situation where the products are antagonistic as indicated by a production possibilities curve showing a decreasing rate of substitution (Fig. 4.15), the farmer would never produce a combination of both products Y_1 and Y_2 under any price ratio. If the isorevenue curve should be of the slope indicated by AB, the farmer would be indifferent between the devoting of all resources to production of Y_1 or to production of Y_2. If the product price ratio should give an isorevenue curve AD, the farmer would produce product Y_1. If the product price ratio should shift as indicated by the isorevenue curve BC, all the resources would be devoted to the production of Y_2. Thus, when the production possibilities curve is convex,

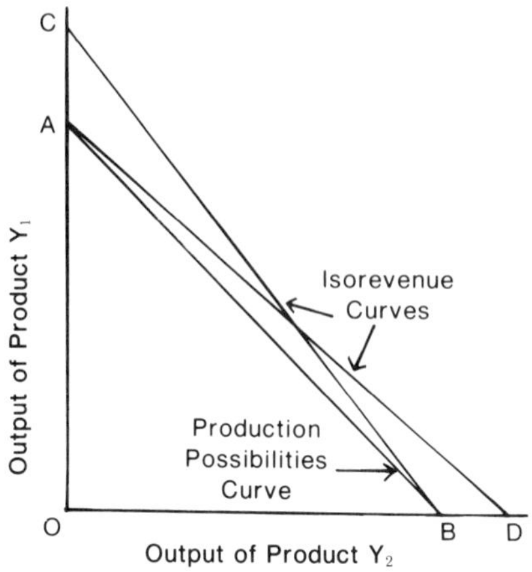

FIG. 4.11. A PRODUCTION POSSIBILITIES CURVE SHOWING A CONSTANT RATE OF SUBSTITUTION AND A CHANGE IN PRODUCT PRICE RATIO

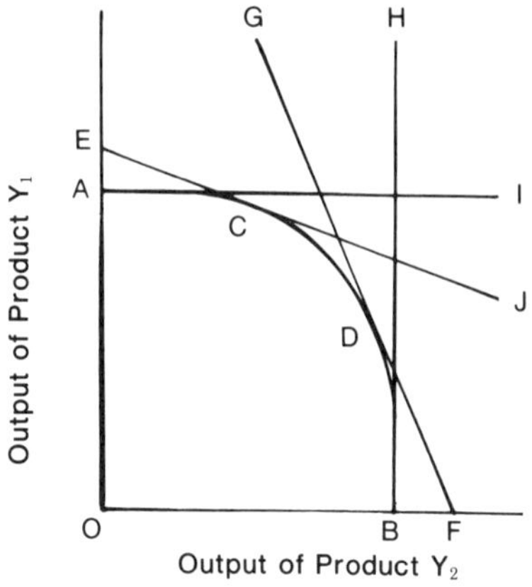

FIG. 4.12. A PRODUCTION POSSIBILITIES CURVE SHOWING INCREASING RATE OF SUBSTITUTION AND CHANGES IN PRODUCT PRICE RATIO

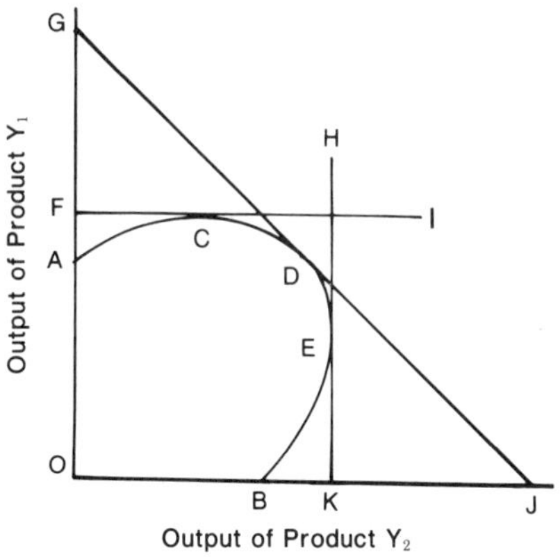

FIG. 4.13. A PRODUCTION POSSIBILITIES CURVE SHOWING COMPLEMENTARY RANGES AND A RANGE OF INCREASING RATE OF SUBSTITUTION WITH CHANGES IN PRODUCT PRICE RATIO

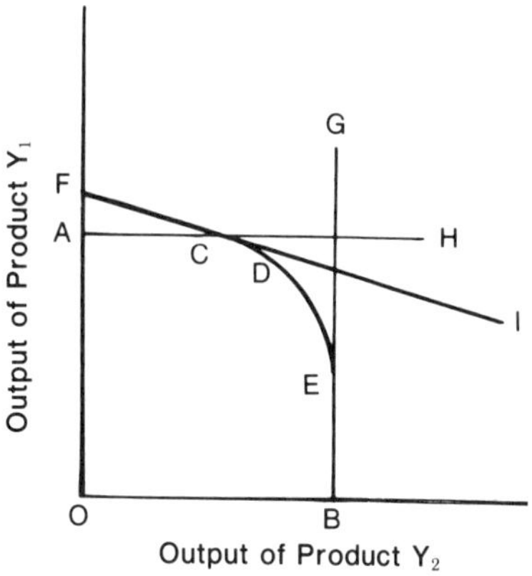

FIG. 4.14. A PRODUCTION POSSIBILITIES CURVE SHOWING SUPPLEMENTARY RANGES AND A RANGE OF INCREASING RATE OF SUBSTITUTION WITH CHANGES IN PRODUCT PRICE RATIO

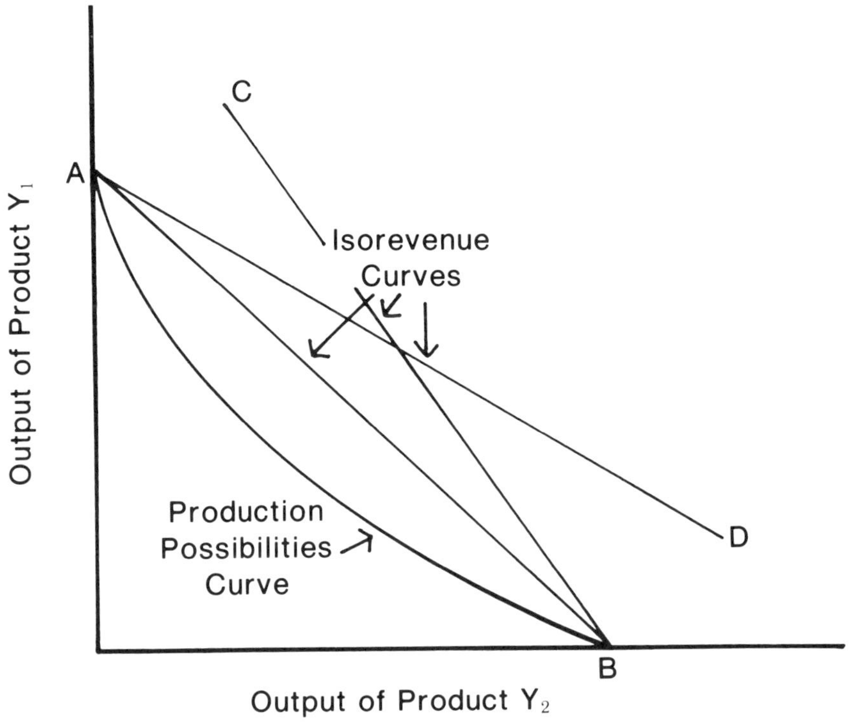

FIG. 4.15. PRODUCTION POSSIBILITIES CURVE SHOWING DECREASING RATE OF SUBSTITUTION WITH CHANGES IN PRODUCT PRICE RATIO

indicating a decreasing marginal rate of substitution, profits are maximized by specialization in a single product and never by diversification.

The foregoing discussion has stressed the principles involved in determining the optimum proportions of the products to produce when given quantities of variable resources are to be used in conjunction with a quantity of fixed resources. If the quantity of resources is permitted to increase, there would be a series of production possibility curves (Fig. 4.16). Each of these curves would have associated with it a given amount of variable resources and may be derived in the same manner as described in a preceding section. Some of these lower curves may be convex which may be due to increasing marginal physical productivity of the underlying production functions, but when more resources are used, diminishing marginal productivity of the underlying production functions gives rise to production possibilities curves of increasing rates of product substitution

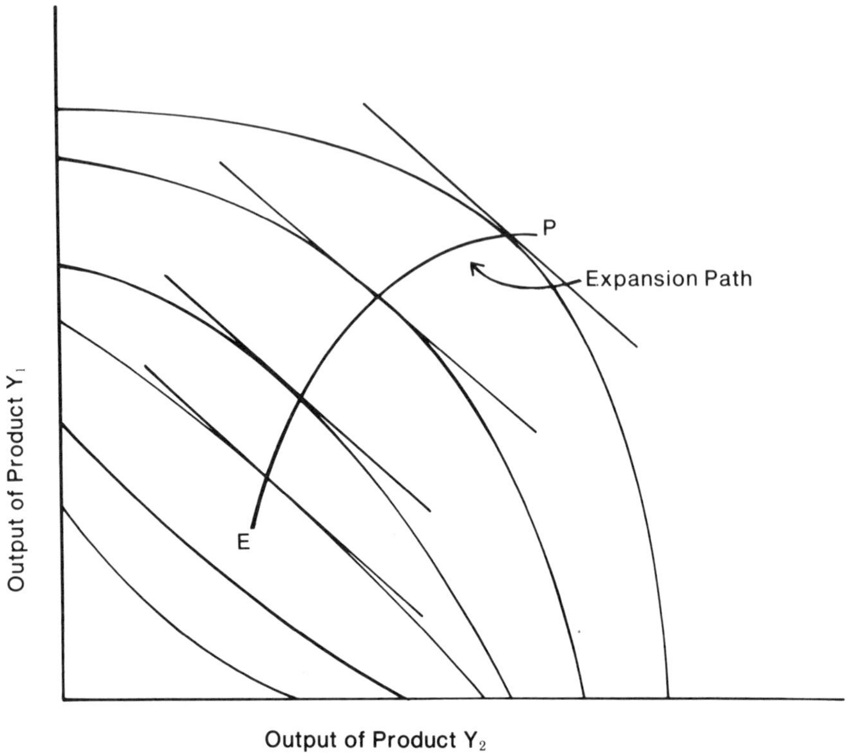

FIG. 4.16. A SERIES OF PRODUCTION POSSIBILITIES CURVES AND ISOREVENUE CURVES SHOWING THE EXPANSION PATH AS THE QUANTITIES OF RESOURCES ARE INCREASED

With a given product price ratio as indicated by the isorevenue curve, the optimum combination of products Y_1 and Y_2 can be defined for each production possibilities curve. By connecting each point of optimum proportion on each production possibilities curve, an *expansion path* (EP, Fig. 4.16) can be generated representing the optimum proportion of Y_1 and Y_2 which should be produced at any given quantity of resources or cost. The expansion path will always fall within the ridge lines as discussed previously. The problem at hand now when the quantity of resources can be varied is to select the proper production possibilities curve. As the expenditures are increased along the expansion path, through increasing the quantities of resources a point is eventually reached beyond which additional expenditures will not produce an equivalent increase in revenue. The point at which the additional resource costs equal additional revenue defines the proper production possibilities curve. This condition may be summarized as

$$\frac{MPP_{X_1, X_2, X_3} P_{Y_1}}{P_{X_1, X_2, X_3}} = \frac{MPP_{X_1, X_2, X_3} P_{Y_2}}{P_{X_1, X_2, X_3}}$$

with $MPP_{X_1,\ X_2,\ X_3}$ referring to the marginal physical product of inputs $x_1,\ x_2,\ x_3$; $P_{X_1,\ X_2,\ X_3}$ referring to their prices; the term P_{Y_1} to the price of product $_{Y_1}$; and P_{Y_2} to the price of product $_{Y_2}$.

Multiple Product Relationships

Until now, the discussion has been devoted to the production of two products in order to simplify the problem. However, the principles are the same for optimum organization of any number of enterprises which may compete for the use of the farmer's limited quantity of resources. It has been pointed out that an optimum combination of two products Y_1 and Y_2 is defined by

$$\frac{-\Delta Y_1}{\Delta Y_2} = \frac{P_{Y_2}}{P_{Y_1}}$$

which is equivalent to saying that

$$\frac{MPP_{Y_2}}{MPP_{Y_1}} = \frac{P_{Y_2}}{P_{Y_1}}$$

which may be rewritten as

$$\frac{MPP_{Y_2}}{P_{Y_2}} = \frac{MPP_{Y_1}}{P_{Y_1}}$$

Now, this relationship may be extended to include any number of products or enterprises and written as

$$\frac{MPP_{Y_1}}{P_{Y_1}} = \frac{MPP_{Y_2}}{P_{Y_2}} = \frac{MPP_{Y_3}}{P_{Y_3}} = , \ldots = \frac{MPP_{Y_n}}{P_{Y_n}}$$

This condition may be expressed alternatively as

$$\frac{\Delta Y_1}{\Delta Y_2} = \frac{P_{Y_2}}{P_{Y_1}};\ \frac{\Delta Y_3}{\Delta Y_2} = \frac{P_{Y_2}}{P_{Y_3}};\ \frac{\Delta Y_3}{\Delta Y_1} = \frac{P_{Y_1}}{P_{Y_3}};\ \text{etc.,}$$

for as many enterprises as desired. These relationships indicate that a producer can maximize the value of his or her output by producing that combination of products which equates the MRS between any two products to the ratio of their market prices. By manipulating these relationships, one can obtain $(\Delta Y_1)(P_{Y_1}) = (\Delta Y_2)(P_{Y_2}) = (\Delta Y_3)(P_{Y_3}) = , \ldots =$ $(\Delta Y_n)(P_{Y_n})$.

CHAPTER 4: REVIEW QUESTIONS

(1) Explain the concepts of joint products and product complementarity.

(2) An increase in the output of one product (A) decreases the marginal cost of a given amount of another product (B). Thus, the products are complementary in production. Explain and appraise this statement.

(3) Using the concepts discussed in the chapter, how would you go about advising a farmer on the most profitable combination of hay and grain to produce on a 240 acre (96 ha) farm? What information would you need?

(4) (a) Complementary relationship between Y and Z.
(b) Supplementary relationship between Y and Z.
(c) Competitive relationship between Y and Z.
(d) Most profitable combination of Y and Z.

Use the above concepts (and others if needed) to explain the basis of international trade and economic development of a country.

(5) In an economy in which 90% of the population is employed in agriculture and in which farming is largely of a subsistence nature, assume a major technological improvement (upward shift in the production function) for the major staple food (probably rice or another grain). Discuss the effect of this change on resource allocation (a) within farms and (b) between the farm and nonfarm sectors. Assume that farmers accept and use the new technology. Will the effect of this change depend upon the income or the demand for the product?

(6) A young farmer who has had college courses in farm management comes to you with the following data from a rotation experiment that had been conducted in his area over the past 45 years. He has converted all the data to a 100 acres (40 ha) of land basis and all other inputs were supposedly constant. He is quite excited about the relationship between grain and hay because he thinks he has found a point where he can get complementary returns.

Cropping System	Acres of Hay	Acres of Grain	Total Production in Thousands of Pounds of Hay	Total Production in Thousands of Pounds of Grain
C	0	100	0	218
CCCWA	20	80	129	230
CWA	33	67	203	215
CCWAA	40	60	316	190
CWAA	50	50	363	166
CWAAA	60	40	330	50

C = Corn—grain
W = Wheat—grain
A = Alfalfa—hay
1 acre = 0.4 ha.
1 lb = 0.45 kg.

He would like to have you help him decide on the most profitable combination of hay and grain to produce on his 240 acre (96 ha) farm. In answering his request you will need to plot his data and tell him about the transformation curves that describe his situation. You may also need to ask him for more information than he has given you. Lay out how you would fulfill his request, using the concepts of production economics.

Paper One: Economic Problems in Feeding Dairy Cows

John C. Redman and Russell O. Olson[6]

Much attention has been focused on government programs designed to improve the returns of dairy farmers and to increase the level of soil conservation. As dairy cows can use large quantities of pasture and hay, programs and policies which make hay and pasture abundant and relatively cheap and grain relatively high make it profitable to use larger quantities of forage in milk production, especially in areas which rely heavily on grain imports. The effects of feed and milk prices on the economic level of milk production and the extent to which it pays to substitute forage for grain in dairy feeding are important so far as profitable management of the dairy herd is concerned and also in appraising the adjustments to various government programs that farmers can or should make.

THE FEEDING PROBLEM

Theoretical Framework

The major feeding problems faced by dairy farmers are: (1) The combination of feeds to include in the dairy ration, and (2) the amount of feed to be fed each cow. A dairy farmer who is interested in operating a herd as profitably as possible must take into account the kind and quantity of his or her cows, the kinds and qualities of feeds available and their prices, the price of milk, the relationship of the feeding system to costs other than feed and many other factors.

If it is assumed that costs other than feed are not significantly affected by the feeding system followed, the most profitable combination of feeds

[6] Abstracted from Redman, J. C. and Olson, R. O. 1956. Economic problems in feeding dairy cows. Kentucky Exp. Stn. Bull. *648*.

for any given level of milk production will be the one that costs least and the most profitable level of feeding per cow will be the one that results in the largest return above feed cost.

A given level of milk output per cow can be produced with any of many different combinations of feeds. Barley or oats can be substituted for corn, soybean meal can be substituted for cottonseed meal and clover hay may be substituted for alfalfa hay. Furthermore, it is possible to substitute, to some extent at least, grain feeds for roughages. When quite similar feeds are substituted for each other, such as wheat for corn, the relative feeding values of the two feeds may not be affected by the proportion of each feed included in the ration. However, when feeds that differ considerably in bulkiness and protein content, such as corn and hay, are substituted for each other, it may be that the relative feeding values of the feeds are significantly influenced by the make-up of the rations. That is, 0.45 kg (1 lb) of grain fed to a cow on all forage ration may have much more feeding value, in terms of its forage equivalent, than 0.45 kg (1 lb) of grain substituted for hay in a ration which already includes a high proportion of grain. Thus, feeds which are quite similar, so that their relative feeding values are not affected by the proportion of each in the ration, substitute for each other at a constant rate. Other feeds, such as grain and forage, may substitute for each other at diminishing rates.

The least-cost combination of two feeds that substitute for each other at a constant rate ordinarily consists of all of one or the other, depending on which has the highest substitution rate relative to their relative costs. But ordinarily, the least-cost combination of feeds that substitute for each other at diminishing rates does not consist of either extreme of all of one or the other. The combination that yields a given quantity of milk at least cost is the one at which the rate of substitution of grain for hay is just equal to the inverse ratio of the cost per unit of each.

The level of feeding (or the rate of production) per cow that will result in the largest return over the costs of feed depends upon the cost of the feeds, the price of milk and the rates at which feeds are transformed into milk. Cows can produce at several different levels, depending upon the quantity and quality of feed consumed. Each level of milk production has its least-cost feed combination. In determining the highest profit level of milk production, the value of the added milk in going from one level of production to a higher level must be compared with the added cost of the feed involved in achieving the higher production. It pays to increase production if the value of the added milk is greater than the difference between the cost of the least-cost feed combination for the higher level and the cost of the least-cost combination for the lower level of production.

Thus, the important feeding problems in dairying are to determine both the least-cost feed combination for any given output of milk and the most profitable level of milk production per cow. In order to solve these two problems the dairy farmer needs a reliable estimate of: (1) the rates at which feeds substitute for each other, (2) the rates at which feeds are transformed into milk, (3) the price of milk, and (4) the cost per unit of each feed. In the sections that follow, guides are developed for estimating each of these factors.

Technical Relationships

The technical relationships in feeding for milk production play a vital role in determining the most profitable system of feeding. If 0.45 kg (1 lb) of corn has the same feeding value relative to 0.45 kg (1 lb) of forage regardless of the proportion of each in the ration, then, except in an unusual situation, the ration would consist entirely of forage or of grain, depending upon the relative prices of the two feeds, and a small change in the feed-milk price ratio logically could induce a farmer to feed to full capacity of the cows to consume feed or not to feed at all and to dispose of the herd, thus minimizing losses. However, if the technical relationships are not linear, such sudden shifts in feeding systems would not be so drastic. Thus, a knowledge of the various technical relationships is essential in working out the optimal feeding program.

Recommendations of dairy specialists for feeding dairy cows have traditionally been based on feeding standards which imply (1) constant rates of substitution between feeds, and (2) constant returns of milk to feed fed.[7] These assumed relationships are inconsistent with much experimental data and with the general concepts of production relationships used by economists. Such gaps in research data on the technical relationships prompted this study which deals with two interrelated problems. The first problem deals with determination of the rates of substitution between roughages and grain at given levels of milk output. The second problem deals with the milk response to different levels of feeding as influenced by different quantities of cows. Then, in subsequent sections, choice indicators are considered in conjunction with these two problems in determining the optimum feeding systems.

Substitution Between Feeds

An important consideration in determining the most profitable feeding system is the possibility of substitution between feeds in producing a

[7] *See* Redman, J.C. 1952. Economic aspects of feeding for milk production. J. Farm Econ. *34* (3) 333–345.

given quantity of milk. Although usual feeding recommendations are generally based upon the assumption of a constant rate of substitution,[8] there is evidence[9] that the inputs of grain and roughage possess a degree of complementarity. Thus, the marginal rate of substitution of two feeds such as hay and grain changes. To feed cows intelligently according to changing price relationships, then, a dairy farmer must know the rates of substitution between forage and grain. These rates will probably vary with factors such as size, quality and breed of cows, quality of forage and level of management.

Nature of Feed Substitution Relationships.—A given quantity of milk, or any other livestock product, can be produced with any one of many different grain-forage combinations. The possible combinations must lie between fixed proportions of grain and forage and a constant rate of substitution. Some feeds, particularly among high-protein feeds such as soybean meal, linseed meal and cottonseed meal, may approach a constant rate of substitution for each other. As grain and forage do not appear to substitute for each other at a constant rate, it becomes necessary to study the nature of their rates of substitution.

The empirical data pertaining to changing rates of substitution of hay and grain are limited. Therefore, it is necessary to synthesize[10] a production function which will provide a basis for determining the optimum combination of grain and hay for a given level of milk production. Synthesized production functions, like the usual budgetary procedure in farm management, may not be highly accurate from an empirical standpoint, but conceptual rather than empircal accuracy is sought in this instance. Ultimately, however, both are essential.

Data from various feeding experiments, such as found in Jensen,[11] were used in a framework of logic to arrive at estimates of the rates of substitution for forage and grain for various levels of production for three

[8] *See* Redman, J.C. *Ibid.*, and Heady, E.O. 1951. A production function and marginal rates of substitution in the utilization of feed resources by dairy cows. J. Farm Econ. *33* (4) 485–498.

[9] For a summary, *see* Redman, J.C. *op. cit.*

[10] The authors wish to make a distinction between synthetic and hypothetical data. Synthetic data have at least some parts based upon experimental results and they are combined in a logical way to construct a model which approaches reality. Hypothetical data are characterized by an assumption of facts merely for the purpose of reasoning and deducing proof or accounting for some fact. In this publication, synthetic data are used to construct a production function which, in the judgment of the authors, approaches reality. For examples of empirical estimates of milk-product contours, *see* Heady, E.O. and Olson, R.O. 1952. *Substitution relationships, resource requirements and income variability in the utilization of forage crops.* Iowa Agric. Exp. Stn. Res. Bull. *390* and Redman, J.C. 1951. Economic considerations of grain-roughage substitution in feeding for milk production. Unpublished doctoral dissertation. University of Kentucky, Lexington. Both studies point out that data used were not well suited to this purpose.

[11] Jensen, E. *et al.* 1942. Input-output relationships in milk production. U.S. Dep. Agric. Tech. Bull. *815.*

different qualities of cows. Roughage of medium quality was used in developing these estimates, which are presented in Table 4.2 and illustrated graphically in Fig. 4.17. These data represent the average substitution relationships over an entire year. Within 1 year it is likely that the substitution rates will vary considerably depending upon: (1) the stage in the cow's lactation period, (2) whether the forage is fed as hay, silage or pasture, and (3) the stage of maturity of the pasture, hay or silage forage.

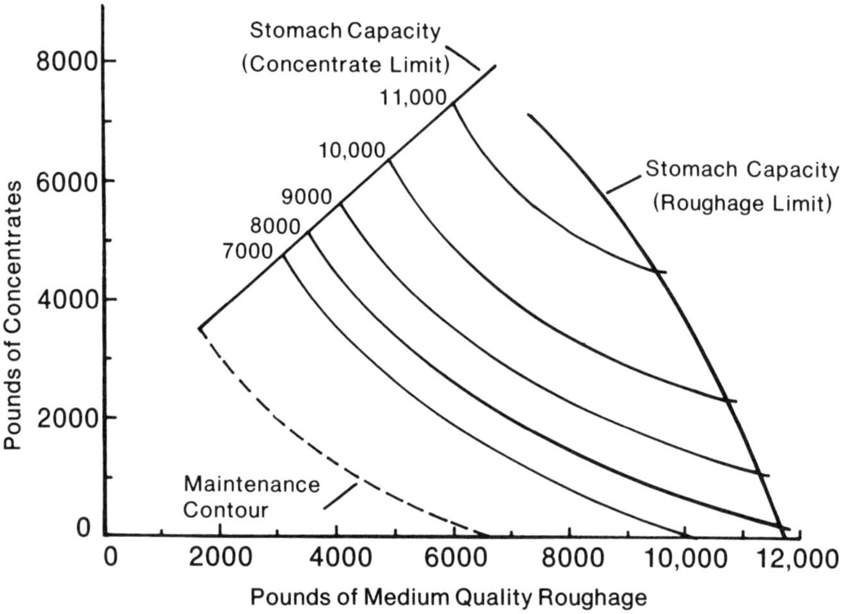

FIG. 4.17. THE ESTIMATED SURFACE OF A PRODUCTION FUNCTION FOR A 1200 LB COW CAPABLE OF GIVING 10,000 LB OF 3.5% MILK WHEN FED AT 1:4 GRAIN-MILK RATIO
1 lb = 0.45 kg.

In Fig. 4.17 forage inputs are measured along the horizontal axis and grain inputs along the vertical axis. Each point in the plane represents a specific combination of grain and forage. If all the various feed combinations which yield a given output of milk, such as 9000 lb (Fig. 4.17), are located and connected, they will form a milk product contour. The curvature of the milk-product contours indicates diminishing marginal rates of substitution between forage and grain. As the reader's eye moves along any one of the contours to the right, in the direction of more forage, it is apparent that each additional unit of forage replaces less and less grain, as the curves become flatter and flatter with respect to the forage

TABLE 4.2. GRAIN-FORAGE COMBINATIONS AND MARGINAL RATES OF SUBSTITUTION OF GRAIN AND FORAGE FOR VARIOUS OUTPUTS OF MILK BY GOOD COWS[a]

	7000 lb Milk			8000 lb Milk			9000 lb Milk			10,000 lb Milk			11,000 lb Milk		
lb of Hay[b]	lb of Grain	MRS H/G[c]	MRS G/H[d]	lb of Grain	MRS H/G[e]	MRS G/H[d]	lb of Grain	MRS H/G[c]	MRS G/H[d]	lb of Grain	MRS H/G[c]	MRS G/H[d]	lb of Grain	MRS H/G[c]	MRS G/H[d]
(1)	(2)	(3)	(4)	(2)	(3)	(4)	(2)	(3)	(4)	(2)	(3)	(4)	(2)	(3)	(4)
3,000	4675	—	—												
3,500	4025	1.30	0.8	5050											
4,000	3500	1.05	1.0	4400	1.30	0.8	5600								
4,500	3050	0.90	1.1	3875	1.05	1.0	5000	1.20	0.8						
5,000	2650	0.80	1.2	3450	0.85	1.2	4500	1.00	1.0	6125					
5,500	2300	0.70	1.4	3050	0.80	1.2	4050	0.90	1.1	5450	1.35	0.7			
6,000	1975	0.65	1.5	2700	0.70	1.4	3625	0.85	1.2	4925	1.05	1.0	7200		
6,500	1675	0.60	1.7	2365	0.67	1.5	3275	0.70	1.4	4450	0.95	1.1	6550	1.30	0.8
7,000	1400	0.55	1.8	2075	0.58	1.7	2950	0.65	1.5	4050	0.80	1.2	6000	1.10	0.9
7,500	1160	0.48	2.1	1820	0.51	2.0	2650	0.60	1.7	3700	0.70	1.4	5575	0.85	1.2
8,000	930	0.46	2.2	1565	0.51	2.0	2375	0.55	1.8	3410	0.58	1.7	5180	0.79	1.3
8,500	705	0.45	2.2	1330	0.47	2.1	2125	0.50	2.0	3160	0.50	2.0	4900	0.56	1.8
9,000	490	0.43	2.3	1115	0.43	2.3	1890	0.47	2.1	2925	0.47	2.1	4680	0.44	2.3
9,500	290	0.40	2.5	900	0.43	2.3	1690	0.40	2.5	2700	0.45	2.2	4500	0.36	2.8
10,000	100	0.38	2.6	730	0.34	2.9	1500	0.38	2.6	2540	0.32	3.1			
10,500				590	0.28	3.6	1360	0.28	3.6	2400	0.28	3.6			
11,000				475	0.23	4.3	1250	0.22	4.5						
11,500				380	0.19	5.3									

Source: Synthesized data based upon the feeding experiments and estimates from dairy scientists and agricultural economists. 1 lb = 0.45 kg.

[a] A 1200 lb cow capable of giving 10,000 lb of 3.5% FCM when fed a grain-milk ratio of 1:4.

[b] Includes silage and pasture converted to hay equivalent consumed. This does not include the portion of hay fed but not consumed, which is normally about 8%.

[c] This is the average marginal rate of substitution of hay for grain, pounds of grain required to substitute for 1 lb of hay within a short range and is the reciprocal of column 4.

[d] This is the average marginal rate of substitution of grain for hay, pounds of hay required to substitute for 1 lb of grain within a short range and is the reciprocal of column 3.

axis. The curvature of the product contours is a measure of the degree of substitutability between the feeds.

In feeding dairy cows, a certain amount of feed is required for maintenance of the cow before any milk is produced. The "zero product contour" may be considered the maintenance contour, that is, the locus of all feed combinations which come short of producing any milk. Any feed combination that falls in the area below the maintenance contour produces no milk and fails to maintain the cow.[12] Any feed combination that falls above the maintenance contour produces some milk. A milk-product contour, which connects all feed combinations that will produce a given quantity of milk, may be obtained for any specified level of milk production within the limits of the cow's capacity to consume feed.

The ability of a cow to consume forage or hay at a given time is determined by the capacity of the stomach to hold feed. The "stomach capacity line" sets the limits within which it is practical to feed forage to dairy cows, and it appears to be a curve concave to the origin (Fig. 4.17).

The extreme right end of each milk-product contour stops or becomes discontinuous at the stomach capacity for forage. When a cow is fed forage to capacity, it is possible to increase milk production, that is, to move to a higher contour, by feeding more grain and reducing the forage intake. This will increase the quantity of feed nutrients passing through the digestive system.

The left end of the milk-product contours as shown in Fig. 4.17 probably stops short of touching the grain axis. How quickly these contours turn up cannot be determined from the available data. There is some evidence, however, that beyond a grain-milk ratio of about 1:1.50 or 1:1.75 the cow will go off feed, at which point the product contours would become vertical. This sets the "physiological limit for grain" beyond which it would be unsafe and impractical under any price condition to feed more concentrates.

Diminishing Returns to Feed

A dairy farmer must determine not only the optimum combination of grain and roughage but also the optimum level of feeding. The level to which the yield of milk should be pushed revolves around the principle of diminishing returns. Higher and higher levels of milk output (higher product contours) may be obtained from a given cow by feeding more feed. However, successive increments of feed will add less and less to total production.

[12] It is recognized, however, that this contour is not so clear cut as cows normally produce some milk at the expense of their own maintenance if feed is limited for a period, especially after calving.

Nature of Feed-milk Relationships.—The law of diminishing returns has been demonstrated many times in both plant and animal sciences. The most comprehensive study of input-output relationships in milk production is that of Jensen *et al.*[13] In one of the series of experiments included in the study, it was assumed that the most economical combination of forage and grain would coincide with the stomach capacity line. The cows were fed hay free choice and increasing quantities of grain. As more grain was fed, the cows ate less roughage, but the total consumption of nutrients increased with each increment of grain. The marginal physical productivity of the feed declined at a decreasing rate from the outset when additional feed above maintenance was fed. In these experiments, heavy feeding of corn silage at all levels did not permit precise separation of grain and roughage. The group of cows fed "roughage alone" actually received a moderate feeding of grain in the silage. Thus, the response to the feeding of grain and forage at low levels of grain feeding was not obtained. However, it appears that the marginal physical productivity of the grain and forage at this level would have been high.

Solution of the problem of determining the economical optimum level of feeding requires a knowledge of the response in milk production to additional increments of feed. Thus, the synthesized function and the empirical data from the Jensen study provided the basis for determining the feed-milk relationships (Tables 4.3–4.5; Fig. 4.18) for cows capable of producing 7000, 10,000 and 13,000 lb of 3.5% fat-corrected milk when fed grain at an average rate of 1 lb for each 4 lb of milk and hay fed free choice. When cows are fed hay free choice, the nutrient intake is usually increased by increasing the grain portion of the ration and letting the cows readjust their hay intake. Farmers then often refer to the increase of milk by feeding grain as a response to grain feeding. Strictly speaking, the production logic involved is open to question,[14] but from a practical standpoint the farmer can consider such relationships as approximate.

Productivity of Cows.—The general assumption made in discussing the milk response to increased level of feeding, as well as the rate of feed substitution, was that other factors such as productivity and size of cows, breed and management practices would be held constant. The rate of feed substitution and productivity of feed depends upon the level at which such factors are fixed. For instance, the milk response to a given quantity of grain is greater with better quality cows. The inherent ability of cows to convert feed into milk sets the economic limits of feeding. The

[13] Jensen, E. *et al.*, *op. cit.*

[14] For a short discussion of this shortcoming, *see* Redman, J.C. 1954. Methodological issues in research in feeding for economical milk production. *J. Farm Econ.* *36* (2) 323–327.

fifth 500 lb unit of grain (the increase from 2000 to 2500 lb) with hay fed free choice produced 205 lb of milk when fed to low-producing cows, 435 lb when fed to good-producing cows and 515 lb when fed to high-producing cows (Fig. 4.18). Thus, a given quantity of grain is not as pro-

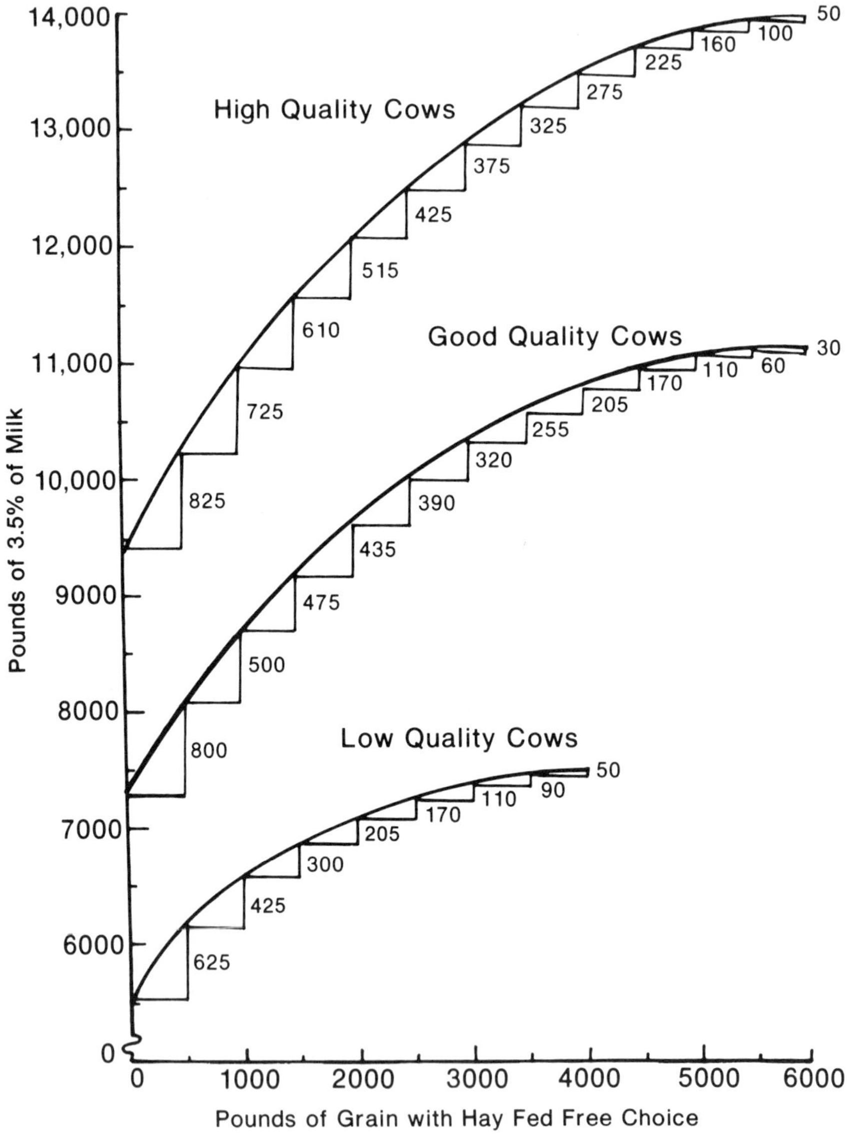

FIG. 4.18. RELATIVE PRODUCTIVITY OF GRAIN WHEN FED WITH HAY FREE CHOICE TO LOW, GOOD AND HIGH QUALITY COWS
1 lb = 0.45 kg.

TABLE 4.3. MILK PRODUCED AND QUANTITIES OF HAY AND GRAIN CONSUMED WHEN LOW-QUALITY HOLSTEIN COWS ARE FED MEDIUM-QUALITY HAY FREE CHOICE

No. of 500 lb Units of Grain	Grain Consumed (lb)	Hay Consumed[1] (lb)	TDN Consumed (lb)	Milk Produced (lb)	Additional 3.5% Milk per 500 lb Additional Grain (lb)	Additional Grain per lb of Additional Milk (lb)	Hay Saved per lb of Additional Milk (lb)
0	0	11,600	5220	5525	—	—	—
1	500	11,400	5505	6150	625	0.80	0.32
2	1000	11,200	5790	6575	425	1.18	0.47
3	1500	10,950	6053	6875	300	1.67	0.83
4	2000	10,725	6326	7080	205	2.44	1.10
5	2500	10,475	6589	7250	170	2.94	1.47
6	3000	10,200	6840	7360	110	4.55	2.50
7	3500	9,800	7035	7450	90	5.55	4.44
8	4000	9,300	7185	7500	50	10.00	10.00

Source: Based on data from U.S. Dep. Agric. Tech. Bull. *815* and estimates from dairy specialists and agricultural economists. These estimates do not include the portion of hay fed but not consumed which is normally about 8%.

[1] It is recognized that a part of the hay (hay equivalent) will be in the form of pasture on most farms.

1 lb = 0.45 kg.

TABLE 4.4. MILK PRODUCED AND QUANTITIES OF HAY AND GRAIN CONSUMED WHEN GOOD HOLSTEIN COWS ARE FED MEDIUM-QUALITY HAY FREE CHOICE

No. of 500 lb Units of Grain	Grain Consumed (lb)	Hay Consumed[1] (lb)	TDN Consumed (lb)	Milk Produced (lb)	Additional 3.5% Milk per 500 lb Additional Grain (lb)	Additional Grain per lb of Additional Milk (lb)	Hay Saved per lb of Additional Milk (lb)
0	0	11,800	5310	7,300	—	—	—
1	500	11,600	5595	8,100	800	0.62	0.25
2	1000	11,400	5880	8,700	600	0.83	0.33
3	1500	11,150	6143	9,175	475	1.05	0.52
4	2000	10,925	6416	9,610	435	1.15	0.52
5	2500	10,675	6679	10,000	390	1.28	0.64
6	3000	10,400	6930	10,320	320	1.56	0.86
7	3500	10,100	7170	10,575	255	1.96	1.18
8	4000	9,800	7410	10,780	205	2.44	1.46
9	4500	9,425	7616	10,950	170	3.24	2.21
10	5000	9,100	7845	11,060	110	4.55	2.95
11	5500	8,725	8051	11,120	60	8.33	10.41
12	6000	8,350	8258	11,150	30	16.67	20.83

Source: Based on data from U.S. Dep. Agric. Tech. Bull. *815* and estimates from dairy specialists and agricultural economists. These estimates do not include the portion of hay fed but not consumed which is normally about 8%.

[1] It is recognized that a part of the hay (hay equivalent) will be in the form of pasture on most farms.

1 lb = 0.45 kg.

TABLE 4.5. MILK PRODUCED AND QUANTITIES OF HAY AND GRAIN CONSUMED WHEN HIGH-QUALITY HOLSTEIN COWS ARE FED MEDIUM-QUALITY HAY FREE CHOICE

No. of 500 lb Units of Grain	Grain Consumed (lb)	Hay Consumed[1] (lb)	TDN Consumed (lb)	Milk Produced (lb)	Additional 3.5% Milk per 500 lb Additional Grain (lb)	Additional Grain per lb of Additional Milk (lb)	Hay Saved per lb of Additional Milk (lb)
0	0	11,950	5378	9,400	—	—	—
1	500	11,750	5663	10,225	825	0.61	0.24
2	1000	11,550	5948	10,950	725	0.69	0.28
3	1500	11,300	6210	11,560	610	0.82	0.41
4	2000	11,075	6484	12,075	515	0.97	0.44
5	2500	10,875	6769	12,500	425	1.18	0.47
6	3000	10,550	6993	12,875	375	1.33	0.87
7	3500	10,250	7237	13,200	325	1.54	0.92
8	4000	9,950	7473	13,475	275	1.82	1.09
9	4500	9,575	7684	13,700	225	2.22	1.67
10	5000	9,250	6912	13,860	160	3.12	2.03
11	5500	8,875	8119	13,960	100	5.00	3.75
12	6000	8,500	8325	14,010	50	10.00	7.50

Source: Based on data from U.S. Dep. Agric. Tech. Bull. *815* and estimates from dairy specialists and agricultural economists. These estimates do not include the portion of hay fed but not consumed which is normally about 8%.

[1] It is recognized that a part of the hay (hay equivalent) will be in the form of pasture on most farms.

1 lb = 0.45 kg.

ductive when fed to low-quality cows as when fed to cows of higher quality. This means that the optimum level of feeding grain varies with the quality of cows.

DETERMINATION OF MOST PROFITABLE FEEDING SYSTEM

The major managerial task of dairy farmers in feeding for milk production is to decide on: (1) The best and most economical ration to be fed for any given level of production, and (2) the amount of the ration to feed for maximum net returns. This involves a knowledge of the marginal rate of substitution of the two categories of feed which have been considered and the marginal rate of transformation of the feeds into milk, both of which are necessary in order to adjust the feeding program to changes in the prices of feed and milk.

Optimum Combination of Feeds.—The technical relationships on substitution of forage for grain for any given level of output were presented in the previous section (Table 4.2). The economic implication is that costs of feed can be minimized for any given output of milk per cow when the grain-hay price ratio (or cost ratios of the feeds as produced on the farm) is equated (inversely) with the average marginal rate of substitution[15] of hay or grain.

The grain-hay price ratio is usually close to 3:1. When this price situation prevails, the optimum combination of grain and hay for all levels of output of milk (the scale line E_2P_2) will follow closely the stomach capacity line for hay except for the 7000 and 8000 lb levels of milk production per cow (Table 4.2 and Fig. 4.17 and 4.19). For the lower level the quantity of hay is restricted, and for the 8000 lb level the complementary effects are such that the substitution rates of grain for hay are very high.

A price ratio of 2:1 would equal the technical ratio of grain for hay on the 7000 lb level of milk production per cow with 1160 lb of grain and 7500 lb of hay, on the 8000 lb level with about 1565 lb of grain and 8000 lb of hay, on the 9000 lb level with 2125 lb of grain and 8500 lb of hay, on the 10,000 lb level with 3160 lb of grain and 8500 lb of hay and on the 11,000 lb level with grain from 4680 to 4900 lb and hay from 8500 to 9000 lb (Table 4.2). It is at these grain-hay combinations that the various levels of milk production are most cheaply produced.

Optimum Level of Feeding.—The optimum level to feed dairy cows for milk production is equally important as determining the most economical and best ration to feed. If only a single feed were involved or if the

[15] Average marginal rate of substitution is used in this study instead of the marginal (instantaneous) rate of substitution for the sake of simplicity.

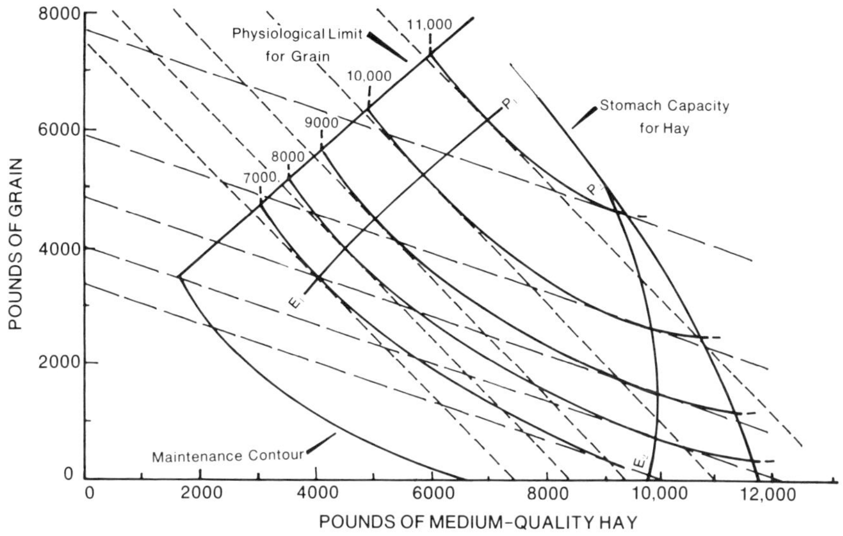

FIG. 4.19. THE ESTIMATED EFFECT OF A CHANGE IN GRAIN-HAY PRICE RATIO ON OPTIMUM COMBINATION OF GRAIN AND HAY ON AN ESTIMATED SURFACE OF A PRODUCTION FUNCTION FOR A 1200 LB COW CAPABLE OF PRODUCING 10,000 LB OF 3.5% MILK WHEN FED AT 1:4 GRAIN-MILK RATIO
1 lb = 0.45 kg.

various feeds were always combined in the same proportions, the optimum quantity to feed a cow could be determined by equating the technical marginal rate of transformation of feed into milk with the ratio of the price of feed to the price of milk. However, feed inputs are not homogeneous units. In going from one level of milk production to higher levels, the proportions of forage and grain that make up the least-cost combination change. The changing composition of the ration means that the price per unit of feed depends on the level of feeding. If the forage component of the feed is free, it is sufficient to equate the grain-milk price ratio and the grain-milk transformation rate along the cow's stomach capacity line. However, this is an unusual situation; ordinarily forage involves at least the cost of harvesting. A convenient way to determine the optimum level of feeding when both grain and forage have a cost is to find the level of production at which the value of the last unit of milk produced just covers the cost of the added feed; the cost of the added feed would include the value of the feeds added minus the value of other feeds saved. Given the price of each feed and the price of milk, the optimum level of milk production can be calculated from the technical data of the previous sections.

If, as is commonly the case, the grain-hay price ratio is 3:1 or more, expansion of production would follow the stomach capacity line. The data in Tables 4.3, 4.4 and 4.5 could then be used to determine the most profitable level of production. For example, assuming the price of milk at $15 per 100 lb, grain at $150 a ton and hay at $50 a ton, the data in Table 4.5 may be used to find the best level of production for high-quality holsteins fed medium-quality hay free choice. The last two columns of the table show the added pounds of grain and decreased pounds of forage for each added pound of milk. With each added pound of milk adding 15¢ to the income, each additional pound of grain adding 75¢ to costs, and each pound of hay worth 26¢, it pays to expand production to slightly over the 13,700 lb level. At that level, each additional pound of milk costs 12.47¢ (2.22 lb of additional grain costing 16.65¢ and a saving of 1.67 lb of hay worth 4.18¢). Expansion of production to the next higher level shown in the table would cost 18.32¢ for each added 15¢ worth of milk.

RELATION OF INDIVIDUAL FARM CONSIDERATIONS TO DAIRY FEEDING DECISIONS

Dairy feeding decisions cannot ordinarily be separated from other important decisions on a farm. The best feed combination depends, among other things, upon the cost of feeds. The cost of feeds may be the purchase price of the feeds for many farms. On many other farms it may be the value of the feeds in alternative uses; that is, their values as feeds for hogs, cattle or sheep, or their sale value; or their value as green manure crops (*see* Chapter 10 for a discussion of the nature of cost).

The cost of forages often depends upon the value of the forage crop in a rotation as a soil builder or deterrent to erosion. Thus, in the absence of a cash market for hay and pasture on many farms, it may pay to grow some forage crops just to maintain the productivity of the soil for production of grain crops even if the forage has no direct use. The cost of forage in the dairy ration in such instances may approach zero, or at least it may be no more than the cost of harvesting. Viewed in another way the value placed on forage in determining the best land use depends upon the feeding value of the forage. Thus, the decisions as to best land use and the feeding system to be followed must often be made jointly as the two are interdependent. Furthermore, these two decisions are related to the decisions as to the combination of livestock enterprises to be kept on the farm. Involved in the latter decision are the relative prices of dairy products and other livestock as well as the relative costs of feed.

5

Elementary Theory of Consumption Economics I

Just as economics of production provides one important aspect of economic activity, the economics of consumption provides another. In fact, one could argue convincingly that practically all economic problems in one way or another find their roots in this dichotomy. The production relationships discussed in the preceding chapters are basic to an understanding of the supply curve of output and, as will be pointed out in subsequent chapters, to the understanding of the demand curve for productive inputs. The purpose of this and the next two chapters is to provide the basic relationships in consumption of commodities necessary for study of the individual and market demand curves.

THE PROBLEM OF CONSUMPTION ECONOMICS

Consumption economics has not been generally regarded as a field with well defined and fixed limits. For some, the technological and physiological aspects of consumption have been the center of activity while others have regarded the field as a study of psychological and sociological aspects of consumption. The economist versed in classical tools of analysis would view the central problem in consumption economics as one of choice.

The problem of choice exists when the number and extent of wants of an individual exceed the means of satisfying them. This problem is analogous to that of production, only the nature of the product is different. The consumer has a limited income or budget to spend in an infinitely large number of ways for the satisfaction of unlimited wants. Thus, a choice must be made with respect to

(1) the quantity of any one commodity to purchase,
(2) the combination of commodities to satisfy a given level of wants or to obtain the maximum level of satisfaction from a given budget, and
(3) the preferred or optimum combination of wants.

At first, one may think that by centering the scope of consumption economics around the problem of choice one is embarking upon a narrow view of the field. After a moment of reflection, this will appear not to be the case. The general assumption of maximization appears to be reasonable since people usually prefer more rather than less satisfaction from any commodity or group of commodities. To make an intelligent choice, one must know the technological aspects of the various commodities, and as these technical aspects change, choices will also change. Other factors such as tastes, population, knowledge and information, governmental and institutional framework (e.g., structure of markets, merchandising techniques and legal restraints), etc., are also not excluded as some have argued. They are held constant at some level for purposes of analysis. The purpose of *ceteris paribus*, which is methodological and not substantive, is essentially involved here. For example, if one wanted to study the effect of one of these factors, say a technological advancement or increased information, on consumption of a particular commodity, the scope of consumption economics centered around the choice-making process would certainly be broad enough to include it and yet be very meaningful. If these factors were allowed to fluctuate or change at will in unknown ways, one would learn very little about individual behavior as related to the demand for commodities.

Subjective Nature

In consumption economics, the decision-making unit is generally the household. This is comparable to the firm on the production side. Just as the farmer or the manager is the one who makes the decisions on the production side, it is the *consumer* on the consumption side who must choose among the alternatives. It is evident that the so-called consumer may consist of an individual or a group of individuals such as the family or any social group. Therefore, the composition of the consumer unit will vary with the particular problem at hand.

Perhaps the most distinguishing feature of consumption economics lies in the nature of the product being produced. In production, the product is physical in nature and can be expressed in dollar value which provides the common basis for comparison. This is essential in making choices pertaining to the products. However, in consumption, the final product from the various goods and services cannot be measured in physical units, yet the consumer still must make a choice. In comparing the things which can be chosen, there must be present a common characteristic which may be called *utility*. The presence of utility or satisfaction may be considered as the ultimate result of human endeavor. Production merely provides the intermediate products and services necessary for the ultimate product, utility, which is often referred to as satisfaction. In fact, it is the utility or satisfaction which can be obtained that gives the intermediate products their value.

The amount of satisfaction or utility obtained from the goods and services varies among individuals since the psychological makeup of each individual differs and is subject to change over time. The time factor can be handled adequately by restriction of analysis to a given moment of time. Thus, utility or satisfaction obtained from the goods and services depends upon the subjective factors present at the time of consumption.

The problem of measurement of utility or satisfaction has been controversial for many years. However, the fact that a successful measuring stick has not been found does not render the utility theory of consumer choice useless. With the assumption of ordinal measurement and the law of transitivity, much can be said about the problem of choice even without exact measurement. The object of our discussion here is to provide an organized and orderly method of thinking about particular problems and to help predict answers concerning the direction and effects in consumption.

Marginal Utility *vs* Indifference Analysis

Much controversy has arisen, much of it needlessly, over the use of marginal utility in analysis. Some seem to infer that marginal utility and indifference analysis are two competing methods and it is a matter of using one or the other. The two do not replace each other since they are tools in the same kit and can be used either singly or together, whichever is applicable. Thus, they are complementary tools in analysis of relationships in consumption. The main criticism of marginal utility has been the alleged implication of cardinal measurability of utility. Much of the criticism was needless because in much of the analysis, the same conclusions are reached whether cardinal or ordinal magnitudes are used. All that is necessary for optimum choice is an ordering of the various alternatives according to some scale of preference. The consumer only needs to determine whether one good or set of goods is preferred to another.

One of the chief advantages claimed for the indifference analysis is that cardinal measurement of utility is not implied or necessary. An indifference curve is a boundary curve separating the area with combinations less preferred than those on the boundary curve from the area with combinations more preferred than those on the boundary curve. Given a field of such curves and the limits of the possibilities of substitution, an ordering of the curves is all that is needed to find an optimum. The expression of preference in determining the difference curve may involve more mental calculation on the part of the consumer than many would admit. However, others claim that this process is not necessarily conscious or deliberate and as such does not require such elaborate calculation. Whether or not measurement is involved is not as important as providing a framework within which to examine problems. Of course, if measurement could be made, it would be of more direct service. The problem of measurability is not confined solely to social sciences as the physical sciences have more or less arbitrarily selected some cardinal measurements of phenomena associated with ordinal magnitures. The problem of measurability doesn't keep the physical sciences from performing useful purposes in those phases.

THE UTILITY FUNCTION

The discussion of the utility function of an individual will not be unfamiliar because of the great similarity between the relationships found in consumption and those found in production. It is helpful to consider the consumer as a "firm" buying and using various quantities of goods and services as inputs and transforming them into a final product, utility. The value of this product will be psychological in nature and peculiar to the individual who makes the decisions relative to the utility gained and the costs involved. Those goods and services purchased are really intermediate products; they have value because they serve as inputs in producing utility, the final product. When consumption relationships are thought of in this nature, many of the concepts employed in the theory of the firm in the preceding chapters are useful in understanding the relationships involved. This close parallel eliminates some of the necessity of detailed discussion of consumption economics.

The consumer buys many goods and services, designated as X, Y, Z, . . . , which are transformed into utility, designated as U. Thus, the amount of utility obtained is a function of the quantity of goods and services consumed per unit of time, as

$$U = f(X, Y, Z, \dots,).$$

In the long run all of the goods and services are variable, but in the short run many of the items such as housing, automobiles, etc., are fixed and cannot be changed readily. The items which are regarded as fixed depend upon the consumer problem at hand. Thus, a subutility function can be noted as

$$U = f(X \mid Y, Z, \dots,)$$

which says that utility is a function of X with Y, Z, etc., fixed at some level of use. When one speaks of the utility of a good it is implicitly assumed that quantities of all other goods and services are held at a certain level.

Total Utility

The entire amount of utility or satisfaction obtained from consuming various quantities of a commodity with all other commodities fixed at some level is referred to as *total utility*. Thus, the magnitude of total utility is a function of the quantities of a good or service consumed per unit of time, and increases up to a point at which the maximum OA utility is reached with consumption of quantity OX (Fig. 5.1). Beyond this point (point a, Fig. 5.1), a consumer will not be able to increase

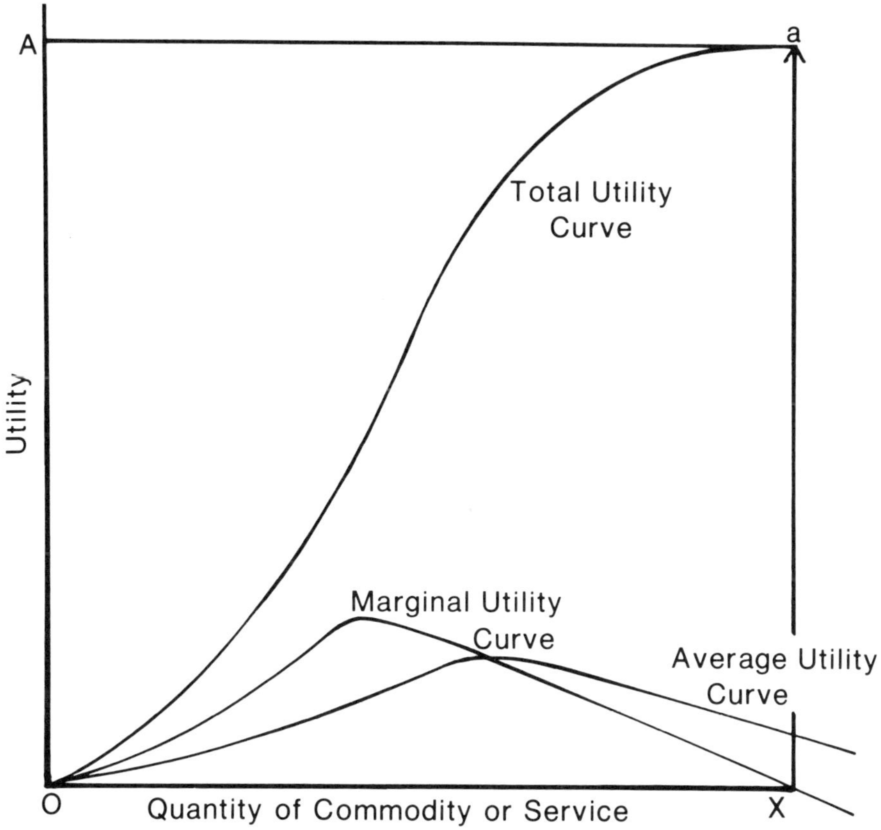

FIG. 5.1. UTILITY FUNCTION SHOWING TOTAL, AVERAGE AND MARGINAL RELATIONSHIPS

satisfaction from consuming additional units, and probably will suffer a loss of total satisfaction if extra consumption does take place. It is known that overeating of large quantities of food can make a person sick or that possession of so many shoes can lead to chaos and confusion. The shape of the total utility curve depends, therefore, on the peculiarities of the utility function and may comprise any possible combination of linear segments, increasing segments and/or decreasing segments.

Average Utility

From the total utility, two additional concepts may be derived—average utility and marginal utility. The *average utility* is found by dividing the total utility by the number of units of the commodity consumed. The average utility concept is to consumption economics what the average physical product is to production relationships. Thus, the same general relationships described in the previous chapters on average physical product have their parallel here. Yet, it must be kept in mind that since utility cannot be cardinally measured, any derived relationship such as average or marginal utility also cannot be cardinally measured.

Marginal Utility

The term *marginal utility* refers to the increase in the total utility which results from each additional unit of commodity consumed per unit of time when the consumption of all other goods is fixed at some level. Thus, the nature of the marginal utility curve depends upon the nature of the total utility curve since the marginal utility function is the first derivative of the total utility function. This means that the value of the slope of the total utility curve determines the marginal utility curve. As the slope of the total utility curve approaches zero, the marginal utility becomes smaller and smaller until it reaches zero (point a, Fig. 5.1).

It is logical to accept without experimental proof the law of diminishing returns as a valid and reasonable concept. Like concepts in other sciences, it can be treated as valid until proven invalid which has never been done. Thus, the marginal utility of any commodity must eventually decline as a consumer increases the consumption of that commodity with the consumption of all other commodities unchanged. There are at least two fundamental, logical reasons why diminishing marginal utility occurs.

First, the satiability of a particular want is generally observable. The point of satiety results when total utility cannot be increased by consuming more of the commodity. This means that the marginal utility of that commodity is zero at that point of consumption. It is also observable that when smaller quantities of the commodity are consumed, then the total utility is rising; thus, the marginal utility of that commodity is positive. Therefore, the marginal utility of a commodity must have been diminishing between the point of consumption where the marginal utility is positive and where it is zero. In a subsequent chapter, it will be pointed out that the demand of an individual consumer for a commodity can be derived from the marginal utility curve and that the speed or ease of satiability of a particular want greatly influences the elasticity of demand for that commodity.

Second, the commodities are imperfect substitutes, or possess a high degree of complementarity. This reason is closely related to the first. Most commodities tend to be consumed in some proportion to each other. When this is true, increased consumption of a given commodity, with consumption of all others remaining constant, will add less and less to the total utility because it is not in the usual proportion with other commodities. Thus, the marginal utility will approach zero and even may become negative.

Choice Indicator

The utility function indicates the relationship between the amount of utility and the quantity of the good or service consumed, with the consumption of all other goods or services unchanged. The consumer is interested in obtaining the maximum amount of satisfaction from consuming commodities while limited by a fixed quantity of resources with which to purchase several commodities. Therefore, the consumer will aim at purchasing the best combination of goods and services to attain the goal of maximum satisfaction. The choice indicator involved here is the relative prices of the commodities. This does not imply that custom, tradition, etc., are unimportant factors in choice making, but here the dominant factor is the prevailing price relationship.

The optimum amount of a commodity to consume depends upon the price-utility ratio, i.e., the utility obtained by consuming another unit of the commodity must be equal to its cost. The cost may be considered as the utility from other commodities that could be purchased with the money involved. Thus, the problem becomes one of determining the optimum allocation of a consumer's income to achieve maximum satisfaction. The general principle involved in maximization of consumer satisfaction is that with a given income, the funds would be allocated in each line of expenditure in such a manner that the marginal utility received for each unit of expenditure, say a dollar, is equal in each line of expenditure. Thus,

$$\frac{MU_A}{P_A} = \frac{MU_B}{P_B} = \frac{MU_C}{P_C} = , \ldots , = \frac{MU_N}{P_N}$$

where MU_A refers to marginal utility of commodity A, MU_B refers to commodity B, etc., and P_A refers to price of commodity A, and so on.[1] This equality means that an expenditure of an extra dollar in all lines of expenditure must have the same result in increasing the utility. Otherwise, one could increase utility by shifting expenditures from one commodity to another. This equimarginal principle is applicable in all types of problems of allocation, such as distribution of one's time, asset holdings, etc. However, it is often very difficult to achieve perfect equality in the marginal returns because

(1) many of the commodities and services consumed are lumpy and indivisible, and
(2) the budget period faced by the consumer is indefinite and difficult to define.

Many of the problems in the first category can be handled if the lumpy and indivisible commodities and services are considered to give off a "flow" of goods and services. Many of the difficulties in the second category also can be handled adequately by the "flow" concept and also by selecting an appropriate length of time period for the problem at hand. The longer the time period, the less troublesome will be the difficulties. Despite the difficulties in achieving perfect equimarginality, the principle still holds.

CHAPTER 5: REVIEW QUESTIONS

(1) Utility, even if unmeasurable, constitutes the driving urge in consumption. True or false?
(2) Elaborate the concept of utility as an ordinal quantity and of utility as a cardinal quantity.
(3) Suppose a college student has $1.60 to spend during an evening of beer and pizza with friends. Since they are sharing the pizzas they order, they agree that each person will contribute 20¢ for each slice that person consumes. Beers cost 40¢ each. Suppose the person's utility functions for beer and pizza are as follows:

[1] Because income is limited for nearly all people, the ratios will not necessarily be equal to 1, much less to zero which the point of satiety would indicate.

Number Beers Consumed	Total Utility for Beer	Number Slices Pizza	Total Utility for Pizza
0	0	0	0
1	12	1	15
2	22	2	25
3	31	3	33
4	39	4	38
5	44	5	41
6	47	6	43
7	47	7	41
8	40	8	37

How much beer and pizza will the person consume?

6

Elementary Theory of Consumption Economics II

For a long time the concept of marginal utility was used exclusively to explain demand, and often was used to explain more than it actually could. Another technique, which made use of indifference curves, was introduced in the early 1880s by the British economist, Francis Y. Edgeworth, modified by the Italian economist Vilfredo Pareto some 25 years later and made popular in the 1930s by two other British economists, John R. Hicks and R.G.D. Allen. Now, no economist can be without this standard equipment in his or her collection of analytical tools. It is basic for a more complete understanding of production and consumption relationships.

OPTIMUM COMBINATION OF COMMODITIES

The consumer is faced with numerous commodities and services which can be used in producing utility. The problem is to determine the properties of the equilibrium position for a consumer who possesses definite tastes and a fixed income. It is assumed that such a consumer faced with externally determined prices makes a choice which will maximize his or her satisfaction.

When the commodities faced by a consumer are many, the utility obtained then depends upon some combination and quantity consumed. Thus,

$$U = f(X, Y, Z, \ldots, n)$$

when X, Y, Z, . . . , n refer to the various commodities to the n number. However, a consumer is faced with a choice among only a few commodities in the short-run planning period; for purposes of simplicity assume two commodities, X and Y. Thus, the function becomes

$$U = f(X, Y \mid Z, \ldots, n).$$

This means that utility is a function of commodities X and Y with all other commodities Z, . . . , n fixed at some level of consumption. More specifically, the problem is to determine the optimum combination of X and Y to purchase with a limited budget given the relative prices of X and Y. A useful tool for this task is the indifference curve.

Indifference Curves

All consumers are assumed to have a scale of preferences for different goods used in consumption and obey the law of transitivity in the ordering process. That is, the consumer will not only be able to state that X is preferred to Y and Y is preferred to Z, but if these are true, then also X is preferred to Z. The indifference curve presents graphically the tastes and preferences of an individual consumer in sufficient detail to permit a wide range of analysis. Each consumer is assumed to be able, when confronted with a choice between two combinations of commodities X and Y, to express either a preference for one of the combinations or an indifference as to which is desired. In other words, the indifference curve rests on the assumption that a consumer can tell which of the many combinations will give equivalent satisfaction and which ones will give greater or less satisfaction. Some economists have argued that this technique will eliminate the implication of measurability of utility; debate still exists on whether or not it does.

An indifference curve[1] represents a schedule of various combinations of commodities that will be equally satisfactory to the individual consumer concerned (Curve I_1, Fig. 6.1). This curve shows all possible combinations of commodities X and Y which occupy the same position in the consumer's scale of preference. It also shows those combinations that will give the consumer a lower or higher level of satisfaction. Any number of additional curves can be drawn which represent other levels of satisfaction (I_2, I_3, etc., Fig. 6.1) that can be obtained by changing the total quantities of the commodities. It is difficult, if not impossible, to measure the levels of satisfaction in the way that physical products are measured. However, one can say whether one indifference schedule will be preferred to another, although not by how much. The family of indifference curves, or the utility surface obtained, represents the preference or taste pattern of the individual consumer; these preferences are assumed to be expressed independently of income or prices.

Properties.—Indifference curves possess some basic and realistic characteristics essential to analysis of consumer behavior. First, the indiffer-

[1] Referred to by some writers as an iso-utility curve.

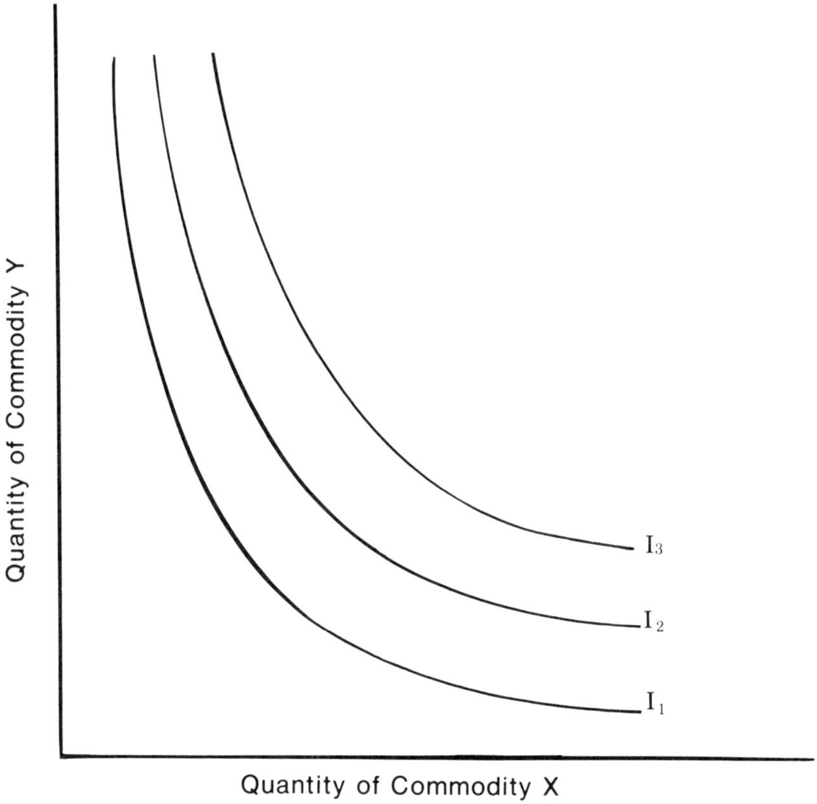

FIG. 6.1. A SET OF INDIFFERENCE CURVES

ence curve necessarily slopes downward from left to right, i.e., the slope of an indifference curve is negative. The necessity of this characteristic can be easily understood by noting the unrealistic implications of assuming a positively sloping curve. This would be saying that the consumer would be indifferent between greater and lesser quantities of goods. Second, the system of the indifference curves cannot have any two curves intersecting. This would lead to contradictory results; it would mean that a greater quantity of goods is sometimes preferred to and sometimes inferior to a lesser quantity. Third, the indifference curve is assumed to be convex to the origin of the indifference map. Actually, the possibility exists that the indifference curve may be concave to the origin, but if such were the case the consumer would specialize in consumption of one good or the other. The reason these three basic properties are assumed rests in the concept of substitution, one of the most powerful concepts in all economics, and in the basic idea of diminishing marginal utility.

The indifference curve of a consumer can be used to reflect the marginal significance of one commodity in terms of the other. The amount of a good which one must give up to acquire a unit of another good and remain on the same indifference curve reflects this significance and permits a little more precise discussion than was possible in the preceding chapter. Thus, a formal definition of the *marginal rate of substitution* (MRS) can be considered as the decrement of Y which will just compensate for an increment in X, without changing the level of satisfaction. The movement must be along the indifference curve and the degree of curvature of the curve will reflect the ease or difficulty with which the commodities will substitute.

Constant Rate of Substitution.—If the decrement of Y which will compensate for an increment in X along the indifference curve never changes, then X is said to substitute for Y at a constant rate (Fig. 6.2). The slope of the indifference curve, $-\Delta Y/\Delta X$, at all points would have the same value. An indifference curve which reflects a constant rate of substitution but at a 1:1 ratio would not only be a limiting case but an impossible case as the two commodities are perfectly equal in every

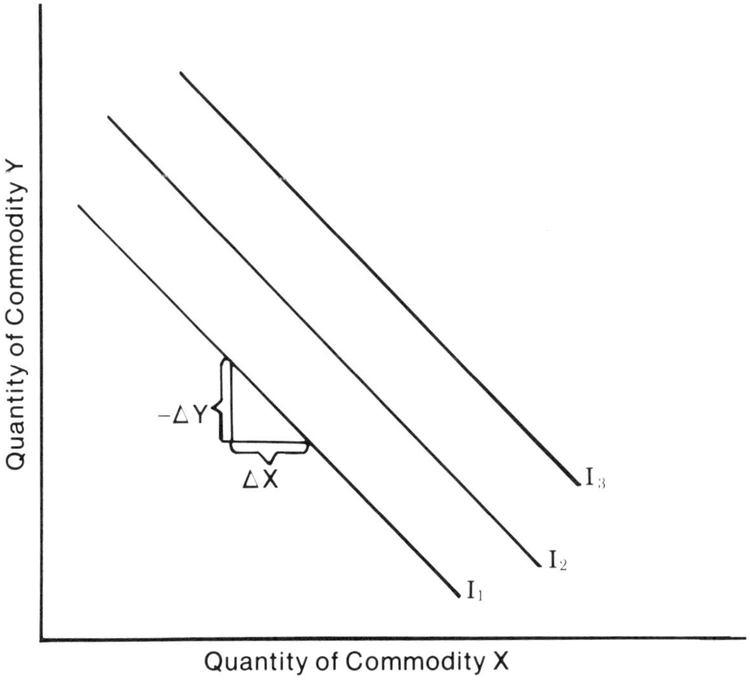

FIG. 6.2. A SET OF INDIFFERENCE CURVES SHOWING CONSTANT RATE OF SUBSTITUTION

respect and must be considered identical. For example, assuming no value for collectors, an Indian head penny is a perfect substitute for a Lincoln head penny in the purchase of a penny postage stamp. Thus, for the purpose, they are considered to be identical commodities.

Complementarity of Commodities.—At the opposite of the limiting case of a constant rate of substitution is another limiting case of complete or perfect complementarity. In cases of complementarity, the amount of Y given up to acquire a unit of X is zero. Thus, there is no possibility of substituting X for Y and the indifference curve would be L-shaped or become right-angled (Fig. 6.3). For example, for a normal adult, right and left shoes may be considered as perfect complements. Commodities that are perfect complements must be considered as a bundle of resources or goods because without full complement of the parts no satisfaction would be produced. Thus, the extreme cases of perfect complements and perfect substitutes must be considered with care in analysis. Most of the real life situations fall in between these two extremes and permit some degree of substitution to occur, whether small or large.

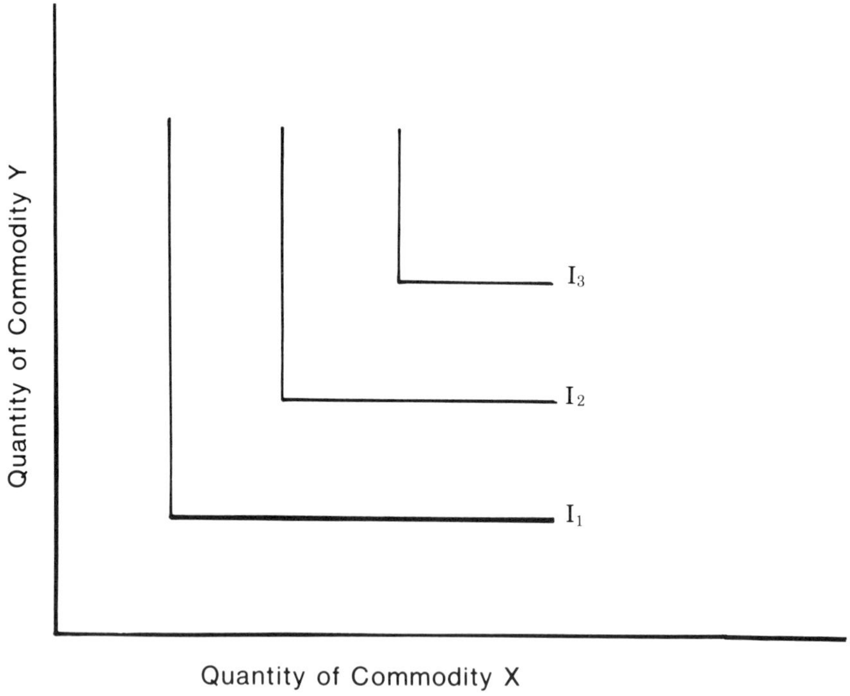

FIG. 6.3. A SET OF INDIFFERENCE CURVES SHOWING PERFECT COMPLEMENTARITY OF TWO COMMODITIES

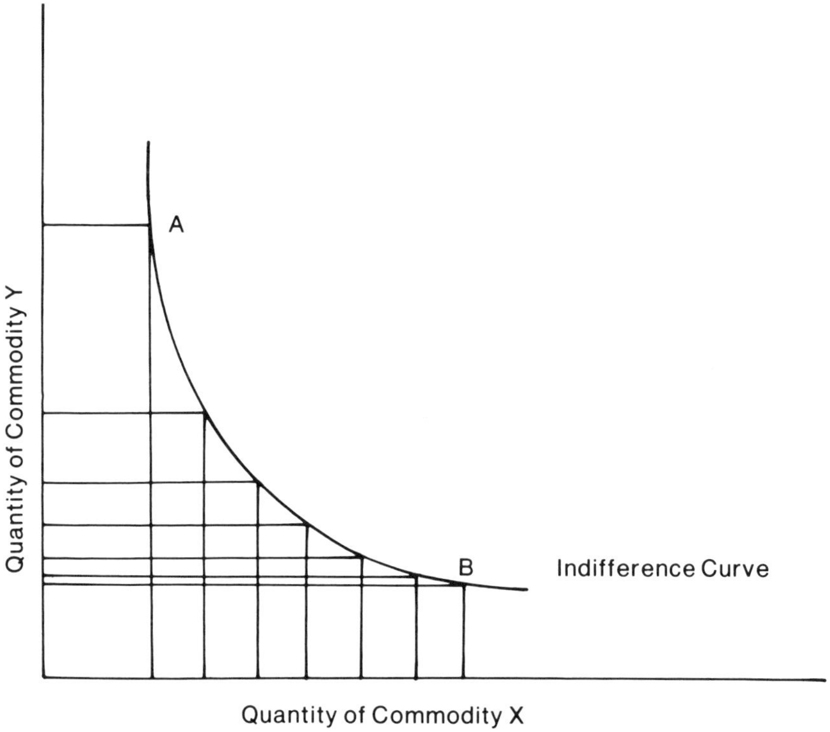

FIG. 6.4. AN INDIFFERENCE CURVE SHOWING DIMINISHING RATE OF SUBSTITUTION

Diminishing Rate of Substitution.—A decreasing marginal rate of substitution results when the decrement of Y which will just compensate for an increment of X decreases as more of X is consumed with the level of satisfaction unchanged (Fig. 6.4). From the graph, it can be seen that a consumer at point A would value a unit of X relatively highly in terms of Y, i.e., the consumer would be willing to give up a considerable amount of Y to acquire another unit of X. Thus, the more of Y a consumer has relative to X, the more important a unit of X becomes relative to Y. As the consumer moves along the indifference curve toward point B, the amount of Y he or she is willing to give up to obtain additional units of X gradually decreases, i.e., the marginal rate of substitution is decreasing. When the consumer is at point B, a unit of Y is relatively more important than a unit of X and he or she would be willing to give up very little of Y to obtain another unit of X. If the marginal rate of substitution is decreasing, the indifference curve must be convex to the origin.

Much of the discussion pertaining to the marginal rate of substitution in the chapter on factor-factor relationships is applicable here. The movement of the MRS can be traced by drawing a tangent to each point on the indifference curve, since the value of each tangent is a measure of the slope or rate of change at that point (Fig. 6.5). The slope of the tangent, which is equal to $-\Delta Y/\Delta X$, will vary from point to point on the indifference curve with a gradual loss of steepness as the stock of X increases relative to that of Y. This indicates a lower $-\Delta Y/\Delta X$ ratio or a decreasing MRS.

Relevant Areas of Consumption

The relevant area of the consumption surface of a consumer includes all segments of the family of indifference curves that are negatively sloping and convex to the origin (Fig. 6.6). If the curve is concave to the origin,

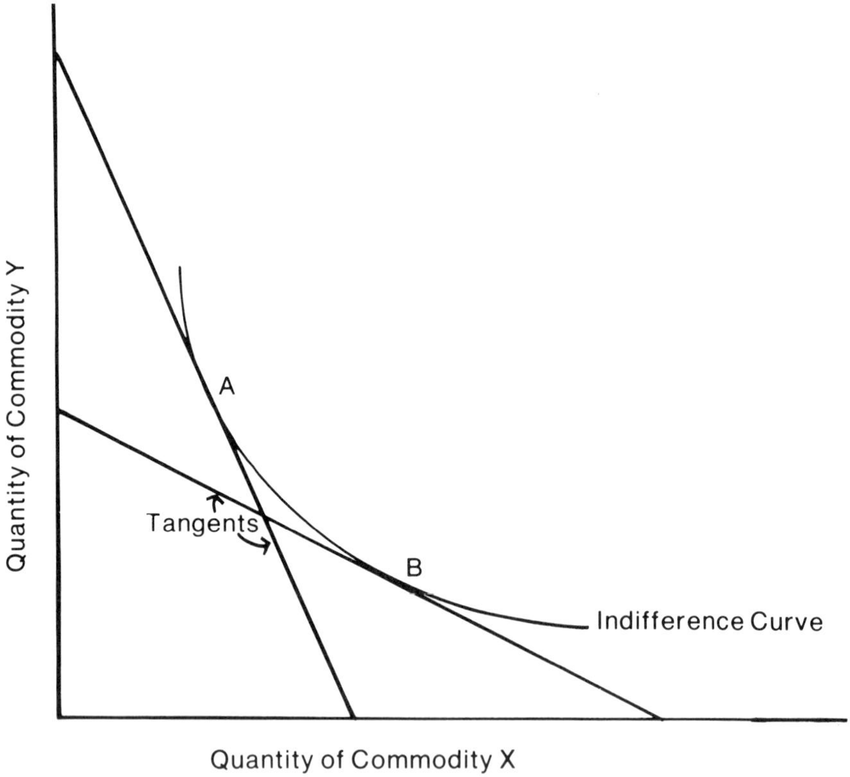

FIG. 6.5. AN INDIFFERENCE CURVE WITH TANGENTS INDICATING NATURE OF SUBSTITUTION

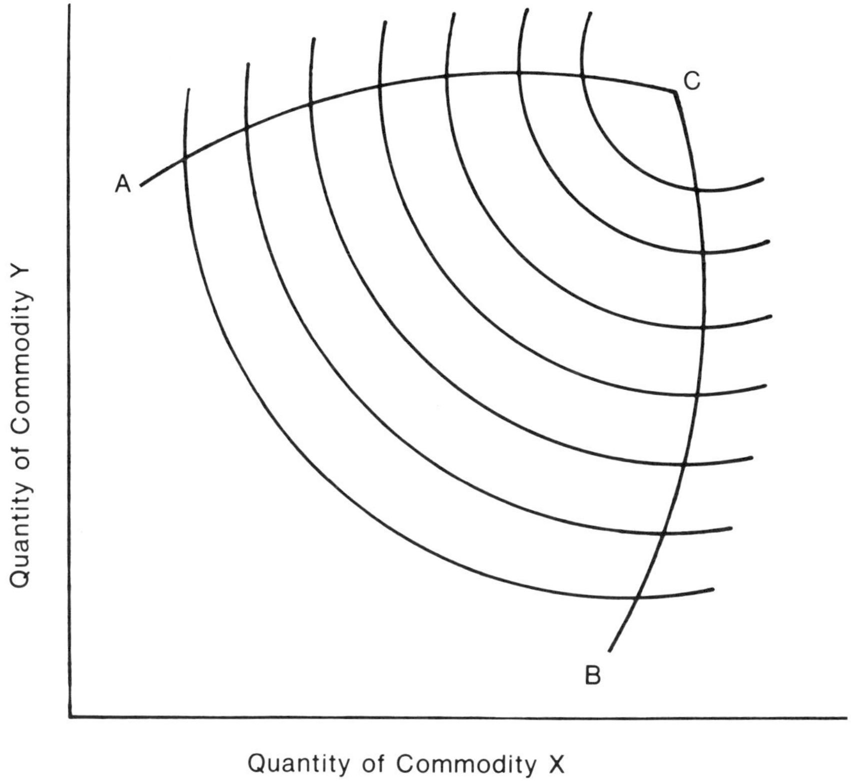

FIG. 6.6. A CONSUMPTION SURFACE WITH RIDGE LINES DEFINING RELEVANT AREAS

the marginal significance of one commodity in terms of another would be increasing and the consumer can never be in equilibrium when purchasing more than one commodity. Thus, he or she would specialize in consuming one commodity. Also, if the indifference curve is positively sloping, it would mean that an increase in consumption of both commodities would be necessary to maintain the same level of satisfaction.

Consumption in this area is not rational because it would be considered an illogical line of action by the consumer. Thus, the relevant areas of consumption can be defined as that within the ridge lines AC and BC (Fig. 6.6). Line AC is obtained by connecting points obtained with vertical tangents to indifference curves and represents the points where the MRS of X for Y is infinite. Line BC is obtained by connecting points obtained with horizontal tangents to the indifference curves and represents points where the MRS of X for Y is zero.

Choice Indicator

The consumer now has an indifference surface reflecting his or her tastes or scale of preferences for combinations of X and Y. Which one of these many possible combinations the consumer will select depends upon income and the respective prices of X and Y. The tastes or scale of preferences are subjectively determined by the consumer but the facts of income and prices are objectively determined. The consumer must spend his or her entire budget on X and Y at prevailing prices, omitting from consideration savings which could be identified as one of the goods. The budget equation will be

$$XP_x + YP_y = I$$

with X and Y representing the commodities, P_x and P_y their respective prices, and I the income. With prices constant and income or budget fixed, the consumer can purchase I/P_y units (OA amount) of Y if all the budget were used on Y, or I/P_x units (OB amount) of X if all were used on X (Fig. 6.7). A straight line joining A and B shows all possible combinations of X and Y given the budget. This line is commonly referred to as the *price line*[2] which represents the opportunities open to the consumer in the market, given the prices and income, while the indifference curve shows the consumer's tastes independent of market conditions.

Optimum Combination

After indicating the quantities of X and Y that can be purchased with a set budget at the prices faced, the problem now is to indicate the quantities of X and Y that will be purchased when tastes and scale of preference are imposed. Generally, there will be only one combination of X and

[2] This line is also referred to as the line of attainable combinations, budget line, price opportunity line, constant outlay curve, isocost curve and perhaps others. In solving the equation $XP_x + YP_y = I$ for Y, one gets

$$Y = \frac{I - XP_x}{P_y} = \frac{I}{P_y} - \frac{P_x}{P_y} X$$

and for X, one gets

$$X = \frac{I - YP_y}{P_x} = \frac{I}{P_x} - \frac{P_y}{P_x} Y$$

which give intercepts I/P_y corresponding to OA and I/P_x corresponding to OB. Thus, the slope becomes

$$\frac{-\Delta Y}{\Delta X} = -\frac{OA}{OB} = -\frac{I/P_y}{I/P_x} = -\frac{P_x}{P_y}$$

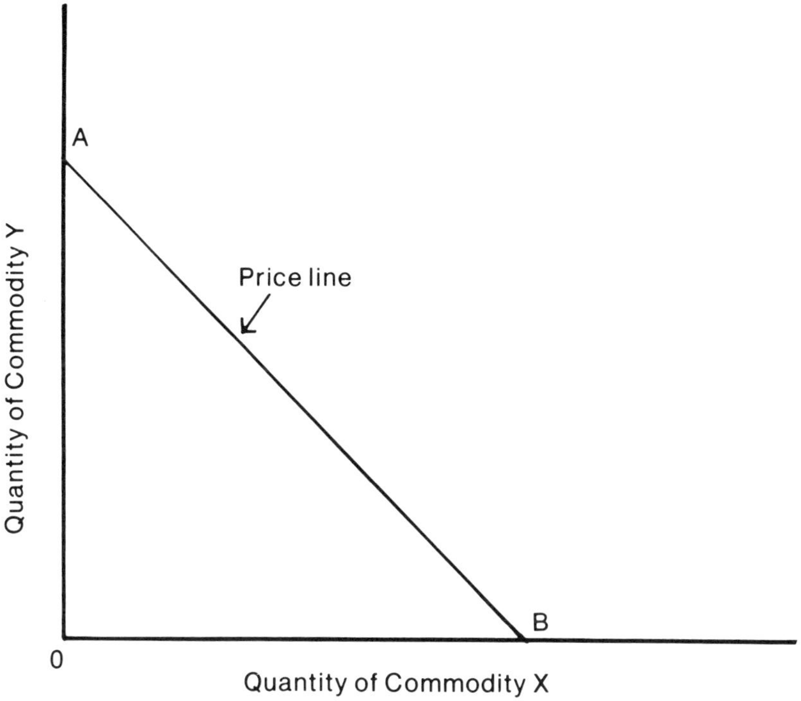

FIG. 6.7. A PRICE LINE AS A CHOICE INDICATOR

Y that can be purchased which will be preferred to all other combinations, i.e., will give the consumer the greatest satisfaction. The consumer will maximize satisfaction by purchasing that combination of X and Y at which the price line is tangent to the highest indifference curve (Fig. 6.8). The price line can be tangent to only one indifference curve, the highest one it touches.

At the point of tangency the slope of the indifference curve measured by $-\Delta Y/\Delta X$, which is equal to MRS, equals the slope of the price line measured also by $-\Delta Y/\Delta X$ which is equal to P_x/P_y. Thus, MRS = P_x/P_y only when the value of $-\Delta Y/\Delta X$ is the same for both the indifference curve and the price line. This will occur only at their point of tangency (point T, Fig. 6.8). For example, at point R, the slope of the indifference curve is greater than the slope of the price line; this means that the amount of Y the consumer is *willing* to forego to obtain a unit of X is greater than the amount of Y that he or she *must* give up to purchase a unit of X, or $-\Delta Y/\Delta X > P_x/P_y$. Obviously, by substituting X for Y the consumer could increase his or her level of satisfaction. At point S, the slope of the indifference curve is less than the slope of the price line,

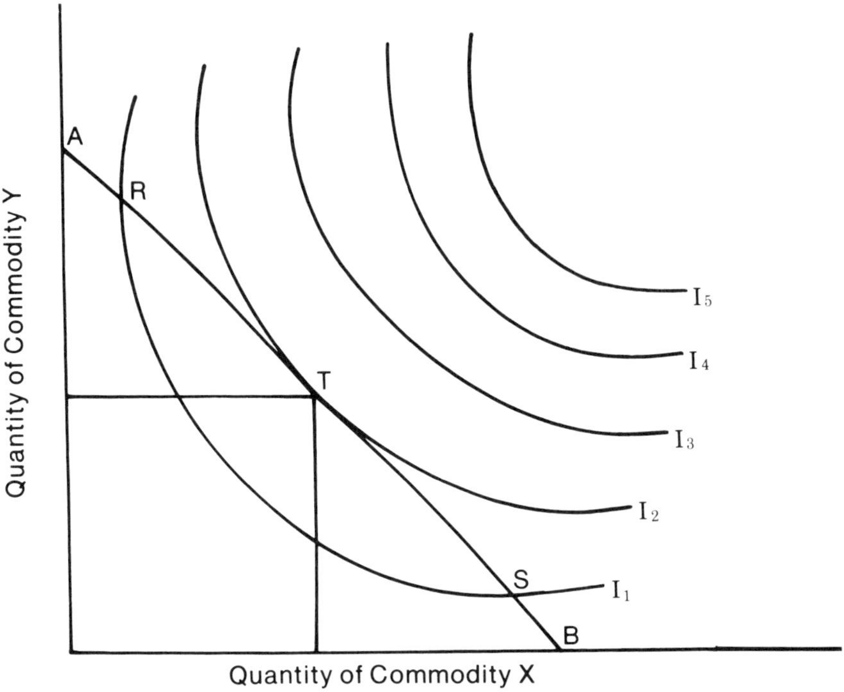

FIG. 6.8. A CHOICE INDICATOR SHOWING THE OPTIMUM COMBINATION OF COMMODITIES

which means that the amount of Y the consumer is willing to give up to obtain a unit of X is less than the amount of Y that he or she must give up to purchase a unit of X, or $-\Delta Y/\Delta X < P_x/P_y$. In this case, shifting from X and using more Y would increase satisfaction. Thus, when the price line is tangent to an indifference curve, which will indicate that their slopes are equal, the incentive to change the purchase combination will no longer be evident. In other words, the subjective factors of tastes and scale of preferences will be consistent with the objective facts of income and prices, and the equilibrium position with respect to the combination of purchases of X and Y has been reached.

Paths of Consumption

The discussion thus far has dealt with the consumer's behavior when income and prices are given. The question now arises as to the response of this behavior to a change in income or a change in prices. Thus, the new optimum combinations of commodities for an individual with a given utility surface depend upon the changes which occur in prices and income. These are the two principal ways in which conditions may affect the equilibrium position indicated by the tangency of the indifference curve and the price line.

The Income Consumption Line.—With prices constant, the consumer's level of satisfaction is a function of income. A consumer with rising income usually spends more in forms of goods and services, but may buy either a larger, the same or a smaller quantity of a single commodity. With tastes and prices constant, an increase in income means that the price line or budget line will shift upward and parallel to the original position (Fig. 6.9). Successive increases in the budget lines will take a consumer to higher and higher indifference curves. By connecting the different points of tangency, a curve or a locus of points is obtained which is known as the *income consumption curve*.[3] This curve shows how this

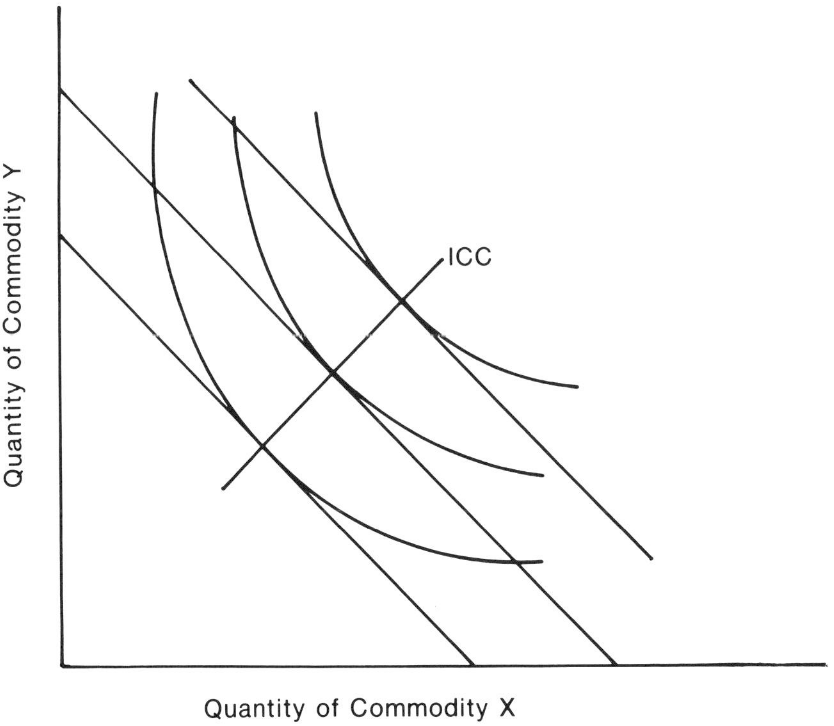

FIG. 6.9. INCOME CONSUMPTION CURVE GENERATED BY CHANGES IN INCOME SHOWING A SUPERIOR COMMODITY

[3] Referred to also as the "standard of life" line.

particular consumer apportions expenditures between commodity X and commodity Y as income increases. The effect of income change on the purchase of X and Y at given prices is generally referred to as the *income effect*. If prices should change there would be, of course, a different income consumption curve since the slope of the price lines will change.

The shape of the income consumption curve, which depends upon the relative position of successive indifference curves, can vary within very wide limits. Three distinct slopes may be noted. First, the curve may slope positively throughout, i.e., slope upwards to the right (Fig. 6.9). This is perhaps the most common and important type which indicates that the amount of both commodities X and Y purchased will increase. When this

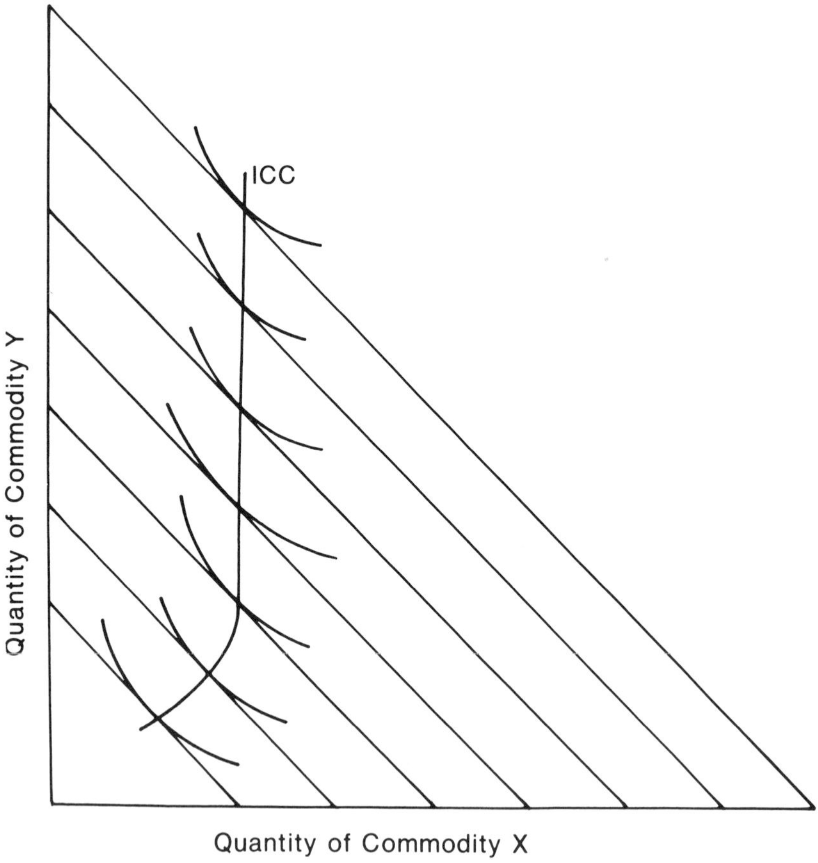

FIG. 6.10. INCOME CONSUMPTION CURVE SHOWING NEUTRAL COMMODITY

situation exists, the income effect is positive for both commodities and both commodities are said to be *normal goods*.

Second, although the income consumption curve may have a positive slope at first, it may become vertical (or horizontal) beyond a certain point (Fig. 6.10). This curve indicates that as income increases the quantity of commodity X purchased will not increase beyond some point, but the quantity of Y will increase. This curve illustrates a situation where the biological need for a commodity X has reached the saturation point and any increase in income will not result in an additional quantity of X purchased. In this situation, commodity X may be termed as a

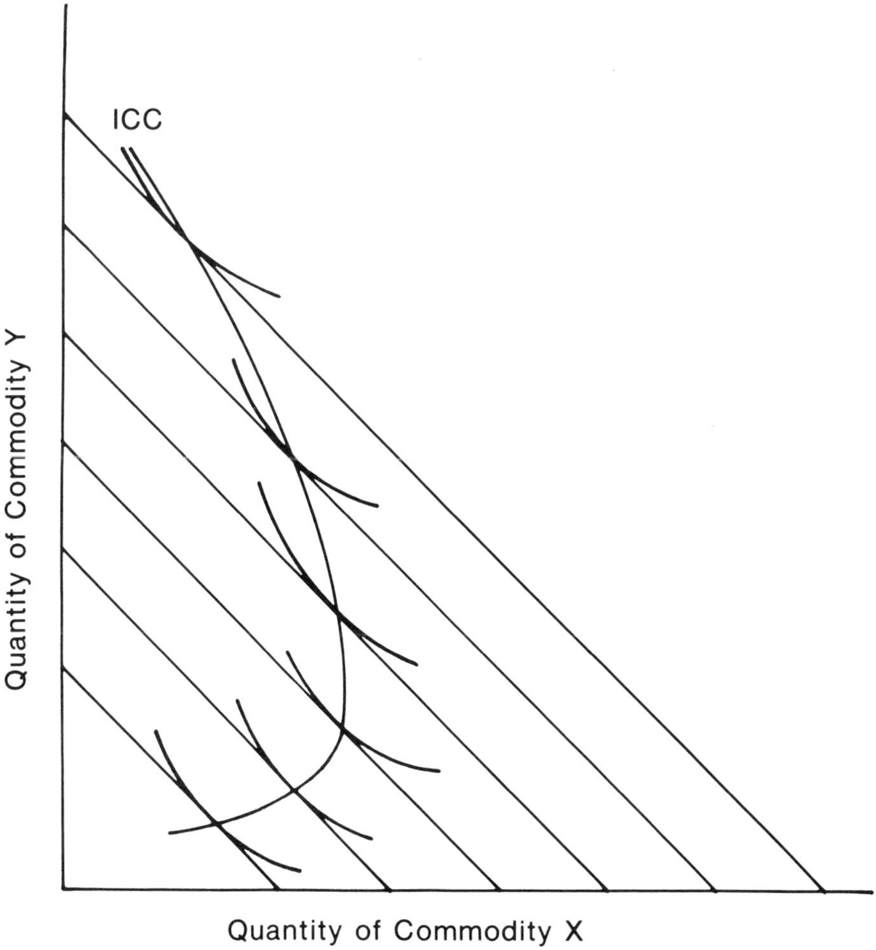

FIG. 6.11. INCOME CONSUMPTION CURVE SHOWING INFERIOR COMMODITY

normal commodity up to some point and then as a *neutral* commodity beyond that point.

Third, the income consumption curve may indicate that the amount of Y (or X) purchased beyond some point will decrease as the income is increased (Fig. 6.11). A commodity which is consumed at low levels of income but drops out of the purchase plan in favor of a superior commodity as income increases is known as an *inferior* commodity. At first, the income consumption curve may have a positive slope, but at higher income levels the slope becomes negative, i.e., it slopes backwards or downwards. The income effect at first is positive for both commodities and later becomes *negative* for commodity X while remaining positive for commodity Y. The concept of negative income effect is important as it offers a logical explanation for many unusual demand situations in which sales fall despite a reduction in price for a commodity.

The Price Consumption Line.—With the consumer's income and tastes constant, the effect of a change in prices on the level of satisfaction may now be noted. This situation may be illustrated graphically by letting the price of one commodity X vary relative to that of the other commodity Y (Fig. 6.12). The price lines will have different slopes as the price of X changes, given the same income and price of Y, because the maximum quantities of X which could be consumed will vary while those of Y will not. Each price line is always tangent to some indifference curve which indicates the highest possible level of satisfaction obtainable with that particular budget and price situation. The locus of all the tangential points of the price lines and indifference curves will give what is known as the consumer's *price consumption curve* (curve PCC, Fig. 6.12). This curve shows the *price effect*, i.e., the way in which the consumer's purchases of commodity X change when the price of X changes, while the income in terms of Y and the price of Y remain constant.

The effect of a price change is in reality the result of (1) the *income effect* which causes a movement on the income consumption curve, i.e., an increase in real income, and (2) the *substitution effect* which causes a movement along an indifference curve, i.e., the consumer will buy more of the commodity X which has fallen in price. The substitution effect occurs when the relative prices of the commodities change, and the change causes the consumer to rearrange his or her purchases in accordance with the new price ratio without changing the level of satisfaction (Fig. 6.13). With the ratio of prices indicated by price line AA′, the optimum combination of commodities X and Y is reflected by coordinates of point P. When the price ratio changes to BB′, the combination of X and Y will shift from coordinates of point P to P′. When the price ratio changes in this respect, the price of Y will have risen but the consumer's income in terms of X also will have risen from OA′ to OB′. This rise of A′B′ in

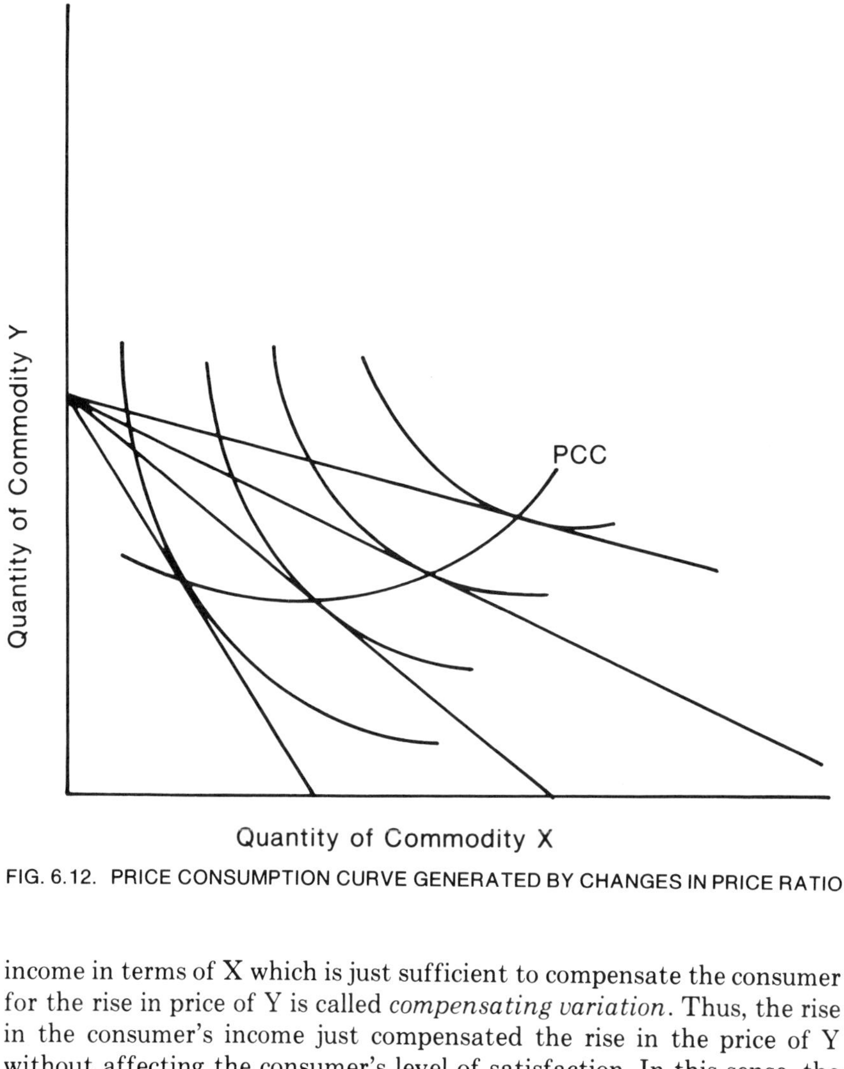

FIG. 6.12. PRICE CONSUMPTION CURVE GENERATED BY CHANGES IN PRICE RATIO

income in terms of X which is just sufficient to compensate the consumer for the rise in price of Y is called *compensating variation*. Thus, the rise in the consumer's income just compensated the rise in the price of Y without affecting the consumer's level of satisfaction. In this sense, the substitution effect can always be illustrated graphically as a movement along an indifference curve.

As the price of the commodity X falls, the resulting increase in real income will cause the price line to move parallel to the original one and generate an income consumption curve (ICC, Fig. 6.14). Both an income effect QR and a substitution effect RP are generated by a fall in price of X. Both of these effects comprise the price effect. The increase in amount of X purchased due to a rise in real income is OM-OL or LM and the amount of X purchased due to a substitution is ON-OM or MN.

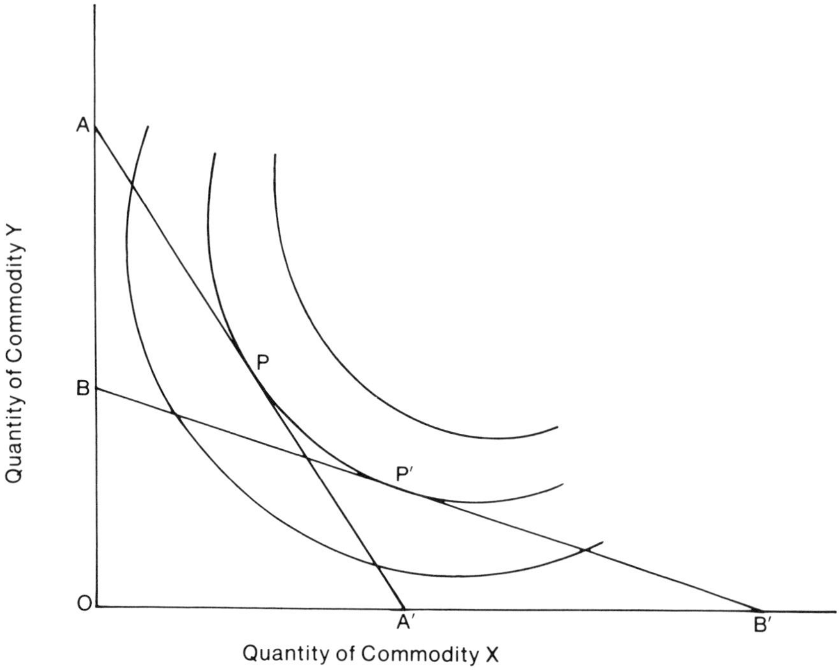

FIG. 6.13. A CHANGE IN PRICE RATIO SHOWING SUBSTITUTION EFFECT

Thus, it is clear that the amount of the commodity X purchased as its price falls depends upon the relative strength and direction of the income effect and of the substitution effect. The substitution effect is always positive for a price decrease (more of X will be consumed as its price falls), and the income effect is usually positive for an income increase which is involved in the price decrease. The positive substitution effect may outweigh the negative income effect in many inferior commodities so that their consumption still increases as price decreases. The income effect can be so strong for some inferior goods as to cause the amount of goods purchased to fall as the price falls.[4]

Multiple Commodity Relationships

For purposes of simplicity and to show the relationships graphically only two commodities were considered in this discussion. Actually, many more commodities are variable and the consumer must equate the mar-

[4] For a discussion of an interesting possible but abnormal situation referred to as "Giffen's Paradox" named after Sir Robert Giffen, *see* Stonier, A.W. and Hague, D.C. 1972. A Textbook of Economic Theory. Longmans, Green and Company, New York.

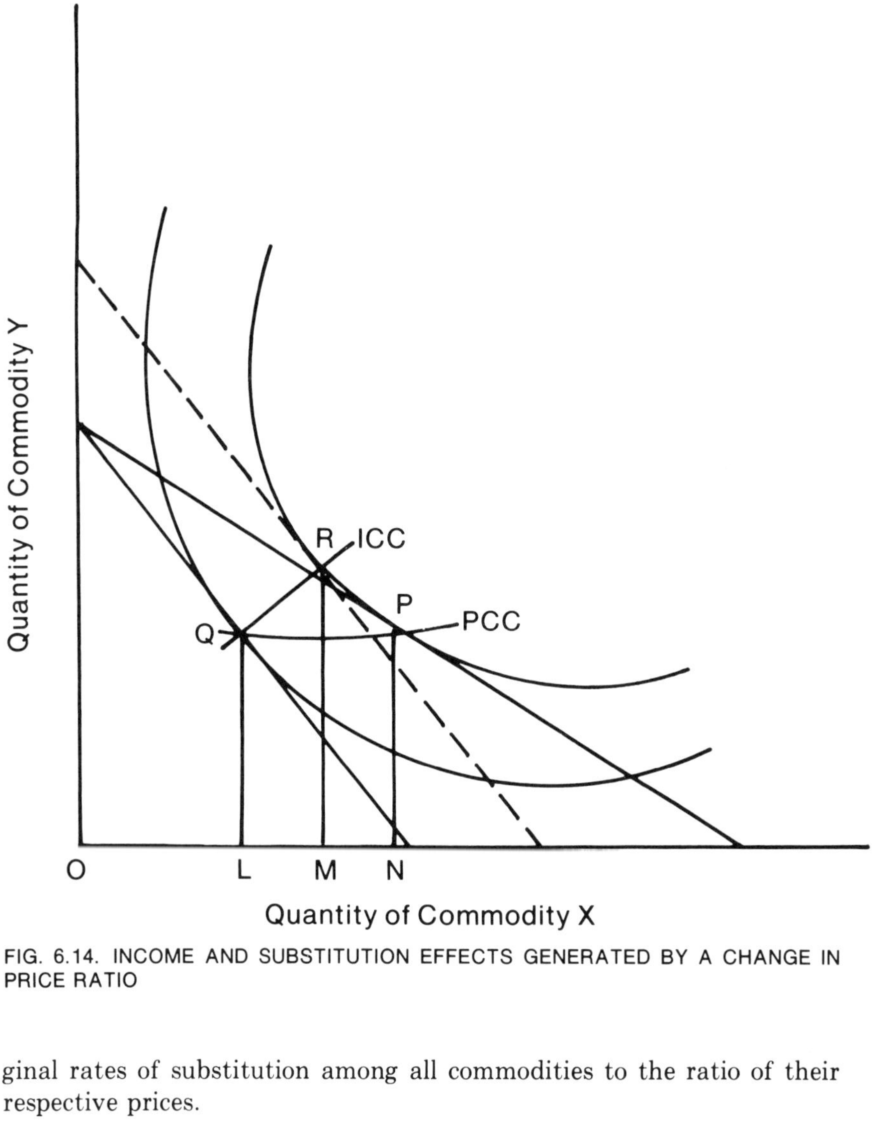

FIG. 6.14. INCOME AND SUBSTITUTION EFFECTS GENERATED BY A CHANGE IN PRICE RATIO

ginal rates of substitution among all commodities to the ratio of their respective prices.

CHAPTER 6: REVIEW QUESTIONS

(1) Describe the fundamental assumptions of the indifference system pointing out its validity and limitations.
(2) Draw the implied indifference curves and budget lines, and appraise the statement, "I wouldn't eat that if you paid me to."

(3) Define the relationship between marginal utility and the marginal rate of substitution.

(4) Draw the appropriate indifference curve through the following indifference combinations:

Commodity X	4	5	8	10	12	14	16	18	22
Commodity Y	20	15	10	7	5	5	3	2	1

(a) Show diagrammatically that the MRS decreases.

(b) Assume income to be \$15 and that P_y = \$1 and P_x = \$1.077. Draw the appropriate price line.

(c) Approximately how many units of the two commodities will be purchased?

(d) If P_y rises to \$1.60 and P_x falls to \$0.833, how many units of each good will be bought?

(5) In the Fig. 6.15, the individual's equilibrium in view of income and prices is at Q, with the purchase combination of OR and OS of x and y, respectively. The prices of x and y, where I denotes income, are

$$P_x = \frac{I}{OT} \text{ and } P_y = \frac{I}{OV}$$

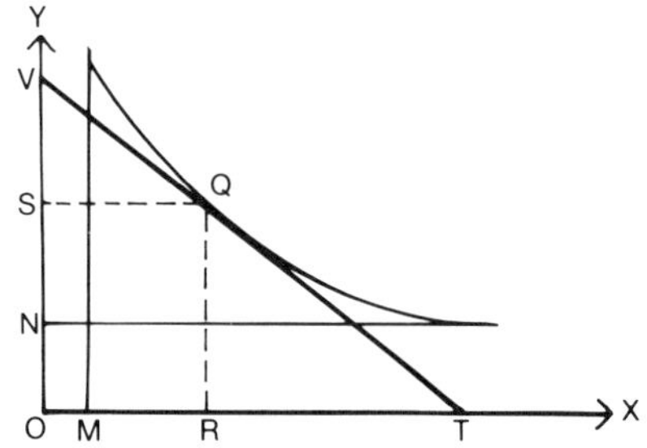

FIG. 6.15. FIGURE FOR PROBLEM 5

(a) Supposing P_x to go up and P_y to go down, at what price of X could we be sure that well-being has fallen?

(b) At what price of Y?

(c) Under what conditions, in terms of purchase quantities of X and Y, could we be sure that well-being has increased?

(d) Referring to (c), through what point must the new price line pass for certainty on the growth of well-being?

(e) If P_x rises so that if the full income were spent on X less than or can be bought, does this necessarily entail a fall in well-being?

(f) If P_y rises so that less than OS of Y can be bought, must this mean a fall in well-being?

(6) It seems that in labor-management negotiations concerning wage contracts a great emphasis is placed upon fringe benefits to be provided by the company. Presumably, the cost of the fringe benefits could be provided in the form of increased wages. These fringe

benefits take on many forms—free hospitalization insurance, purchases from the company at discounts, etc. Prove by indifference curves that a given employee would prefer an increase in income.

7

Elementary Theory of Consumption Economics III

In the preceding chapter, those relationships were discussed which would enable a consumer to select, out of many possible choices, the one which stands highest on some scale of preference. This chapter presents the framework which the consumer can use to choose the optimum combination of many wants. This framework does not attempt to appraise the goodness or badness of different wants or consider the relationships in the normative economic sense, but to suggest that all wants may be classified into those possible and those impossible to attain by the consumer with a fixed level of income or resources.

OPTIMUM COMBINATION OF WANTS

In present-day society, the consumer is faced with the enormous problem of deciding which of the infinitely large number of wants are attainable and which are not attainable with the limited income or resources at hand. Also, the consumer is faced with the problem of choosing the optimum combination of those wants that are attainable. The selection of these wants by a consumer must entail some idea of their relative importance in his or her scale of preferences, and also how much of one desire or want must be sacrificed in order to obtain another and still stay within the income limitation. These preferences are individually and subjectively determined.

The Function

The functional relationships involved in determining the optimum combination of wants are no different conceptually from those found in production. The main difference lies in the degree of measurability of the subjective aspects of consumption. Nevertheless, a person's income or other resources are fixed in quantity at a given instant of time and can be used to obtain or purchase many different wants. Suppose for purposes of simplicity there are only two wants involved, A and B, and the consumer can use his or her limited income X_1 in connection with a given quantity of other resources $X_2, X_3, \ldots, X_n$ to obtain want A or want B or some combination of both. Thus, at a given level of prices the amount of A and B obtained depends upon the functional relationship

$$A = f(X_1 \mid X_2, X_3, \ldots, X_n)$$

$$B = f(X_1 \mid X_2, X_3, \ldots, X_n)$$

Therefore, A = f (B) which means that for a given income the amount of want A obtainable depends upon the amount of want B, and vice versa. This relationship when graphed is known as the *consumption possibilities curve* which indicates the amount of one want that must be sacrificed in order to obtain a unit of the other want (Fig. 7.1). The curve divides the entire utility surface of an individual consumer into two parts:

(1) those combinations which are possible and attainable which lie within or on the curve, and
(2) those combinations not possible nor attainable with the resources or income available which lie outside the curve and contain very little interest for the consumer.

Basic Relationships

The relationships that can exist are many, varied and often complex. The consumption possibilities curve may take on numerous shapes, depending upon how the individual views the characteristics of individual wants obtained. The consumer must also have some idea of the order of preferences, i.e., there must be some estimate of how much of a given want A he or she would be willing to give up in order to acquire some amount of another want B. Otherwise, there would be no logical basis on which the consumer could make decisions. The curves will be of the same general nature as found in product-product relationships discussed in a preceding chapter on production; corresponding to the production functions underlying the production possibilities curve are the utility functions underlying the consumption possibilities curve.

Complementary Relationships.—Two or more wants are complementary in nature when an increase in the amount of one want A attained results in an increase in the amount of another want B attained from a given quantity of income or resources (segments db and eh, Fig. 7.1).

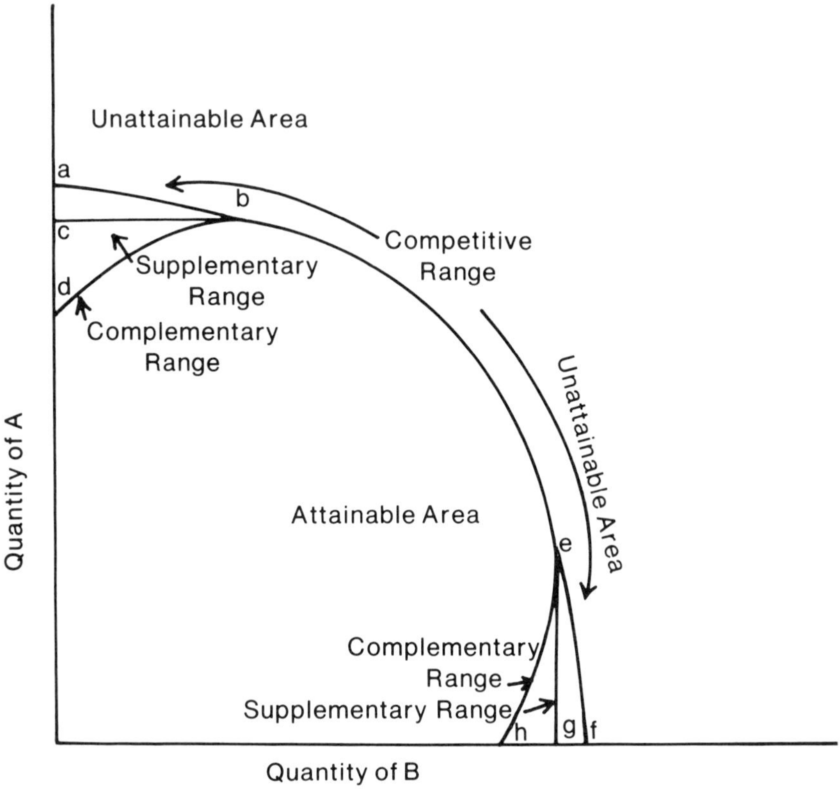

FIG. 7.1. CONSUMPTION POSSIBILITIES CURVE SHOWING VARIOUS RELATIONSHIPS

Some students would argue that studying and recreation are complementary in nature within certain ranges within a given time period. Vacations and work may also be complementary within a time span of a year or so. To realize full complementary effects from resources, time must be considered. At a given instant of time the wants may be competetive instead of complementary. While it may be somewhat difficult to imagine how complementarity of wants can result fom the first and third ways as discussed in a previous chapter (Chapter 4), it is clear the complementarity can result from the second way, i.e., withdrawal of the surplus resource which has pushed the utility obtained over into Stage III, the stage of negative marginal utility, and the allocation of those resources withdrawn toward the attainment of another want which is still in Stage I or Stage II. This action would increase the amount of both wants, and when this readjustment is possible, the consumer would not logically remain within the complementary ranges of the consumption possibilities curve.

Supplementary Relationships.—The wants of a consumer may be supplementary in nature when an increase in the amount of one want A attained does not influence the amount of another want B attained with the use of a given quantity of income or resources (segments cb and eg, Fig. 7.1). This relationship arises from the fact that some fixed resources used in consumption continue to provide services not used at certain points in the time period in attaining want A but which can be used in attaining want B during those periods of disuse. Several examples of this relationship may be cited in the household area of economics. The car may be used for business and yet used for shopping or for vacation purposes, thereby using it to attain one want without affecting the level of another want. The supplementary relationship exists wherever a stock of consumer resources is continuing to render services available but cannot be utilized entirely in securing one particular want.

Competitive Relationships.—Perhaps most of the wants desired by consumers are competitive in nature. A competitive relationship exists between two consumer wants when from a given quantity of resources or income the quantity of one want B can be increased only through the reduction in quantity of the other want A (curve abef, Fig. 7.1). This means that a consumer with a limited or fixed income may have to forego purchasing a new car in order to purchase new home laundry appliances, or forego the purchase of nonhuman goods and services in order to raise children which may be considered another form of consumer goods. How much of one good or want A a consumer is willing to give up to acquire a unit of another want B depends upon the peculiarity of the utility or preference functions underlying the wants under consideration. The degree by which one want substitutes for another can vary from one extreme of a constant rate of substitution to the other extreme of no substitution. In consumption, however, the less extreme situations are most commonly found which are illustrated by a moderately curved[1] consumption possibilities curve (curve abef, Fig. 7.1). The curve illustrates the increasing rate of substitution and as such indicates that increasing sacrifices in the amount of want A must be made for each unit of want B attained. This curve is usually considered to be concave to the origin or otherwise there would be specialization. However, in nonmarket relationships this doesn't necessarily have to follow. As will be indicated subsequently, the indifference curve which is usually convex to the origin may be the choice indicator.

[1] The curve may not be continuous throughout the whole range of possibilities.

Choice Indicator and Optimum Combination

The underlying objective of determining the relationships which exist among the many different wants of the consumer is to provide the necessary conditions for maximizing the satisfaction obtained from a given income or quantity of resources at the consumer's disposal. Many possibilities obviously exist for the consumer to spend or allocate his or her resources but the possibility which offers the highest level of satisfaction represented by the highest indifference curve would logically be the one chosen (Fig. 7.2). It is obvious that a consumer logically would not

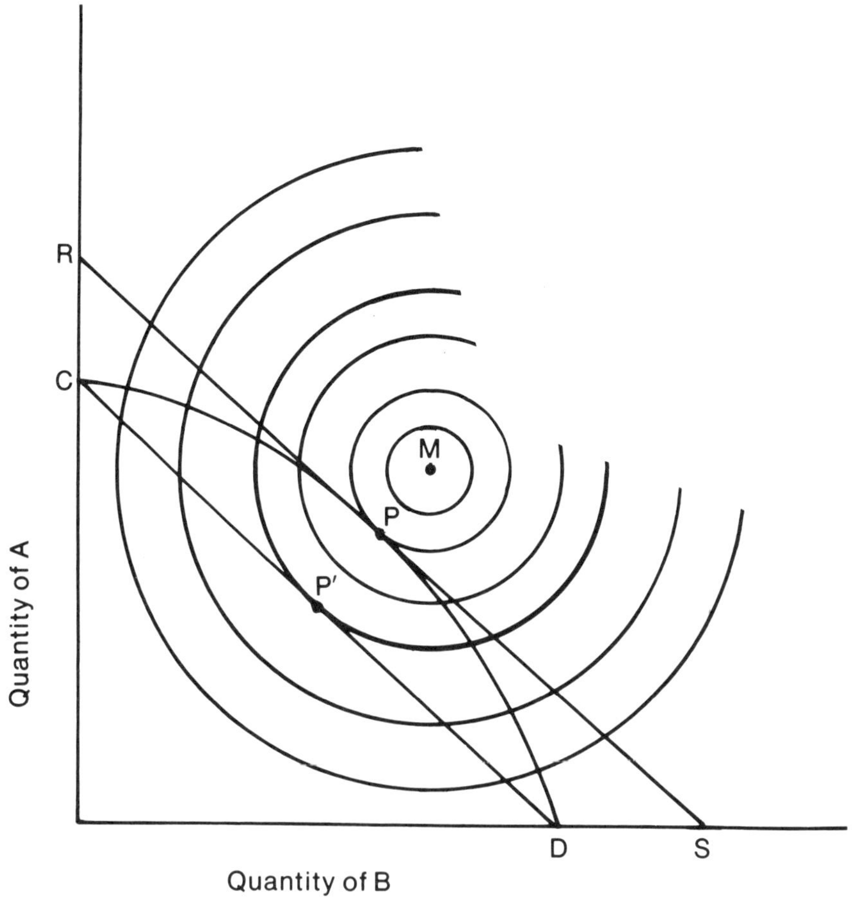

FIG. 7.2. RELATIONSHIP OF INDIFFERENCE CURVES TO THE CONSUMPTION POSSIBILITIES CURVE

select those possibilities that are complementary or supplementary in nature because other combinations can be found which would put the consumer on a higher indifference curve. By this, it is seen that the consumer's indifference curve expressing the consumer's pattern of preferences serves as the choice indicator.

The problem is now to determine the preferred or optimum combination among all those which are possible since those impossible combinations are not of any particular interest. The optimum combination is where the highest indifference curve touches or lies within the consumption possibilities curve (Fig. 7.2). The highest indifference curve touches the consumption possibilities curve CPD at point P. At any other point on the consumption possibilities curve, it would be possible to move to a higher indifference curve and still be on the curve CPD. At point P, the slope of the indifference curve which reflects the marginal rate of substitution of A and B used in consumption is equal to the slope of the price line RPS which expresses the relative value of the two wants.

The consumption possibilities curve CPD reflects the maximum quantity of satisfaction that can be "produced" from various combinations of wants A and B. The line RPS expressing the relative value of A and B may be referred to as the isosatisfaction or level of consumption curve. The optimum combination of wants A and B to "produce" is at point P where the marginal rate of substitution is equal to the slope of line RPS. Since at point P the MRS of A and B in the consumption process is equal to the slope of RPS, and at point P the MRS of A and B in the consumer's ability to provide them with a given quantity of resources or income is equal to the slope of RPS, it can be said that the MRS of A and B in the consumption process is equal to the MRS of A and B in the ability to provide them.

Basically, the problem facing the consumer with a given level of income, RPS, is one of choosing that combination of goods and services, A and B, to achieve the highest indifference curve possible within the constraints imposed by the possibilities available, CPD. That is achieved at point P. If at the same ratio of prices the consumer finds that P′ expresses the present combination of A and B being consumed, a higher indifference curve can be achieved from the same quantity of resources or income available by moving from P′ to P.

In summary, a theory of optimum choice involves establishing a set of relationships which describes the available options among which to choose, and a set of relationships which enables a person to select from the possible choices the one which will be highest on some scale of value.

CHAPTER 7: REVIEW QUESTIONS

(1) Analyze the similarities and differences between production and consumption theory.

(2) Explain why the indifference curve serves as a choice indicator for the optimum combination of wants to be attained.

(3) How may consumption theory be useful in everyday decision-making processes?

8

Demand Analysis

Modern demand analysis involves a thorough understanding of the economic forces which affect the commodity under study and also adequate data on which modern techniques of analysis can be used effectively. More important is a full understanding of the essential economic theory needed for analysis of these forces. Theory contributes meaningfully to the design of all economic investigations and is most useful in the evaluation of empirical results.

The theory of production and the theory of consumption, discussed in the preceding chapters, provide the underlying basic relationships necessary for the study of demand for goods and services used in production and consumption. Actually, the desire to satisfy human wants and needs motivates all human activity. To satisfy their desires or wants, people are willing to pay or forego something in return for the goods and services obtained.

CONCEPT OF DEMAND

The analytical concept of demand is most helpful when used to logically explain everyday economic problems. Needless to say, abuse of the concept doubtless will lead to erroneous conclusions. In a free enterprise economy, nothing can influence price except as it influences demand and supply. A thorough knowledge of the concept of demand and the influence it has on the determination of price and thus output of a good should help prevent many costly decisions. The volume of production is greatly influenced by the demand structure. Appropriate governmental policy also depends to a large extent on the structure of the many demand relationships.

Demand Schedule

The demand by an individual for a commodity or service may be defined as the schedule of the amounts of a good that would be purchased by the person at various prices, at a given time and place. A horizontal summation of individual demand schedules for a good in a particular market constitutes the total or market demand for that good. The demand schedules of various individuals for a particular article may differ widely because of variations in the determinants of demand, such as varying tastes or incomes. The demand schedule can be shown easily by graphical means to give a demand curve which clearly depicts the relationship between quantity and price (Fig. 8.1). This relationship illustrates the so-called law of demand; the quantity of a commodity purchased by a consumer will vary inversely with its price, given the time and place.

Changes in Demand

A change in demand is a shift in the demand schedule which will be graphically shown by a shift in the demand curve, i.e., consumers will be

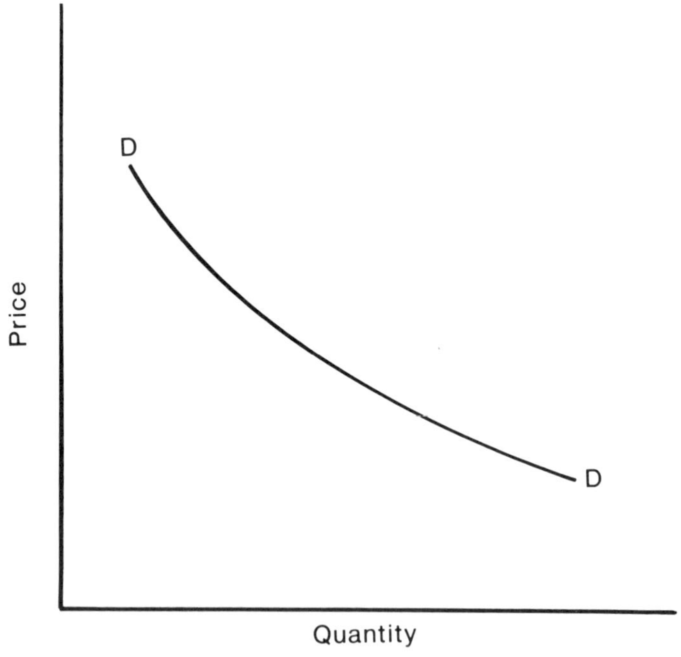

FIG. 8.1. A HYPOTHETICAL DEMAND CURVE

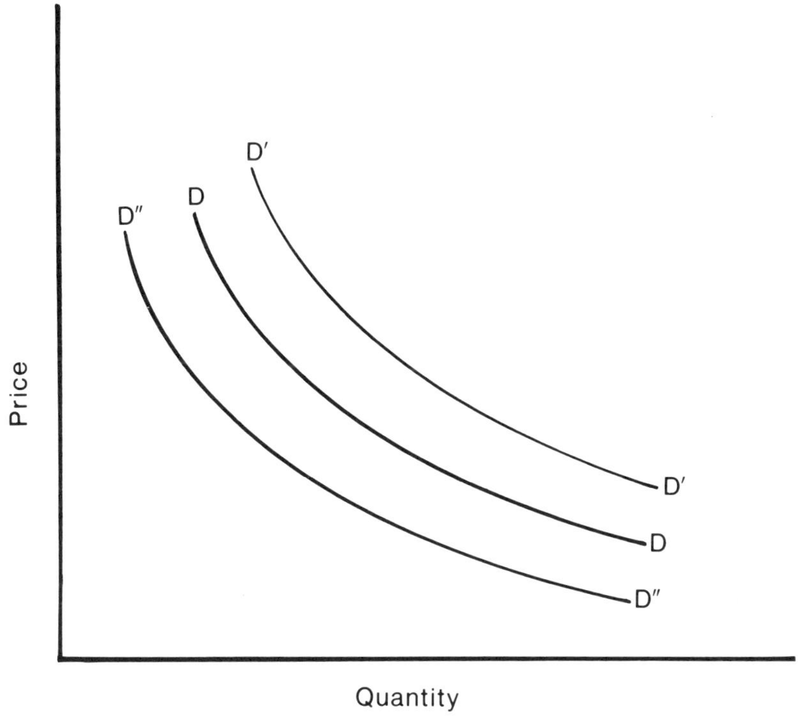

FIG. 8.2. SHIFTS IN THE DEMAND CURVE

willing to buy more (or less) of the commodity at the same price, or pay a higher price (or less) for the same quantity (Fig. 8.2). A change in the quantity demanded as a result of a price change does not constitute a change in demand since it represents a movement from point to point on the same demand schedule. Thus, the common expression "as the price goes down, the demand increases" is a misconception.

Assumptions Underlying the Demand Schedule

There are several factors which determine the level of the demand schedule for a particular commodity by an individual consumer. For a given demand schedule, these factors are assumed to be constant or given; any changes in these given factors will cause a shift in the demand schedule.

First, the scale of consumer preferences or tastes determines the level of the demand schedule for a commodity and thus any shift in the scale of preferences will lead to a change in the demand. Of course, the scale of preferences is conditioned by many factors such as custom, tradition, education, advertising, etc. These tastes are represented by means of a family of indifference curves. As can be seen subsequently, a shift in the pattern of indifference curves must lead to a change in the derived demand curve. Thus, an increase in the desire for a commodity in relation to other commodities will constitute a shift to another demand curve.

Second, the income at the disposal of a consumer will determine the level of the demand schedule. A consumer whose income changes will likely purchase different quantities of a commodity at the various prices than before the change. Thus, the consumer's demand schedule for a commodity will shift. An increase in income may lead to an increase in demand for several commodities or it may lead to an increase in demand for some commodities known as "normal" or "superior" and a decrease in demand for other commodities known as "inferior." The change in demand may lag behind the change in income since expenditures are influenced not entirely by the income of the current period but also by incomes of preceding periods.

Third, the level of the prices of other commodities is also a major determinant of the level of a particular demand schedule. When the price of commodity A rises relative to a substitute commodity B, consumers will purchase more of B and less of A. (If the goods are complementary in consumption, i.e., they tend to be used together, consumers would purchase less of both goods.) Prices of close substitutes are far more influential in altering the demand schedule for a particular commodity than are the prices of poor substitutes. The strength of the influence of the price change of one good on the demand for another good can be estimated by use of the concept of *cross elasticity*, which will be discussed subsequently.

Fourth, expectations regarding future prices of commodities affect the height of the demand schedule of a consumer for a particular commodity. The current price is sufficient for only nonpostponable needs, but there appear to be only a few commodities which cannot be postponed at least for a short time. When the price of bananas is very high a consumer can postpone purchase of bananas until the price is lower. If a commodity is storable, the consumer can vary the rate of purchase in order to take care of nonpostponable needs, or to carry him or her through periods of seasonably high prices. At any particular time, expectations can be of substantial importance and can cause major shifts in demand schedules. However, the influence of expectations is governed by

(1) the inconvenience and storage costs of postponing consumption,
(2) the extent and amplitude of anticipated fluctuations of future prices, and

(3) the amount of available funds to invest in the stock of commodities.

As was indicated, the market demand schedule for a commodity is a horizontal sum of the individual consumer demand schedules. The number of consumers in the market affects the height of the total demand schedule. Of course, the number of consumers can be increased by population growth or by enlargement of market area by reducing trade barriers or improving transportation.

DERIVATION OF DEMAND CURVE

The necessity of holding the above factors constant becomes evident when the process of deriving a demand curve is understood. The demand curve for a particular commodity can be derived logically and precisely if either the utility function or the indifference map of the particular consumer for that commodity is known. The utility function provides the simplest approach to the derivation of the demand curve but, as pointed out previously, objections have been raised on the grounds that it assumes measurability of utility. The critics of the utility approach have suggested another technique using a system of indifference curves.

The Utility Technique

To derive the demand curve for a particular commodity using the utility function, one needs to know the utility schedule of the individual for that commodity and the marginal utility of money. The marginal utility of money can be considered as the utility of all the other commodities expressed in monetary value. Because a single consumer's purchases usually do not affect the price of the goods purchased, the price of a unit of the commodity will be constant, i.e., the consumer can purchase all he or she desires at the same price. The problem facing the consumer now is to equate the marginal utility of a unit of the commodity with the utility of the amount of money required to purchase a unit in order to consciously or subconsciously maximize satisfaction.

As discussed in Chapter 5, satisfaction is maximized when $\frac{MU_x}{P_x} = \frac{MU_y}{P_y}$. Since the demand curve represents the relationship between the price of a good and the quantity of that good consumed, and the marginal utility curve represents the relationship between the quantity of a good consumed and the extra satisfaction derived from that unit consumed, the demand curve may be derived from the marginal utility curve.

Let Y represent all other goods which may be consumed, and P_y their collective price. (Alternatively, MU_y may indicate the marginal utility of the money used to purchase them.) Assume the price, consumption and marginal utility of these other goods are constant. Suppose that initially $MU_x = 2$, $P_x = \$1$, $MU_y = 6$, $P_y = \$3$; $\frac{2}{1} = \frac{6}{3}$. Then let the price of good X rise, say to \$2. Since the right-hand side of the equation is constant, in order to maintain the equality the marginal utility of X must also rise, to 4. Since the marginal utility curve is downward sloping in the rational range (Fig. 8.3), if the marginal utility of X is to rise then the quantity consumed of X must fall. If one knows the marginal utility schedule, one can determine by how much the quantity consumed must fall in order to achieve the new equilibrium position.

This technique has its counterpart in production, where it avoids the difficulties of subjectivity involved in consumption. In production, the

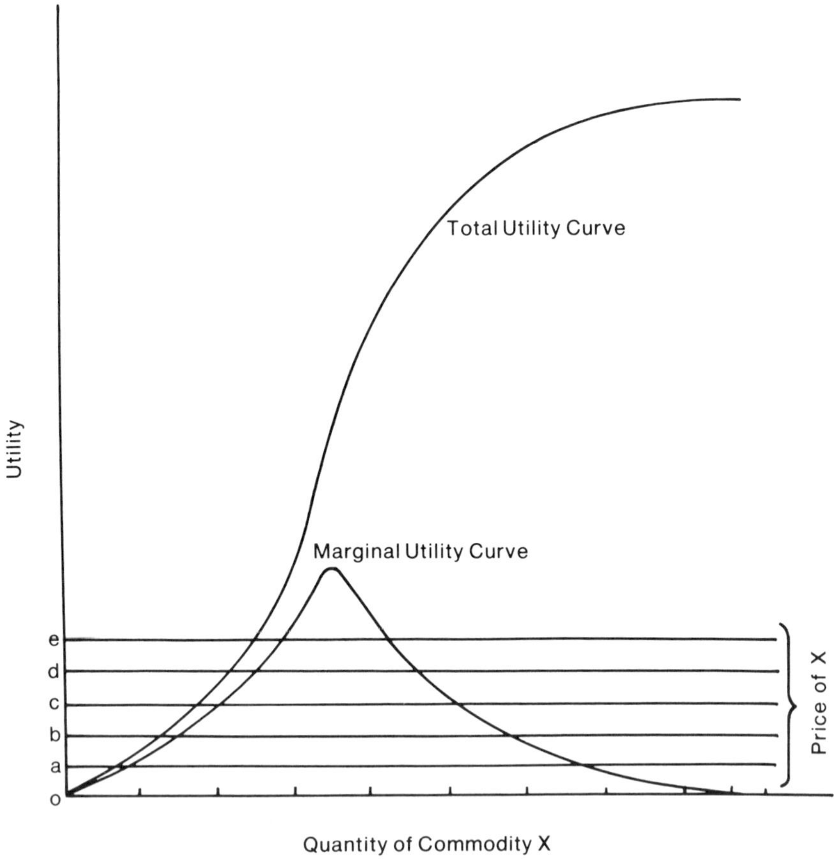

FIG. 8.3. MARGINAL UTILITY CURVE AS A DEMAND CURVE FOR COMMODITY X

marginal physical product curve of a factor multiplied by the price of a unit of product gives a marginal value product (MVP), and the cost of a unit of the factor is known as marginal factor cost (MFC) which for perfectly competitive input markets (*see* Chapter 12) does not vary with the quantity of input used. The optimum quantity of the factor to purchase results when MVP = MFC, where MVP is declining. Thus, by varying the MFC of the unit, the quantity of the factor that will be purchased by the producer can be ascertained, giving a demand schedule for the factor of production (Fig. 8.4). Thus, the marginal value productivity curve is the demand curve for the input used in production.

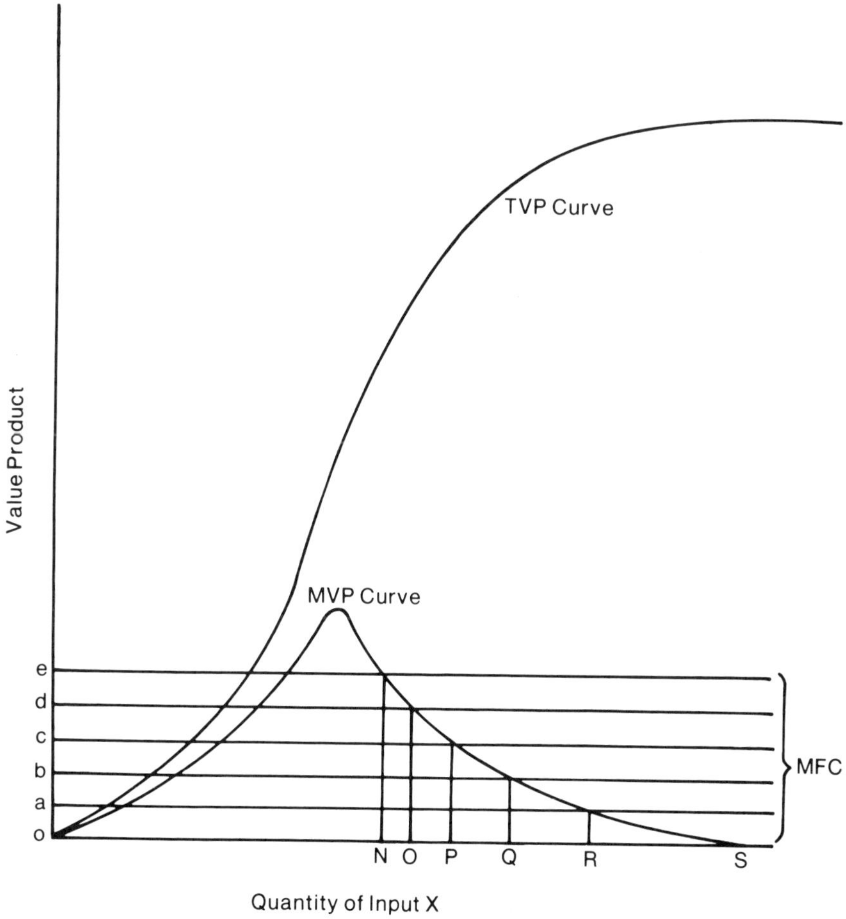

FIG. 8.4. MARGINAL VALUE PRODUCT CURVE AS A DEMAND CURVE FOR INPUT

The Indifference Technique

To avoid the alleged assumption of measurability of utility, many economists have suggested the use of a family of indifference curves as an alternative approach in deriving the demand curve. Although empirical demand relations do not emerge out of the use of the indifference technique, it does provide an insight into the importance of the many factors affecting the characteristics of a particular demand curve.

Discussed in the preceding chapters was the theory of consumer behavior which provides the basis for derivation of the demand curve. An individual's demand curve for a commodity X must be related to the individual's price consumption curve for that commodity. In fact, the price consumption curve provides the necessary information for a demand curve. Held constant are the nature of the indifference surface and the size of the income. The indifference map, with money on the Y axis and commodity X on the X axis, expresses along a given curve the various combinations of the commodity and money to which the consumer is indifferent (Fig. 8.5). Money can be considered to represent all other commodities which in some degree substitute for X. This assumption permits the substitution between X and all other commodities which the demand relationships imply.

When the price of a unit of X is known (with the price of money assumed constant), the outlay curve or budget line can be constructed and made tangent to an indifference curve, giving the equilibrium quantities of X and money at point A. Other points of equilibrium, B, C, D, can be determined in a like manner by letting the price of X vary, i.e., to decrease as in this example. As indicated in a previous chapter, a locus of these points gives a price consumption curve ABCD. At these points of equilibrium, the consumer will purchase quantities of OE″ (1½ units), OE (5 units), OG″ (9½ units) and OH″ (12 units) of X, respectively. The prices are indicated by the slopes of KE, KF, KG and KH; the prices paid per unit for these quantities of X are KL/OE″, KM/OE, KN/OG″ and KP/OH″, respectively. The total amount of money is OK; the consumer at point A, for example, has indicated a combination of OE″ quantity of X and OL quantity of money and so exchanges KL quantity of money for OE″ quantity of X. Similar decisions are made by the consumer at points B, C and D. The price consumption curve is really a total outlay curve, upside down, for any given quantity of X purchased.

A demand curve only indicates the quantity of X purchased at any given price and is not concerned with the size of the income or how much is left over after the purchase. The only requirement is that size of income must be constant. However, a reduction in the price of X enables a consumer to buy more X with a given income and this affects the

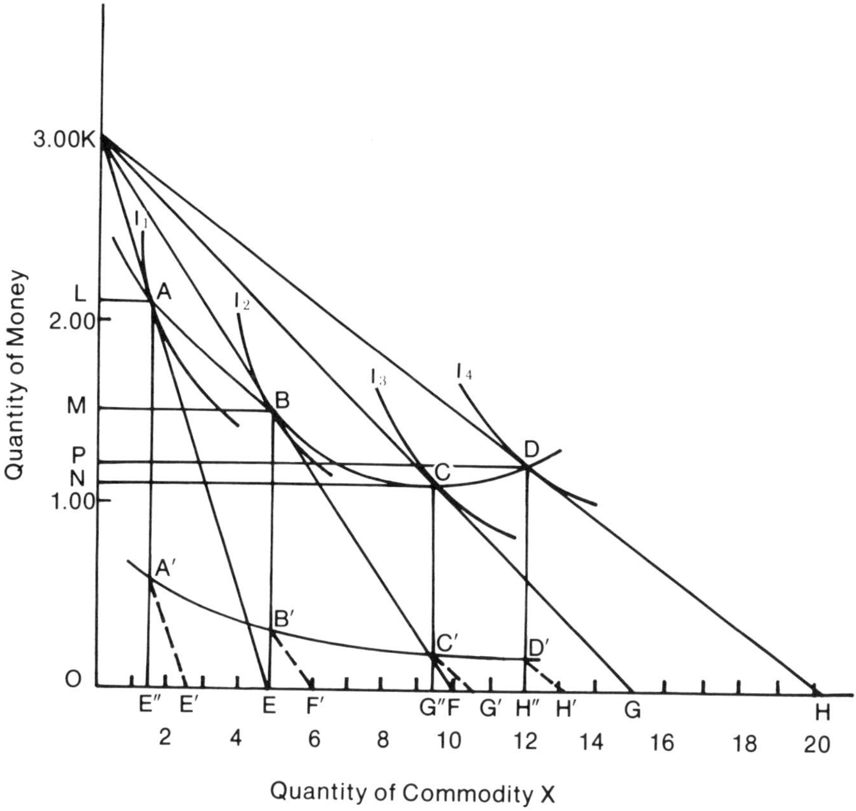

FIG. 8.5. DERIVATION OF DEMAND CURVE FROM INDIFFERENCE CURVES

consumer's welfare in the same way as an increase in income.[1] The price per unit of X must be known for any given quantity of X purchased. The graphical technique of determining the unit price of X is easy. For example, consider line AE″ which shows OE″ units of X purchased at a unit price of KL/OE″ or OK/OE. To find the unit price of X, mark off one unit of X along the axis to the right of AE″, which is E″E′ and then draw a line A′E′ parallel to budget line KE. The slope of line KE (i.e., OK/OE) indicates the unit price of X and is equal to the slope of line A′E′ which also indicates the price of one unit (E″E′) of X. Thus, E″A′ indicates the price of a unit of X when OE″ quantity is bought and A′ is a

[1] For a discussion of this refinement of the Marshallian demand curve, *see* Friedman, M. 1949. The Marshallian demand curve. J. Pol. Econ. 57 (6), or Friedman, M. 1953. Essays in Positive Economics. Part II. University of Chicago Press, Chicago.

point on the consumer's demand curve for X. In other words, point A′ indicates how much of X will be purchased when one unit costs E″A′. Other points—B′, C′, D′—can be located and connected to form a demand curve A′ B′ C′ D′ which shows the amount of X which the consumer will purchase at various prices of X.[2]

Most individual demand curves will be negatively sloping throughout because in most cases both the income effect and the price effect are positive. There may be certain situations in which the Giffen paradox seems to hold and the demand curve will be positively sloping within a range (Fig. 8.6). If the income effect is positive or unimportant at the beginning, the segment AB of the demand curve will be negatively sloping. When the price falls farther, the income effect becomes strongly negative, outweighing the positive substitution effect, which causes the BC segment of the demand curve to be positively sloping. At this point the price is low and thus total outlay is small. This will cause the income effect, even if still negative, to be outweighed again by the stronger positive substitution effect, which will induce the CD segment to be once again negatively sloping. Thus, the positively sloping segment will be only over those price ranges where the income effect is strongly negative, i.e., strong enough to offset the positive substitution effect. In a market demand curve, which is a horizontal sum of the individual demand curves, the Giffen paradox may not be present. A commodity may be inferior for some individuals and not for others, and individuals for whom the commodity is normal may buy in sufficient quantities to more than offset the behavior of those for whom the commodity is inferior, thus making the market demand curve appear normal.

In the above derivation of the ordinary demand curve, the price of the commodity was permitted to change and the price line was permitted to pivot on a point on the vertical axis. This method permits the real income to change as the commodity price changes. This really violates a basic assumption underlying the demand curve, namely, that income remains constant. Two modifications have been suggested in order to keep real income constant. One suggested by Slutsky involves rotating the price

[2] The relationship of the price consumption curve ABCD and the demand curve A′ B′ C′ D′ can be shown by a table.

Explanation	A	B	C	D
Slope of price line (Ratio of intercepts)	$\frac{3.00}{5}$	$\frac{3.00}{10}$	$\frac{3.00}{15}$	$\frac{3.00}{20}$
Price of X	0.60	0.30	0.20	0.15
Quantity of X taken at each price, units	1½	5	9½	12

line around a given point (D, Fig. 8.7) which represents a combination of commodities. The points of tangency of the resulting various price lines to indifference curves can be used to generate a demand curve D′S′ which holds real income constant in the sense that money income when deflated by a price index gives constant purchasing power. The other modification, which follows the work of Hicks, involves a set of price lines abutting a given indifference curve. This keeps real income constant in the sense of keeping utility constant. A decrease in the price of a commodity would involve a reduction in income to keep the consumer on the same indifference curve. The points of tangency of the price lines to the indifference curve can be used to generate the demand curve D′H′ which is lower than the Slutsky curve. Both of these demand curves lie below the usual or ordinary demand curve D′U′ at the right of the intersection at D′ (Fig. 8.7).

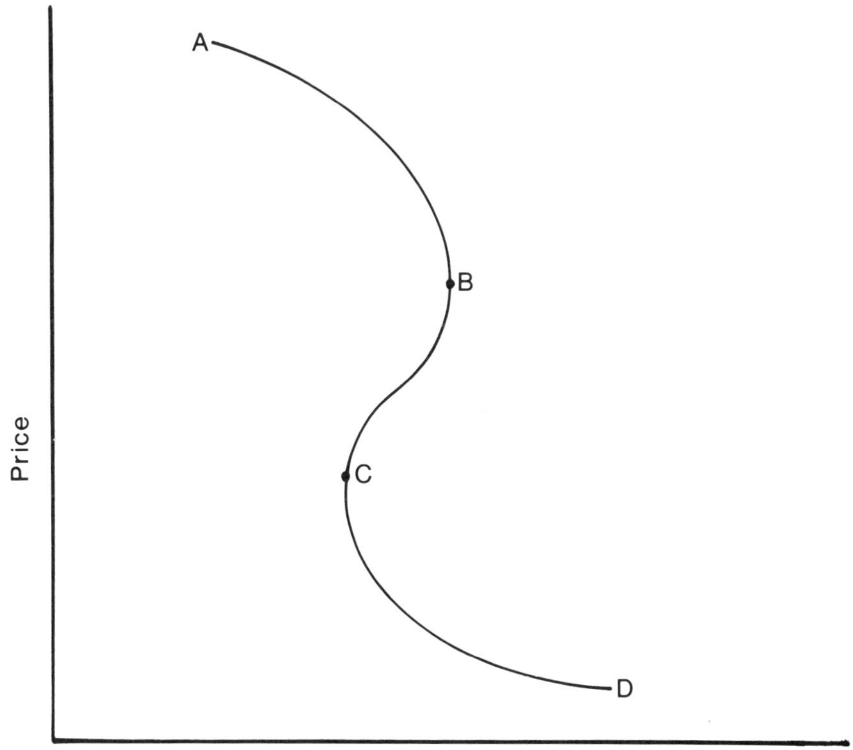

FIG. 8.6. SEGMENTS OF POSITIVELY AND NEGATIVELY SLOPING DEMAND CURVES

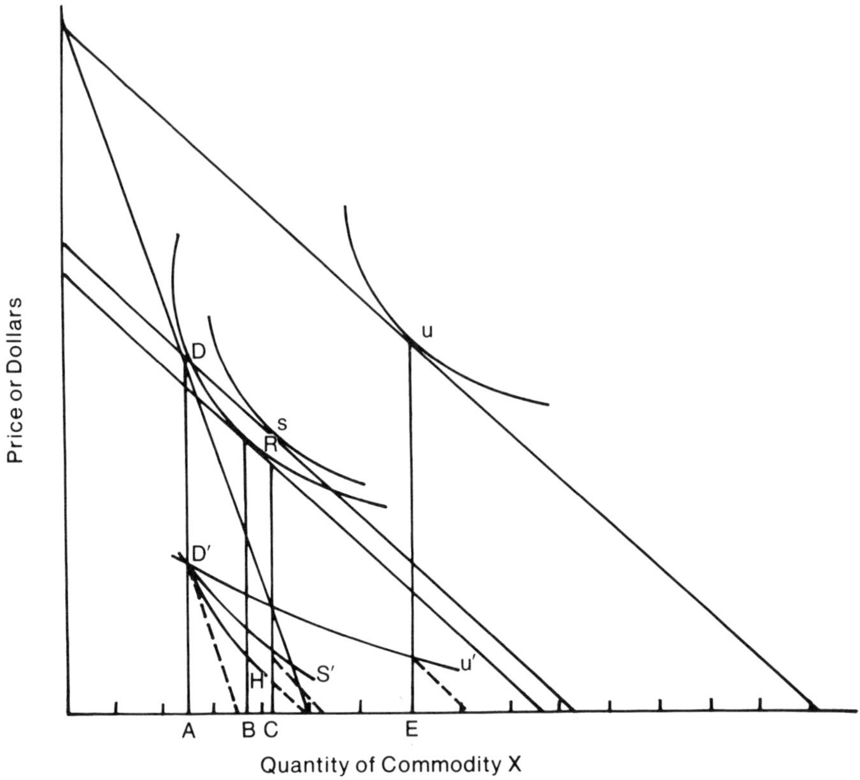

FIG. 8.7. DERIVATION OF THREE DIFFERENT DEMAND CURVES

Because the price of X declined, the quantity taken increased from OA to OE as a result of both the income and substitution effects as previously explained. The quantity AE can be allocated between the two effects. Following Hicks, the

Total Effect		Income Effect		Substitution Effect
AE	=	BE	+	AB

Following Slutsky, the

Total Effect		Income Effect		Substitution Effect
AE	=	CE	+	AC

The difference between the two approaches is BC; as the price change approaches zero, BC approaches zero more rapidly than the other amounts CE, AC, BE and AB. Thus, the smaller the change in the price of the commodity, the less significant is the difference between the two approaches. A knowledge of the indifference curves is necessary to follow the Hicks approach, but the Slutsky approach can be used directly with observations obtained in the market.

Engel Curves

Through the indifference technique one can derive the Engel curve for a commodity.[3] An Engel curve shows the different quantities of a commodity which a consumer will purchase at different levels of income. The Engel curve for commodity X may be obtained from the family of indifference curves with money on the vertical axis and commodity X on the horizontal axis. Given the price of X, an increase in income will shift the point of optimum combination from P to P′; the locus of such points obtained as income changes is called the income consumption curve as discussed in a preceding chapter (Fig. 8.8). The income consumption curve is not always an Engel curve although they may appear very similar graphically and portray the same information. To understand more precisely what an Engel curve is, it is necessary to go into more detail. When the income was OB, the optimum combination was OM of X and OE of money which means that the consumer spent BE amount to obtain OM quantity of X. After the increase of income from OB to OA, or by the amount of BA which also equals EC since BB′ and AA′ are parallel, the optimum combination becomes ON of X and OD of money which means that the consumer spends AD amount of money to obtain ON quantity of X. One should note that of the increase in income EC only CD is spent on X while ED is held in the form of money to be used on other commodities. Thus, when the increase in quantity MN is placed on the horizontal axis and the increase in income AB is placed on the vertical axis, an Engel curve is generated (Fig. 8.9). If X is a normal good, the higher the income the greater will be the quantity of X purchased.

Engel curves are useful in studying consumption patterns for different commodities by different individuals. They may help in understanding the reasons why certain food commodities, i.e., beef *vs* eggs, are purchased in differing quantities as the income level rises.

ELASTICITY OF DEMAND

The concept of elasticity in economic analysis describes a particular property of a relationship. It is embodied in a comparison of the rates of change of two variables, i.e., a response of one variable to a change in

[3] The Engel curve is named after Ernst Engel, a German pioneer in the field of budget studies.

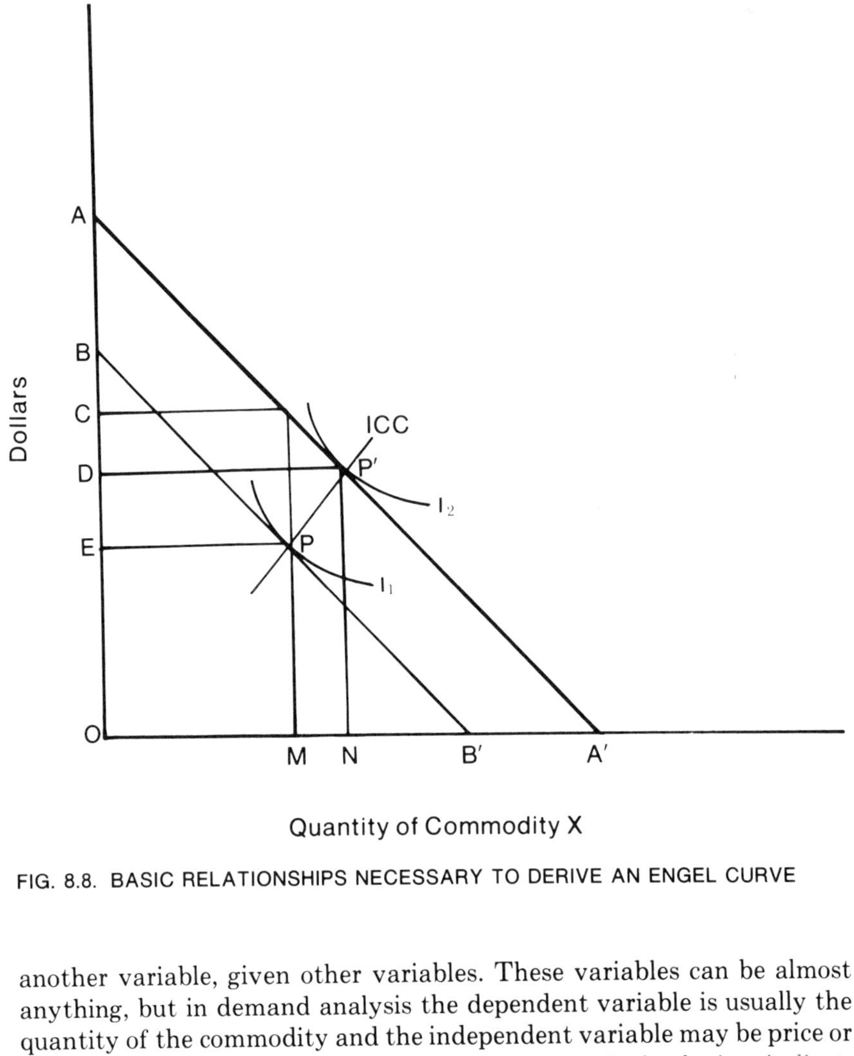

FIG. 8.8. BASIC RELATIONSHIPS NECESSARY TO DERIVE AN ENGEL CURVE

another variable, given other variables. These variables can be almost anything, but in demand analysis the dependent variable is usually the quantity of the commodity and the independent variable may be price or income. Since most price demand curves are negatively sloping, indicating an inverse relationship between price and quantity, consumers will respond to lowering of the price with an increase in quantity demanded. However, the amount of response will depend upon the elasticity of the demand. A knowledge of the response to a change in price is valuable to the grocer, for example, in determining the prices for many items. When a price is cut, the grocer knows he or she can sell more but how much more depends on the responsiveness of the customers to the price cut. On those commodities that have a big response to a price change the grocer

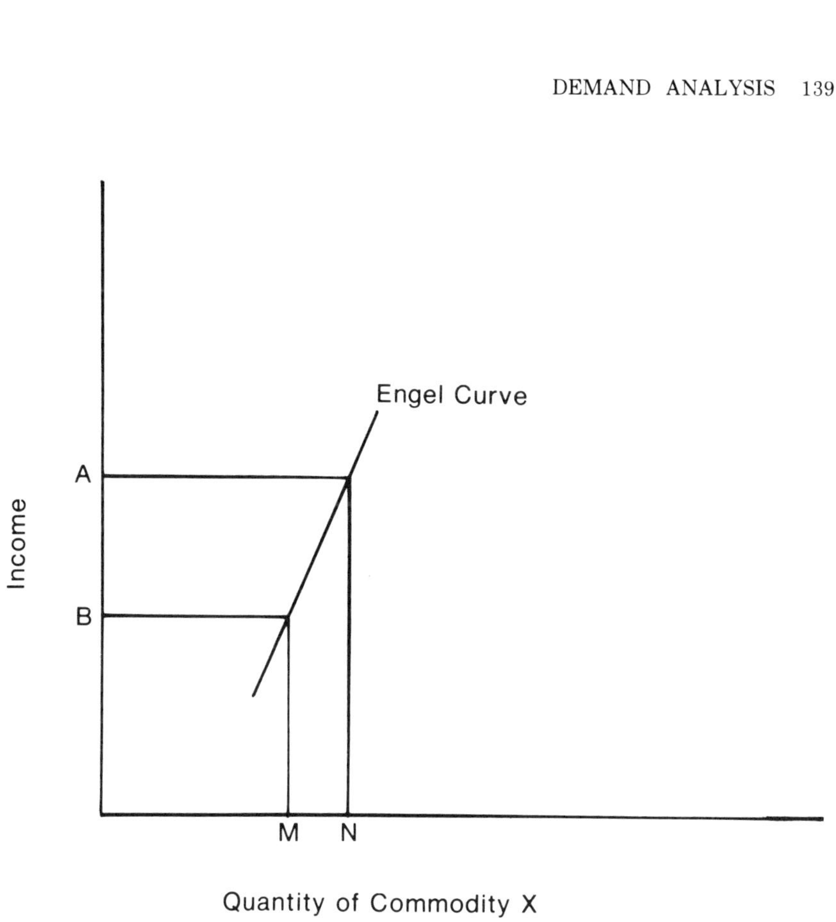

FIG. 8.9. AN ENGEL CURVE

will soon learn to cut prices, and on those with a small response to a price change he or she will maintain a higher price. Thus, the grocer soon becomes very familiar with the working of the concept even though perhaps not familiar with the formal theoretical concept.

The price elasticity of demand for a commodity, which usually is referred to simply as elasticity of demand, depends on the structure of the demand for that commodity. Since the demand curve is derived from the price consumption curve, the elasticity of demand depends on the structure or shape of the price consumption curve which in turn depends on the nature of the income effect and of the substitution effect. Thus, elasticity of demand is actually dependent on *income elasticity* of demand and on *elasticity of substitution*. Price elasticity of demand may be considered as a sort of a composite of the underlying income and taste components.

Elasticity of Substitution

The concept of elasticity of substitution is very important in understanding the elasticity of demand. It provides a numerical measure of the extent to which one commodity can be substituted for another and still remain on the same indifference curve. Elasticity of substitution (E_{ss}) between any two commodities in consumption may be defined as the relative change in the ratio of the commodities as compared to the relative change in the marginal rate of substitution of the commodities. Since the concept is formulated in terms of proportional units, the measure is independent of the scale or size of units used along the axes. The measurement at any point on a single indifference curve is given by the formula $E_{ss} = [\Delta(X_1/X_2) \;/\; (X_1/X_2)] \div [\Delta(\Delta X_1/\Delta X_2) \;/\; (\Delta X_1/\Delta X_2)]$ where $\Delta(X_1/X_2)$ refers to the change in the ratio at which commodities combine, (X_1/X_2) refers to the original ratio or combination of commodities, $\Delta(\Delta X_1/\Delta X_2)$ refers to the change in the marginal rate of substitution, and $(\Delta X_1/\Delta X_2)$ refers to the original marginal rate of substitution between the commodities. All other commodities are assumed to be fixed in quantity while X_1 and X_2 vary, because if other commodities should vary then the marginal rates of substitution, the original quantities and hence the elasticity of substitution between X_1 and X_2 would change.

The elasticity of substitution can range from one extreme of infinity to the other extreme of zero. The infinite elasticity occurs when the two commodities are perfect substitutes as represented by a linear indifference curve. On such indifference curves, the proportionate change in the ratio between the holdings of X_1 and X_2 is very large as compared with the relative change in the marginal rate of substitution. The change in the MRS is zero, making the numerical value of elasticity of substitution infinity. In practice, one may never find a linear indifference curve; if two commodities are perfect substitutes they are economically the same commodity. However, many commodities are likely to have high elasticities of substitution. The zero elasticity occurs when two commodities cannot be substituted for each other, as indicated by an L-shaped indifference curve. This means that as the indifference curve approaches the perfect L-shape, the proportionate change in the ratio between the holdings of X_1 and X_2 is very small (in the limit, zero) as compared to the relative change in MRS which also approaches zero, thus giving a zero elasticity of substitution. Again, in practice, one may not find very many commodities that are perfect complements but there are many that have a very low elasticity of substitution.

Income Elasticity

The level of income has a substantial effect on the amount of a given commodity a person will purchase. The income elasticity (E_i) gives a numerical indication of the responsiveness of a consumer's purchases of a commodity to a change in income. It may be defined as $E_i = \frac{\text{relative change in quantity of commodity purchased}}{\text{relative change in income}}$, or $E_i = dq/q \div dI/I$ which is equivalent to $(dq/dI)\,(I/q)$. This concept explains how the purchases by a consumer of a given commodity change as income changes with prices remaining constant. The income elasticity can have various positive or negative values. For example, if a 1% increase in income causes a 5% increase in the amount of commodity X purchased, the E_i for commodity X would be 5; if a 1% increase in income causes a 0.2 or 0.3% increase in quantity, as is apparently the case of food, the E_i would be 0.2 or 0.3 which means that commodity X is normal since E_i is positive. All income elasticities of normal goods are positive, and income elasticities of inferior goods are negative. A commodity with a negative income elasticity is one for which an increase in income leads to a decrease in the amount purchased. Some food commodities such as potatoes have a negative income elasticity. If the E_i of demand for a commodity is greater than one, it indicates that an increasing proportion of the consumer's income is spent on the commodity as the income increases. Likewise, if the E_i is less than one, the proportion of income spent on the good falls as income increases. It has been suggested that unitary income elasticity can be considered roughly as the dividing line which separates luxury commodities from those in the necessity category. Under this suggestion, those commodities with income elasticities greater than one would be luxuries and those with income elasticities less than one would be necessities.

In cases where exactly all of the increase in income is spent on the commodity, the income elasticity is equal to the reciprocal of the proportion of the consumer's income spent on the commodity. Thus,

$$E_i = \frac{1}{kX}$$

where kX refers to the proportion of the income spent on X. This means that if a person is spending 5% (1/20) of his or her income on X and if the person has a 1% increase in income and spends it all on X, he or she will increase the expenditure on X by 20%, thus giving an E_i of 20 for commodity X. If less than all of the increase in income is spent on X, then the $E_i < \frac{1}{kX}$ and vice versa.

Price Elasticity

Price elasticity of demand is perhaps the most frequently used elasticity concept in economic theory and is defined as the ratio of the proportionate change in quantity purchased in response to the proportionate change in price. Thus,

$$E_p = \frac{\text{relative change in quantity}}{\text{corresponding relative change in price}}$$

or $E_p = dq/q \div dp/p$ which is equivalent to $(dq/dp)\,(p/q)$ or $p(dq) / q(dp)$. This definition makes the measure independent of the units used along the axes. Price elasticity of demand (E_P) depends upon both the elasticity of substitution and the income elasticity of demand. Thus,

$$E_P = (kX)\,(E_i) + (1 - kX)\,(E_{ss})$$

where E_{ss} refers to elasticity of substitution, E_i refers to income elasticity, and kX refers to the proportion of income spent on X. First, when a change in price of a commodity X occurs, the size of the change in quantity purchased depends on the income effect. The income effect, in turn, partly depends upon the proportion of the consumer's income spent on X, as this indicates the amount available for new spending if the price (and thus expenditure) has fallen. Given the income elasticity, the greater the amount of one's income spent on the commodity X whose price has decreased, the greater will be the amount of income that is free for all new expenditures, including the commodity X. Also, the income effect partly depends upon the size of the income elasticity of demand for commodity X because this determines what proportion of the income set free by a price decline will be spent on X.

Second, the size of the change in quantity of the commodity X purchased as a result of a decline in its price and increase in real income depends in part on the elasticity of substitution between X and other commodities Y. Since X is now relatively cheaper compared to Y, a consumer would want to substitute X for Y if possible. Also, it depends in part on the amount of the other commodity Y that was purchased before the decline in price of X. Given the elasticity of substitution, a decline in the price of X will cause a shift of purchase from Y to X only to the extent that Y was previously bought. Thus, $1-kX$ indicates the proportion of income not spent on X and the proportion within which it is possible to substitute X for Y.

One may note immediately that when the elasticity of substitution and the income elasticity are both equal to one, the price elasticity of demand must also be equal to one. For example, with one tenth of a person's income spent on X, $E_P = (1/10)(1) + (9/10)(1) = 1$. This does not mean that all unitary price elasticities of demand require that the elasticity of substitution and income elasticity be unity, e.g.,

$$E_P = (1/2)(3/10) + (1/2)(17/10) = 1$$

with one-half of income spent on X, an income elasticity of 0.3 and an elasticity of substitution of 1.7. For another example, if the E_i of food is about 0.3, the E_{ss} of food and other goods and services is about 0.2, and the consumers are spending about one-fourth of their incomes on food, the price elasticity of demand for food would be 0.225, i.e.,

$$E_P = (1/4)(3/10) + (3/4)(2/10) = 0.225$$

Salt is often cited as a classical example of a commodity whose price elasticity of demand is low, i.e., inelastic. The reason for the low elasticity can be easily understood. The proportion of income spent on salt is very low and the income effect of a price decline can never be great. In addition, income elasticity of demand for salt is perhaps very low. Also, since no good substitutes exist for salt, the elasticity of substitution between salt and other goods would be very low. This means that the indifference curves between salt and other commodities would have a very high degree of convexity and would indicate that a taste for salt would be quickly satisfied.

Often, a knowledge of income elasticity and elasticity of substitution of a commodity is not available and the need exists for a measure of price elasticity of demand. Elasticity at a point on the demand curve can be determined geometrically. A tangent can be drawn to a demand curve at point P and extended to cut the axes at C and D (Fig. 8.10). Suppose the price falls from OB to OA. Then the quantity purchased would increase from OG to OE; however, as the change in price becomes smaller, then OE will approach OF. Thus, for a small price change from OB to OA then the quantity change will be from OG to OF. Applying the formula for price elasticity,

$$E_p = \frac{\frac{\Delta q}{q}}{\frac{\Delta p}{p}} = \frac{\frac{GF}{OG}}{\frac{BA}{OB}} = \frac{GF}{OG} \cdot \frac{OB}{BA} = \frac{GF}{BA} \cdot \frac{OB}{OG}$$

Since right triangles PHI and PGD are similar, GF/BA can be written as DG/OB. The equation $\frac{GF}{BA} \cdot \frac{OB}{OG}$

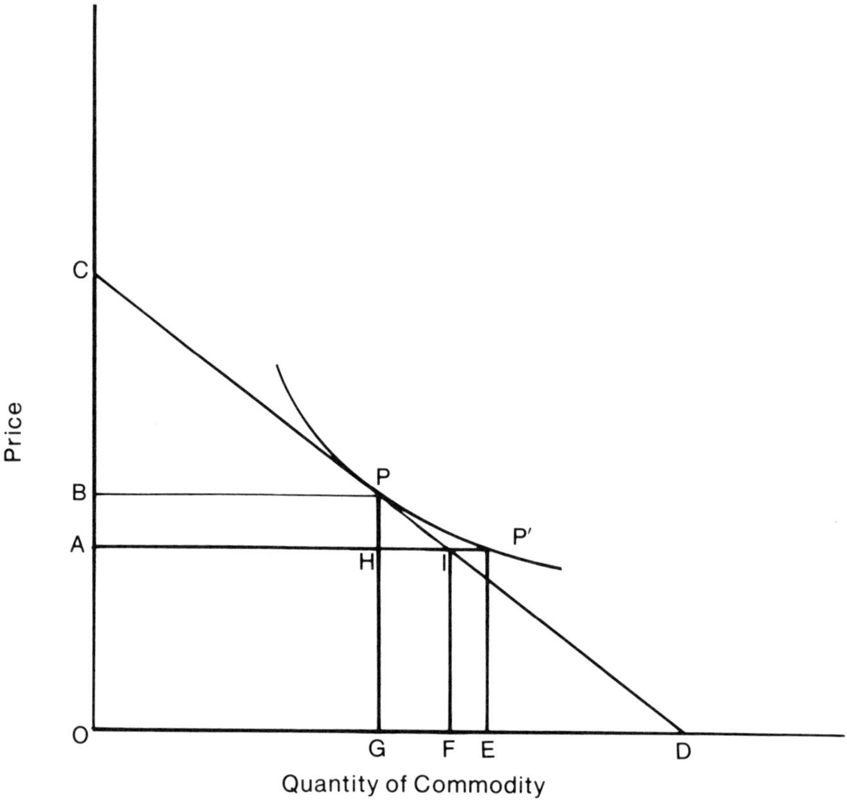

FIG. 8.10. GEOMETRICAL DERIVATION OF PRICE ELASTICITY OF DEMAND

becomes $$\frac{GD}{OB} \cdot \frac{OB}{OG} \text{ or } \frac{GD}{OG}$$

which is the elasticity of demand at point P. Since triangles GDP and BPC are similar, $$\frac{GD}{OG} = \frac{PD}{PC}$$

Thus, point elasticity of demand on a demand curve can always be found by drawing any tangent CD to the curve at any point P and calculating PD/PC. If the numerical value at any point P is 1, the elasticity is said to be unity; if greater than 1, the demand is said to be relatively elastic; if less than 1, it is said to be relatively inelastic. The elasticity of demand, which can range from zero to infinite values, is always negative except in backward bending demand curves, but in practice the negative sign is often dropped.

An alternative method of showing the elasticity of demand at a point has been suggested.[4] This method emphasizes the fact that elasticity and the slope of the demand curve are not the same thing. A tangent BC may be drawn to the demand curve at point P showing the slope of the demand curve at that point, i.e., dp/dq, and then a total revenue rectangle OAPD may be completed (Fig. 8.11). Within the revenue rectangle, a diagonal AD can be drawn showing the ratio of price to quantity, p/q. Elasticity of demand at point P is the ratio of the slope of the diagonal line to the slope of the tangent, or p/q ÷ dp/dq. If the two lines

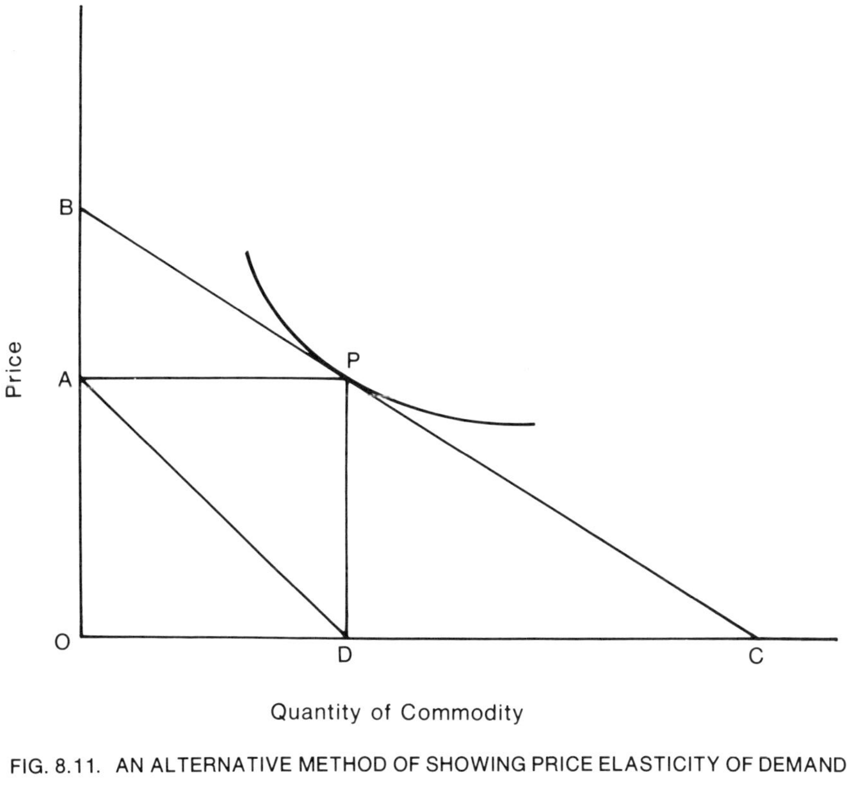

FIG. 8.11. AN ALTERNATIVE METHOD OF SHOWING PRICE ELASTICITY OF DEMAND

[4] *See* Holt, C. and Samuelson, P. A. 1946. The graphic depiction of elasticity of demand. J. Pol. Econ. *54* (4) 354–357.

AD and BC are parallel, meaning that the slopes are of equal value, the elasticity of demand at point P is unitary. If the diagonal AD has a lesser slope than the tangent BC, or in other words the two lines tend to meet toward the horizontal axis, the elasticity will be less than one or relatively inelastic. If they tend to converge toward the vertical axis, the elasticity of demand will be greater than one or relatively elastic.

A graphic method exists also by which the demand elasticities at points on different demand curves can be compared.[5] In order to compare the elasticity at points S and T on the demand curves D_1 and D_2, a tangent can be drawn to each point, extending to cut both axes (Fig. 8.12). After

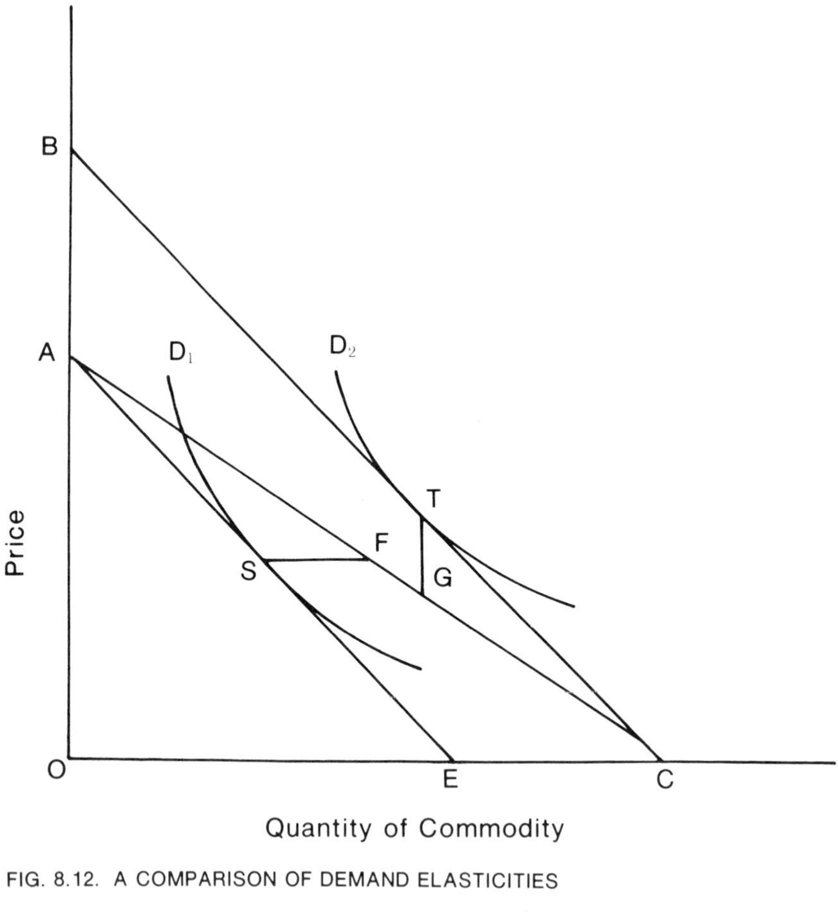

FIG. 8.12. A COMPARISON OF DEMAND ELASTICITIES

[5] *See* Lerner, A. P. 1947. Geometrical comparison of elasticities. Am. Econ. Rev. *37*(1).

connecting the alternative extremities A and C to form line AC, draw a horizontal line from point S and a vertical line from point T to cut line AC at F and G, respectively. The elasticity of demand at point T is TC/TB which is equal to GC/GA by the geometric theorem of similar right triangles. Likewise, the elasticity of demand at point S is SE/SA which is equal to FC/FA. This procedure relates the elasticities to a common line AC. If points F and G are equal, the elasticities at S and T would be equal and point T would be directly above point F. If FC is greater than GC, then FA is less than GA which makes the elasticity at point S greater than the elasticity at point T.

Elasticity of demand refers to instantaneous movement from point to point along the demand curve. Often it is not possible to measure the elasticity at a point. The data may be for only two observations without knowledge of the continuity of the mathematical function. However, an approximation to the actual point elasticity can be made over the arc extending between two points, hence, *arc elasticity*. A number of formulae exist that could be used to measure the arc elasticity but none provides the same answer as the point elasticity. A simple and workable formula is one which is equivalent to passing a straight line through the points A and B and finding the point elasticity at the midpoint (Fig. 8.12). Thus,

$$E_{arc} = \frac{Q_2 - Q_1}{P_1 - P_2} \cdot \frac{P_1 + P_2}{Q_1 + Q_2}.$$

It will be noted that the $(Q_2 - Q_1) / (P_1 - P_2)$ portion of the formula is equivalent to the $\Delta q/\Delta p$ component (not taken to the limit to give dq/dp) of the point elasticity formula. The $(P_1 + P_2) / (Q_1 + Q_2)$ portion is the counterpart of p/q of the point elasticity formula but it is the average of P_1 and P_2, and Q_1 and Q_2 (Fig. 8.13). Thus,

$$E_{arc} = \frac{\Delta q}{\Delta p} \cdot \frac{\frac{P_1 + P_2}{2}}{\frac{Q_1 + Q_2}{2}} = \frac{\Delta q}{\Delta p} \cdot \frac{P_1 + P_2}{Q_1 + Q_2} = \frac{Q_2 - Q_1}{P_1 - P_2} \cdot \frac{P_1 + P_2}{Q_1 + Q_2}$$

With $P_1 = \$5$, $P_2 = \$4$, $Q_1 = 2$ units, and $Q_2 = 3$ units, the

$$E_{arc} = \frac{3 - 2}{5 - 4} \cdot \frac{5 + 4}{2 + 3} = \frac{9}{5}$$

or 1.8 at point M. The farther apart A and B become, the greater will be the degree of discrepancy between point elasticity and arc elasticity.

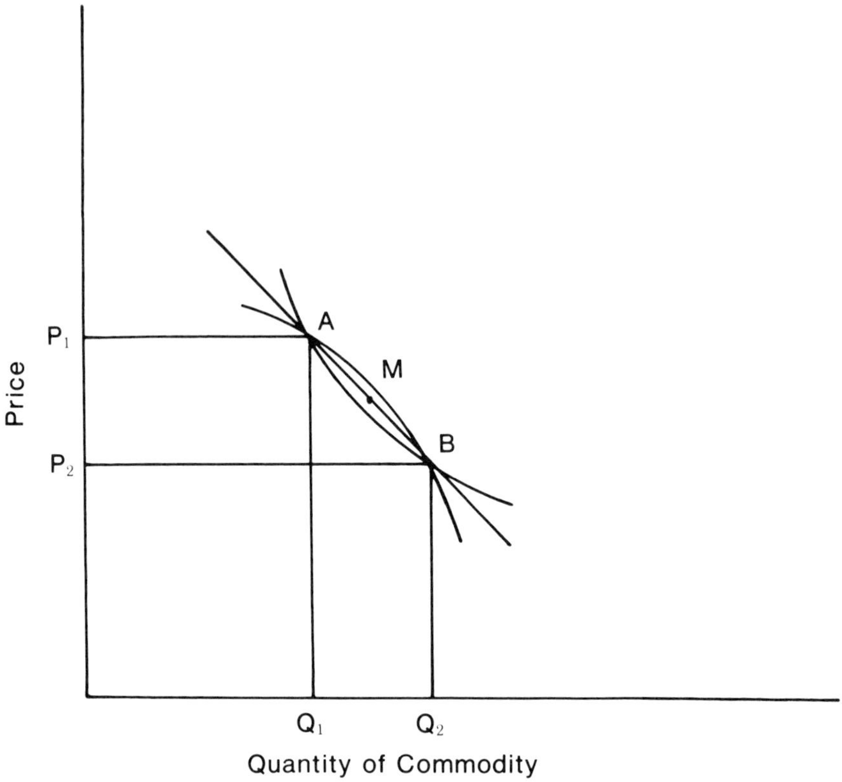

FIG. 8.13. ARC ELASTICITY OF DEMAND

The elasticity concept is important when studying the demand curve because it provides a very convenient indication of the behavior of total receipts. The change in price and the change in quantity have opposite effects on total receipts from a negatively sloped demand curve; a decline in price reduces the receipts while the corresponding increase in quantity increases receipts. If no change occurs in total receipts, the two effects will have exactly offset each other and the demand curve will have an elasticity of unity and will be a rectangular hyperbola in shape. If the effect of the price change dominates, the total revenue will move in the same direction as the price change; a rise in price results in a rise in total receipts and the elasticity of demand will range from unity to zero. Demand in this case is relatively inelastic. If the effect of the quantity increase dominates, the total revenue will move in the opposite direction of the price change; a rise in price results in a decrease in total receipts, and the elasticity of demand will range from unity to infinity which means that the demand curve is relatively elastic. The numerical value of elasticity is negative in all cases for normal goods.

The change in total receipts can be computed algebraically. For a change in price, ΔP, there will be a corresponding change in quantity, ΔQ. For a given reduction in price $(P - \Delta P)$, there will be an increase in quantity $(Q + \Delta Q)$. To obtain the total receipts after changes, multiply

$$(P - \Delta P)(Q + \Delta Q) = PQ + P\Delta Q - Q\Delta P - \Delta P\Delta Q$$

Since $-\Delta P\Delta Q$ will be of a very small magnitude it can be ignored; the original total receipts before the change took place, PQ, can be subtracted to give the change in total receipts, or

Total Change in Revenue = $P\Delta Q - Q\Delta P$ = (Marginal Revenue per Unit Sold) (Change in Quantity Sold)

Since $E_p = \dfrac{P\Delta Q}{Q\Delta P}$,

then, $E_p = \dfrac{P\Delta Q}{P\Delta Q - (MR)\Delta Q}$ or $\dfrac{P}{P - MR}$

Thus, $MR = \dfrac{P(E_p - 1)}{E_p}$ or $P\left(1 - \dfrac{1}{E_p}\right)$

At any output, the $MR = P\left(1 - \dfrac{1}{E}\right)$ where E_P equals the elasticity of demand. If $E_P = 1$, then $MR = P\left(1 - \dfrac{1}{1}\right) = 0$ which means that total revenue is constant. Marginal revenue is always positive at any output where $E_P > 1$, and always negative at any output where $E_P < 1$. Thus, it is possible to determine the marginal revenue at any output from the price at that output if the point elasticity of demand is known.

Cross Elasticity

Often commodities are related in such a way that a change in the price of one leads the consumer to change his or her purchases of another. The cross elasticity of demand measures the extent to which various commodities are related to each other, i.e., the strength of substitution or complementarity. Where there are two commodities, A and B, the cross elasticity of demand is obtained by considering the percentage change in quantity of B purchased resulting from a given percentage change in the

price of A, with the price of B held constant.
Thus,

$$E_c = \frac{\frac{\Delta A}{A}}{\frac{\Delta P_b}{P_b}} = \frac{\text{relative change in purchase of A}}{\text{relative change in price of B}}$$

The cross-elasticity values can be positive, zero or negative. If E_c is positive, the commodities are good substitutes, which means that if the price of A rises, a large shift to the purchase of B will occur. If E_c is zero, then there is no relationship between the commodities, i.e., if the price of A rises, there would be no change in the quantity of B purchased. If E_c is large and negative, the commodities can be considered good complements, which means that if the price of A should rise and the quantity of A purchased should fall, the quantity of B purchased would decrease also.

The concept of cross elasticity is useful in defining *commodity*, a term which has been used throughout these chapters without a formal definition. All items which have infinite cross elasticities can be considered items of the same commodity. Cross elasticities also furnish a guide to the boundaries of industries; one may consider those commodities which have high cross elasticities to comprise an industry. However, cross elasticities cannot be considered exact or precise determinants of industry classification.

CHAPTER 8: REVIEW QUESTIONS

(1) What are the assumptions underlying the demand curve and why are they important in demand analysis?

(2) What are the essential differences between the demand curves derived by Hicks, Slutsky and Marshall? Under what assumptions is each generated?

(3) Evaluate Marshall's observation that "the one universal rule to which the demand curve conforms is that it is inclined negatively throughout its whole length."

(4) In the theory of consumer demand, the *total effect* of a change in the price of a consumer good on the quantity of that good purchased is described to be the result of an *income effect* and a *substitution effect*.
Explain carefully (using graphs) how this is the case. Introduce and employ such concepts as indifference curves, budget lines and the price consumption curve.

(5) Define and explain the following concepts:
   (a) Income consumption curve
   (b) Engel curve
   (c) Substitution and income effects; the Slutsky equation
   (d) Price elasticity, income elasticity, and elasticity of substitution
   (e) Inferior goods and Giffen goods

(6) "Elasticity of demand with respect to price is 0.25"; what does this mean?

(7) "Price elasticity is dependent upon income elasticity and elasticity of substitution." Discuss.

(8) "The Giffen paradox results from the impact of income effects and substitution effects." Discuss.

(9) "As income rises, the demand curve shifts to the right, indicating a willingness on the part of the consumer to buy greater quantities of a good than before." Appraise.

(10) "I buy only one automobile because I need only one." Why is this explanation imprecise in a scientific treatment of demand phenomena?

(11) "Demand is desire plus ability to pay." Discuss the shortcomings of this definition as an aid in understanding demand phenomena.

(12) "Commodities may be defined and distinguished according to the nature of their demand schedules." Defend or criticize.

(13) "An increase in income will shift the demand curve to the right." Criticize and give illustrations.

(14) Discuss several geometrical methods for ascertaining and comparing demand elasticities.

(15) "The demand for such necessities as bread, meat and sugar is inelastic." Criticize.

(16) Describe certain difficulties that would confront an investigator who attempts to measure the elasticity of demand for sugar, bread, etc.

(17) "If the cross-elasticity of demand is positive, the commodities (according to the definition) will be substitutes." Discuss.

(18) "Market demand for a commodity class is likely to be less elastic than for each commodity comprising the group." Discuss.

(19) Discuss the concept of elasticity of demand with respect to price. Upon what assumptions is it based? How is it related to income elasticity and elasticity of substitution? Using these ideas, offer an explanation of why the demand for salt is inelastic with respect to price.

(20) Discuss those factors which influence the price elasticity of demand for a commodity.

(21) Discuss the relationship of time to demand elasticities and their estimation, indicating significant generalizations and limitations, if any.

(22) What are the differences among cross elasticity, point elasticity and arc elasticity?

(23) Is the price elasticity of demand greater for food or for meat? For meat or for pork? For strawberries or vegetables? Why?

(24) With a demand equation of $P = a/X$,
   (a) What is the elasticity of demand?
   (b) Does this vary?
   (c) What is true of all the rectangles fitted under the demand curve?

(25) Prove that demand is perfectly elastic at the point at which the demand curve cuts the vertical axis, and zero elastic at the intersection with the horizontal axis.

(26) If the demand curve is of the following form, in which the quantity demanded of commodity A depends on the price of commodities A and B, as $X_a = b + cP_a + gP_b$:
   (a) What is the relation between the goods if g is positive? negative?
   (b) What is the influence on the demand for A of $\pm \Delta P_b$?

(27) Explain how the demand for gasoline would be affected by each of the following:
   (a) a tax on bus tickets
   (b) growing traffic congestion in a city
   (c) a tax on horsepower of automobile engines
   (d) a subsidy on lubricating oil produced in fixed proportion with gasoline

(28) Given the following situations, graph possible indifference curves and the price-consumption curve, and compute the price elasticity. Income throughout is constant at \$6, and the price of Y at \$1. Price of X is originally \$1, and changed to \$2.

   (a) $P_{X_0} = \$1, X_0 = 4, Y_0 = 2$ (Initial situation)

   $P_{X_1} = \$2, X_1 = 2, Y_1 = 2$ (New situation)

   (b) $P_{X_0} = \$1, X_0 = 5, Y_0 = 1$

   $P_{X_1} = \$2, X_1 = 2, Y_1 = 2$

   (c) $P_{X_0} = \$1, X_0 = 3, Y_0 = 3$

   $P_{X_1} = \$2, X_1 = 2, Y_1 = 2$

(d) $P_{X_0} = \$1, X_0 = 2, Y_0 = 4$

$P_{X_1} = \$2, X_1 = 2, Y_0 = 2$

(29a) Assume the following information relative to the market demand for beef cattle this year:

(1) Elasticity of demand for beef cattle w/respect to price= − 0.8.
(2) Elasticity of demand for beef cattle w/respect to income =0.6.
(3) The relevant length of run is short run.
(4) Current per capita consumption of beef = 165 lb (live weight basis).
(5) Current price per cwt (live weight basis) = $18.50.
(6) Current disposable income per capita = $1800.00.

The following expressions are furnished for your reference.

$$\text{Demand elasticity} = \frac{Q}{P} \cdot \frac{dP}{dQ}$$

$$\text{Income elasticity} = \frac{Q}{I} \cdot \frac{dI}{dQ}$$

If you had the following estimates available to you for next year, what would be your estimate of the pricc consumption and marketing situation for beef cattle for next year?

(1) Estimated salable beef cattle (per capita live weight) = 155 lb.
(2) Estimated disposable income per capita = $2000.

Indicate the steps by which you arrive at your estimate.

Make and specify whatever added assumptions you feel are *needed* to arrive at useful answers. For those components of the market situation for beef cattle which you feel cannot be specified from the information at hand, indicate the reasons for this opinion.

(29b) If you had the following additional information at hand, how would you modify your answer to part (a)?

A recent study suggests that the cross elasticity of beef consumption with respect to pork prices is −3.6 at the farm level. The forecast for pork production for next year as indicated by sows to farrow in the fall is up 11%. The demand elasticity for hogs is estimated at −0.4 at the farm and the income elasticity of demand for hogs is estimated at 0.4. You may again add assumptions *needed* to arrive at an answer, specifying those which you add.

The following expression is furnished for your reference.

$$\text{Cross elasticity of x relative to price of y} = \frac{dQx}{dPy} \cdot \frac{Py}{Qx}$$

Paper Two: The Demand for Major Foods in Canada

Zuhair A. Hassan and S.R. Johnson[6]

It has become increasingly apparent that effective policies for agriculture require a comprehensive view of the industry. Such policies, whether private or public, must account for interrelationships within the agricultural sector as well as the functional role of the industry in the economic system. For Canada, this aspect of policy analysis is even more crucial because of the importance of its agriculture in international trade. Policies that fail to incorporate these interrelationships adequately may be highly sensitive to the changing nature of the industry and the economy. Consequently, they may require continual updating and revision and, correspondingly, unnecessarily high adjustment costs and uncertainty for agents in the agricultural sector.

Consumer demand for food is an obvious and important component of the economic structure within which the agricultural sector must operate. Since the demand for food is, in general, unresponsive to price changes and since the production and supply of agricultural commodities is somewhat variable, accurate estimates of demand relationships are important inputs in the development of national price stabilization, trade, storage and production control policies. These policies in turn affect the decision making of farm operators and other micro-units in the food and agricultural sector.

This paper reports the results of a major study designed to provide estimates of consumer demand for food commodity groups in Canada (Hassan and Johnson 1976). Estimates of the demand structure for 27 food commodity groups and a nonfood group are presented. The purpose of these estimates is to explain consumer behavior in the marketplace—

---

[6] From Hassan, Z.A. and Johnson, S.R. 1977. The demand for major foods in Canada. Can. Farm Econ. *12* (2) 7–15.

that is, to explain what commodities consumers will purchase and in what quantities, and how consumers can be expected to respond to changes in commodity prices and income.

DEMAND FUNCTIONS

According to the theory of consumer behavior, individuals or households arrange purchases of goods and services so as to maximize satisfaction (utility) subject to limited money income. Given this assumption, demand functions can be easily derived.[7] These demand functions show that the amount of a particular commodity an individual will purchase is related to the price of the commodity in question, prices of other commodities and income. For example, a consumer deciding on the purchase of beef might well consider its price in relation to prices of other meats, other foods and, more generally, prices of nonfood items, as well as his/her income.

Demand theory suggests an inverse (negative) relationship between the quantity demanded of a product and its (own) price. This relationship —called a *direct-price effect*—means that an increase in the price of the commodity results in a decrease in the quantity purchased with other factors remaining constant.

Relationships between the quantity demanded of one product and the prices of other products may be positive, negative or zero. This is called a *cross-price effect*. Relationships are expected to be positive for rival (substitute) products like beef and pork; for example, an increase in pork prices can be expected to result in an increase in beef consumption. For cooperating (complementary) products like bread and butter the relationship is likely to be negative; an increase in the price of one will trigger a decrease in demand for the other. For independent products like salt and tea the relationship is expected to be zero, meaning that the price of one does not affect the demand for the other.

Finally, an increase in income will affect demand. A positive *income effect* is expected for a product considered superior (beef), meaning that more of the product will be purchased, while a negative income effect is

---

[7] In mathematical notation these demand functions can be written as:

$$q_i = f_i(P_1, P_2, \ldots, P_i, \ldots P_n, m) \quad i = 1, \ldots, n$$

where q_i is the quantity of the (ith) commodity, P_i is the price of the (ith) commodity and m is consumer income.

[8] The terms "superior" and "inferior" do not refer to the nutritional value or the quality of the product but refer to the sign of the income coefficient.

associated with a good considered inferior (lard).[8]

To apply these theoretical results, it is assumed that the individual consumer is "representative" of an aggregate group. This assumption is necessitated by the fact that most of the data required for estimating the demand functions are available only in aggregate form. In addition it is assumed that other factors (e.g., tastes, age, composition of household, habits, etc.) affecting consumption remain constant or change sufficiently slowly that they can be omitted from the analysis. Finally, it is often presumed that prices of other commodities not closely related to the one in question can be omitted from the demand function because their effects on observed consumption levels are not systematic.

Recently, this latter assumption, implicit in most applied demand analyses, has come under increased attention (Brandow 1961; George and King 1971).[9] The contention has been that consumer demands for food commodities are so highly interrelated that the use of estimated demand functions that consider only income, direct (own) price and perhaps the price of another related commodity give results that are too simplified for accurate policy analysis. But this observation has brought with it a dilemma. The theory indicates that all prices are important. Yet, the data series on which the estimates for the demand systems are based are much too short to permit statistical estimation of the required parameters. The compromise made in approaching the food demand estimation problem has been one of estimating the basic or important parameters, i.e., parameters for direct price, income and selected cross-price effects and then using restrictions[10] following from the consumer demand theory to generate the remaining cross-price effects (Brandow 1971; George and King 1971; Hassan and Johnson 1976). The restrictions following from the theory of consumer demand are included in the resulting demand system and hence, they are not exploited for their possible information content in the estimation of the basic parameters from the sample data.

ESTIMATION METHOD

Parameter estimates used in constructing the full demand system are direct-price elasticities of demand, selected cross-price elasticities, in-

[9] The rest of this section plus the section "Estimation Method" may be of interest only to economists. Other readers may wish to proceed directly to the section "The Full Demand System for Food."

[10] For a detailed treatment of these restrictions (Engel, Cournot, Symmetry and Homogeneity) see Hassan and Johnson (1976).

come elasticities[11] and expenditure proportions.[12] The estimated price and income elasticities employed in constructing the system are reported in Table 8.1. The price elasticity estimates used are from selected time series studies for the Canadian economy. Details relating to these estimates and their relationships to others for the Canadian and United States economies are contained in the monograph by Hassan and Johnson (1976). Income elasticities are from a study (Hassan and Lu 1974) based on the *1969 Family Food Expenditure Survey*.[13] In the latter cross section data, the period of observation is sufficiently short that prices can be presumed constant. Differences in family food consumption patterns can thus be related to income levels.

Restrictions from the theory that are used in the construction of the estimated food demand structure are also detailed in the more extensive report (Hassan and Johnson 1976). Briefly, these restrictions relate to the internal consistency of the system with respect to cross-price effects, income elasticities and the assumption that individuals make a basic budget decision on food and nonfood expenditures and then proceed from it to select among food commodities.

In summary, although the underlying parameters are estimated from different data sources and by different statistical estimation methods, once they are obtained the rules derived from the theory fix all of the elasticities except those for cross-price effects. There is considerable latitude with the cross-price effects in that a number of them can be prespecified. In past studies this alternative has been used when fairly reliable statistical information has existed on the nature of the cross-price effects.

THE FULL DEMAND SYSTEM FOR FOOD

The full demand system for food obtained by applying the methods outlined in the preceding section is presented in Table 8.2. As already indicated, parameter estimates used in constructing the demand matrix are presented in Table 8.1. Before explaining the various estimated coefficients in the demand matrix, it will be useful to discuss the preliminary statistical results contained in Table 8.1.

---

[11] The various elasticity concepts will be defined in the next section.

[12] Expenditure proportion = expenditure for a particular commodity as a proportion of total expenditure. In Table 8.2, these proportions are in decimal form. To convert to percentages, multiply by 100.

[13] Statistics Canada, Catalogue No. 62-537.

TABLE 8.1. DIRECT PRICE AND INCOME ELASTICITIES

Commodity	Direct-Price Elasticity	Commodity	Income Elasticity
Elastic		*Superior*	
Veal	-2.59	Lamb	0.68
Lamb	-1.87	Frozen Foods	0.54
Turkey	-1.09	Cheese	0.52
Frozen Foods	-1.03	Turkey	0.52
		Veal	0.51
Inelastic		Beef	0.51
		Canned Fruits	0.40
Shortening	-0.97	Prepared Foods	0.33
Pork	-0.95	Salad Dressing	0.30
Salad Dressing	-0.93	Butter	0.29
Cheese	-0.91	Fresh Fruits	0.23
Butter	-0.86	Shortening	0.22
Beef	-0.85	Fish	0.22
Fish	-0.80	Fluid Milk	0.21
Canned Fruits	-0.75	Cereals	0.16
Prepared Foods	-0.67	Beverages	0.15
Margarine	-0.63	Chicken	0.15
Chicken	-0.56	Pork	0.13
Lard	-0.46	Sugar	0.12
Fresh Fruits	-0.45	Other Dairy Products	0.11
Fluid Milk	-0.44	Canned Vegetables	0.11
Beverages	-0.37	Margarine	0.10
Other Dairy Products	-0.33	Fresh Vegetables	0.09
Canned Vegetables	-0.32	Miscellaneous Foods	0.04
Fresh Vegetables	-0.24		
Sugar	-0.24	Eggs	0.0
		Skim Milk Powder	0.0
Cereals	-0.20		
Skim Milk Powder	-0.19	*Inferior*	
Miscellaneous Foods	-0.12		
Eggs	-0.12	Lard	-0.10

The information shown in Table 8.1 reveals that:

(1) All of the estimated direct-price elasticities[14] have the expected negative sign, which demand theory would lead one to expect. That is, an increase in the price of the product results in a decrease in the quantity purchased, other factors remaining unchanged.

(2) For veal, lamb, turkey and frozen foods, the percentage change in quantity is greater than the corresponding percentage change in

[14] The direct-price elasticity of demand is a measure of the responsiveness of consumption of a product to changes in its own price. It is simply a ratio that expresses the percentage change in quantity associated with a 1% change in price. If the direct-price elasticity is greater than one in absolute terms, demand is said to be elastic. If the ratio is less than one in absolute terms, demand is said to be inelastic. The terms thus refer to more and less than proportionate responses in consumption to (own) price changes.

price. This means that the quantity demanded is relatively highly responsive to price changes. In other words, a given change in price will result in a more than proportionate percentage change in the amount purchased.

(3) In the case of beef, pork, cheese, etc., the percentage change in quantity purchased is less than the corresponding percentage change in price. That is, the quantity demanded exhibits a lower responsiveness to price changes. A change in the price has a smaller effect on the amount purchased than in the case of veal, lamb, turkey and frozen food.

(4) The demand for other commodities, such as skim milk powder, miscellaneous food and eggs, is apparently unresponsive to changes in prices. For example, the ratio of percentage change in quantity to percentage change in price for eggs is 0.12. This means consumption of eggs drops only 0.12 percent when the price rises one percent.

(5) The estimated income elasticities[15] are positive (with only one[16] exception) which implies that all commodity groups are superior.

(6) The consumption of superior goods such as beef, cheese, etc., follows response patterns that differ from those for only modestly superior and inferior goods (e.g., lard). On the one hand, the income elasticities for strongly superior goods suggest that consumption of these items increases by a factor of about one-half of 1% with a 1% increase in income. The income elasticity for the inferior good, on the other hand, shows that its consumption decreases with increased income.

(7) The income elasticities of demand for eggs and skim milk powder indicate that consumption of these commodities is unresponsive to changes in the level of income. Thus, consumers are not likely to increase their consumption of these commodities when their incomes rise.

The Demand Matrix

Table 8.2 provides numerical estimates of the effects of changing prices and incomes on the type and amount of food we consume. These results include the income and price elasticities shown in Table 8.1, as well as the

---

[15] Income elasticity of demand is a measure of the responsiveness of the quantity demanded to changes in income. It is the ratio of the percentage change in quantity purchased to the percentage change in income.

[16] Superior commodities are those with an income elasticity that is positive. Inferior commodities have a negative income elasticity. Commodities with income elasticities between zero and one are considered necessities, while those with elasticities greater than one are defined as luxuries.

TABLE 8.2. ELASTICITY MATRIX FOR FOOD AND NONFOOD COMMODITY GROUPS

	Beef 1	Pork 2	Lamb 3	Veal 4	Chicken 5	Turkey 6	Fish 7	Eggs 8	Cereals 9	Milk 10
1 Beef	−.85220	.06330	.00930	.01108	.03447	.00398	.00762	.00011	.00243	.00597
2 Pork	.10908	−.95470	.01621	.03435	.03146	.01086	.04681	.01583	.09833	.06108
3 Lamb	.40600	.46502	−1.86600	.01404	.00942	.00468	.00943	.00017	.00178	.00616
4 Veal	.26735	.54290	.00779	−2.59300	.10688	.04165	.09354	.03064	.01262	.11642
5 Chicken	.18330	.10280	.00149	.02237	−.56370	.00272	.00432	.00037	.00483	.00619
6 Turkey	.05618	.09330	.00164	.02454	.00505	−1.09000	.02019	.00409	.02962	.02199
7 Fish	.07061	.24237	.00206	.03084	.00635	.01192	−.79290	.00299	.02111	.01598
8 Eggs	.01950	.05806	.00059	.00739	.00152	.00286	.00302	−.12070	.00232	.00422
9 Cereals	.01968	.06754	.00057	.00125	.00177	.00332	.00351	.00012	−.20000	.00645
10 Milk	.02320	.07963	.00068	.01013	.00209	.00392	.00414	.00014	.00691	−.43900
11 Butter	.06676	.22917	.00194	.02916	.00601	.01127	.01191	.00042	.01989	.01485
12 Cheese	.03028	.10394	.00088	.01323	.00272	.00511	.00540	.00019	.00902	.00673
13 Skim milk powder	.02696	.00950	.00079	.00360	.00243	.00455	.00481	.00017	.00803	.08950
14 Other dairy products	.02576	.08842	.00075	.01125	.00232	.00435	.00459	.00016	.00767	.00573
15 Margarine	.06895	.00900	.00201	.00300	.00620	.01164	.01230	.00043	.02054	.01533
16 Lard	.08349	.00900	.00243	.00300	.00751	.01409	.01489	.00052	.02487	.01857
17 Shortening	.01600	.32429	.00275	.04126	.00850	.01595	.01685	.00059	.02815	.02101
18 Salad dressing	.07458	.25601	.00217	.03257	.00671	.01259	.01330	.00047	.02222	.01659
19 Fresh fruits	.02173	.07460	.00063	.00949	.00195	.00367	.00388	.00014	.00647	.00483
20 Canned fruits	.03052	.10476	.00089	.01333	.00275	.00515	.00544	.00019	.00909	.00679
21 Fresh vegetables	.01689	.05796	.00049	.00737	.00152	.00285	.00301	.00011	.00503	.00376
22 Canned vegetables	.02485	.08529	.00072	.01085	.00224	.00419	.00443	.00016	.00740	.00553
23 Sugar	.01500	.00380	.00051	.00210	.00106	.00198	.00209	.00007	.00350	.00261
24 Beverages	.02342	.08038	.00068	.01023	.00211	.00395	.00418	.00015	.00698	.00521
25 Frozen foods	.04472	.15350	.00130	.01953	.00402	.00755	.00797	.00028	.01332	.00994
26 Prepared foods	.03280	.11260	.00096	.01433	.00295	.00554	.00585	.00020	.00977	.00730
27 Other foods	.01078	.03700	.00031	.00471	.00097	.00182	.00192	.00007	.00321	.00240
28 All food	−.09646	−.02085	−.00285	−.00406	−.00694	−.00693	−.00588	−.00158	−.01605	−.02201
29 Nonfood	−.01931	−.02616	−.00023	−.00078	−.00779	−.00131	−.00443	−.00893	−.04406	−.01766
30 Expenditure proportion	.03743	.02491	.00084	.00155	.00759	.00263	.00477	.00720	.03748	.01868

TABLE 8.2. *(Continued)*

	Butter 11	Cheese 12	Skim Milk Powder 13	Other Dairy Products 14	Marga-rine 15	Lard 16	Short-ening 17	Salad Dress-ing 18	Fresh Fruits 19	Canned Fruits 20
1 Beef	.01036	.00409	.00013	.00194	.00271	.00030	.00022	.00209	.00368	.00408
2 Pork	.06192	.02264	.00015	.02337	.00062	.00002	.02003	.01226	.03787	.02569
3 Lamb	.01267	.00441	.00015	.00214	.00339	.00039	.00429	.00258	.00367	.00446
4 Veal	.12311	.04242	.00106	.04545	.00287	.00025	.04025	.02443	.07161	.04877
5 Chicken	.00615	.00362	.00010	.00176	.00145	.00014	.00182	.00121	.00409	.00352
6 Turkey	.02685	.00966	.00071	.00826	.00755	.00089	.00882	.00536	.01353	.01058
7 Fish	.01699	.00712	.00046	.00567	.00463	.00052	.00540	.00337	.01006	.00760
8 Eggs	.00228	.00271	.00001	.00088	.00030	-.00001	.00046	.00042	.00299	.00245
9 Cereals	.00512	.00355	.00010	.00179	.00114	.00010	.00142	.00099	.00433	.00343
10 Milk	.00580	.00335	.00269	.00140	.00135	.00013	.00174	.00115	.00341	.00320
11 Butter	-.85830	.00344	.00007	.00141	.05995	.00023	.00209	.00134	.00328	.00331
12 Cheese	.00304	-.90770	.00017	.00240	.00310	.00035	.00387	.00236	.00438	.00457
13 Skim milk powder	.00271	.00401	-.19240	.00244	.00149	.00014	.00179	.00123	.00544	.00406
14 Other dairy products	.00258	.00383	.00015	-.33000	.00138	.00013	.00172	.00116	.00428	.00355
15 Margarine	.21220	.01026	.00041	.00491	-.62760	.00091	.00896	.00556	.01773	.01238
16 Lard	.01085	.01243	.00049	.00595	.00955	-.46280	.31263	.00291	.01144	.00777
17 Shortening	.00948	.01406	.00056	.00673	.01081	.03820	-.96800	.00662	.01993	.01410
18 Salad dressing	.00748	.01110	.00044	.00531	.00854	.00039	.00850	-.92700	.00964	.00751
19 Fresh fruits	.00218	.00323	.00013	.00155	.00249	.00011	.00248	.00101	-.45460	.00336
20 Canned fruits	.00306	.00454	.00018	.00217	.00349	.00016	.00348	.00141	.00502	-.74980
21 Fresh vegetables	.00169	.00240	.00010	.00120	.00193	.00009	.00192	.00078	.00278	.00245
22 Canned vegetables	.00249	.00370	.00015	.00177	.00284	.00013	.00283	.00115	.00409	.00361
23 Sugar	.00118	.00210	.00007	.00084	.00134	.00006	.00134	.00054	.00193	.00170
24 Beverages	.00235	.00349	.00014	.00167	.00268	.00012	.00267	.00109	.00385	.00340
25 Frozen foods	.00449	.00666	.00026	.00319	.00512	.00023	.00509	.00207	.00736	.00649
26 Prepared foods	.00329	.00488	.00019	.00234	.00375	.00017	.00374	.00152	.00540	.00476
27 Other foods	.00108	.00160	.00006	.00077	.00123	.00006	.00123	.00050	.00177	.00156
28 All food	-.01031	-.01313	-.00013	-.00485	-.00131	.00005	-.00191	-.00188	-.01557	-.01197
29 Nonfood	-.00549	-.00246	-.00073	-.00717	-.00206	-.00026	-.00141	-.00096	-.01125	-.00383
30 Expenditure proportion	.00662	.00497	.00059	.00663	.00188	.00019	.00153	.00117	.01227	.00574

TABLE 8.2. *(Continued)*

	Fresh Vege-tables 21	Canned Vege-tables 22	Sugar 23	Bev-erages 24	Frozen Foods 25	Pre-pared Foods 26	Other Foods 27	All Food 28	Non-food 29	Income 30
1 Beef	.00042	.00169	.00002	.00345	.00413	.00374	−.00166	−.67258	.16688	.50570
2 Pork	.02735	.02151	.00021	.04080	.02214	.02521	.01266	−.17623	.04373	.13250
3 Lamb	−.00004	.00183	.00007	.00360	.00473	.00419	−.00245	−.89921	.22311	.67610
4 Veal	.05192	.04176	.00147	.07839	.04260	.04845	.02333	.68508	.16998	.51510
5 Chicken	.00169	.00161	.00017	.00355	.00309	.00304	.00013	−.19817	.04917	.14900
6 Turkey	.00786	.00750	.00054	.01432	.00975	.01025	.00191	−.68907	.17097	.51810
7 Fish	.00603	.00519	.00052	.01021	.00671	.00715	.00202	−.28901	.07171	.21730
8 Eggs	.00125	.00082	.00020	.00220	.00194	.00191	.00041	−0.00000	0.00000	0.00000
9 Cereals	.00215	.00165	.00026	.00372	.00286	.00291	.00070	−.05958	.01478	.04480
10 Milk	.00102	.00126	.00008	.00286	.00291	.00274	−.00038	−.27345	.06785	.20560
11 Butter	.00070	.00125	.00001	.00279	.00313	.00288	−.00080	−.38184	.09474	.28710
12 Cheese	.00064	.00211	.00003	.00423	.00458	.00423	−.00147	−.69160	.17160	.52000
13 Skim milk powder	.00311	.00226	.00036	.00489	.00332	.00352	.00131	−0.00000	0.00000	0.00000
14 Other dairy products	.00193	.00168	.00021	.00372	.00306	.00305	.00038	−.14617	.03627	.10990
15 Margarine	.01216	.00961	.00112	.01855	.01064	.01188	.00537	−.13553	.03363	.10190
16 Lard	.00792	.00571	.00084	.01141	.00636	.00719	.00398	.13300	−.03300	−.10000
17 Shortening	.01350	.01101	.00119	.02109	.01231	.01365	.00564	−.29380	.07290	.22090
18 Salad dressing	.00550	.00501	.00044	.00982	.00676	.00709	.00150	−.39474	.09794	.29680
19 Fresh fruits	.00109	.00137	.00008	.00306	.00307	.00290	−.00041	−.29952	.07432	.22520
20 Canned fruits	.00140	.00213	.00002	.00435	.00427	.00405	−.00084	−.53200	.13200	.40000
21 Fresh vegetables	−.24020	.00063	.00010	.00177	.00200	.00185	−.00017	−.11970	.02970	.09000
22 Canned vegetables	.00097	−.32150	.00015	.00273	.00255	.00246	.00006	−.14417	.03577	.10840
23 Sugar	.00046	.00054	−.24000	.01547	.00911	.01007	.00427	−.15628	.03878	.11750
24 Beverages	.00091	.00108	.00184	−.37260	.00250	.00234	−.00029	−.20549	.05099	.15450
25 Frozen foods	.00174	.00207	.00351	.00453	−1.03200	.00520	−.00103	−.71288	.17688	.53600
26 Prepared foods	.00128	.00152	.00257	.00332	.00398	−.67100	−.00092	−.43891	.10841	.32850
27 Other foods	.00042	.00050	.00085	.00109	.00131	.00103	−.12440	−.04748	.01178	.03570
28 All food	−.00765	−.00459	−.00118	−.01180	−.00917	−.00936	−.00352	−.29188	.07242	.21946
29 Nonfood	−.01330	−.00686	−.00165	−.01279	−.00159	−.00411	−.01083	−.21742	−1.02224	1.23965
30 Expenditure proportion	.01197	.00633	.00154	.01256	.00337	.00535	.00912	.23491	.76509	1.00000

cross-price effects. What the demand matrix adds then is a basis for showing how price, income and consumption are related.

In Table 8.2, the 27 food commodities, their sum (an all-foods category) and a nonfood group are listed. The expenditure proportions are indicated in row 30 and the income elasticities are recorded in column 30. Numerical entries in the main body of the table refer to the commodity names heading the rows and columns in which they are located. To illustrate, in row two, column two, the entry is −0.9547. This is the column and row identified with pork. The entry is the direct-price elasticity, which can be found also in Table 8.1. The comparability of Tables 8.1 and 8.2 can in fact be confirmed by observing that the direct-price elasticities, located in like-identified rows and columns, and the income elasticities, located in column 30, are the same as those shown in Table 8.1. Other entries in the main body of Table 8.2 are cross-price elasticities of demand.[17]

Interpretations of the results presented in Table 8.2 are straightforward. The income and direct-price elasticities of demand can be interpreted as indicated by the discussion of Table 8.1. The cross-price elasticities simply express the percentage change in the quantity consumed of one commodity resulting from a 1% change in the price of another. The effect of a 10% change in prices can be found simply by multiplying the coefficients by 10.

As an example of how the results in Table 8.2 can be used, observe that the entry in row one, column one (beef) shows that a 1% increase in the price of beef is expected to reduce its estimated consumption by 0.852%—a direct-price effect. Alternatively, a 1% increase in the price of pork is projected to increase beef consumption by 0.063%. This estimate is made on the basis of the entry in row one, column two and is a cross-price effect. Relatedly, if nonfood prices (clothing, housing, fuel, etc.) increase by 1%, beef consumption is estimated to rise approximately 0.167%. This cross-price effect is obtained from the entry in row one, column 29. Finally, from row one, column 30, it is observed that a 1% increase in consumer income will increase beef consumption 0.506%.

Similar exercises can be conducted to obtain the implications of the results in Table 8.2 for effects of selected price and income changes on estimated consumption levels for each of the commodities. On a more general basis, the results in Table 8.2 suggest some additional observations. First, from what is called a "homogeneity condition," the effect of a given percentage increase in all prices and income is to leave consumption unchanged. Again, using beef as an example, the results in

[17] Cross- price elasticity of demand is a measure of the responsiveness of consumption of a good, for example, beef, to changes in the price of another commodity, such as pork.

Table 8.2 show that a 1% increase in the prices of beef, of all other foods, of nonfoods, and income would have no effect on beef consumption.[18]

Second, the entries in the demand matrix presented in Table 8.2 show that most of the estimated cross-price elasticities are positive. This implies that consumers generally view food commodities as substitutes (rivals) rather than complements. For example, the cross-price elasticity of demand for beef with respect to the price of pork is 0.063, i.e., a 1% increase in the price of pork increases beef consumption by 0.063%. Alternatively, the cross-price elasticity of demand for pork with respect to the price of beef is 0.109. A 1% increase in the price of beef increases pork consumption by 0.109%. These results suggest that changes in beef prices have a much greater effect on pork consumption than changes in pork prices have on beef consumption. Another example is the case of margarine and butter. The table shows that a change in the price of butter has a far greater effect on the consumption of margarine than vice-versa.

In short, the results provided by the demand matrix in Table 8.2 are generally self-explanatory. The purpose of this discussion has been to demonstrate the importance of such a set of elasticity estimates as a component of a comprehensive food policy. The effects of ignoring these cross-price effects and the interrelationships imposed by such a system may be substantial. This is particularly evident when one considers the relative magnitudes of some of the cross-price elasticity estimates.

SUMMARY

The purpose of this discussion has been to outline the more detailed development of the final demand matrix for food commodities contained in the report by Hassan and Johnson (1976). The present discussion has focused on an outline of the construction of the final demand matrix, definitions and applications of some of the standard elasticity concepts and selected implications of the coefficients provided by the estimated demand matrix. The emphasis has been on the cross-price effects provided by the demand matrix. This information, showing the interrelatedness of final demands for agricultural commodities, is the major contribution of the larger study.

The more complete report of these results includes a full theoretical development of the consumer demand theory on which the estimates are based, a collection and comparison of alternatively available estimates for the parameters reported in Table 8.1, a step-by-step review of the procedures used to construct the final demand matrix and a detailed

[18] (−0.852% + 0.180% + 0.167% + 0.506% = 0.0%).

discussion of policy implications of the estimated matrix. The discussion of policy implications features alternative structures for translating final to farm demand estimates and the derivation of price-flexibility estimates. These flexibility estimates show price changes associated with the supply of different quantities of foods and thus are more directly applicable to many of the standard policy questions for agriculture. It is hoped this abbreviated treatment of the results has served to indicate their importance, provide some of the basic parameter estimates and highlight the potential of the more comprehensive report for private and public policy analysis.

REFERENCES

BRANDOW, G.E. 1961. Interrelationships among demands for farm products and implications for control of market supply. Penn. Agric. Exp. Stn. Bull. *680*.

GEORGE, P.S. and KING, G.A. 1971. Consumer Demand for Food Commodities in the United States with Projections for 1980. Giannini Found., Monogr. *26*, University of California, Davis.

HASSAN, Z.A. and JOHNSON, S.R. 1976. Consumer Demand for Major Foods in Canada. Agric. Can. Econ. Branch Publ. *76/2*.

9

The Production of Capital

INTERRELATIONSHIP OF PRODUCTION AND CONSUMPTION DECISIONS

The subject of capital is one which involves both production and consumption decisions. Capital goods are those used in production of other goods. These goods, intermediate goods, must themselves be produced. However, they do not directly benefit the consumer in the time period the choice is made. They cannot be consumed in themselves. Their value lies in their use in production of other goods. A time lag exists between the production of capital goods and the production of these final goods for consumption, since capital goods in general cannot be produced instantaneously. In the decision to produce capital goods, then, the decision agent as consumer is choosing between consumption of final goods now and consumption of final goods later. Presumably, the investment in more capital production will mean more consumption goods possible in the future than at present through greater quantities of input resources available. It then becomes an issue of intertemporal choice, whether to consume now or later.

INTERTEMPORAL CHOICE

Other things equal, a person would prefer to have any given item now rather than later. This is known as time preference for present consumption. In a world of uncertainty, many things could happen to prevent or diminish the later enjoyment. Therefore, a person must be paid a premium to abstain from present consumption. A person in order not to consume now must expect greater consumption in the future to compensate for the present inconvenience. As people are different, different persons have different requirements for premiums to abstain from present consumption. When speaking of money saved instead of spent, that premium becomes known as interest. At an interest rate of 6% increased from 5%, one person may decide to save instead of spend while another person with a stronger time preference for current consumption may continue unrestrained current spending. That money saved (not spent on present consumption) by the individual can then be used (borrowed) by investors or firms to hire factors of production to produce capital goods (or consumption goods, though capital is the most frequent rationale). Borrowed funds are particularly important because they form the source of most investment and future economic growth, which in turn expands the future supply of inputs available for production of goods. These investors pay interest for having the use of this money now instead of in the future when they may have increased their own financial reserves. Again, different investors have different time preferences and as such make different borrowing responses to changes in the lending interest rate. The market interest rate is determined by the time preferences of all potential borrowers and lenders.

It should be intuitively clear that a firm will borrow money if it expects the rate of return on the intended project to exceed the rate of interest it must pay for that borrowed money. However, this says nothing about the supply of borrowed funds (at their source, the households), nor about the individuals who also form part of the borrowing sector, nor about the nature of time preference per se.

An individual will have preferences, expressed by an indifference map,

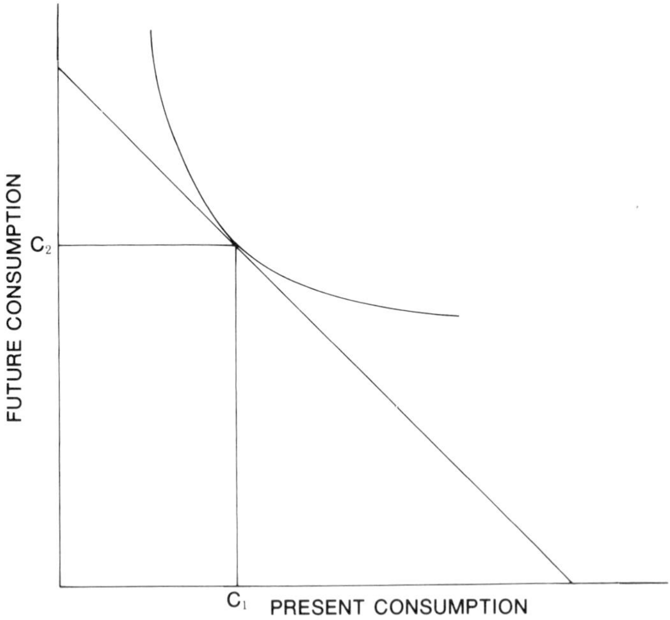

FIG. 9.1. AN INDIVIDUAL'S CHOICE OF PRESENT CONSUMPTION (C_1) AND FUTURE CONSUMPTION (C_2)

between present and future consumption (Fig. 9.1). The price line or budget line between them reflects the person's income and the interest rate [more precisely, its slope is $-(1 + r)$]. To increase present consumption, one must borrow from the future; if one desires less present consumption, one may consume more in the future. The X-intercept is the maximum possible current consumption, or what a person could consume in the present if he or she reduced next-period consumption to zero. The Y-intercept is the maximum possible future consumption, or what a person would consume in the future if he or she consumed nothing at all in the present and invested it at interest rate r. Since a person would rather have a given amount now than the same amount next year, that person must be paid a premium to induce him or her to forego present consumption. That premium per dollar which the person requires also measures the person's time preference for present over future consumption and as such the slope of the person's indifference curve. The person will choose the mix of present and future consumption where the budget line is tangent to the highest indifference curve or, alternatively, where the marginal rate of substitution of future for present consumption equals $-(1 + r)$.

According to Fisher (1930), the marginal rate of substitution of future for present consumption is simply the person's rate of impatience for present consumption. Factors determining the rate of impatience include the size, shape, composition and uncertainty of one's income stream, as well as personal characteristics of foresight, self-control, habit, life expectancy and love for posterity. The greater the foresight and self-control a person has, the less the rate of impatience for present consumption. Those expecting a longer life ahead and those with greater love for the financial well-being of their heirs will also experience less impatience. Those in the habit of saving will have a lower rate of impatience than will those in the habit of extravagant spending. A person who has little income now, or who expects income to increase in the future, or who is reasonably certain about these prospects will have greater impatience for present consumption than will a person with the opposites of these income characteristics. It may be noticed that the determinants of impatience and thus of borrowing behavior depend heavily on psychological factors. This has become evident in consideration of the effects of monetary policy, which operates as much on people's expectations as it does on physical quantities of money in existence.

A person in an initial position confronted with a change in the interest rate (which rotates the budget line about the initial allocation) will react differently according to the nature of his or her preferences. A strong saver will probably continue saving though at a different rate, a strong borrower will continue to borrow; intermediate cases may shift back and forth between saving and borrowing. In general, a lower interest rate will favor increasing present income at the expense of future income (Fig. 9.2), whether this means increased borrowing or decreased saving. A higher interest rate creates greater incentive to save and less to borrow, and so future consumption should increase and present consumption decrease (Fig. 9.3).

This-period analysis also does not indicate the changes in resources for the borrower *vs* saver in the periods 2 *vs* 3 decision. With wage income constant, in period 2 the budget line the saver encounters will shift outward, due to interest income (Fig. 9.4). The borrower's budget line will shift inward, due to interest payments as a drain on period 2 income. However, if the borrower uses the borrowed funds for investment and manages thereby to increase period 2 income, the borrower's period 2 income may increase by more than the interest-payment decrease and, depending upon the profitability of the investment, may increase beyond the increase of the saver. Firms (and some individuals) which borrow money for investment purposes do so in anticipation that the yield on that investment, net of borrowing costs, will exceed that which could be obtained from other investments such as bonds or Treasury bills. Further, they will choose that investment which offers the greatest shift outward of the budget line.

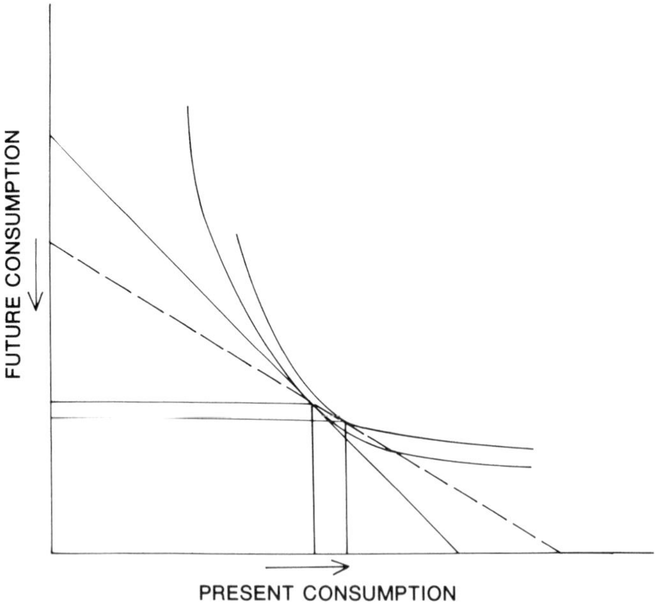

FIG. 9.2. SHIFT TO PRESENT CONSUMPTION DUE TO A LOWER INTEREST RATE

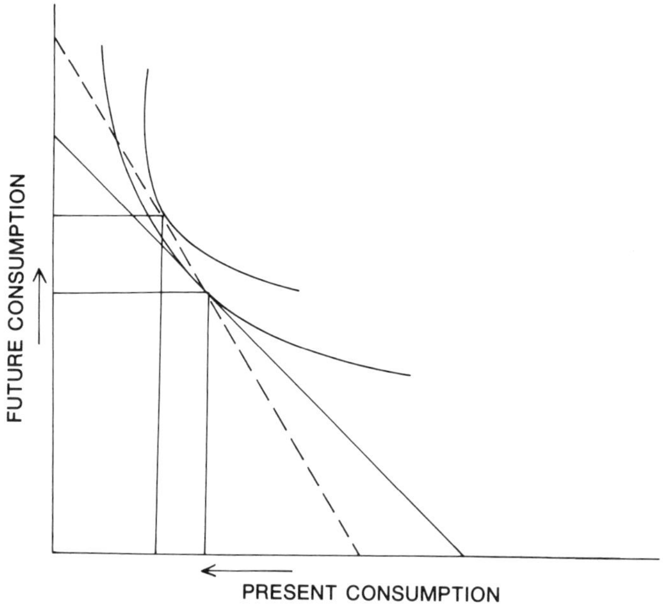

FIG. 9.3. SHIFT AWAY FROM PRESENT CONSUMPTION DUE TO RISE IN INTEREST RATE

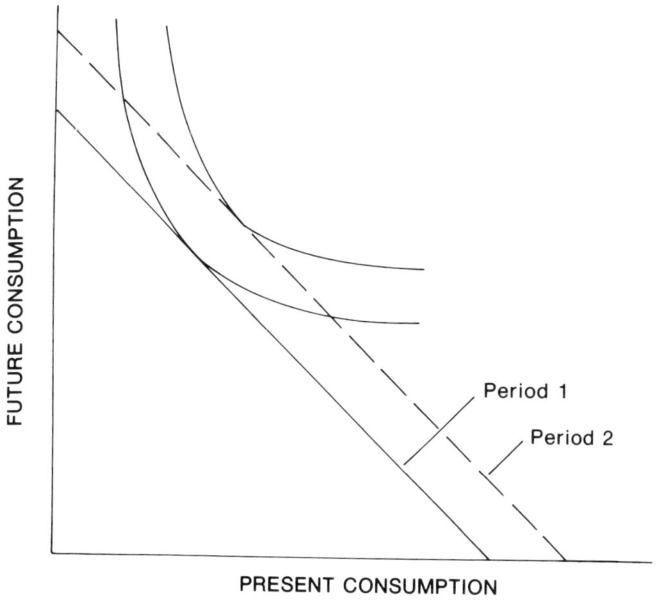

FIG. 9.4. OUTWARD SHIFT IN BUDGET LINE DUE TO SAVING IN PREVIOUS PERIOD

In multiperiod horizons, different investments may have differing income streams. In order to compare an investment with rapid payoff and an investment with a larger but more distant benefit, one must convert all measures of future income to what they are worth in the present. One dollar today invested for 1 year at interest rate r yields a future income of $\$1\ (1 + r)$. This amount reinvested for a second year yields $[\$1(1 + r)]\ (1 + r) = \$1(1 + r)^2$; for t years, $\$1\ (1 + r)^t$. If the future value of the present \$1 invested for t years is $\$1(1 + r)^t$, the present value of \$1 to received t years from now equals $\frac{\$1}{(1 + r)^t}$. The firm will choose the investment which offers the highest total present value or $\sum_{t=1}^{n} \frac{Y_t}{(1 + r)^t}$, where Y_t is the income from the investment in a given time period t. In many cases, an equivalent criterion for investment would be to choose that investment which yields the highest rate of return.

Given that individuals in an economy will have varying rates of impatience or time preference, the interest rate serves to equate the amount of funds to be saved with the amount to be borrowed. Its mechanisms may be seen in the above diagrams; those with intermediate rates of impatience may decide to save or borrow depending on the interest rate while for others the amounts saved or borrowed may vary. In considering the effects of determinants of impatience on the rate of interest, one would expect that in periods of rising incomes where expectations are that such would continue, impatience would increase, borrowing would increase, saving would decrease; so the interest rate must also rise to equalize borrowing and saving. This has happened in the last few decades, even aside from inflationary considerations. Although the analysis presented is somewhat oversimplified (for example, the borrowing and lending rates of interest in fact differ, in part due to the necessity of some return to the saving/lending institutions), it presents the basic principles of behavior.

HUMAN CAPITAL

Capital may be considered as an intermediate good in production. Used in conjunction with labor and other inputs, it assists in the production of the final product. It requires scarce resources to create it, and in turn provides a stream of resources for current and future consumption. So far, we have seen the use of capital as one input of production in the factor-factor relations. We have seen the production of this intermediate good of capital itself in the factor-product relationships. We have seen how resources may be allocated in one time period to the production of capital in the next time period, through intertemporal consumption. However, this analysis need not be limited to only physical capital. The same reasoning applies to human capital.

Human capital is capital embodied in human beings. People invest in themselves and in their future productivity. They do this through formal and informal schooling and acquisition of information, acquisition and maintenance of good health, and (for their progeny) the bearing and raising of children.

Human capital does differ in some respects from physical capital. Since it is embodied in the human, it travels with its owner (who must be present at its use) and can only be rented rather than sold. The differences most important for its analysis are twofold:

(1) it is more often produced outside the market than in physical capital, and
(2) its production is much more time-intensive than is that of physical capital and the major portion of its cost is the opportunity cost of foregone earnings.

Because of this latter consideration, the allocation of the individual's time becomes most relevant. Because of the former consideration, one must eventually include a three-way choice between work in the market, work at nonmarket production (whether household production or human capital production) and leisure.

The first step in analysis is the theory of the allocation of time (Becker 1965). Consider first the division of time between market work and leisure. An individual's utility is derived from two elements: a composite market good (X) and leisure (L). Available time $T^\circ = L + t_w$, i.e., a fixed number of hours in the day (or week) can either be devoted to leisure (L) or time at work in the marketplace (t_w). Total nominal income is comprised of both nonearnings income (V) and earnings (which equals the wage rate (w) times t_w), which in turn equals total expenditures or PX (where P is the price of X). Thus, $V + wt_w = PX$, or, substituting, $V + w(T^\circ - L) = PX$. Full income, or the maximum income possible with no leisure, equals $F = V + wT^\circ = PX + wL$. If one defines F in terms of X to get real income, $F^* = \frac{F}{P} = \frac{V}{P} + \frac{w}{P} T^\circ = X + \frac{w}{P} L$. One is then back to the familiar problem of maximization of utility $U = U(X, L)$ subject to the budget constraint F^*, and the resulting equilibrium choice is where $\frac{MU_L}{MU_X} = \frac{w}{P}$. As the real wage increases, the opportunity cost of leisure rises so time spent in leisure falls, which raises its marginal utility. Time spent in market work rises. Graphically, under indifference curve analysis the situation is as Fig. 9.5. Effects of changes in the wage rates include the income and substitution effects described in Chapter 6.

As the inputs of production need not be physical, neither must the outputs. Increased attention has been given in recent years to household

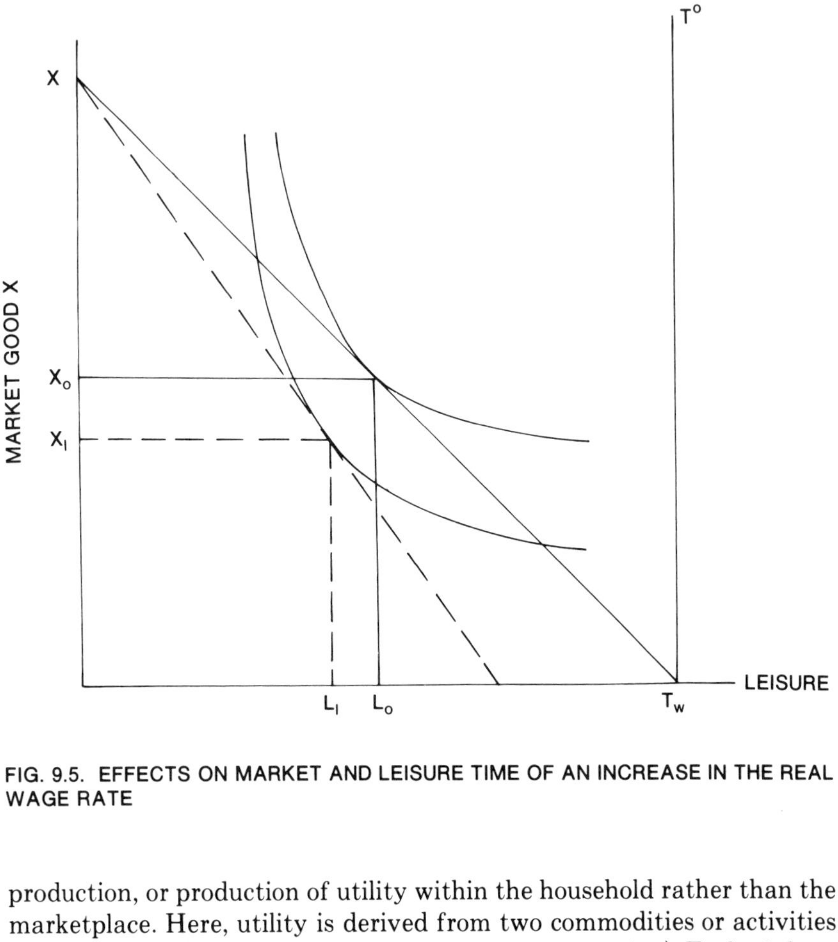

FIG. 9.5. EFFECTS ON MARKET AND LEISURE TIME OF AN INCREASE IN THE REAL WAGE RATE

production, or production of utility within the household rather than the marketplace. Here, utility is derived from two commodities or activities Z_1 and Z_2 (for example, the activity of movie consumption). Each of these is produced as a function of intermediate market goods (i.e., a movie ticket) and time, and subject also to a host of environmental influences. The time constraint becomes $T^\circ = t_w + \sum_{i=1}^{2} t_i$, where the t_i are nonmarket amounts of time allocated to production of Z_i. Otherwise, the analysis proceeds according to that in the previous paragraph in the maximization of $U = U(Z_1, Z_2)$ subject to full income. The results:

(1) $$\frac{MU_{z_1}}{P_{z_1}} = \frac{MU_{z_2}}{P_{z_2}}.$$

The choice of Z_1 and Z_2 to be produced depends on the ratios of their marginal utilities to their prices. Since the household consumes as well as produces the entire output, the prices are equal to the marginal costs of production (*see* Chapter 10).

$$(2) \qquad \frac{MP_{x_i}}{P_i} = \frac{MP_{t_i}}{w} = 1.$$

The factor combination used in producing Z_1 and Z_2 follows the principles laid out in Chapter 3. One can extend this analysis to include intertemporal allocation of time as well, and to households of more than one member (Gronau 1977).

The production of human capital involves the intertemporal allocation of consumption and production. Utility is a function of consumption goods produced over present and future time periods. The production of either consumption or investment goods is a function of intermediate market goods and a stream of services from the person's stock of human capital. Additions to the stock of human capital are the investment goods produced. The stock of human capital, like physical capital, is subject to depreciation through disuse and obsolescence. Therefore, the stock of human capital from which services may be drawn for production in any given time period consists of last period's beginning stock less depreciation plus additions made in the last period. The conditions to be satisfied in factor and product choice again follow those described in earlier chapters. This model has often been applied to investment in schooling and effects on lifetime earnings (Ben-Porath 1967).

IMPLICATIONS OF CAPITAL PRODUCTION FOR FUTURE CHOICES

An increase in human capital indicates greater productivity of existing human resources, whether in labor or in management, whether in market production or household production, and should result in greater returns for that person's services. An increase in physical capital generally implies greater quantities of capital equipment available for potentially greater physical market production, although quality of capital may also be included if an adequate measure of it exists. An increase in either sort of capital is made possible through the use of money diverted from present consumption to future consumption via time preferences and saving/borrowing of individuals.

The expansion of the budget line (through borrowing) to a greater extent than possible through saving carries considerable implications for not only the dynamic allocation of resources in the present, but also (as a consequence) the static allocation of resources in the future. The present quantities of resources which can be used in production, especially the quantities of available capital, are a function of the saving and borrowing behaviors of previous periods. As savings must finance the borrowings for investment (aside from some government monetary policy tools), what is also involved in economic growth is a static reallocation of resources in those previous periods from savers to investors. The interest rates which provide the incentives for such reallocation, as should be clear by now, depend on the collective time preferences or rates of impatience of the members of that society, which in turn depend on individual and income characteristics.

REFERENCES

BECKER, G.S. 1965. A theory of the allocation of time. Econ. J. *75* (September) 493–517.

BEN-PORATH, Y. 1967. The production of human capital and the life cycle of earnings. J. Pol. Econ. *75* (August) 352–365.

FISHER, I. 1930. The Theory of Interest. Macmillan, New York.

GRONAU, R. 1977. Leisure, home production and work—the theory of the allocation of time revisited. J. Pol. Econ. *85* (6) 1099–1124.

CHAPTER 9: REVIEW QUESTIONS

(1) "The optimum allocation of income between (1) consumption and (2) capital accumulation depends upon the nature of the time-opportunity curve facing the family (individual) and the time-indifference curve involved." Evaluate this statement and use as a tool of analysis to explain the differential in ratios of capital accumulation in areas like eastern and central Kentucky.

(2) Leisure is becoming a very important activity in the United States. The progressive Federal Income Tax affects the choice of leisure as a nonmarket activity and labor as a market activity in a different way than a proportional tax. Analyze

- (a) the effects of a progressive *vs* proportional income tax with respect to work and leisure
- (b) income elasticity for leisure
- (c) elasticity of substitution of leisure and labor
- (d) price elasticity of demand for leisure
- (e) the effect on the worker of the requirement that one be paid time and a half for overtime, and the implications if all overtime pay were tax exempt

(3) Why has the bulk of the analytic literature on price and output determination traditionally been devoted to static economics instead of dynamic economics?

10

Cost Relationships

In the preceding chapters, the forces affecting the determination of price through the demand side have been discussed. The discussion on the supply side is somewhat incomplete even though many of the basic relationships which give rise to the structure of supply have been discussed in the chapters concerning resource allocation. Thus, in the next two chapters, the supply and cost relationships will be examined separately and more completely. As supply depends heavily on cost to the producer, the cost relationships must be discussed first.

THE CONCEPT OF COSTS

The term cost, like many other terms in economic analysis, can have a variety of meanings and interpretations. Cost considerations enter into almost every business decision and the use of the appropriate cost concept is very important. The kind of cost concept which is most useful depends upon the decision to be made. While conventional accounting techniques may be well suited for legal and other financial purposes, they are not well suited for many economic decisions. However, they do provide much raw material which when supplemented by additional data makes appropriate and useful cost estimates. In economic analysis, it is generally more useful to have a rough estimate of the correct cost concept for a particular decision than to have an accurate estimate of an irrelevant concept. The quantity of a commodity a producer is willing to produce and place on the market at a given price is influenced largely by his or her cost of production.

It must be pointed out that cost usually refers to the compensations which must be received by the owners of the factors of production if the producer continues to obtain and use the factors in production.

Opportunity Cost

The quantity of resources available in an economy is limited with respect to human wants. Also, when these resources are used by a firm to produce a given product, other products which the resources may be able to produce must be foregone by the society. The value of the products foregone by society is the social cost of securing the product actually produced. Likewise, a firm, in order to continue to receive productive services, must pay those prices which the owners can command from other opportunities, i.e., from producers of other or competitive products. In this sense, the cost of producing a product is at least the highest value of the product foregone by not using resources in their best alternative uses, hence the term alternative cost or opportunity cost. This is a very useful concept in economic analysis and is easily overlooked.

Opportunity costs are more important than actual outlay costs in many decisions. Numerous examples can be cited to illustrate this generalization. If a manager investing money in a forest can receive only 4% per year return, it is often argued that the enterprise is profitable. But, if that money, which is of course limited, could return 20% from fertilizer applied on crops, the forest investments then become relatively unprofitable. The fact that farmers can obtain a higher return from the capital and land resources in enterprises other than timber production explains a large part of the disinvestment in farm woodland.[1] A farmer investing $6000 in a portable sprinkler irrigation system cannot consider only the net return from using the system but the net return that could be obtained if the investment had been used for other purposes. The fact that farmers during economic depressions tend to produce more than during periods of high prices can be explained with this concept. When a farmer has no better alternative for his or her land, labor force and other resources, he or she will continue to use these resources in producing farm products. In producing hogs, for instance, the cost of production is really the value of corn, labor and other resources used if they had been sold or used for other purposes. For the purpose of determining the profitability of the feeding operation in deciding whether to feed corn to hogs or sell it, the opportunity cost here is the relevant concept. The cost of a college education is not merely the outlay for tuition, board, room, books, etc., but includes the earnings the student foregoes by not working full-time. As the supply of input factors becomes relatively more scarce, the role of opportunity costs becomes increasingly important. An unlimited number of examples can be cited, but all point out that the nature of sacrifice provides the basis for distinguishing opportunity costs from other costs.

---

[1] *See* Redman, J. C. 1956. Economic aspects of the farm woodland enterprise. J. Farm Econ. *38* (4).

Opportunity costs which take the form of sacrificed alternatives are never recorded in financial records. Thus, it is very dangerous to confine cost information only to financial records since what is not done, yet could be done, will have been ignored.

The popular definition of opportunity cost—the cost of productive service X used in production of A is equal to the highest value of the marginal physical product of X in its use in producing other products, B, C, etc.—implies that if the service has no alternative use, the service has no cost. If the service can be used only in one industry, the opportunity cost to the industry is zero, but to each firm in the industry the cost of the service is what it is worth to or earns from other firms. Perhaps resources with no alternative use are rare; yet, in a great many cases, a given resource may be very productive in one use relative to all other uses. The excess return on the best use over the best alternative can be called a *rent*. Under these conditions, the services are regarded as being specialized. Skilled techniques acquired by sections of the labor force may be cited as specific examples.

The theory of opportunity cost is internally consistent, directs attention to relevant aspects of resource allocation and provides an essential aid in studying the problem of efficiency. Opportunity cost theory gives rise to the equimarginal principle which points out, among other things, that the marginal value productivity of a given resource must be equal in all uses. Thus,

$$\frac{MVP_x(Y_1)}{P_x} = \frac{MVP_x(Y_2)}{P_x} = ,\ldots, = \frac{MVP_x(Y_n)}{P_x}$$

where MVP_x refers to marginal value productivity of resource X, P_x refers to its price and Y_1, Y_2, Y_n refer to various uses to which the resource is devoted. If the opportunity cost of X (i.e., the MVP_x in producing Y_2 or Y_n) exceeds the MVP_x in producing Y_1, the resource X would shift to the production of Y_2 or Y_n and away from Y_1, which will maximize output. When the equality expressed in the equation above is not present, there exists a degree of inefficiency to the extent of the inequality. This concept of opportunity cost was illustrated in previous chapters by use of the production possibilities curve or isocost curve. Likewise, the concept of opportunity cost is equally applicable to the production counterpart in consumption—the consumption possibilities curve.

Opportunity costs also provide the basis of the much discussed idea of *comparative costs* or comparative advantage. Wheat may be grown in the corn belt at a lower cost per bushel than in the plain states. However, the resources in the corn belt are more productive in growing corn than in growing wheat and resources in the plain states are more productive in growing wheat than in growing corn. Thus, the aggregate of resources in both regions are devoted to their best alternative uses when wheat is grown in the wheat belt and corn in the corn belt. The traditional definition of comparative advantage—each area, region, person or firm tends to produce those commodities and services for which the relative advantage is the greatest or the relative disadvantage is the least—fits well into the explanation of the opportunity cost. A corn crop has the advantage over wheat in the corn belt, wheat has the advantage over corn in the plain states; wheat can be grown in the corn belt better than it can be grown in the plain states, but wheat is grown in the plain states because it has the least disadvantage.

Cost and Rate of Output

Entrepreneurs in their many decisions are obviously conscious of the monetary outlays for factor services used in production. The behavior of the relationship of the structure of costs to output is not so clear to most entrepreneurs, but nevertheless, it plays the key role in decision making with respect to the level of production and size of business. The behavior of the cost schedule of an individual firm is closely associated with three important interrelated variables which are

(1) the length of the time period available to the firm in which adjustments in output to a change in demand for the products can be made
(2) size of the firm, and
(3) prices paid for the services of the productive factors, with other determinants such as technology given

A knowledge of the impact of each determinant on the cost structure, using the appropriate cost concept, is essential in economic analysis.

The time period is somewhat arbitrarily defined, but it is generally referred to as the interval during which the quantity of productive factors used by the firm is fixed or is variable. There is no clear-cut line of distinction, but the longer the length of run the greater will be the quantity of factors that are variable and the fewer that are fixed. Likewise, the shorter the length of run, the greater the quantity of factors that are fixed and fewer that are variable. There is no particular chronological time interval applicable to all firms and to all resources.

Short-run Costs.—In the short run, the firm has some factors fixed in quantity and some which can be varied. The firm can vary output by varying the quantity of the variable factors used, i.e., by varying the proportion between fixed and variable factors. In an extremely short-run time period often referred to as the *market run*, all resources are virtually fixed. In the market run, the product has been produced with virtually no resources moving in or out of production. Changes in demand can only affect the prices and distribution of the existing quantity of goods available. The market run period cannot be longer, but may be shorter, than the time required to produce more goods.

The short-run time period is one in which the firm is unable to vary the quantities of some resources while able to vary the quantity of others used. There is no clear-cut line separating the time periods since when a time period under consideration is extended, it becomes possible for the firm to vary the quantities of more resources until finally all resources fall into the variable category. Strictly speaking, the time between the period in which no resources can be varied and that in which all resources except one can be varied is known as the *short-run period*. However, in practice, the definition is greatly restricted to refer to the situation in which only a few of the resources can be varied, depending upon their nature and the costs of the resources. Obviously, the length of the time period will vary from industry to industry and even within an industry. In agriculture, the short-run period usually considered for milk production is different and will involve different variable resources than does broiler production. Generally, however, the short-run period is one in which the plant is fixed and output is adjusted by changing the quantities of factors not fixed.

The short-run cost analysis is based upon the assumption that

(1) certain factors are fixed in quantity which gives rise to the fixed costs
(2) the fixed factors require some quantity of variable factors for production and can use various quantities of the variable factor
(3) some variable factors are "lumpy" in that they are not perfectly divisible, and which in an extreme short run can be regarded as fixed but in the long-run variable
(4) the state of technology and factor prices are given for the period under consideration, and
(5) all successive factor inputs and units of output are of same quality

(1) *The Total Costs.*—The classification of resources in the short run as fixed and variable gives rise to the classification of costs as fixed and variable. The costs associated with all the fixed factors as output expands are known as *total fixed costs* and the costs associated with all the variable factors are known as *total variable costs*. The sum of the total fixed costs and total variable costs is known as *total costs* (Fig. 10.1). More precisely, fixed costs are those that remain the same regardless of output (TFC, Fig. 10.1). These fixed costs may be classified further into those involving continual outlay during the period known as *recurrent*

costs, and those involving a share allocated to the period of the costs of factors used over several time periods known as *allocable costs*. The recurrent costs involve such expenditures as taxes, interest, utilities, insurance and perhaps some labor for maintenance. These costs must be met continually if operations are to continue. The only way of avoiding such payments will be for the firm to disestablish itself.

The allocable fixed costs do not necessarily involve cash outlays during the short-run time period. Thus, the firm can continue to operate during this period even if these costs are not covered, but these costs must be covered over the life of the resource if the firm is to continue to operate. Depreciation due to obsolescence and the return on the capital supplied by the owners constitute examples of allocable fixed costs. Depreciation due to use is actually a variable cost, but in practice this distinction is not usually made.

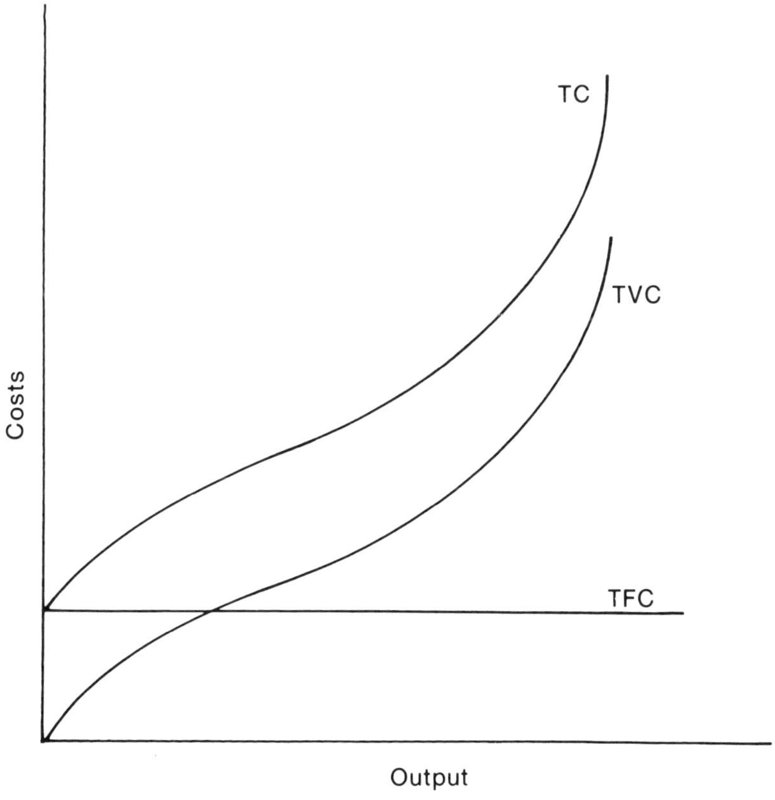

FIG. 10.1. TOTAL COST CURVES

Variable costs are those which are associated with the variable factors of production and are dependent upon the volume of output (TVC, Fig. 10.1). If no production is carried on, then these costs can be eliminated since purchases of such resources as raw materials, fuel and most labor will not be made. Thus, the behavior of the costs as output changes is dependent on the cost-productivity relationship of the variable factors of production. As larger quantities of the variable resources are used with the fixed resources, the law of diminishing returns eventually comes into operation. In Stage II, the total physical product is increasing but at a decreasing rate. Thus, the product arising from an expenditure on the variable factor declines which makes the total variable cost curve concave upward (TVC, Fig. 10.1). When the fixed factors have reached their absolute capacity, with no increase in output regardless of the quantity of variable input used, the total variable cost curve will be vertical.

Sometimes, the total variable costs are classified further into *direct variable costs* which vary in relation to output such as raw materials and *constant variable costs* which change very little if any with changes in output but which could be avoided if production were to cease. Constant variable costs arise out of the indivisibilities of the factor units which are really fixed costs for the time period under consideration. The classification of costs in the short run into fixed and variable is not so clear-cut and simple as may at first appear, and the distinction is significant only in the short run since in the long run all factors of production and costs are variable.

The *total costs* of a firm are the sum of the total fixed costs and the total variable costs for the given output (TC, Fig. 10.1). Since the total fixed costs and the total variable costs are summed vertically, and the increase in output will not affect the fixed cost, the total cost curve will have the same shape as the total variable cost curve. In the short run the behavior of the total variable cost curve is important in decision making.

(2) *The Unit Costs.*—The cost schedule in a particular time period depends mainly upon the technique of production, the productivity of the factors used and the prices paid for the factor units. In studying the cost schedule of a firm these determinants are given. When a change in one of these occurs, the whole cost schedule will shift. This is represented by a shifting of the curve and not by a movement along the curve.

The unit cost relationships probably are used more often than the total costs in economic analysis, yet the same information is conveyed by total costs in a different form. The *average fixed costs* or the fixed costs per unit of product at various levels of output are obtained by dividing the total fixed costs involved by those outputs. Since the total fixed cost remains the same regardless of output, obviously the average fixed cost will decline as output expands, i.e., each unit of output carries a smaller share of the total fixed costs which means that the AFC curve is negatively sloping throughout and approaching but never touching the horizontal axis (Fig. 10.2).

The *average variable costs* at various levels of output are obtained by dividing the total variable costs by the outputs (AVC, Fig. 10.2). The average variable cost curve generally will have a U-shape which is determined by the underlying production function, as AVC = P_x/APP where P_x refers to the price of the variable factor and APP refers to the average physical product. This can be proven rather easily by use of the definitions. By definition, AVC = $\frac{TVC}{Y}$ where Y refers to the output, but TVC = P_xX where P_x refers to price of the factor and X to the quantity used. Therefore, AVC = $\frac{P_xX}{Y}$. Divide both numerator and denominator of P_xX/Y by X to obtain AVC = $\frac{P_x}{\frac{Y}{X}}$ and since Y/X = APP, then AVC = $\frac{P_x}{APP}$. Thus, throughout Stage I, the APP is increasing which will cause the AVC curve to decrease, and throughout Stage II the APP is decreasing which will cause the AVC to increase. The AVC curve may take on different degrees of U-shapes varying from almost a V-shape to a range of considerable flatness or constant average variable cost. There is some indication that in activities operated below capacity of the fixed factors, the AVC curve may be flat and continue to be flat until the capacity of the fixed factors is reached. For example, in portable supplemental irrigation, the AVC appears to be constant or nearly constant up to the capacity of the system. It can be seen easily that the behavior of the average variable cost for a particular firm is dependent upon the characteristics of the production function involved.

The *average total cost* or simply the *average cost* at any particular output is the sum of both the average fixed cost and the average variable costs, or simply the total costs involved divided by the corresponding output. The AC curve is the vertical summation of the AFC and AVC curve, with the minimum point on the AC curve occurring at a higher level of output than the minimum point of the AVC curve. This is because for a while the increase in the AVC curve is more than offset by the decrease in the AFC curve, which causes the AC curve to continue to decrease. However, a point is eventually reached where the increase in the AVC curve is not offset by the declining AFC curve, hereafter making the AC curve rise.

The term *marginal cost* may be defined as the increase in the total cost resulting from producing an additional unit of output. Since marginal cost depends in no way on fixed costs, it is obtained from an increase in the total variable cost which results from producing another unit output. Marginal cost is thus the derivative of the total cost or the total variable cost. When the derivative of the TC or TVC function is plotted, the curve at first declines because the TC or TVC is increasing at a decreasing rate, due to increasing physical returns, and then rises because the TC or TVC is increasing at an increasing rate. This latter situation occurs where the diminishing physical returns to the resources are evidenced (MC, Fig. 10.2). The inflexion point on the TC or TVC curves will give the minimum point on the MC curve. There can be a considerable range on either side of the inflexion point of the TC or TVC curves that will give a range of flatness in the MC curve. The determinants of the behavior of the marginal cost are the same as those of average costs. It is easily seen that MC bears a definite relationship to the marginal physical product of the variable factors. By definition, $MC = \frac{\Delta C}{\Delta Y}$, where ΔC refers to the increment in cost and ΔY refers to an increment in product, but $\Delta C = P_x \Delta X$ where P_x refers to the price of the resource and ΔX refers to the increment of resource used. P_x will be constant whenever the change in quantity of X used will not affect the price of X one must pay. Therefore, $MC = \frac{P_x \Delta X}{\Delta Y}$; divide both sides of $(P_x \Delta X)/\Delta Y$ by ΔX to obtain $MC = \frac{P_x}{\frac{\Delta Y}{\Delta X}}$ and since $\Delta Y/\Delta X = MPP$, the $MC = \frac{P_x}{MPP}$. It can be seen that when the MPP curve is increasing, the MC curve will be decreasing, with the lowest point on the MC curve occurring at that output where the MPP curve is the highest. Since the MPP is a derivative of the total physical product, it is thus dependent upon the nature of the response curve.

(3) *Relationships Between Unit Cost Curves.*—The total cost curve gives rise to the marginal cost curve and the average variable cost curve. In this way, marginal cost and average variable cost bear a unique interdependent relationship. It can be reasoned easily from the preceding sections that when MPP is greater than the APP, then the MC would be less than the AVC. Also, when the MPP is less than the APP, the MC would be greater than the AVC. Thus, when AVC is decreasing, the MC will be less than the average variable cost, and when AVC is increasing, the MC will be greater than the average variable cost. Therefore, AVC and MC must be equal and MC must intersect the AVC curve at the lowest point on the AVC curve (Fig. 10.2).

The average variable cost curve for many situations may be constant over a considerable range of output. Throughout this range, a doubling of

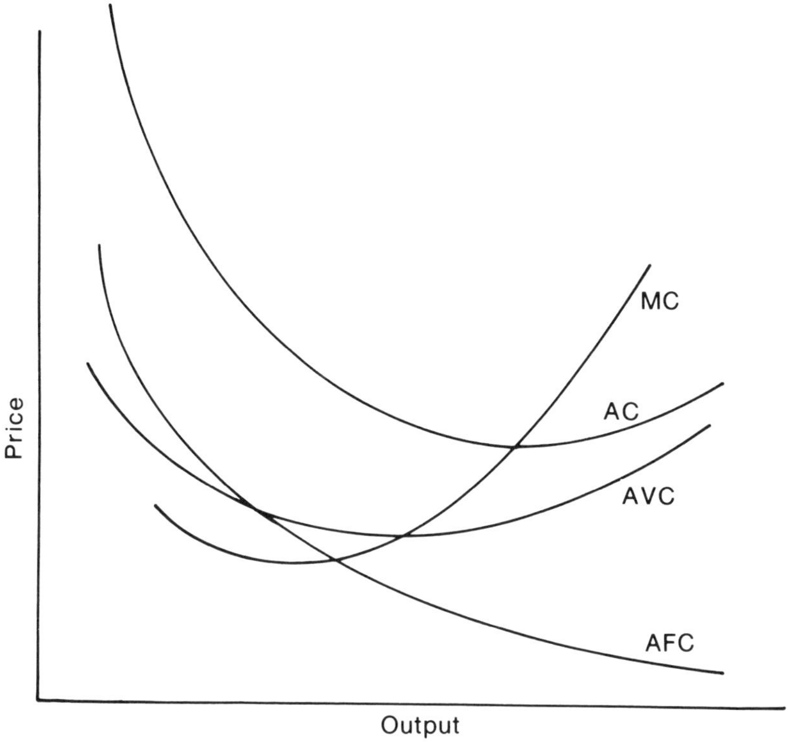

FIG. 10.2. HYPOTHETICAL AVERAGE COST CURVES

the variable factors will double the output causing the average physical product to remain at the same level. With the APP constant, the AVC curve will also be constant. This situation may occur when the fixed inputs, such as buildings, are not completely utilized and the variable inputs, in the form of several complete units such as machines with a fixed complement of labor, are added. The return to each machine unit with other inputs fixed may be constant over a considerable range, giving rise to constant average variable cost. When the average variable cost is constant for given outputs, the marginal cost is also constant for these outputs and is equal to the average variable cost. Both MC and AVC curves will be represented by the same line which will be horizontal. Empirical studies of cost functions in recent years confirm the belief that a range of constant average variable cost is not only important but also realistic.

The marginal cost curve intersects the average total cost curve (AC) at its lowest point for the same reasons given above. The AC curve incorporates the average fixed costs which causes the curve to shift upward and to the right of the AVC curve. Any increase in the fixed costs would also cause such a shift and so the MC would still intersect it at its minimum point.[2]

(4) *Optimum Output.*—A firm or plant of a given size is most efficient when maximum output can be produced at the lowest average cost. At this point of output, the value of the inputs per unit of output is the least and is referred to as the most efficient output. The most efficient rate of output for a particular firm will not necessarily be the most profitable output since profits depend both upon the prices of the output and the prices of the inputs. Under the assumption of perfect competition used here, the prices of resources for given firms would not vary as output varies. Thus, the nature and the efficiency of the production function under study is reflected in the shape of the cost curves.

Long-run Costs.—A firm is in a position to vary all resources if the time period is sufficiently long. The actual time interval depends on the nature of the productive process and especially on the "lumpiness" and durability of the factors of production. It would require a longer period of time for a steel mill to adjust all factors of production than perhaps a hog farmer or a grocery store. When all factors of production are variable, all costs are variable also. In the short run the firm can adjust to the changes in demand for its product by combining more or less of a particular variable resource with the fixed resources. If the expectation is for a more or less permanent change in demand, the firm can adjust the output through changes in use of all resources, the resources that are normally fixed in the short run as well as the variable. Once the new adjustment is made in firm size, the short-term fluctuations in demand for its output will, therefore, be met by adjusting the quantity of variable resources used.

---

[2] Perhaps an algebraic proof would be interesting. Let c = average cost of q units and c_1 = average cost of $q-1$ units, therefore cq = total cost of q units and $c_1(q-1)$ = total cost of $q-1$ units. The marginal cost of q units will be the difference between the two total costs,

$$cq - c_1(q-1) = cq - c_1q + c_1 = q(c-c_1) + c_1$$

As output is increased, $c < c_1$ if average cost falls, resulting in a negative quantity for $q(c-c_1)$. Therefore, marginal cost which is $q(c-c_1) + c_1$ will be equal to a quantity smaller than c_1 which means that marginal costs range below the average costs when the total average costs are declining. Likewise, as output is increased, $c > c_1$ if average total cost rises, resulting in a positive quantity for $q(c-c_1)$. Thus, marginal cost, or $q(c-c_1) + c_1$ will be equal to a quantity larger than c_1 which means that marginal cost will exceed average cost when average cost begins to rise. Also, at a given output, $c = c_1$ if the average total cost is constant, resulting in a zero value for $q(c-c_1)$. Then marginal cost, or $q(c-c_1) + c_1$, will equal c_1 which means that marginal cost is equal to average costs when average cost is neither rising nor declining. It follows then that marginal cost curve intersects the average total cost curve at its minimum point.

(1) *Long-run Cost Curves.*—Since the firm can vary all resources in the long run, there is no long-run average fixed cost curve. Thus, the chief concern is with the long-run average cost curve, which is identical with long-run variable cost, and with the long-run marginal cost curve.

A schedule of long-run cost shows the lowest possible cost of producing various quantities of output. The long-run average cost for the production of a product is obtained by dividing the long-run total cost by the number of units of output. It shows the least possible cost for producing a unit of product at various output levels when the firm has time to adjust the quantity of resources used or vary its size (Fig. 10.3).

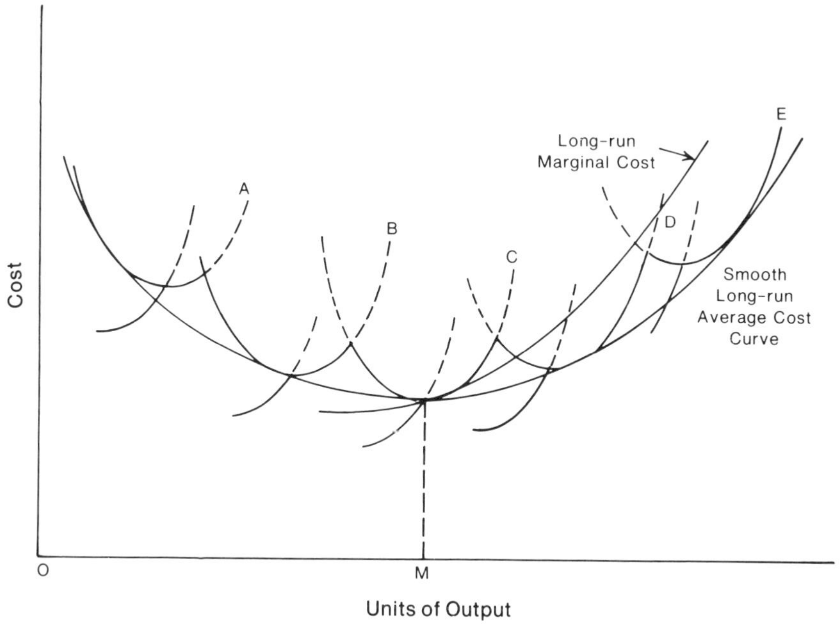

FIG. 10.3. RELATIONSHIP BETWEEN VARIOUS SHORT-RUN AVERAGE COST CURVES OF A FIRM AND THE LONG-RUN AVERAGE COST CURVE

A firm has an unlimited number of possible scales of production that it can effect. For any given size plant, there will be another size infinitesimally smaller or larger. Thus, there are a very large number of short-run average cost curves, commonly called *plant* curves, that can exist. If there is a sufficient number of plant curves such as A, B, C, D and E, the outer portion of these curves will form a solid smooth curve which is the long-run average cost curve, commonly called the *planning* curve or the *envelope* curve (Fig. 10.3). Other plant curves may exist, but due to their high cost they will not form a part of the planning curve. When the factors of production are lumpy, the successive scales of operation will not be close to one another, causing the long-run average cost curve to be scalloped (Fig. 10.3). The long-run average cost curve is pertinent only when the firm is making plans with regard to the scale of output over a long period of time and prior to the commitment of resources. The long-run cost curve is not a historical but rather a subjectively estimated cost curve since it shows the various cost output relationships if various sized plants were built. After the plant is built, the long-run cost curve has only historic interest. At any particular time, a firm already in operation must base its output decisions upon the cost schedule of the existing plant indicated by the appropriate short-run cost curve which is then the relevant decision-making cost curve.

The long-run average cost curve does not coincide with, nor is it tangent to, the minimum short-run average cost curves of the various plant sizes.[3] The sole exception arises when the long-run average cost is minimum, i.e., output OM, where the optimum scale of operations occurs (Fig. 10.3). At this scale of operations, the firm would make adjustments according to the short-run cost curve of plant C.

The long-run average cost curve may be considered also in terms of least-cost combination, i.e., the cost is the least when all resources used are combined in such proportions that the marginal physical product per unit value of one resource is equal to the marginal physical product per unit value of every other resource used. Thus, the following condition must hold on the scale line,

$$\frac{MPP_{x_1}}{P_{x_1}} = \frac{MPP_{x_2}}{P_{x_2}} = \frac{MPP_{x_3}}{P_{x_3}} =, \dots = \frac{MPP_{x_n}}{P_{x_n}}$$

with X_1, X_2, X_3, . . . , X_n referring to the various resources used in the productive process. As pointed out in a previous chapter, should this condition not be fulfilled then shifts in the expenditure from one resource to another will increase the total output without increasing cost which is the same as decreasing the cost while holding the output constant. Thus, only when the various firms use the least-cost resource combinations for the respective given outputs can the long-run average cost relationships be attained.

The long-run average cost curve, like the short-run average cost curve, normally is slightly U-shaped. When this relationship exists, a long-run

[3] The student may note that all humans make errors at times. For example, *see* Jacob Viner's famous article, "Cost Curves and Supply Curves," reprinted in Stigler, G. J. and Bouldings, K. E. 1952. Readings in Price Theory. Richard D. Irwin, Homewood, Illinois.

marginal cost curve similar to the short-run marginal cost curve also exists. It is defined as the increase in the total cost resulting from an increase in output of one unit when the firm has sufficient time to adjust its scale. This definition is essentially the same as that of the short-run marginal cost except that it is considered from the long-run standpoint. The long-run marginal cost curve bears the same relationship to the long-run average cost curve as the short-run marginal cost curve bears to the short-run average cost curve (Fig. 10.3). The long-run average cost curve is intersected at its minimum point with output OM by the long-run marginal cost curve. Since the long-run average cost curve and the short-run average cost curve are tangent at their minimum points, the respective marginal cost curves intersect at the point of tangency of the average cost curves.[4]

(2) Economies of Scale.—As indicated, there is a certain size of plant or a certain range of sizes that is more efficient to operate than either larger or smaller plants. The upper limit to size measured by output is not set by this fact since a firm can operate several plants of optimum size, but since a firm cannot be less than one plant some lower limit tends to be set. Nevertheless, small firms may exist, though their costs probably will be higher than larger firms. Higher costs place firms with small plants at a disadvantage and provide the incentive for these firms to increase the scale of output to achieve lower cost. When plants on successively larger scales are more efficient than the smaller plants, it is said that economies of scale exist, i.e., the long-run average cost curve is decreasing (*see* Fig. 10.3, OM portion).

The forces which cause the long-run average cost curve to decrease as the output is increased, i.e., economies of scale, may be external or internal in nature. Internal economies of scale may be of a monetary nature arising out of the market structure or of a technological nature arising from the reduction of technological coefficients of production. However, all economies ultimately result from physical relationships. Internal monetary or market economies are usually related to volume purchases of factors of production. Such internal economies can result also from expansion of output from a given plant.

Perhaps the greatest internal economies can be realized from reducing costs through changes in coefficients of production. This may occur through division and specialization of labor or through the use of ad-

[4] It can be shown that long-run marginal cost = LAC $(1 + \frac{1}{E}$ LAC) and short-run marginal cost = SAC $(1 + \frac{1}{E}$ SAC) with LAC and SAC referring to long-run and short-run costs, respectively, and E_{LAC} and E_{SAC} their respective elasticities. Since LAC = SAC and $E_{LAC} = E_{SAC}$, then long-run marginal cost must be equal to the short-run marginal cost.

vanced technological methods adapted only to large outputs. In most cases, the cheapest way of producing a small output would not utilize the most advanced technological information. If a person wants to dig a small fish pond 3 ft wide, 6 ft long and 2 ft deep (0.9 m × 1.8 m × 0.6 m), the cheapest way to move 1 ft^3 (0.03 m^3) of dirt probably would be by use of "hand methods," that is, either a spade or shovel. The cost may be relatively high per unit of dirt moved in terms of energy spent, since there is no relatively cheap way of producing a small output. On the other hand, if the person wanted to create a very large reservoir for boating, irrigation, etc., the cheapest way to move 1 ft^3 (0.03 m^3) of dirt probably would be through the use of large machinery which can move several cubic yards (m^3) at once. Also farmers who have a small quantity of resources, small land area, little capital, etc., would most probably find that the cheapest way of producing a unit of output would be by the so-called inefficient hand methods. A farmer may not have the necessary scale of operations to justify the use of modern equipment. The cost of production might be high if a value is placed on the farmer's labor, but probably would be much higher if modern equipment were used for that particular output. In other words, as output is increased through increased scale of operations, the use of the more advanced technological methods becomes more and more feasible with the usual result in decreased unit costs. Also, economies can be created by using large units of resources rather than a larger number of smaller units. For example, it will cost less per ton (0.9 MT) to haul heavy equipment if a single 10 ton (9 MT) truck is used rather than 20 half-ton (0.45 MT) trucks. Thus, possibilities of a technical nature represent an explanation, in part, of the increasing economies as the scale of the plant is increased.

Another possibility which contributes to the internal economies of scale consists of the advantages of division and specialization of labor. A large plant which employs a large number of people can have a division of labor so the workers can become more proficient in their special assignments. A small plant which employs a few people will not have the opportunity for specialization since workers may be required to perform several tasks. Thus, their proficiency at some tasks will not be as great as in larger plants. In extreme specialization, monotony may become so great that it will begin to counteract the possible increases in efficiency.

Economies of scale by a given plant can result from forces external to the plant, yet which are independent of the output of an individual plant; for example, economies can accrue to a particular plant as the result of increased output by the whole industry. Like internal economies, external economies can be either pecuniary or technological in nature. Technical economies appear to be somewhat difficult to find, but could result from a widespread program to eradicate brucellosis among cattle or from a better organization of resources. This might occur where a sufficient number of complementary and supplementary firms are properly located. Trade associations can also be developed to promote the exchange of ideas or the improvement of the product.

External market economies are common and can result from a reduction in the cost of services and materials due to the quantities of such services and materials purchased by the entire industry. Reductions in cost for the industry's purchases, consequently the plant, are likely to result from internal or external economies to the supplying industry. Other possible market economies can result from improved organization and operation of market facilities such as storage, transportation and credit.

(3) *Diseconomies of Scale.*—As the size of a plant is increased, sooner or later forces will come into play that will cause the long-run average cost curve to rise. However, for some types of firms there may well be a range of scales of output for which there are no economies or diseconomies. Thus, there may be a series of minimum points of equal value, rather than a single minimum point, which gives the long-run cost curve a horizontal segment indicating no economies or diseconomies of scale. When the scale of plant has become sufficiently large for diseconomies of scale to occur, the long-run average cost curve begins to rise upward. Actually, economies of scale in the use of certain resources can continue to occur while diseconomies in the use of other resources are prevalent. If the diseconomies of scale more than offset the economies of scale, the net result will cause the long-run average cost curve to rise.

Diseconomies of scale can be either internal or external to the plant. Internal diseconomies of scale do not appear to be as widespread as external, but can result from complexities of large-scale management. It can be argued that by increasing all factors of production in proportion, the "red tape" and difficulty of coordination of managerial activities will multiply rapidly and cause diseconomies. At one time it was thought by some people that the family farm was the optimum size and anything larger was subject to diseconomies to scale. Whether or not this is true remains a debatable question although it is probable that the above can be refuted.

External diseconomies of scale can occur to a particular firm as a result of the expansion of the industry and may be pecuniary or technological in nature. These are very common and are very important. Pecuniary diseconomies can result from increased output as all firms in the industry bid for resources which result in higher unit prices for those resources. As long as there is full employment, these diseconomies will exist unless there is a corresponding and simultaneous decrease in demand for those resources by other firms or there is an increase in supply of resources. Also, unit prices may not increase should the resources have negatively sloping supply curves because of the net external and internal economies involved in their production. In many cases pecuniary external diseconomies may be offset by technological external economies with no net external diseconomies for the firm. However, pecuniary external diseconomies coupled with technological external diseconomies may result in considerable net diseconomies to scale.

Technological external diseconomies of scale can result because the output of one firm causes the cost for other firms to rise. In fishing, for example, heavy catches by one firm make it more expensive for others to maintain their output.[5] The use of more water by farmers in irrigation causes less to be available for other farmers. The effect of external diseconomies is to make the long-run average cost curve rise at a faster rate, i.e., more inelastic.

(4) *Optimum Size of Firm.*—Since there are many possible scales that a firm faces, an important decision involves the optimum scale on which to operate. The optimum scale is one whose short-run average cost curve is tangent to the minimum point on the long-run average cost curve. The least cost per unit of output varies with the size of the firm. For scales of operation larger or smaller than the optimum, the cost per unit will be higher. In the long run, firms will adjust under perfectly competitive conditions to the optimum scale of operations. However, for any output the firm must use that scale of plant where the short-run average cost curve is tangent to the long-run average cost curve if costs are to be minimized. In the long run, to produce at the least unit cost, the scale of plant must be such that the short-run average cost curve is tangent to the long-run average cost curve. At the output of this tangency, the short-run marginal cost will be equal to the long-run marginal cost.

In the short run, however, the firm must operate on its short-run average cost curve. As the tangency of short-run average cost to long-run average cost does not occur at minimum short-run average cost (except at minimum LAC), the firm will be able to reduce costs somewhat further given the choice of scale.

A firm will not always operate at minimum average cost, just as it will not always (and usually will not) operate at maximum average physical product. It needs a choice indicator, i.e., price, to indicate where in the realm of rational production to operate. As in Chapter 2 the marginalities of production were the critical elements, so the marginalities of cost are crucial in production decisions.

As discussed in Chapter 2, with unrestricted supplies of factors for a given price and with a given price for the product regardless of output,

---

[5] For a very stimulating article *see* Gordon, H. S. 1954. The economic theory of a common property resource: The fishery. J. Pol. Econ. *62* (2).

the optimal condition for profit maximization is $MPP_x(y) = \frac{P_x}{P_y}$. This can be rewritten as $P_y = \frac{P_x}{MPP_{x(y)}}$. From the introduction to marginal cost earlier in this chapter, $MC = \frac{P_x}{MPP_x}$. Therefore, under these specified conditions (which suggest perfect competition and which will be discussed in Chapter 12), the firm will operate where $P_y = MC$. It can thus be seen that marginal cost, not average cost, is the primary element in choice of output.

CHAPTER 10: REVIEW QUESTIONS

(1) Explain the concept of opportunity cost.

(2) Outline the main problems encountered in using cost functions or cost of production data to analyze the problem of optimum resource allocation on an individual farm. Leaving aside the problems of estimating these functions, what can be done with them and what cannot be done with them?

(3) Explain why the use of the word "costs," without a qualifying adjective, is useless.

(4) Suppose that you are a production economist employed by a lumbering firm. The firm manager wishes to know how many trees to harvest this year.
The accounting department has two sets of excellent data:

SET A: Complete information regarding
- (1) the demand for saw logs
- (2) the basic technical input-output information for the company (i.e., a saw log production function)
- (3) prices of factors used in saw log production

SET B: Complete information regarding
- (1) the demand for saw logs
- (2) the costs of producing saw logs (i.e., a saw log cost function)

Which set of data would you choose in order to answer the manager? Why? (Use static framework.)

(5) "The law of costs is that total costs increase as output expands." Discuss.

(6) "Because of economies of large-scale enterprise, average costs fall when output increases." Criticize.

(7) "If productivity rises and factor prices rise, marginal costs may be constant." Analyze this statement.

(8) "Costs are high because productivity is low." Clarify and discuss.

(9) Explain why average and marginal costs are equal at the minimum AC point.

(10) "The principle that the marginal cost eventually rises as output increases is essentially the same as the principle that marginal productivity declines as the employment of an input is increased." Discuss.

(11) What is the relationship, if any, between economic efficiency, profit maximization and scale or plant size?

(12) Two farmers are arguing on the sidewalk in front of the county courthouse. One says, "I've got the most efficient farm in the county." The other hotly replies "I've got the most profitable farm in the county." Hearing these two farmers argue, another farmer horns in and says, "Why you old coots, you're possibly both right." And the inebriated official town light pole holder-upper (performing his duty in an efficient manner) mutters, "Two of you are crazy or drunk—there can only be one best farm in the county." Resolve this predicament before it starts a town riot.

(13) Theoretically, what is the difference between "minimizing cost of producing a specified output" and "maximizing profit?" More specifically, will output and the cost of that output be any different under the two goals and, if so, why?

(14) Prove that $\frac{P_x}{APP} = AVC$ and that $\frac{P_x}{MPP} = MC$.

(15) Prove that if productivity rises and factor prices rise, then:

(a) marginal costs may be constant
(b) average costs may be constant

(16) Prove AC = AVC + AFC. (Hint: TC = TVC + TFC).

(17) Prove that when MC > AC, AC rises and when MC < AC, AC falls.

(18) Using a typical TC curve, prove geometrically that the derived AC curve is U-shaped.

(19) The definition of marginal cost is the amount added to total costs by the last unit of output. It can be derived from the total costs or the variable costs. Further, the marginal cost of output is equal to the ratio:

$$\frac{\text{input price}}{\text{marginal productivity}}$$

Explain these statements using whatever tools of mathematics you think are necessary.

(20) The total function for a firm is represented by $TC = \frac{1}{5}X^2 + 3X + 150$.

(a) Write the equation for average cost.
(b) Select certain output values and plot the average and total cost curves.
(c) If the price is 20¢ per unit, what quantities can be produced profitably?
(d) If the price is 30¢ per unit?
(e) If the marginal cost curve is given by the equation $MC = \frac{2}{5}X + 3$, how many units will be produced at 30¢ per unit?
(f) What is the total profit on this quantity?
(g) Prove that total profit on this quantity is greater than the total profit from a little more sales or a little less sales.

(21) If the average cost curve is as indicated in (20), what is the lowest price at which the firm can still remain in business?

(22) Economies of scale is an important concept in market structure research. Carefully define the concept of the long-run average cost curve and its relationship to economies of scale. What does economic theory have to say about its shape and the various factors that determine its shape?

11

Supply Relationships and Market Equilibrium

THE CONCEPT OF SUPPLY

The supply of a commodity can be considered as that amount which is presented to the market for sale to consumers and will therefore be determined by the cost of producing the commodity and its price at that time. The supply curve of a commodity, therefore, can be defined as *a graphic representation of a schedule of quantities that producers are willing to offer at various prices, given the time and place* (Fig. 11.1). Since the higher the price the more producers will offer, the law of supply can be defined as *the quantity offered will vary directly with the price, given the time and place*. The supply curve may be thought of as a boundary line, separating the attainable from the unattainable points and representing graphically the price-quantity combinations. The attainable points are those at which producers would be willing to supply the indicated quantity at the indicated price, or if so desired, supply smaller amounts at the indicated price. The attainable points would be located above and to the left of the separation line (shaded area, Fig. 11.1). The supply curve can be described in one or both of two ways depending on the structure or shape of the curve. With the usual shape (Fig. 11.1), it can be thought of both as a curve indicating the maximum amount that will be supplied at a given price and as a curve indicating the minimum price at which a specific quantity would be supplied. If the supply curve is "backward bending," the supply curve can then describe only the maximum quantity that would be supplied at a given price (Fig. 11.2). If the curve is "forward falling," then it reflects the minimum price at which a given quantity would be supplied (Fig. 11.3). If the segment of a supply curve is negatively sloping throughout, there is no way of knowing whether it is the negative portion of the backward bending supply curve or the negative portion of the forward falling supply curve. Thus, the area of attainable points cannot be defined completely.

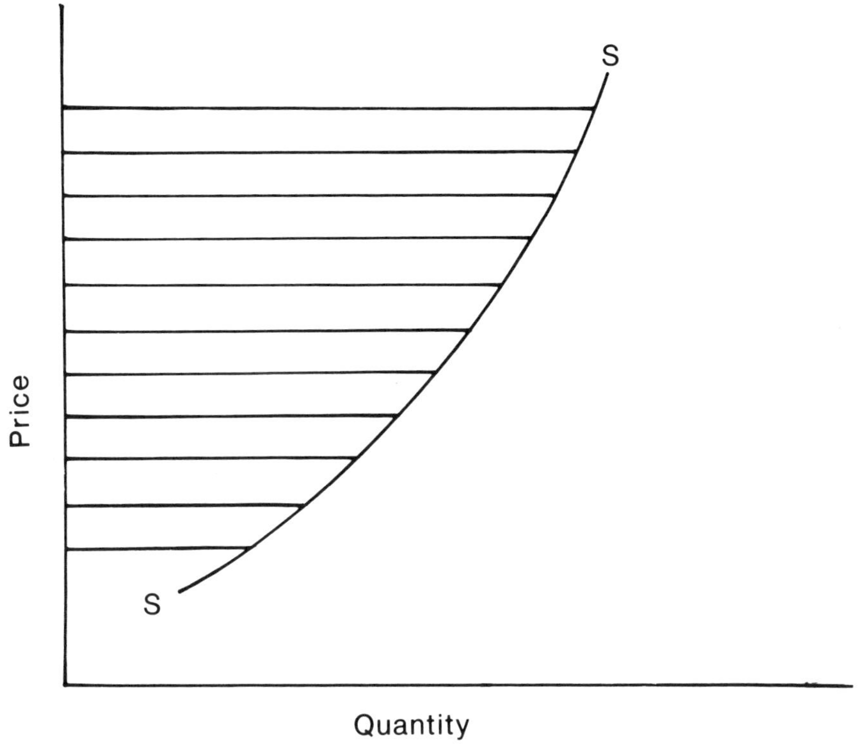

FIG. 11.1. A SUPPLY CURVE

A change in the supply results when there is a shift in the supply schedule, i.e., a shift in the supply curve which represents the schedule. A change in the quantity supplied consists merely of moving either up or down the supply schedule and does not express a change in the schedule. The quantity of a commodity a producer is willing to offer at a given price, except possibly in extremely short-run conditions, depends on the cost structure in production. In the extreme short run, commonly referred to as the market run, the supply schedule is more greatly influenced by expectations of future prices than by cost of production. Cost of production does, perhaps, affect the producer's expectations and, therefore, the amount the producer is willing to supply at various prices.

THE SUPPLY CURVE

The perfectly competitive firm such as described in the preceding chapter always chooses its output such that the marginal cost associated with

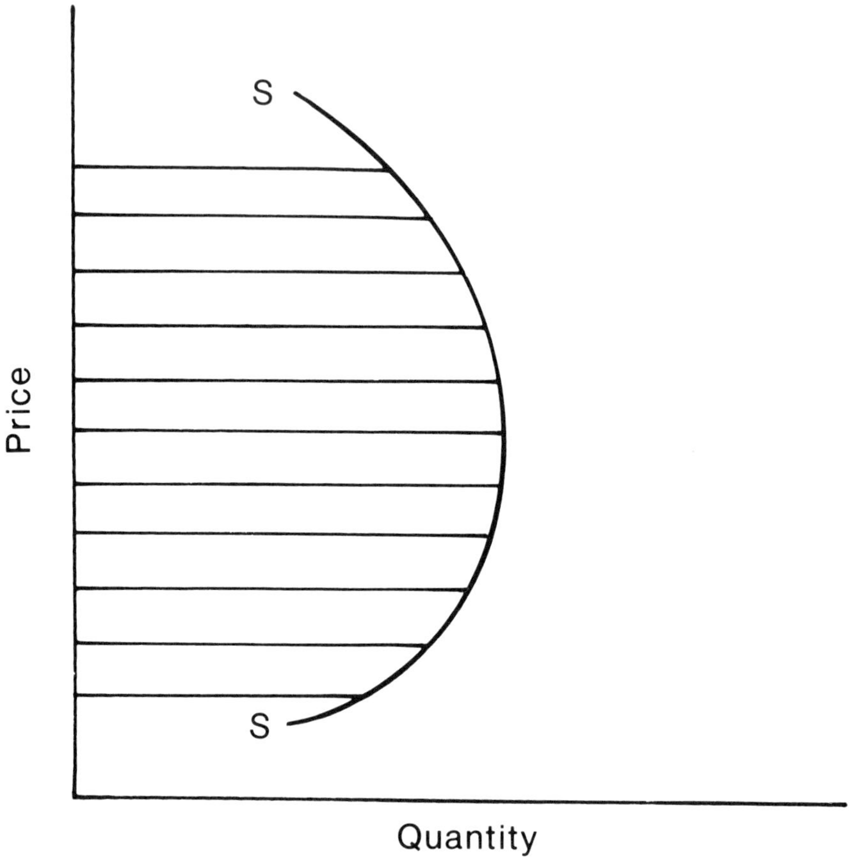

FIG. 11.2. A BACKWARD BENDING SUPPLY CURVE

it equals the (constant) price it commands. Thus, in graphical terms the portion of the rising short-run marginal cost curve above the average variable cost curve may be regarded as the firm's short-run supply curve, i.e., the curve which indicates the amount of output forthcoming at various prices. Since marginal cost must equal the price for a competitive firm to maximize profits, as will be discussed in the next chapter, price may be substituted for cost on the Y-axis to show the output a firm will provide at each price. The declining portion of the marginal cost curve has no significance with respect to supply since greater net returns can be obtained by extending production to quantities corresponding to their respective prices on the rising portion of the marginal cost curve, assuming that sufficient plant capacity exists. This rising portion of the

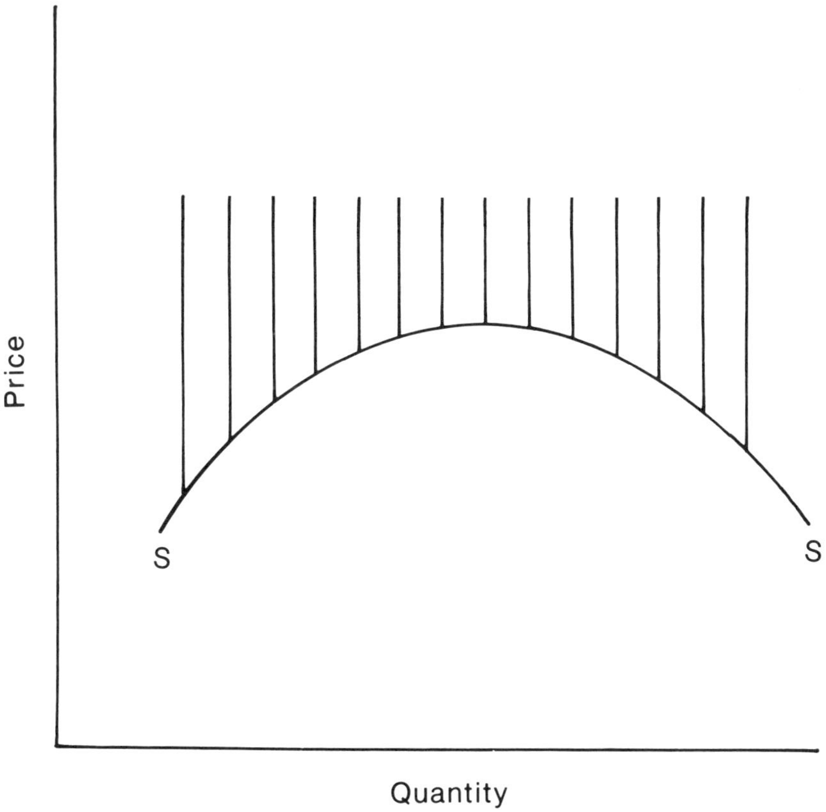

FIG. 11.3. A FORWARD FALLING SUPPLY CURVE

marginal cost curve which is below the average variable cost curve is also irrelevant; at these outputs and prices the firm cannot cover its variable costs of operation much less its fixed costs, so it will go progressively further into debt by continuing operations. By shutting down altogether, it would lose only its fixed costs. Therefore, at prices below average variable cost a firm's output will be zero.

(1) Basic Cost-Productivity Relationships

It has been shown in previous chapters that the output of an enterprise depends on the nature of the production function and that the optimum output depends on the factor cost-product price ratio for the length of run under consideration. It has also been shown that the marginal cost of producing a unit of product depends on the nature of the marginal

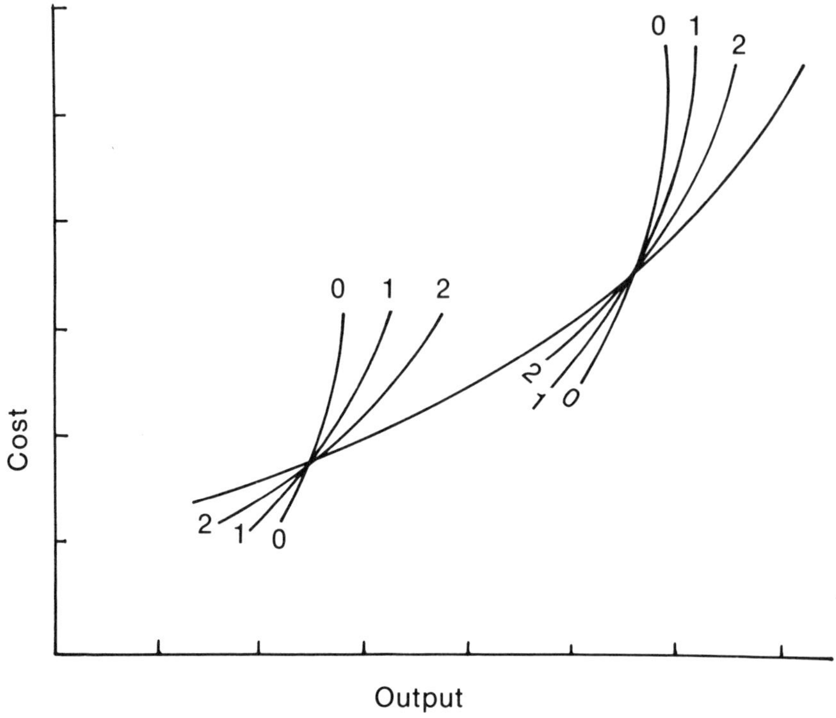

FIG. 11.4. LONG-RUN AND SHORT-RUN COST

physical productivity of the inputs when the marginal factor cost is given.

There can be any number of lengths of run for which a supply curve can be considered but the degree of elasticity may be different for each length of run. In the shortest of runs, all supply curves will have a perfectly inelastic segment; i.e., all factors are fixed and cannot be brought into productive use. On the other hand, in the longest possible length of run, all supply curves will be perfectly elastic; i.e., all factors of production are variable and can be put to a productive use. Through every point on the long-run marginal cost curve, a set of short-run marginal cost curves will pass. The shortest run of the short-run curves will be the steepest curve, and as the firm utilizes more factors that become variable the marginal cost curves become progressively flatter (Fig. 11.4). In most problems the elasticity of the supply curve will probably be somewhere between the two extremes of perfectly elastic and perfectly inelastic. In firms with unused plant capacity, there can be linear segments (perfectly elastic) of the marginal cost curve over a rather wide range of output before a rise in marginal cost takes place as the firm nears its output capacity.

At any given output of a firm, there will be some combination of factors of production that would minimize the cost of producing that output. The condition,

$$\frac{MFC_{x_1}}{MPP_{x_1}} = \frac{MFC_{x_2}}{MPP_{x_2}} = , \ldots , = \frac{MFC_{x_n}}{MPP_{x_n}} = MC_y$$

of the function $Y = f(X_1, X_2, \ldots, X_n)$, with Y referring to specific output, is valid regardless of the shape of the supply curve for the factors of production. The supply curves of factors to a firm may be perfectly elastic and considered as variable factors, or they may be perfectly elastic for one segment but perfectly inelastic for another segment in which they can be considered as fixed factors. In the latter case, there is a maximum quantity of the factor available for the adjustment in question. In many problems, only the horizontal segment of the supply curve may be relevant and it can be treated as if it were horizontal throughout.

In summary, the marginal cost curve of a perfectly competitive firm shows what will be the most profitable (or least unprofitable) output to produce at a series of prices. At a high price for its product, the firm will produce more than at a low price, following the marginal cost curve in expansion of output. The price at which a given quantity will be supplied by a firm is known as the supply price for that quantity. Thus, the supply curve relates the various supply prices to the respective quantities supplied.

(2) Industry Supply Curves

The supply curve for an industry is simply the sum of the marginal cost curves of individual firms for the particular length of run if there are no external economies or diseconomies present. As the supply price increases, the output of the industry increases because the output of each existing firm increases and new firms enter the industry.

Firms will enter or leave the industry according to changes in the supply price. An industry is said to be in equilibrium where there is no tendency for it to expand or contract. The marginal firm (the least profitable firm) must make at least normal profits or it eventually will leave the industry. On the other hand, if the firm's profits are above normal, other firms will be coming into the industry and the industry will expand.

The normal supply curve[1] of an industry can be derived from the cost curves of the component firms (Fig. 11.5 and 11.6). Suppose for reasons of simplicity an industry has four firms with firm A having the lowest cost position and firm D having the highest cost position. When the price of the product is less than OP_1, nothing will be produced as no firm will enter or continue in production. However, at price of OP_1, firm A will find it profitable to enter the industry and produce eight units (Table 11.1). As the price rises to OP_2, firm A will expand production to 12 units following its marginal cost curve and generating the supply curve (Fig. 11.6). At the price OP_2, firm B will find it profitable to enter the industry and will produce seven units at this price, making a total industry

TABLE 11.1. TOTAL SUPPLY SCHEDULE FOR INDUSTRY

Supply Price Output (Units)	P_1	P_2	P_3	P_4
Firm A	8	12	14	15½
Firm B	0	7	11	12½
Firm C	0	0	6	10
Firm D	0	0	0	8
TOTAL	8	19	31	46

output of 19 units at this price. As the price rises to OP_3, firm A will expand its output to 14 units, firm B to 11 units, and a new firm C will find it profitable to enter the industry and will produce six units, making a total industry output of 31 at this price. Further, if the supply price should rise to OP_4, firm A will expand its output to 15 ½ units, firm B to 12 ½ units, firm C to 10 units, and another new firm D will find it profitable to enter the industry and will produce eight units, making a total output of 46 units for the industry at price OP_4 (Fig. 11.6).

If the industry supply curve (Fig. 11.6) is a long-run supply curve, and the cost curves of individual firms remained unchanged, a series of declines in demand will cause first the high cost firm D, then other firms in order, to liquidate or go out of existence, returning the industry to the original equilibrium positions. This is to say, the long-run supply curve has the property of being reversible; i.e., the same supply curve will show the output response to either a rise or fall in price.

Economic rent can be defined as any payment to a supplier of a product which is in excess of the amount necessary to keep this supply forthcoming. Thus, economic rent comes into being when the industry supply curve is less than perfectly elastic. Since some firms have high costs and others have low costs, it is evident that if the price is high enough to keep the high cost firm producing, it is greater than necessary to keep the low

[1] The normal supply curve will include normal profits. Normal profits are essential for an industry to remain in equilibrium.

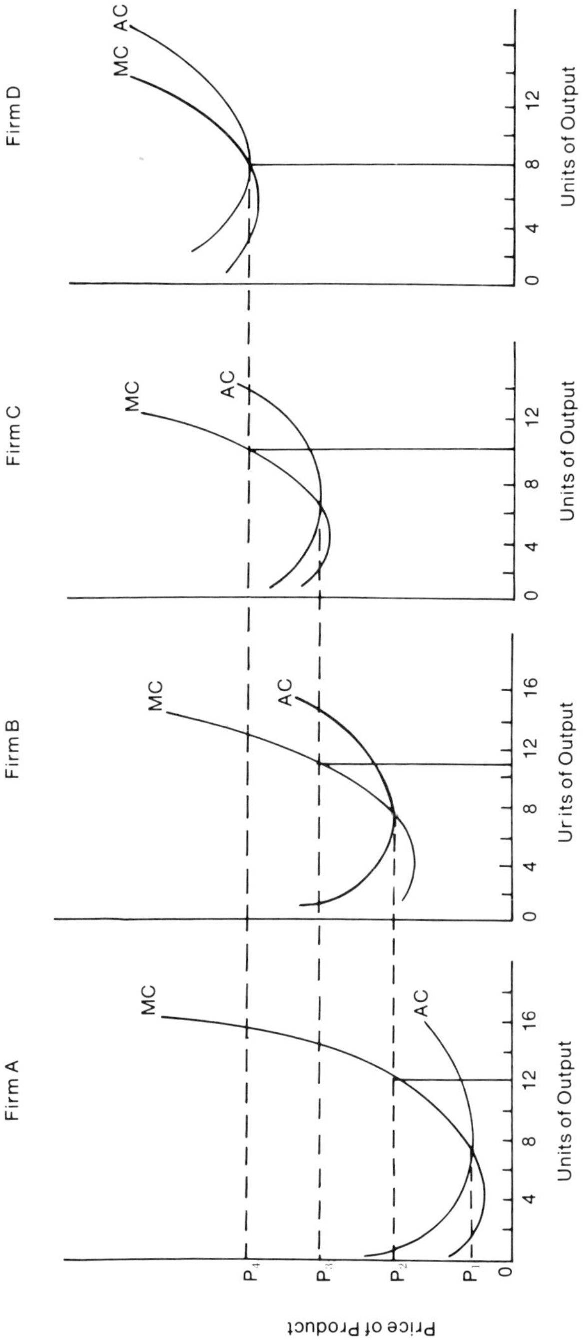

FIG. 11.5. COST CURVES OF COMPONENT FIRMS OF AN INDUSTRY

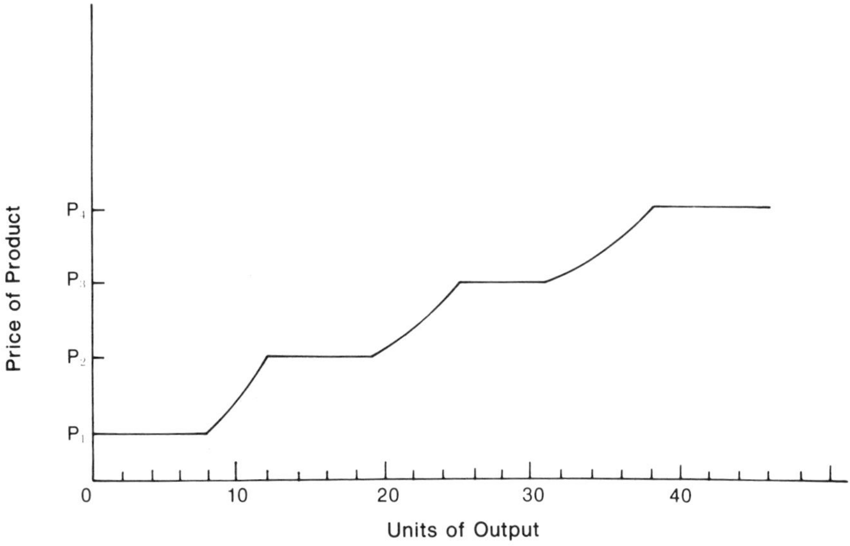

FIG. 11.6. SUPPLY CURVE DERIVED FROM COST CURVES

cost firms in the industry. Thus, the low cost firms are receiving economic rent if the price is high enough to keep firm D in the industry (Fig. 11.5). If all the firms in the industry had identical cost curves, the industry supply curve would be horizontal, i.e., perfectly elastic, and no economic rent would be received by any firm.

With the introduction of external economies or diseconomies the industry supply curve will diverge from the sum of the marginal cost curves of individual firms, and the degree of divergence may differ for different lengths of run. The supply curve of the firm and its contribution to the industry's output will not correspond with its marginal cost curve (Fig. 11.7). Due to an increase in demand from DD to D′D′, the firm in order to expand output from OM to ON will bid up the price of the resources to obtain them from other firms. Thus, the rise in the price of resources will cause the MC curve to shift to MC′. The equilibrium point for the industry is higher than before. A locus of such equilibrium points will generate an industry supply curve, SS, which is more inelastic than the MC curve, due to monetary diseconomies to the firms.

External technological diseconomies may generate the same general relationships (Fig. 11.7). When resources are common to all firms and not owned or controlled, such as fishing, common oil pools, etc., the costs may be raised for other firms as one firm or a group of firms expands. Heavy catches by one firm in fishing waters may make it more difficult and, thus, more expensive for other firms. As industry expands, smoke control problems become more severe and expensive. These technological diseconomies will make the industry supply curve more inelastic.

No external diseconomies will result when the firm can get factors from other firms without increasing the price. Increasing technology or underemployment of factors is a condition that can provide an additional quantity of resources at no rise in price; i.e., the supply of these resources is perfectly elastic. Also, an industry may expand if there is a decrease in the demand for other products which will release resources for use in the expanding firm without increasing the price.

Often when external diseconomies are operating in the use of some resources, certain external economies are operating in the use of other resources which may or may not offset each other. External economies may be of sufficient weight to yield a negatively sloping supply curve to the industry while the marginal cost curve of a particular firm is rising.

(3) Elasticity of Supply

The concept of elasticity of supply is very similar to that of demand. The supply curve as has been stated can be described as showing the

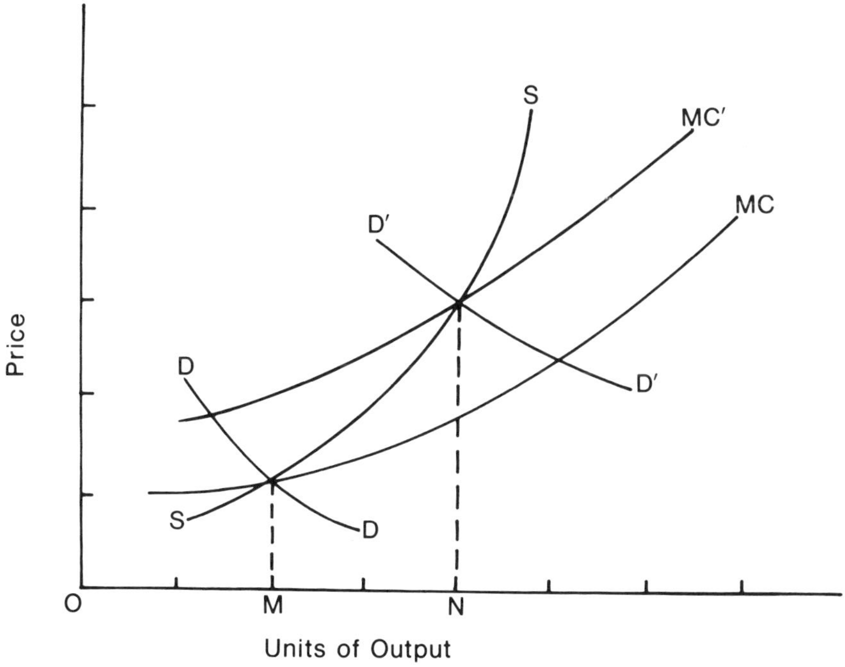

FIG. 11.7. SUPPLY CURVE AND MARGINAL COST CURVES

quantities of goods and services that will be offered for sale at various prices. Elasticity of supply refers to the ratio of the relative change in quantity offered for sale in response to a relative change in price, i.e., the percentage change in quantity offered in response to a 1% change in price. The concept measures the degree of responsiveness of sellers to changes in price. The formula for the numerical measurement is similar to that of demand, i.e.,

$$Es = \frac{\Delta q}{q} \div \frac{\Delta p}{p} = \frac{\Delta q}{\Delta p} \cdot \frac{p}{q}$$

which may be equal to, less than or greater than unity. During a given time period, if it is easy for a firm to expand its output and if it is easy for new firms to enter the industry, then the supply will be elastic because for a given increase in price a large increase in output will result. On the other hand, if it is difficult for the firm to expand its output or it is difficult for new firms to enter the industry, the supply curve will be inelastic. The degree of difficulty in expanding output is reflected in the size of the rate of increase in the marginal cost. The supply curve will be perfectly elastic if output can be expanded without any increase in marginal cost. Also, the supply will be perfectly inelastic if the absolute capacity has been reached so that an increase in output will cause an infinite increase in marginal cost and no new firms can enter the industry. Therefore, the elasticity of supply may be regarded as a measure of ease with which a firm or an industry may expand output.

A simple graphic test may be employed to determine whether or not a point on a supply curve is elastic or inelastic. This may be done by extending the tangent to a point in question until it intersects an axis. If the tangent intersects the X axis, the elasticity of supply at the point P would be inelastic or have a point elasticity less than one and this would imply that the tangent would intersect the Y axis at a negative point (Fig. 11.8B). If the tangent intersects the Y axis at a positive point, the elasticity of supply at point P would be elastic, or have a point elasticity greater than one (Fig. 11.8A). Thus, a tangent passed through the origin 0 would denote the elasticity of supply at the point of tangency as unity. This would require that a supply curve of unit elasticity be a straight line through the origin.

It has been noted previously that elasticity of supply equals

$$\frac{\Delta Q}{Q} \div \frac{\Delta P}{P}$$

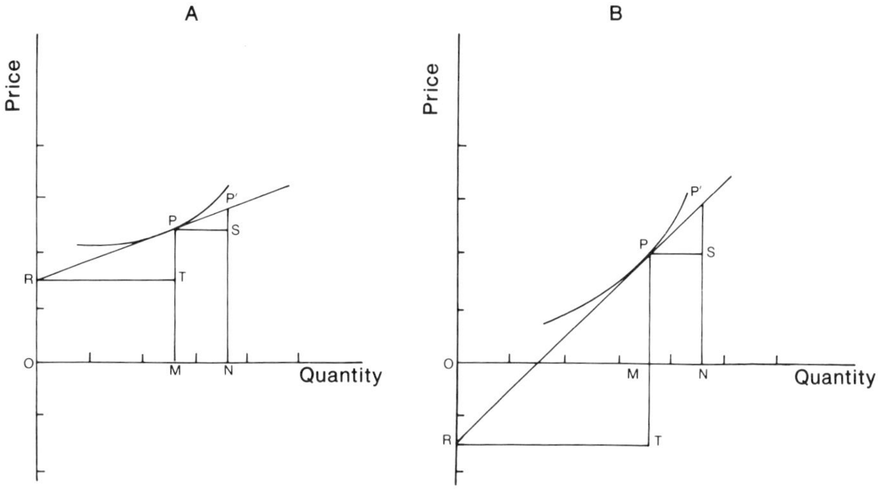

FIG. 11.8. DIAGRAMMATIC TEST OF ELASTICITY OF SUPPLY

Therefore, over the range PP′ on the supply curve RP′, the elasticity is equal to

$$\frac{MN}{OM} \div \frac{SP'}{MP}$$

or alternatively written as

$$\frac{PS}{OM} \div \frac{SP'}{MP} = \frac{PS}{SP'} \cdot \frac{MP}{\underset{(RT)}{OM}},$$

but since triangle RTP is similar to triangle PSP′, then PS/SP′ = RT/TP. By substituting, then

$$\frac{RT}{TP} \cdot \frac{MP}{RT} = \frac{MP}{TP}.$$

If MP is greater than TP (Fig. 11.8A), the elasticity of supply will be elastic or greater than unity, which means that relatively large output expansion will result from a small change in price. If MP is less than TP (Fig. 11.8B), the elasticity of supply will be inelastic or less than unity, which denotes a slight increase in output from a price change. If the

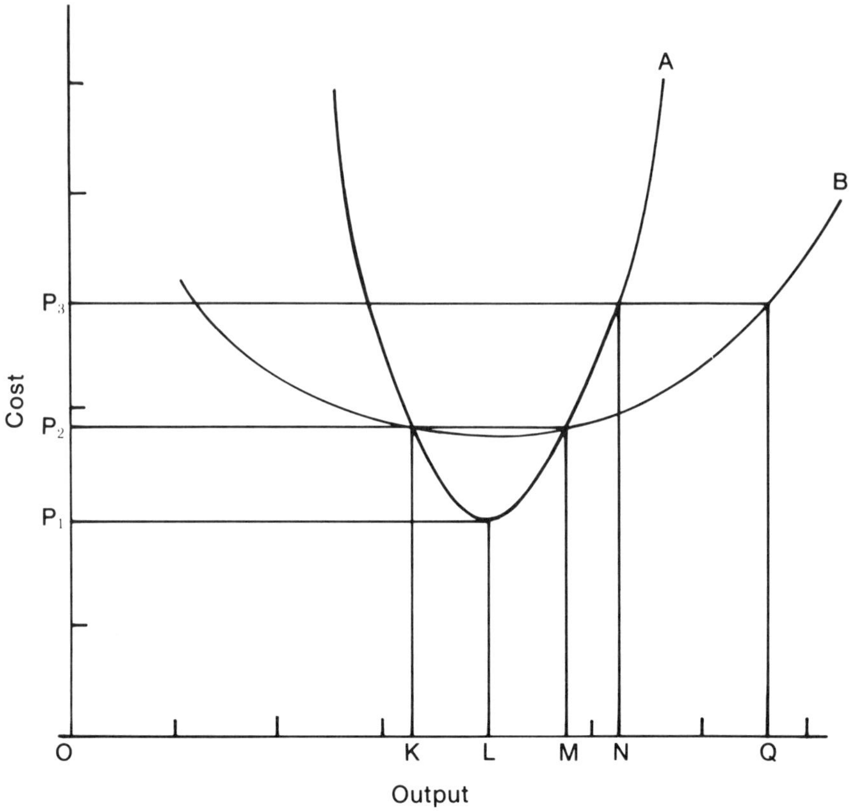

FIG. 11.9. OUTPUT FLEXIBILITY OF TWO FIRMS

supply curve is horizontal because the marginal cost curves of each firm are horizontal, the supply curve will be perfectly elastic since MP/TP will be infinity. On the other hand, if the output is completely inflexible as indicated by a vertical marginal cost curve, the elasticity of supply becomes perfectly inelastic since MP/TP will be zero.

(4) Output Flexibility

If economic phenomena were always constant, the firm would select that combination of resources to produce that output which would maximize profits or minimize costs. Because the economic phenomena may change, the firm will likely want to vary the output. In such situations, the firm may desire that combination of resources which, although not the least costly for any one particular level of output, would be less costly for a wide range of possible outputs (Fig. 11.9).

If the firm expected to produce only at one output, obviously output OL would be at the least cost. This would involve specialized equipment of a given size with other inputs such as labor and materials in more or less a constant flow and to adjust output would involve a rapid increase in cost along the cost curve (Curve A). Substantial fluctuations in output without a very great increase in cost (Curve B) could be made if the divisibility of the plant had been done in the planning stage. At output OL, in fact from output OK to OM, the unit cost of the inflexible plant would be lower than the flexible plant. However, the firm with cost curve B can expand output from OM to OQ while the relatively inflexible firm can expand only from OM to ON when the price is raised from P_2 to P_3. Thus, the firm with cost curve B is said to be more flexible.

Flexibility in plants can be achieved by constructing several smaller but identical units rather than one gigantic plant that must be used entirely or not at all. Adjustment in output can be achieved by adjusting the number of units. Also, flexibility can be achieved by substituting more variable factors for the fixed or bulky factors, e.g., substitute hand labor for larger automatic machinery. In addition, in many firms multipurpose equipment can be installed and plant layout so arranged so that built-in flexibility will permit adjustments to other uses or other products. By doing these things, the unit costs can become more nearly constant as output varies over rather wide ranges.

PRICE AND OUTPUT DETERMINATION

As mentioned previously, firms will not always produce at the output which corresponds to minimum average cost. A choice indicator is needed in the form of demand for the product which influences the price prevailing in the market. Although an individual firm may possibly face a situation where the price received per unit is uninfluenced by the amount sold (the assumption involved in a firm's choice of minimum-cost output, as will be seen in the next chapter), this is extremely unlikely to hold for an industry as a whole. More attention must thus be paid to the interaction of firm production with consumer choice, to the interaction of supply with demand which determines the market price and the quantity produced and sold. The effects vary somewhat depending on the length of the time period under consideration.

The Market Run

Price is the mechanism which allocates or rations a fixed quantity among those who want it. The equilibrium market price is one at which the quantity the buyers are willing to take is equal to the quantity the sellers are willing to offer. It is the price at which the market is cleared

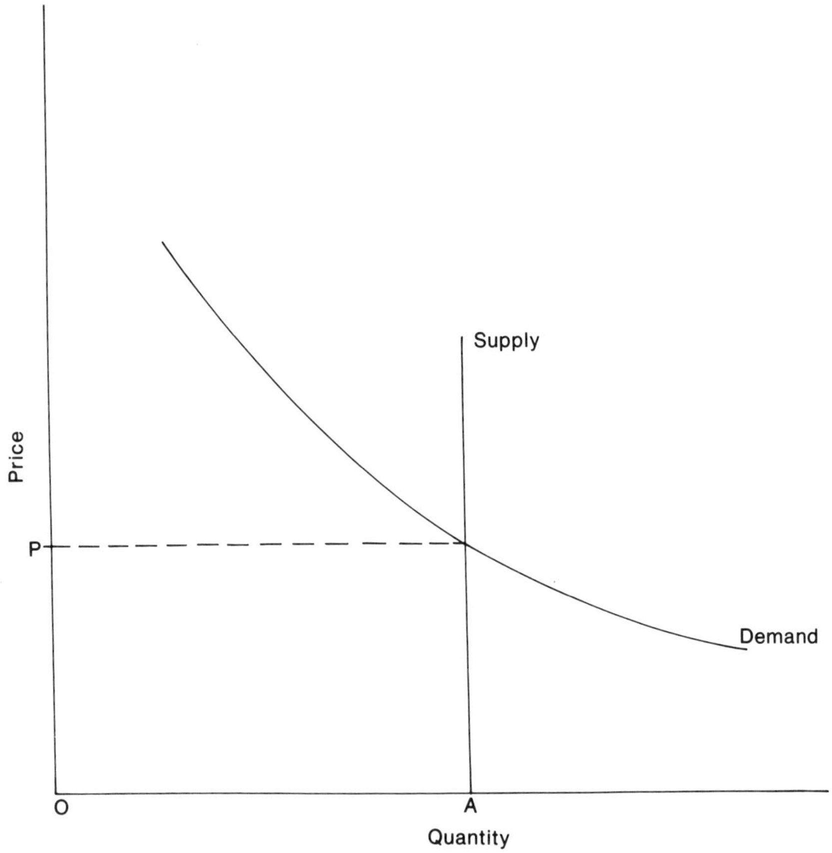

FIG. 11.10. PRICE DETERMINATION IN THE MARKET RUN

and is illustrated graphically by the intersection of the market supply and demand curves. For the market-run period, which has a fixed (unstorable) quantity of the product available from prior production, the price will be determined by the demand. Whatever pricc buyers are willing to pay for that quantity in that marketplace will prevail (price OP for quantity OA in Fig. 11.10). In this situation, the seller is at the mercy of the buyer. Should there by only a limited number of sellers in the market, they could behave like monopolists and sell only a part of OA and at a price higher than OP (and throw away the rest), which may realize a greater total return depending on the elasticity of demand.

Prices also function to ration a fixed quantity over time, but this function is more complex. When sellers have the alternative of holding the commodity for a possibly better price in the future, they can have a reservation price (below which they would refuse to sell) which could make their offerings variable. The relationship between the market price and reservation price will determine whether or not a seller will sell a part or all he or she has on hand. Many factors will influence the reservation price, such as the expectations for an improved price, storability of the commodity and need for immediate cash. In such situations, the market-run supply curve is not vertical; this means that as the market price rises the sellers are willing to place more on the market (Fig. 11.11). As the price rises, the expectation increases that the price will fall and the likelihood decreases that it will go higher.

During the first part of the market run, the supply curve will slope upward; sellers may, for example, offer OC quantity at OP_1 price (curve S, Fig. 11.11). The supply curve for another portion of the market-run period (curve S′) will be less elastic and will lie above the supply curve for the first part. The quantity sold would be OB at price OP_2. The pos-

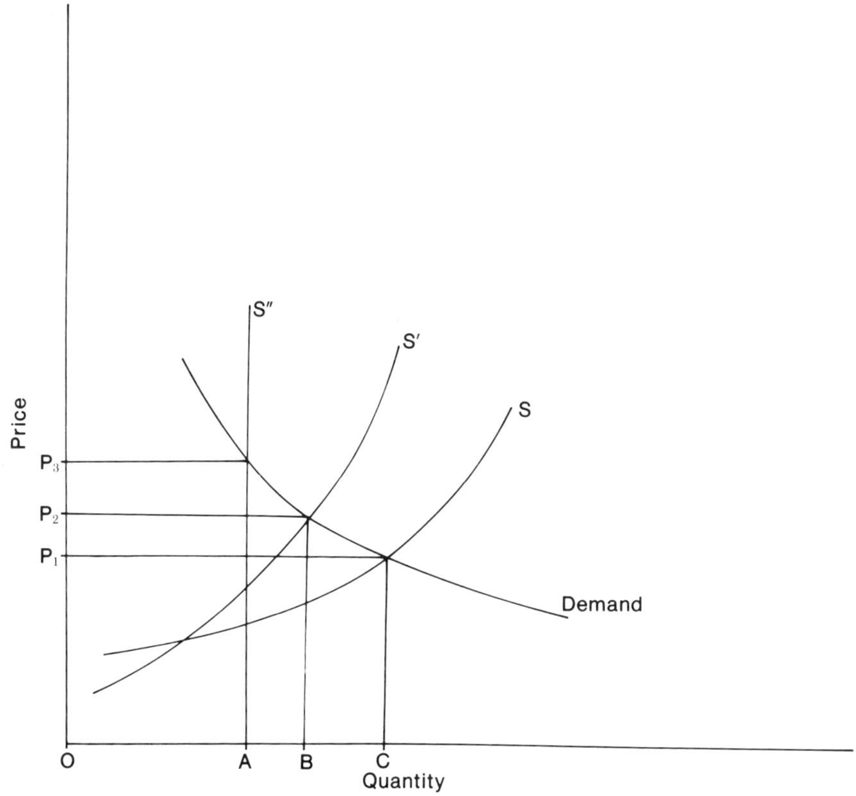

FIG. 11.11. PRICE DETERMINATION WITH VARIABLE OFFERINGS OVER TIME

sibility of low prices in the second part of the period would become more serious for sellers because the opportunities for disposing of the quantity during the time period become more limited. Unless the quantity is disposed of before the last opportunity to hold the commodity, the seller is faced with the same situation as those who do not have reservation prices, i.e., the necessity of disposing of the remaining quantity OA at price OP_3. If the sellers' anticipations prove correct, the prices for each period of delay should be enough to pay storage costs, normal rate of return on investment, risk involved, etc. Activity of this nature by the sellers which is speculative in character does much to narrow the differential in prices between the early and the late portions of the market-run time periods.

The market-run analysis explains prices and sales in situations where the quantity is already in existence. Costs of production are considered only when there is some possibility of varying the quantity produced over the period under consideration. In both short-run and long-run time periods such possibilities exist.

The Short Run

In the short-run time period the firm can adjust output by adjusting the quantity of variable inputs used with the fixed factors. The length of the time period depends on the nature of the production function. Producing more or less must come about within the present capacity by controlling the outlays for the services of the variable factors of production. In this time period, the resources such as the plant size and equipment cannot be adjusted and consequently will not affect the behavior of the variable cost. What is true of all costs in the market-run period holds true of the fixed costs in the short-run period.

(1) Nature of the Supply Schedule.—The firm will adjust output to the level at which the marginal cost with the existing plant equals the marginal revenue received from the sale of the product. Production will be carried on at the range of prices equal to or above the lowest variable cost. If output is offered for sale beyond the level at which marginal revenue and marginal cost are equal, additional units will add more to total cost than to revenue and will either reduce profits or increase losses. Thus, the firm will place on the market the number of units for which the marginal cost of the last unit is equal to marginal revenue; where marginal revenue equals price, the marginal cost curve (above its intersection with the average variable cost curve) becomes equivalent to the supply curve (Fig. 11.12). Special cases of the marginal cost/marginal revenue principle will be discussed in Chapter 12.

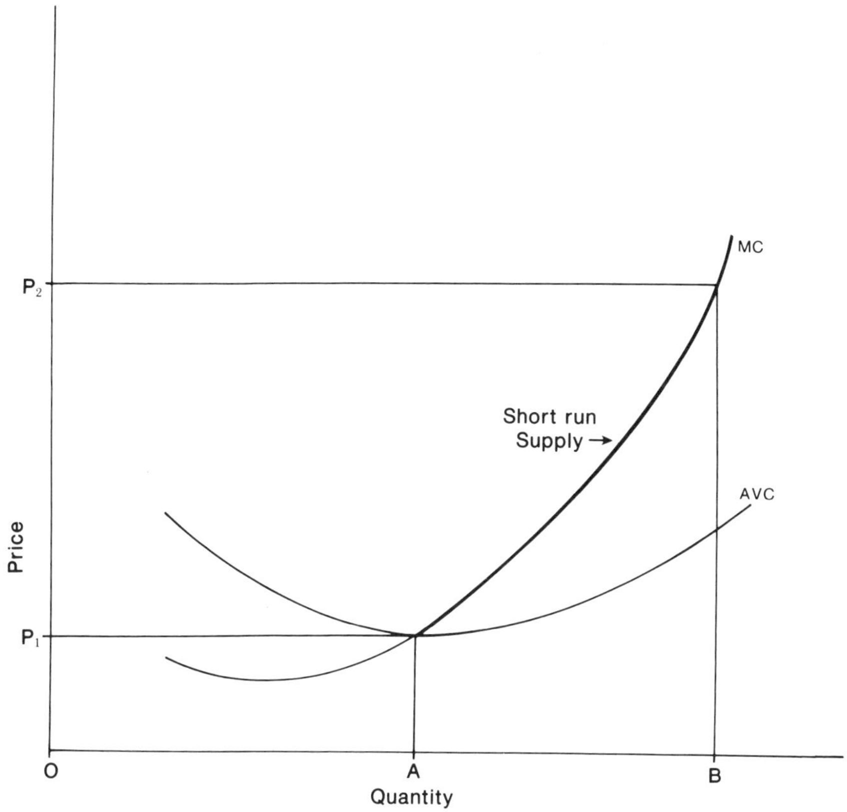

FIG. 11.12. SHORT-RUN COST CURVES AND SUPPLY CURVE

It has been shown in a preceding chapter that the marginal cost curve depends on the marginal physical productivity relationship to the factor prices, i.e., the price of the variable factors divided by the marginal physical product of the factors used in increasing output. Thus, the elasticity of the supply curve expresses the degree of difficulty in adjusting output by adjusting the quantity of inputs used.

The industry short-run supply curve can be viewed as a horizontal summation of all the short-run supply curves of the firms in the industry. Such an industry short-run supply curve is accurate if the supply of resources to the industry is perfectly elastic, i.e., the increased use of resources in adjusting output has no effect upon resource prices. If the resource supply curve should be rising, the quantities supplied at higher prices will be somewhat less than they would be on the basis of horizontal summation.

(2) Equilibrium of Prices.—The short-run equilibrium price level is reached when the quantity demanded for the product and the short-run quantity supplied of the product are equal. The sellers will produce with a given plant and place on the market at some price the same quantity that the buyers will purchase in the same interval of time. The firm is in equilibrium when it cannot improve its profit position by a change in output through changes in resource use.

There is a difference between the market-run equilibrium and the short-run equilibrium. The market-run equilibrium is attained when the buyers are willing to purchase at a certain price the whole existing stock of a perishable commodity or a portion of a stock already produced which the sellers are willing to sell at a given time. The short-run equilibrium is reached when at a certain price the rate and flow of production in which adjustments are achieved by changes in the use of variable resources approximates the rate of consumption or purchases for each time period involved.

The Long Run

The long run operates much like the short in that firms may vary output to meet demand conditions. Again, market equilibrium occurs when the quantity supplied at a given price matches the quantity demanded at the price. However, in the long run, firms have more flexibility and are more likely to achieve efficient operation since all resources are variable. The long-run elasticity of supply will likely exceed the short-run elasticity, at least given unchanging input prices. Long-run industry adjustment of output includes in addition the entry or exit of firms from the industry and thus the addition or subtraction of these firms' output. As previously discussed, the change in industry demand for inputs which results from changes in industry output may affect input prices for the industry as a whole, and in turn a given firm's variable costs and individual supply curve (*see* also Chapter 12). Effects on input prices may thus reduce the long-run elasticity of supply for a firm compared to its long-run elasticity under unchanging input prices, while external economies previously discussed may increase long-run elasticity.

A firm in the long run must be able to operate at a profit or at least not at a loss in order to stay in business. Firms will be attracted to an industry by the existence of profits for existing firms, and will exit an industry if in the long run they are unable to avoid a loss. The effects of firm entry and exit will be discussed in Chapter 12.

Changes in Market Demand and Supply Curves

A shift in either the demand curve or the supply curve will change the equilibrium price and quantity sold. Assume that initially Q_o is bought and sold at P_o. If demand increases through a change in one of the variables assumed constant (for example, a change in consumer preferences), more of a commodity will be demanded at the initial equilibrium price than before and as such more will be demanded (Q'_d) than is supplied (Q_o) at that price (Fig. 11.13). The market price then rises so as to eliminate from the market those who value the commodity at the lower price and no higher, and also entice extra quantities to the market from suppliers with higher reservation prices. This process continues (as indicated by the arrows) until quantities supplied and demanded are again equal, this time at Q_1. A higher market quantity will be bought and sold than before and at a higher price (P_1).

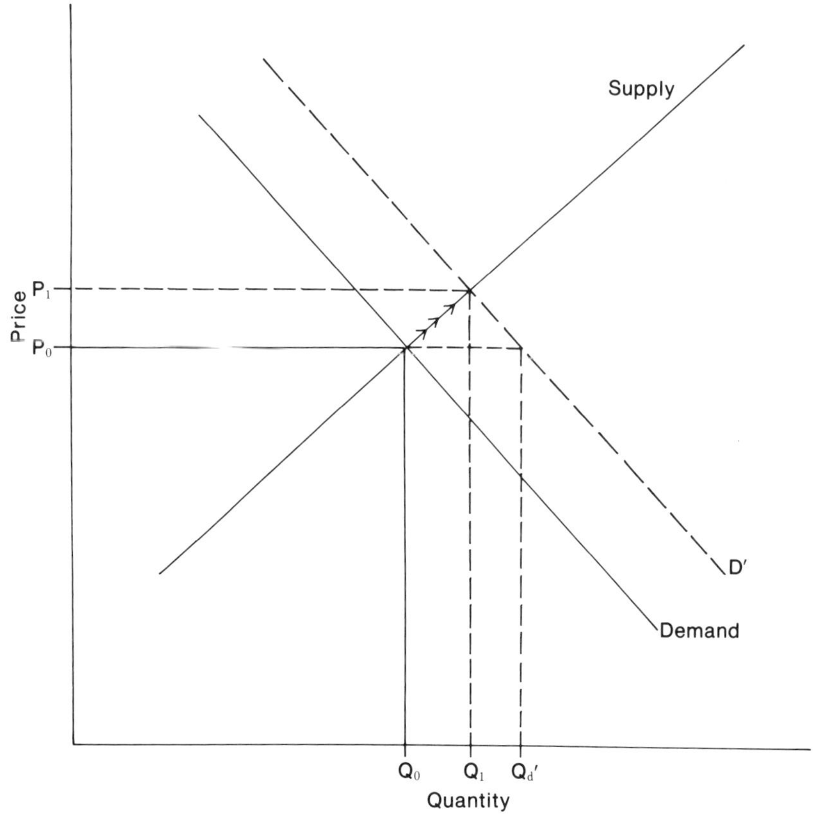

FIG. 11.13. AN INCREASE IN EQUILIBRIUM PRICE AND QUANTITY SOLD DUE TO AN INCREASE IN DEMAND

A restriction in supply (perhaps due to crop failure, higher input prices or the imposition of a tax (to be paid by sellers) on each unit of a good sold) has a similar effect on price, but the reverse effect on quantity (Fig. 11.14). Again, the initial effect is an excess of quantity demanded over quantity supplied ($Q_o - Q'_s$) which will result in an increase in price. However, the equilibrium quantity traded (a compromise between the initial difference of quantities demanded and supplied) will be less than the original equilibrium quantity.

If demand falls, quantity supplied will exceed quantity demanded. Price will fall until it goes below the reservation price for some sellers which then will reduce quantity supplied. At the same time, lower prices will increase the quantity demanded. Equilibrium in this case will occur at a lower price and quantity than before the shift in demand (Fig.

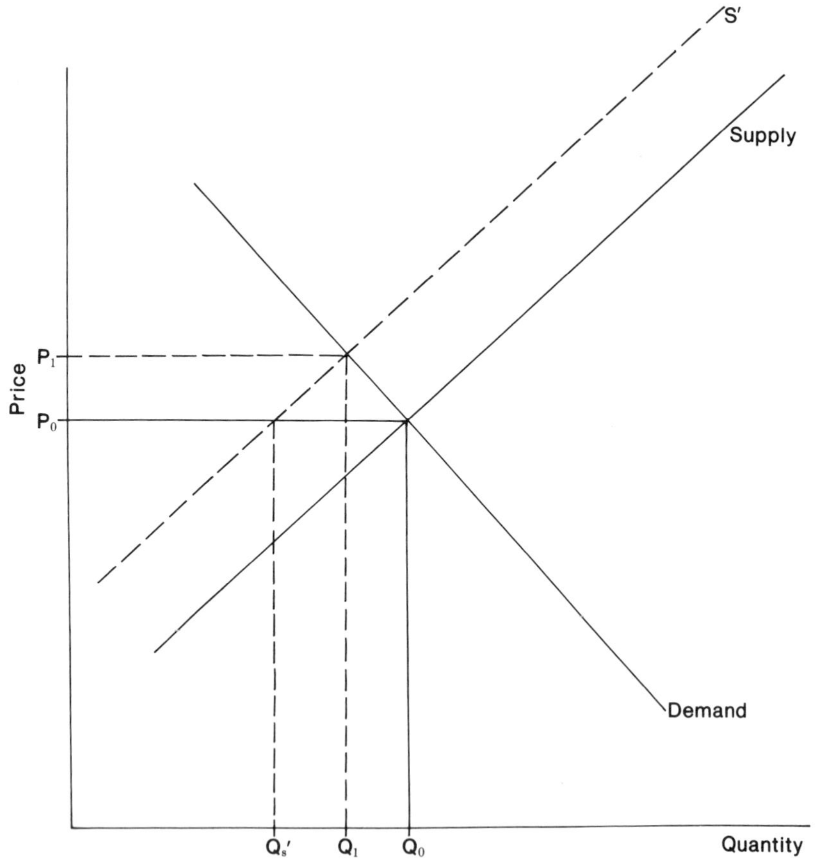

FIG. 11.14 AN INCREASE IN EQUILIBRIUM QUANTITY DUE TO A DECREASE IN SUPPLY

11.15). An increase in supply will also lower price (Fig. 11.16), but will increase the quantity sold from the initial equilibrium.

For an example consider the demand and supply curves for beer on a college campus. Assume that the price of beer is flexible. A sustained increase in partying by students would lead to an increase in demand for beer, since beer is a complementary good to many campus parties. The price and quantity consumed of beer would both rise (Fig. 11.13). If the state raised its tax on alcoholic beverages (which must be paid by the sellers), this would amount to an increase in the cost of offering a can of beer on the market, and so the supply curve would shift upward and inward (Fig. 11.14). Students must pay a higher price for their beer and consume less through the law of demand, as the demand curve has not changed in this case. If government aid to students were cut, this would

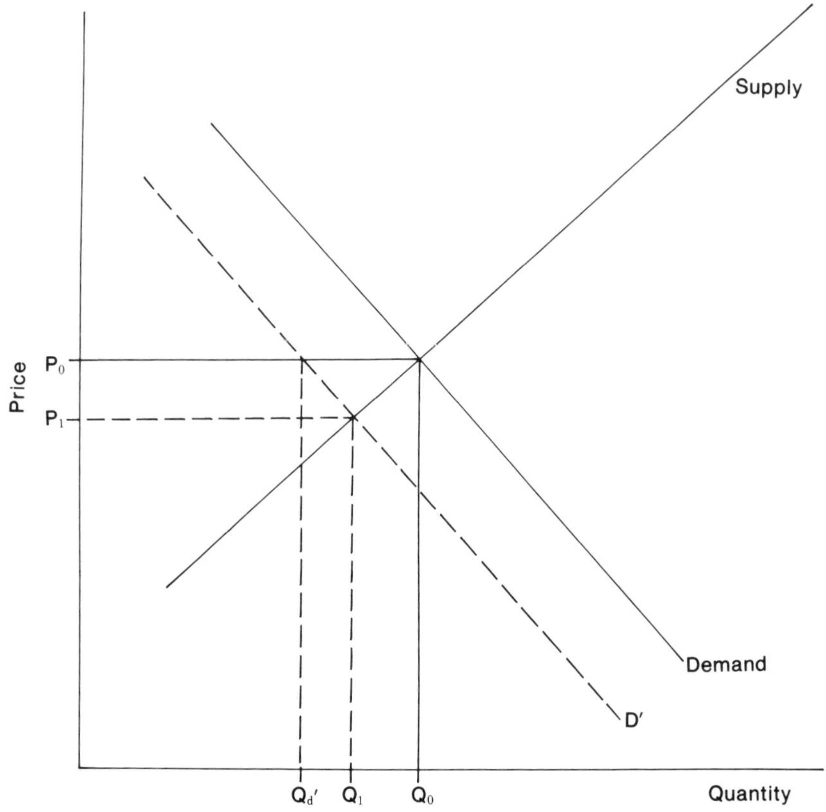

FIG. 11.15. A DECREASE IN EQUILIBRIUM PRICE AND QUANTITY DUE TO A DECREASE IN DEMAND

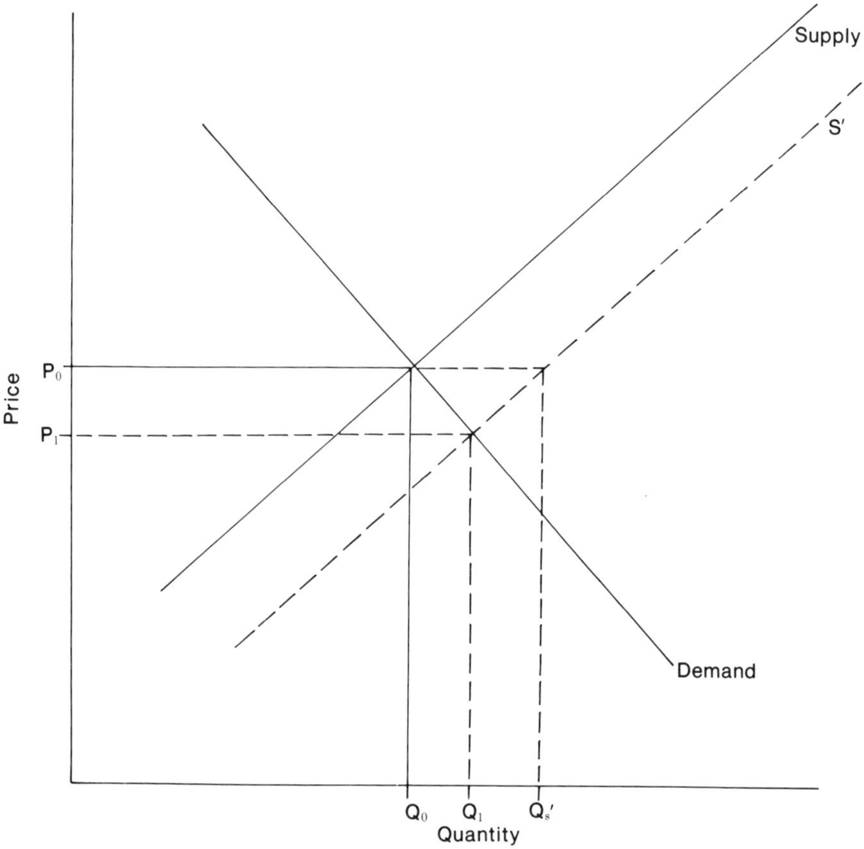

FIG. 11.16. A DECREASE IN EQUILIBRIUM PRICE AND AN INCREASE IN EQUILIBRIUM QUANTITY DUE TO AN INCREASE IN SUPPLY

result in a lowering of student income in the aggregate (though not all students would be affected nor to the same degree). This decrease in income would lead to a decrease in demand for beer, which would drive down the price of beer and decrease its consumption (Fig. 11.15). Suppose the college now allowed beer to be served on campus and a few campus bars opened. This would have the effect of increasing the supply of beer in the campus market. The price should go down and consumption should go up (Fig. 11.16). Besides the effects described by this demand/supply analysis, the change in the number of establishments occasioned by campus policy may affect the market structure of beer which has further implications, as the next chapter will indicate.

CHAPTER 11: REVIEW QUESTIONS

(1) Most of the usual geometric figures (in two dimensions) used in economic analysis can be viewed as exercises in what Boulding calls "plausibility topology." Thus, most of the curves we ordinarily think of as representing functional relations in production economics can also be thought of as representing boundaries between attainable and not attainable points of two-dimensional space.
For the functions listed show by diagram the two half-spaces that are attainable or not attainable if they exist. Indicate briefly the rationale for your answer.

(a) The isocost contours for the production of two commodities, X and Y.
(b) The budget line for two factors of production A and B (assume perfect competition).
(c) The demand curve for a firm for a factor of production, where the demand curve represents the maximum quantity the firm will take at a given price.
(d) A production function relating one input and one output.
(e) A negatively sloped supply curve that indicates the minimum price for which a given quantity would be supplied.
(f) The age of a farmer and the farmer's average hourly labor output.
(g) The marginal cost curve.
(h) The marginal revenue curve.

(2) Suppose you know that the aggregate production function for wheat produced in the United States conforms to the following mathematical form:

$$Y = 10N^{.5}K^{.25}$$

where Y = wheat output (bushels), N = hours of labor services and K = units of capital services.
Also, you know that the price of N is constant at \$1 per hour and the price of K is constant at \$2 per unit.
Using this information:

(a) Derive a variable cost function of the form $C_v = g(Y)$, where C_v = variable cost.
(b) Derive an aggregate supply function.

(3) Agricultural economists have developed an impressive number of useful production functions. It follows that aggregate supply is well estimated. *Discuss.*

(4) Discuss the concept of irreversibility of supply.

(5) Discuss the factors determining elasticity of supply.

(6) "The elasticity of supply is likely to be greater when the firm is operating at lower levels of output." Discuss.

(7) Assume a firm is producing one product with two variable inputs. It can buy both inputs at a given price up to a certain point; after this point the prices of both inputs are 50% higher. Demonstrate what this does to the firm's supply curve. Discuss what happens to the elasticity of supply at various points.

(8) "The supply curve for a firm using a common resource (e.g., the ocean for a fishing industry, or a pool of oil) is likely to have a different elasticity than supply curves for firms using resources owned or controlled by the firm." Evaluate this statement and explain why this is true or false.

(9) Discuss the effect of the labor (or capital) input market characteristics on the supply function for a farm product (say, wheat).

(10) "Due to a technological discovery, an increase in productivity of labor used in a furniture factory resulted in a shift in the supply curve for chairs." Discuss.

(11) "A tax on a commodity will raise the price to the consumer by the amount of the tax per unit if and only if the supply of the commodity is perfectly elastic." Discuss and prove.

(12) Assume that the following is a valid set of relationships for hogs:

Supply: $X_1 = 700 + 0.1X_2 + 0.04X_3 + 0.6X_2^2$

Demand: $X_1 = 810 - 0.9X_2 + 0.03X_3 - 0.4X_2^2$

where X_1 = live weight of hogs slaughtered (000000), X_2 = farm price of hogs (cents per pound) and X_3 = disposable consumer income per capita (dollars).

Given this set of relationships, determine the equilibrium price and quantity when consumer disposable income levels equal $2000.

(13) Prove by graphics the following:

(a) A change in demand will cause no change in price when the supply of a commodity is perfectly elastic.

(b) A change in demand will cause no change in the quantity supplied when the supply of a commodity is perfectly inelastic.

(c) A change in supply will cause no change in the price when the demand for a commodity is perfectly elastic.

(d) A change in supply will cause no change in the quantity bought when the demand for a commodity is perfectly inelastic.

(e) When the demand for a commodity is relatively inelastic, a fall in supply will increase the price and decrease the quantity supplied, but the decrease in quantity will be proportionately smaller than the increase in price.

(f) When the supply of a commodity is relatively elastic, a fall in demand will decrease both the price and the quantity supplied, but the fall in price will be proportionately smaller than the fall in quantity.

(14) The effect of a shift in either a supply or demand curve on price and quantity exchanged will be determined by the elasticity of the other curve. In the first column, indicate which curve has shifted by writing S for supply curve or D for demand curve. In the second column indicate the elasticity of the curve which has not shifted by writing E if the curve is relatively elastic or I if relatively inelastic.

Curve Shifted	*Elasticity of Other Curve*	*Quote*
____________	________	(1) "Despite the fact that many new producers have come into the field, price has fallen only slightly."
____________	________	(2) "Although a subsidy on each unit produced is now paid by the government the quantity sold has increased very little."
____________	________	(3) "The price of the commodity has increased sharply as a result of the rise in consumer preference."
____________	________	(4) "As a result of levying an excise tax upon the production of the good, its price has increased considerably."
____________	________	(5) "The quantity of a good purchased has decreased little although excellent new substitutes for it have appeared in production"

Curve Shifted	*Elasticity of Other Curve*	*Quote*
__________	________	(6) "Although the prices of substitute goods have fallen, the price of this good has fallen only slightly."
__________	________	(7) "Despite the fact that people want this commodity more than they did before, they do not have to pay more for it."
__________	________	(8) "There are many good substitutes for this good so the rise in the cost of producing it has not led to much increase in its price."

(15) Assume that it is socially desirable to support agricultural prices above the free market equilibrium level in order to improve the economic well-being of the farmer. Obviously society is interested in developing a proposal to do this at the least cost. After a careful study of several possibilities, the conclusions reached were:

(a) For those products which have a price elasticity of demand less than the price elasticity of supply, a program restricting output would be the cheapest.
(b) For those products which have a price elasticity of demand greater than the price elasticity of supply, a program of compensatory payments would be the cheapest.
(c) The program to buy at support price all products that are offered—a guaranteed minimum price—and sell out of stock whenever price exceeds the support level would be the most expensive program.

Develop and evaluate the rationale that may lead to such conclusions.

Paper Three: Social Cost Effects of Agricultural Price Support Schemes

John C. Redman[2]

Efforts to manipulate supply and demand of agricultural commodities are practiced throughout the world with the use of foreign trade and with internal marketing and production regulations. In the more highly developed countries, the concern is with the relatively low farm income while in underdeveloped countries the emphasis is on increased production. Nearly all free world countries provide price and income support for their agriculture.

The question of the appropriate farm price support program in the United States is far from being settled. Further modifications and change of direction can be expected because of the pressures that build up when the equilibrium position of the forces of supply and demand is not permitted to occur. Many schemes have been advanced and some have been tried in an effort to hold the price of agricultural commodities above the equilibrium price. In recent years, many such schemes have ceased to be operative because of the high equilibrium price of agricultural commodities. When society accepts a policy scheme that forces the price from that determined by the free play of supply and demand, it does so at a net cost to itself, either to the consumers or to the producer, or both.

OBJECTIVES OF STUDY

The society is interested in which of the several pricing schemes will be less costly in terms of cost to itself. Thus, the purpose of this paper is (1)

[2] The main ideas used in this paper were developed while the junior author was a postdoctoral fellow of the Social Science Research Council at the University of Chicago. Acknowledgement is due Professor A. C. Harberger, University of Chicago, who in a classroom lecture provided some of the conceptual ideas used in this paper.

to discuss the social cost society imposes on itself by adopting one of the several schemes, and (2) to suggest the hypothesis that supply and demand characteristics of the farm commodities supported must determine the appropriate price support scheme to minimize the net social cost involved. If the government intends to influence the play of economic forces, it is logical that they should be directed to minimize the net social cost.

THE CONCEPT OF SOCIAL COST

The social cost as used here consists of that experienced by producers or that by consumers or both. In an economy where the output of a commodity is being expanded, resources are diverted from some alternative use to its production. In this case, the cost to the economy is the value of those commodities sacrificed which would have been produced. A social cost line may be drawn which indicates the locus of minimum prices that must be paid to pull the resources from other uses to produce a unit increase in the output of the commodity being expanded (Fig. 11.17).

This line represents the price that must be paid to the owners of resources to entice them to shift from producing other commodities to

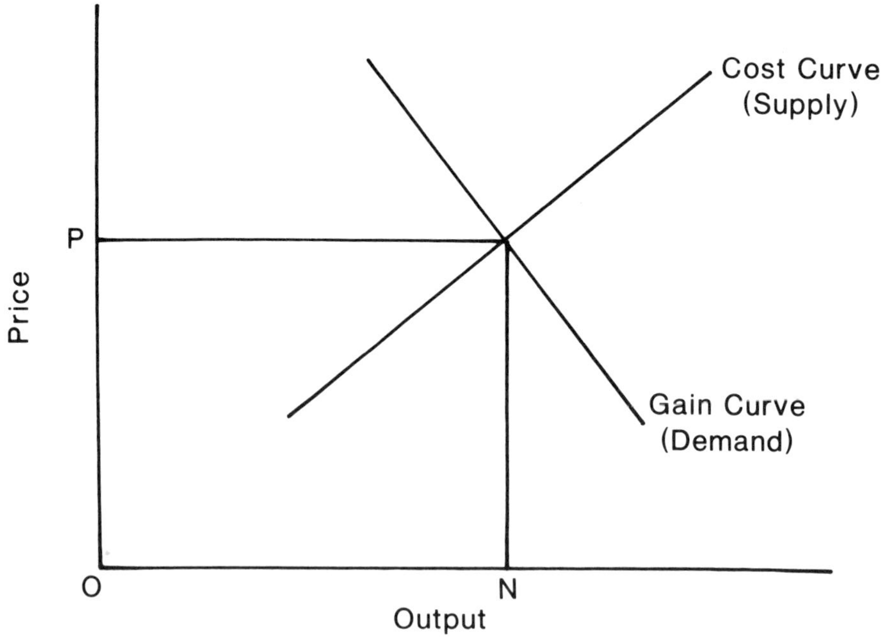

FIG. 11.17. PRICE DETERMINATION UNDER FREE PLAY OF SUPPLY AND DEMAND

the production of the new commodity.

The social cost curve will have a nonnegative slope throughout and in most cases will be positively inclined. If more of commodity A is being produced, less of commodity B must be produced from a given quantity of resources. The further the production of A is pushed, the more of B must be given up to produce a unit of A. Thus, long-run tendencies are such that increasing output of a commodity, other conditions remaining the same, must increase its cost of production. More specifically, there are at least two good reasons for increasing cost. Probably the most important one is largely technological in nature. Many of the resources used in producing these commodities being sacrificed are not as useful in production of that being increased. As a consequence, resources which are transferred are used in progressively larger proportions in the production of the commodity being expanded and in smaller proportions in the production of other commodities in combination with resources that are specialized and well suited to the two industries, respectively. This means there is a diminishing marginal rate of substitution between a resource and numeraire resource to produce the output. Thus, the factors are not homogenous in quality. As the resources are transferred from production of B to A, it will be that labor, capital, land and management become progressively more suitable for B and less suitable for A. Thus, each unit suffers a progressively greater reduction in its value in terms of units of either commodity.

The second important reason for a possible increasing cost curve is due to monetary external diseconomics to scale. In a fully employed economy, when an additional unit of A is being produced and factors transferred from production of other commodities are raised in price, the quantities of these factors already used to produce A will rise in price along with those added to the production of A. In a sense, the social cost of production of the last unit of A would be all the increased cost caused by its production. But for a transfer of resources to take place, there must be a shift in the market estimate of A in comparison to the commodities competing for the resources to justify it, making all units of A equal in value. The increase in the total value of A must be greater than the decrease in value of output of the commodities competing for the resources. However, there would be no external diseconomies if there is no rise in prices of the resources to secure the services, i.e., the resources are underemployed making the supply of them perfectly elastic. Underemployed resources could result from a sudden shift in the demand of the product they produce. Thus, no need exists to bid up price to obtain them.

All of these reasons contribute to the degree of slope of the cost curve indicating the ease of expanding production of a commodity. Thus, the supply price of a given quantity of A, assuming perfect competition, will be equal to the ordinate of the social cost curve.[3]

On the other hand, as the output of a commodity is expanded the society will gain from the increase. The gain curve can be defined as the maximum amount that can be charged and paid by the consumer for each unit of output as it is expanded (Fig. 11.17). In other words, it is the locus of points defining the maximum amount that will be paid per unit of output at every level of output. Corresponding to any given quantity of output, the demand price will be equal to the ordinate of the gain curve. The curve will have a negative slope throughout because there is a diminishing marginal rate of substitution between the commodity and a numeraire good (representing all other goods), making the revenue obtained for each unit of output diminish as output increases. In this situation, the gain curve is identical with the price schedule of a perfectly discriminating monopolist.

NET SOCIAL COST OF SELECTED SCHEMES

It is the relationship which exists between these two curves—the gain curve and the cost curve—that determines the nature and incidence of the social cost when prices are supported above the free equilibrium level. Only when the gain is equal to the cost will there not be any net social cost and this occurs only when the free equilibrium price OP equates the cost and gain schedules at output ON (Fig. 11.17). This situation therefore can serve as the base by which any social costs encountered either by producers or consumers can be compared.

Scheme I

Suppose the governmental authority sets the support price of a commodity above the free equilibrium price, say by 20%, and places no restriction on the output of any sort. This scheme is approximately what was applied to potatoes in the late 1940s. In this case the producers will supply a unit at ON quantity at OP_1 price at the cost of not producing other products (Fig. 11.18).

The consumers, because of their collective taste pattern, will purchase a unit at OL quantity at OP_1 price. The cost to society encountered through excess production is the area MEBN. The cost to society encountered through reducing consumption of its members is the area MLAE. Thus, the total social cost for this scheme is the area AEBNL.

[3] Pigou calls this Social Opportunity Cost which is defined as the price that has to be paid to attract further supplies of resources and represents nothing but a measure of increasing quantities of satisfaction which consumers have to forego elsewhere.

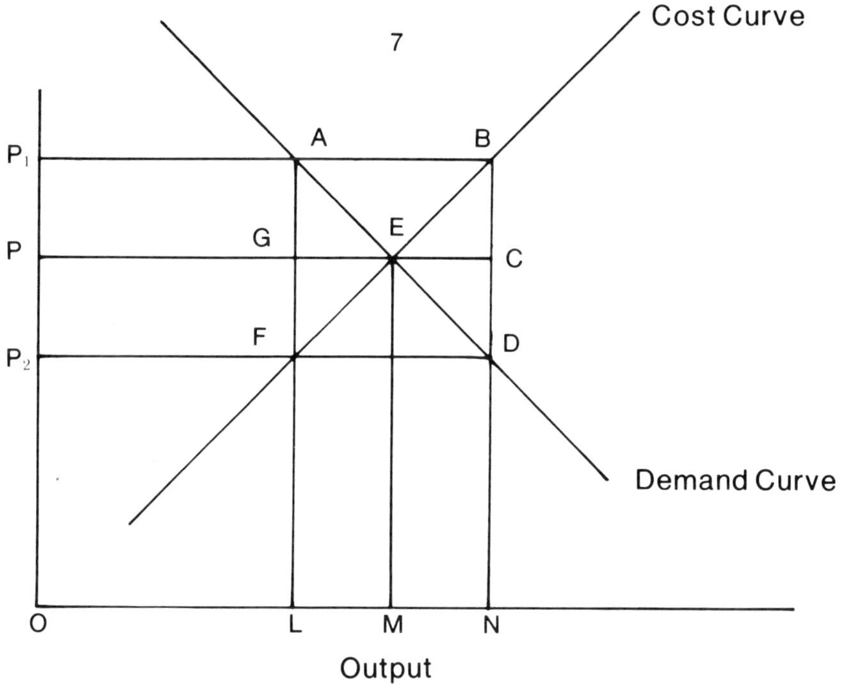

FIG. 11.18. PRICE DETERMINATION AND SOCIAL COST UNDER VARIOUS PRICE MANIPULATING SCHEMES WITH THE ASSUMPTION THAT SUPPLY AND DEMAND CHARACTERISTICS OF ALL COMMODITIES ARE THE SAME

The area AEB is a net transfer payment from consumers to the producer with no social cost involved (what the producer receives as a gain is exactly equal to what consumers lose).

Scheme II

Suppose the governmental authority decides to make a compensatory payment which will make the total price received for the commodity 20% above the free equilibrium price that would prevail. Under this scheme the producers will supply ON quantity at OP_1 price but the consumers will pay only OP_2 price for a unit at that quantity (Fig. 11.18). The total cost to society due to excess production and not producing something else is the area MEBN but the gain to society through consuming this quantity is the area MEDN, leaving as a net social cost the area EBD.

A modified compensatory scheme has been suggested which will permit a payment to be made on a large fraction but not all the commodity produced.[4] It is argued that this modification will permit producer decisions to expand or contract production to be governed mainly by the value of the marginal output which is the value of the portion at "free" market prices not included for compensation. The quota on which compensation is made is to be 75% of the three preceding years of production and no restrictions would be necessary on production. While this modification will involve less social cost than the one with compensatory payments on the full quantity produced, it will not be free of social cost since any sort of subsidy on any portion of the production will encourage output greater than what will be called for by free price. There would be a desire on the part of the producers to increase their quota by producing more.[5] As the percentage of the production on which the compensatory payments is made is reduced, the social cost will reduce until no compensatory payment is paid.

Scheme III

In many circles, the export-dumping scheme has been suggested to support the domestic price above the free market equilibrium price. Under this scheme, the government would support price at OP_1 which would call forth ON quantity (Fig. 11.18). The consumers will purchase only OL quantity at that price. The quantity LN or ON-OL would be "dumped" on the world market at OP price, the free equilibrium price. The net social cost to the consumers is the area AEG and to the producers is the area EBC, making the total net social cost the sum of these two areas (AEG + EBC). In addition to the social cost, there may be many international political difficulties which would arise with this scheme.

Scheme IV

The scheme with which society has had the most experience is the output-restriction type. Under this scheme, the support price is maintained primarily by restricting output to the level necessary to force the price to the desired level, OP_1, called the support price (Fig. 11.18). Most of the United States programs when combined with the Commodity Credit Corporation's activities are really a combination of this scheme and Scheme I. However, strict marketing quotas can be imposed which will put a tight control on the amount placed on the market, making this

[4] *See* Brandow, G. E. 1955. A modified compensatory price program for agriculture. J. Farm Econ. *37* (4).

[5] This practice was followed by some tobacco producers. They grew the tobacco in excess and paid the penalty in order to have a larger acreage allotment.

scheme strictly an output-restriction type. The social cost under this scheme is all encountered by the consumers and is represented by area AEF. No social cost is incurred by the producers since they would be able to place their resources in alternative production.

ROLE OF ELASTICITIES

The concept of price elasticity is very important in economic analysis and it plays a fundamental role here. It measures the responsiveness of consumers and producers to changes in the price. The shape of the demand curve and the supply curve for a commodity is determined by the degree of elasticity present. Unfortunately, like information on all important problems, the knowledge of the price elasticities of the demand and particularly the supply is not in very good shape. However, the estimates as rough as they may be can give an indication of the importance of the relative elasticities in determining the support program with the least social cost.

The price elasticity of demand for all farm products is between 0.2 and 0.4 which is relatively inelastic. Demand for individual commodities is in general much more elastic due largely to the possibilities of substitution. Mehren[6] gave a list of price elasticities for particular farm commodities only for the year of 1949 at the farm level. These, as he points out, do not represent long-run estimates and are relevant to commercial sales and 1949 conditions. W. A. Cromarty made some estimates on price elasticity of supply for several commodities. These were made on the basis of either the current or lagged price and do not include an expectation factor.

	Price Elasticity of	
Commodity	*Demand*	*Supply*
Beef	0.80	0.037
Hogs	0.80	0.130
Soybeans	0.60	0.171
Cotton	0.60	0.361
Feed grains	0.50–0.65	0.364
Eggs	0.42	0.298
Wheat	0.41	0.129
Flue-cured tobacco	0.45	0.516
Burley tobacco	0.20	0.381

[6] *See* Mehren, G. L. 1951. Comparative costs of agricultural price supports in 1949. Am. Econ. Rev. *41* (2).

Which of the schemes involves the least social cost will depend on the relative elasticities of supply and demand. Clearly, under almost any relationship, Scheme I would involve the greatest social cost. For those commodities like flue-cured tobacco and burley tobacco where the price elasticity of supply is *greater* than the price elasticity of demand, Scheme IV which is the output restriction type would involve the least social cost (Fig. 11.19).

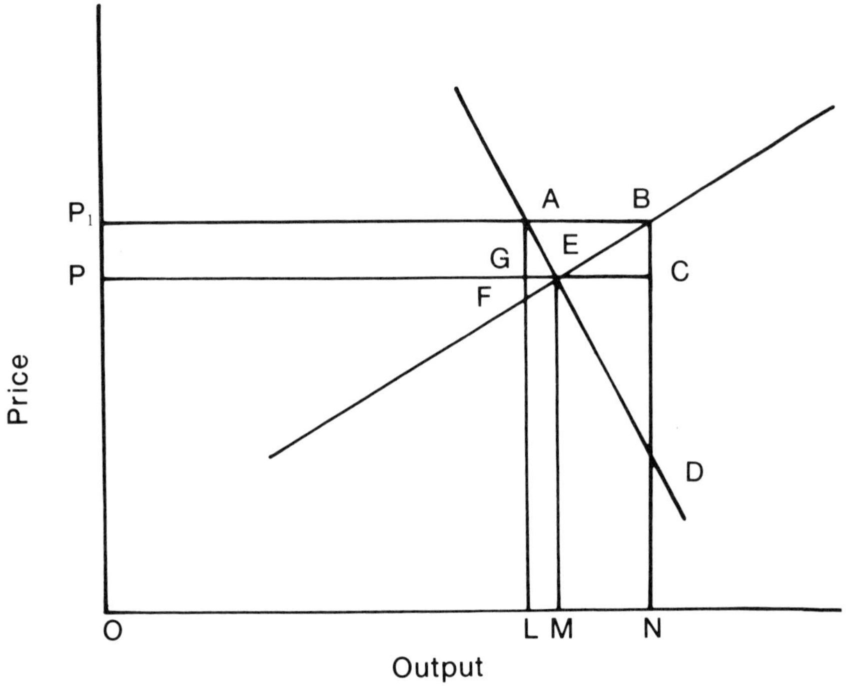

FIG. 11.19. PRICE DETERMINATION AND SOCIAL COST OF PRICE MANIPULATION SCHEME WITH THE SUPPLY AND DEMAND CHARACTERISTICS ASSUMED TO SUGGEST AN OUTPUT RESTRICTION SCHEME

The area AEF which indicates the amount of social cost under Scheme IV is much smaller than area EBD which indicates the amount of social cost under Scheme II which in this case would be also more expensive than Scheme III.

For those commodities like beef, hogs, soybeans, cotton, feed grains, eggs and wheat which have price elasticities of supply *less* than the price elasticities of demand, Scheme II which is the compensatory type will involve the least social cost (Fig. 11.20).

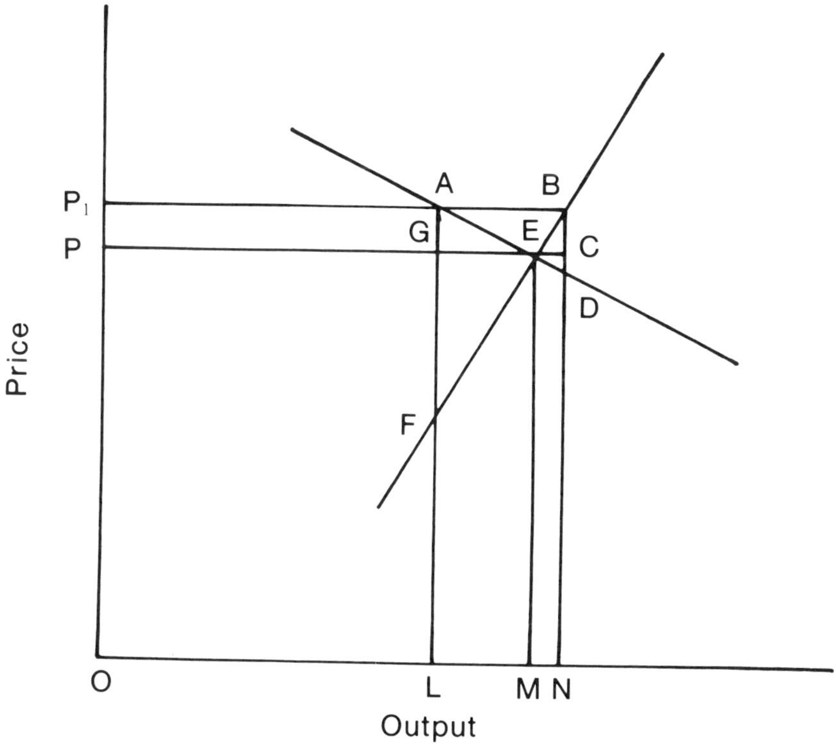

FIG. 11.20. PRICE DETERMINATION AND SOCIAL COST OF PRICE MANIPULATION SCHEME WITH SUPPLY AND DEMAND CHARACTERISTICS ASSUMED TO SUGGEST A COMPENSATORY PAYMENT SCHEME

The area EBD which illustrates the amount of social cost under this scheme is smaller than area AEF which indicates the amount of social cost under Scheme IV which in this case would be more expensive than Scheme III.

The determining factor is whether or not the price elasticity of demand is greater or less than the price elasticity of supply. If it is uncertain what these behavioral characteristics of commodities are, then Scheme III, the export-dumping type, would be a middle-of-road scheme. However, it will without doubt involve international politics.

CONCLUSIONS

It is evident that a price support scheme regardless of its nature will impose a social cost. It is also evident that different support schemes impose different amounts of social cost depending on the characteristics of the supply and demand for the commodity. If the society is interested in achieving the support level at the least social cost, then it is essential that the most appropriate price support scheme be used. Thus, this study suggests that for that commodity group whose price elasticity of demand is *less* than the price elasticity of supply, Scheme IV, the output restriction type, be used. For that commodity group whose price elasticity of demand is *greater* than the price elasticity of supply, Scheme II, the compensatory type, should be used. For the commodity group whose price elasticity of demand is *equal* to the price elasticity of supply, all three schemes—Scheme II, Scheme III and Scheme IV—will have the same social cost.

Because of the importance of the relative elasticities of supply and demand in determining the amount of social cost involved and in suggesting which price support scheme should be used, it is obvious that the knowledge about the price elasticities of all agricultural commodities should be improved. This does not deny other important reasons for improving the knowledge of price elasticities.

The proponents of the compensatory payment type should gain strong support if the scheme is used only for those commodities for which it has the advantage. Likewise, proponents for the restriction type can have strong support if it is used only for those commodities, e.g., tobacco, which have the supply and demand characteristics suited for it.

12

Market Structure: Ideal Types

IDEAL TYPES IN THEORY

The analysis of market structure in traditional economic theory relies heavily on the use of ideal types. Ideal types are limiting concepts, that is, abstractions from instead of representations of reality. They are never found in all their characteristics in the real world, though they may be approximated, but rather are meant as interpretive or explanatory schema of real-world phenomena. They do not attempt to cover all real-world characteristics at once, but only to explain some of them. They consist of the specification of a set of characteristics and a set of general hypotheses connecting these characteristics. The importance of ideal types lies not in their actual existence or in description of the real world, but in the characteristics they contain (which do carry empirical interpretation) and the theoretical implications of those characteristics. As such, they are theories rather than descriptions; the functions of explanation and prediction served by theory are not identical with the function of description.

Ideal types should not be confused with extreme types. The latter are found in the real world, though rarely, and serve as (opposing) poles between which to order other real-world phenomena. Extreme types serve little purpose other than that of comparison; one may declare a phenomenon to be more one type than another, but this does little for theoretical analysis from that point onward. In recent years, attempts have been made to modify the ideal types of perfect competition and monopoly into extreme types which may actually exist, through modifications of assumptions and introduction of such concepts as "workable" and "effective" competition. Although these provide a more realistic model of the real-world market, and as such may serve as a yardstick of competition, they add nothing from a theoretical standpoint. They merely continue to make use of the predictions derived from the ideal types, corresponding to those characteristics of the ideal type which prevail in their particular setting.

Market structure analysis may thus be viewed linearly:

Perfect competition	Effective competition	Monopolistic competition	Oligopoly	Pure monopoly

Market organization follows a continuum along dimensions to be described in the next chapter, with discontinuities between the extreme type concepts of effective competition and the ideal type of perfect competition, between extreme cases of oligopoly (few sellers) and the ideal type of monopoly. Although the intermediate cases of oligopoly and monopolistic competition have been noted in the literature, precise identification of their bounds and adequate analysis have so far eluded economists. The present discussion will content itself with describing the dimensions of the continuum along which they exist. The ideal types will be analyzed to uncover basic principles of behavior, which are followed through the less clear-cut and real-world market types as well.

PERFECT COMPETITION

Definitional Assumptions

One of the ideal types most frequently used in market analysis is perfect competition. In fact, much of the analysis in the preceding chapter has utilized its assumptions, for the purpose of clarity of exposition. Perfect competition is defined by four characteristics:

(1) *There is a very large number of very small firms.* No firm is large enough to be able by itself and its own actions to influence the prevailing market price or the price it receives, and there are so many firms that it is impossible to form effective coalitions to alter the market price. Each firm, therefore, must accept the prevailing market price as determined by market demand and supply, and adjust the quantity it produces to maximize its profits.

(2) *All firms produce a homogeneous product.* For example, there is very little difference between the whole milk produced by different companies. Whole milk would be a fairly homogeneous product, although milk as a whole would not because of the alternatives of whole *vs* lowfat *vs* skim *vs* buttermilk. Homogeneity of product ensures that the products of different sellers are perfect substitutes for each other, i.e., their cross elasticities are infinite. This eliminates differences in service, quality, location and brand images

which could exist, for these serve to differentiate products at least in the minds of consumers and as such result in a violation of the assumption of a homogeneous product.

(3) *There are no barriers to movement of resources, either among firms in the industry or into or out of the industry.* Resources are perfectly mobile, and firms can easily enter or leave the industry. This implies that there are no specialized skills for labor and no large capital costs to opening a business and starting production.

(4) *Perfect knowledge on the part of buyers and sellers concerning all other market transactions.* This means that one seller cannot secretly undercut another in price, and if a price difference among sellers did exist, all buyers would immediately know it and flock to the lower-priced seller. (Since the product is homogeneous, no reason exists not to buy at the lowest price.) Perfect knowledge thus forces identical pricing behavior among sellers.

The above characteristics imply that the demand curve facing an individual firm is perfectly elastic and thus horizontal (Fig. 12.1). Any seller who lowers price below $\bar{p}$ would attract an extremely large amount of business, for the reasons mentioned under perfect knowledge. Actually, the seller would attract the (finite) entire market quantity demanded, but since the firm normally accounts for such a tiny fraction of the market, the effect appears infinitely large. Any seller who raises price above $\bar{p}$ would lose all business, for the same reasons.

This horizontal demand curve is also the marginal revenue curve. Since price does not change as quantity varies, the extra total revenue generated by an increase in quantity sold is simply that change in quantity times the price per unit. Thus, the marginal revenue (equalling the extra total revenue divided by the extra quantity) equals the price, and the marginal revenue curve equals the demand curve.

Output Determination

The firm in the short run will produce where marginal revenue equals marginal cost. This is the profit-maximizing output; at any other, the firm could do better. At outputs less than where marginal revenue equals marginal cost, marginal revenue will exceed marginal cost. Production of the next unit will add more to revenue than to cost, so the firm should produce it. This continues until the next unit will add more to cost than to revenue. At this point the firm stops expanding production, but at this point the firm is at the equality (intersection) of marginal cost and marginal revenue. Therefore, this intersection determines the firm's profit maximizing output. This holds for any kind of firm. But in the previous paragraph it was noted that for perfectly competitive firms

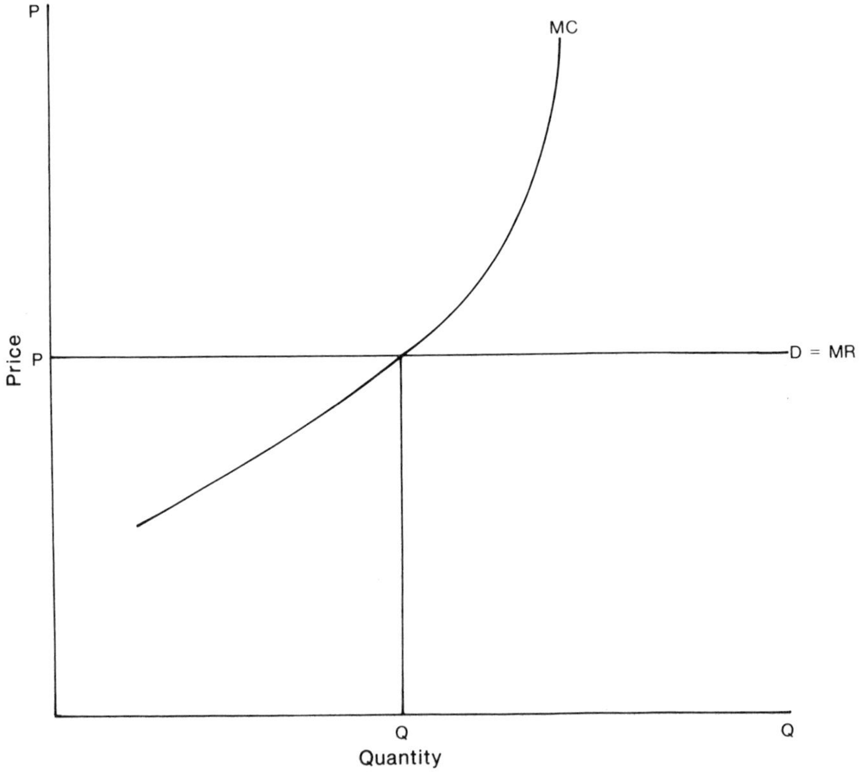

FIG. 12.1. OUTPUT DETERMINATION BY A FIRM UNDER PERFECT COMPETITION

marginal revenue equals price. Thus, by varying the price and noting the intersection with the firm's marginal cost curve, it becomes evident that a firm's supply curve is its marginal cost curve as described in Chapter 11.

This in itself says nothing about whether the firms will in fact make a profit, or if so how much. This depends on the short-run average cost curve. If SAC is below price at the above intersection (Fig. 12.2), the firm will earn a short-run profit (ABCD). If SAC is above price (Fig. 12.3), the firm will have a short-run loss (AEFG).

Not included in the defining characteristics of perfect competition was any assumption on firm costs. At least in the short run, firms may have differing cost structures, so it is possible for one firm to earn a profit and another a loss. In the long run, given the assumption of resource mobility,

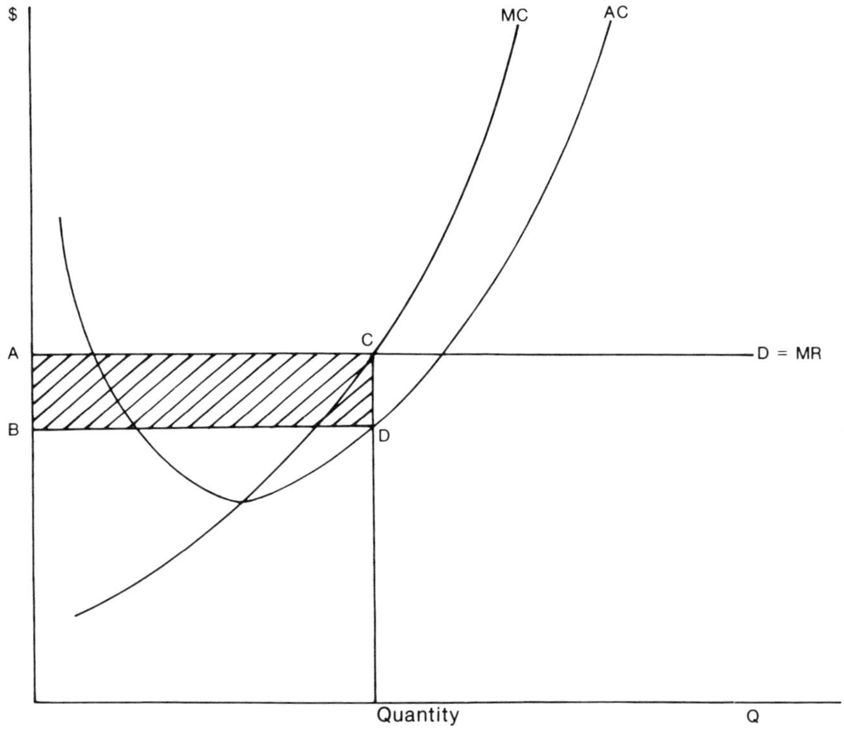

FIG. 12.2. A PERFECTLY COMPETITIVE FIRM WHICH EARNS A SHORT-RUN PROFIT

this will not continue. The higher-cost firms earning losses will eventually go out of business and enter some more profitable industry or other use of their resources. The existence of pure profits in an industry will attract new firms to the industry; this expands the market supply (Fig. 12.4) and lowers the market price, which lowers the profits to each firm (Fig. 12.5). Because of the perfect mobility assumption, then, the long-run tendency is toward zero pure profit for each firm.

Costs may also change in the long run. In the short run, a firm must operate out of a given size plant. This may not be the most efficient size in the long run. In the long run, firms are able to adjust plant size as well as output, as described in Chapter 10. Therefore, the long-run equilibrium for a firm in a perfectly competitive industry is at minimum long-run average cost, which coincides with minimum short-run average cost, with the intersection of the marginal cost curve, and with the tangency of the demand curve (Fig. 12.6).

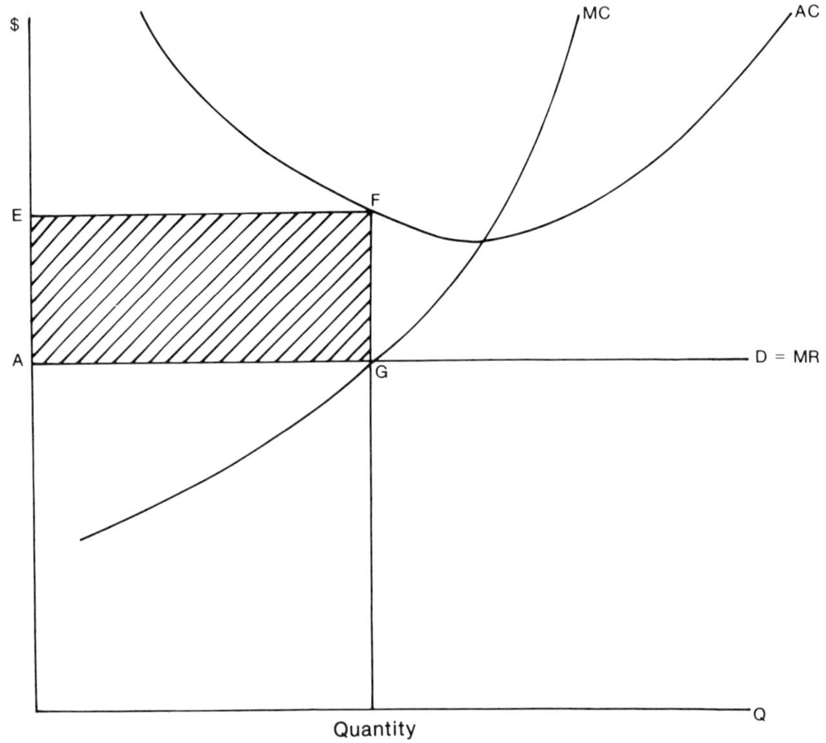

FIG. 12.3. A PERFECTLY COMPETITIVE FIRM WHICH EARNS A SHORT-RUN LOSS

The preceding analysis has more or less assumed that the industry experiences unchanging costs as industry output changes (Fig. 12.7). More specifically, the increased use of resources occasioned by expanded output (i.e., if more firms enter) does not lead to an increase in the prices of these resources. In other words, the supply of these resources is perfectly elastic. This may be approximated in the case of unspecialized resources such as unskilled labor. In other cases, however, this may not hold. In these situations (increasing or decreasing cost industries), changing industry output may result in changed cost curves for firms; new firms then enter or leave until the new tangency of LRAC to price is reached (Fig. 12.8). For example, if more skilled technicians are required because of an increase in an industry output, technician wages will most likely increase and thus raise the variable cost curve of a given firm. Less efficient firms may then be forced to exit the industry, even while new firms enter.

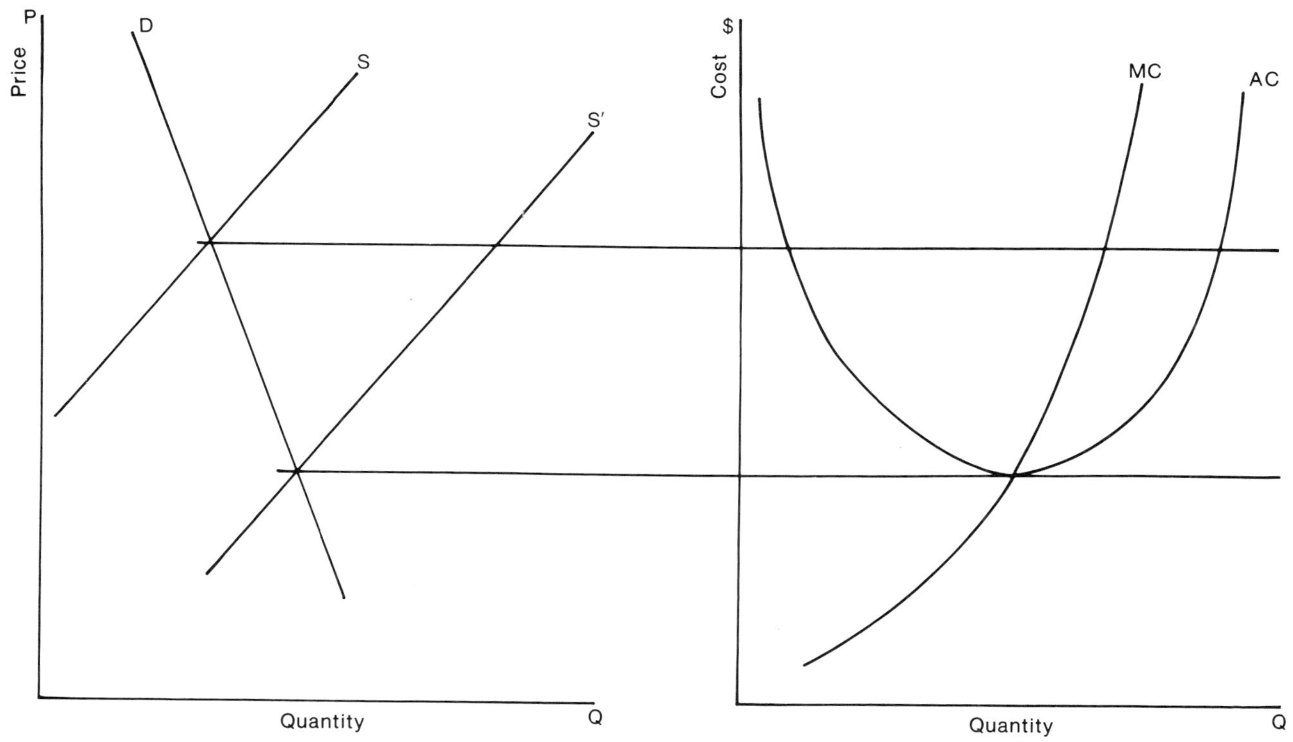

FIG. 12.4 AND FIG. 12.5. EFFECT OF NEW ENTRANTS ON FIRM PROFITS IN A PERFECTLY COMPETITIVE INDUSTRY

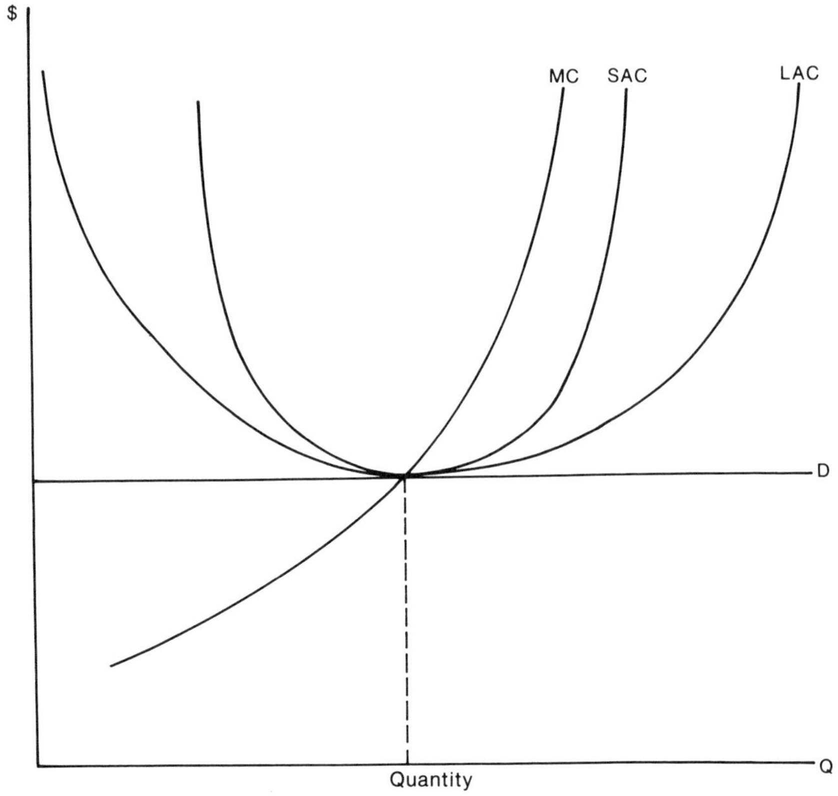

FIG. 12.6. LONG-RUN EQUILIBRIUM FOR A FIRM IN PERFECT COMPETITION

MONOPOLY

Definitional Assumptions

The other ideal typc used in market analysis is monopoly. The major definitional characteristic of monopoly is that only one seller exists in the industry. To justify such an assumption, though, a few others must also hold.

First, there must be no substitutes for the products. If there were, the seller would not have full control over market conditions since the buyer would have alternatives. In monopoly, the seller constitutes the entire industry; the firm's demand and cost curves are identical with those of the industry.

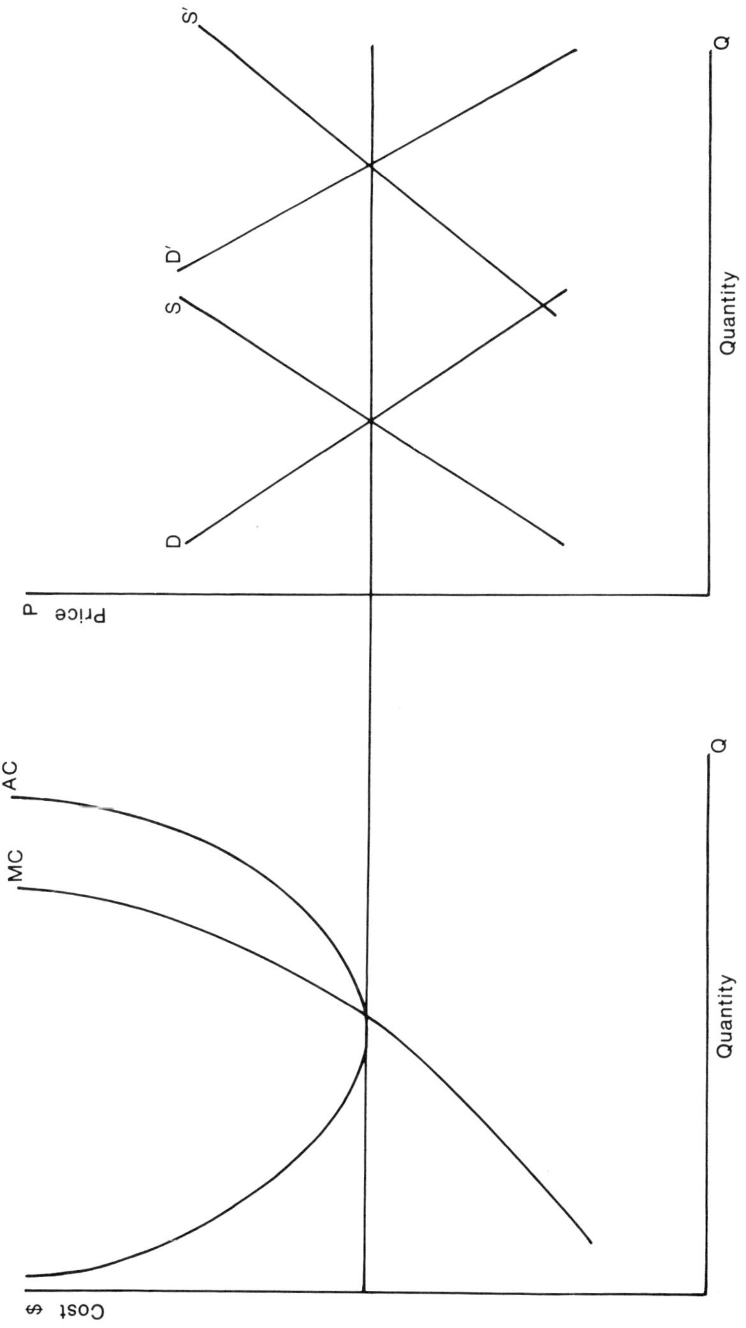

FIG. 12.7. A PERFECTLY COMPETITIVE INDUSTRY WHICH EXPERIENCES UNCHANGING COSTS OF INPUTS

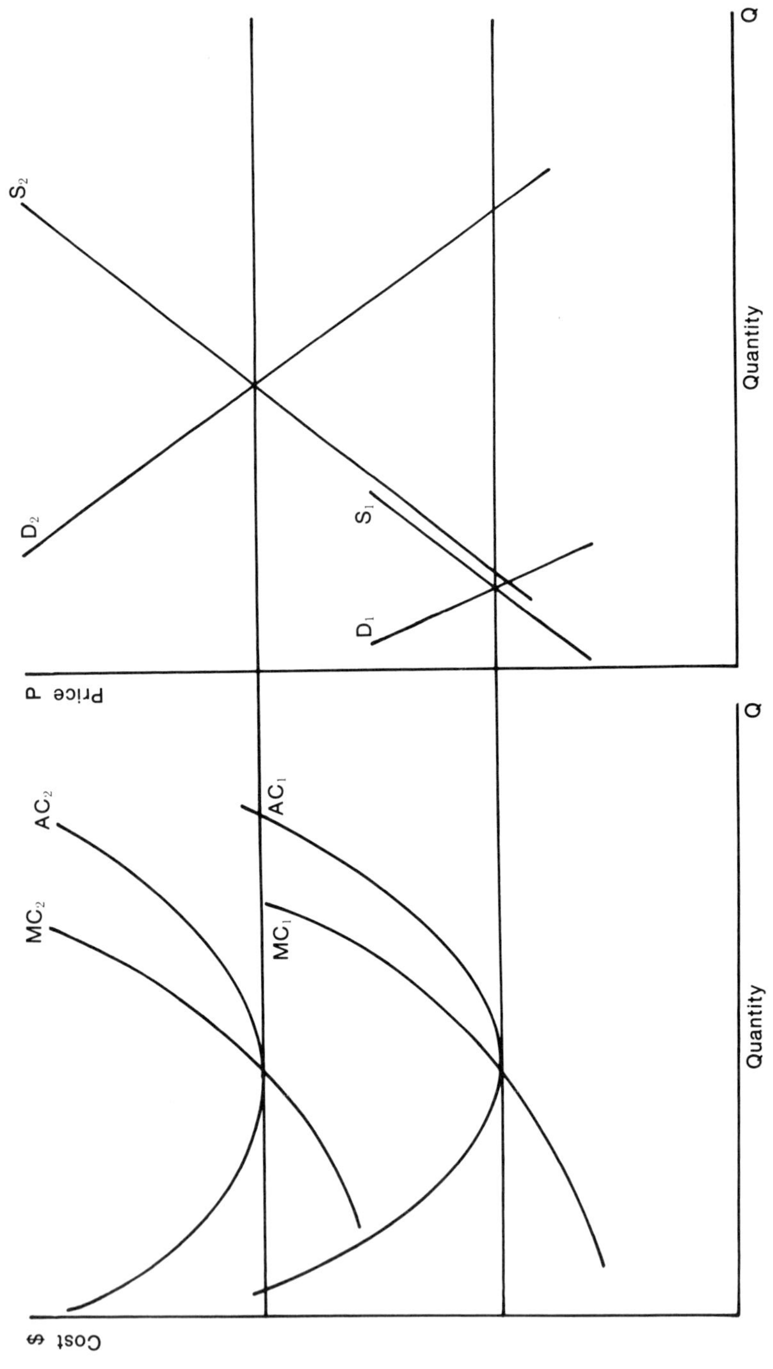

FIG. 12.8. A PERFECTLY COMPETITIVE INDUSTRY WHICH EXPERIENCES INCREASED COSTS WITH INCREASED OUTPUT

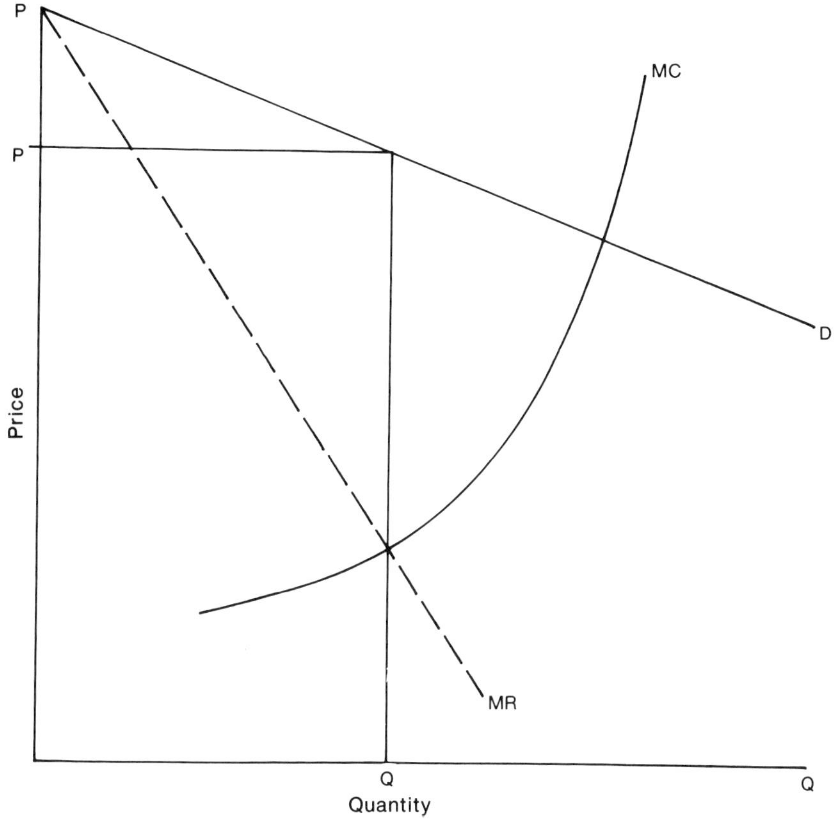

FIG. 12.9. PRICE AND OUTPUT DETERMINATION FOR A MONOPOLIST

Second, in order to maintain this state of affairs, other firms must not be able to enter the industry. Impassible barriers to entry must exist, to protect the monopolist's position. While present government regulations prevent the erection or maintenance of these barriers to entry in most private industries, it is the no-substitutes assumption which truly makes monopoly an ideal type rather than an extreme type. In practice, no products exist for which there is not some kind of substitute available. Close substitutes are not necessary for a buyer to have a choice and it is the element of buyer choice which distinguishes monopoly. Also, though a monopoly may be able to bar production of its own product by another firm, through patents, government franchises, extremely large economies of scale, or control over raw material supplies, it is extremely difficult for it to bar production of a substitute. Therefore, the no-substitute assumption is crucial.

Price and Output Determination

The monopolist is dependent on market demand as well as cost in determining profit-maximizing price and output. (While the perfectly competitive firm only adjusts output, the monopolist can adjust both price and output.) The monopolist also operates where marginal cost equals marginal revenue. However, marginal revenue no longer equals price. As the market demand curve is the monopolist's demand curve, the monopolist no longer faces the horizontal demand curve of the perfect competitor. Now, as quantity to be sold increases, price per unit must decrease. As the price per unit applies to all units sold, not just the extra unit, the increase in revenue from an extra unit sold is less than the price paid for that unit (Fig. 12.9). The quantity produced is $\bar{Q}$, and price

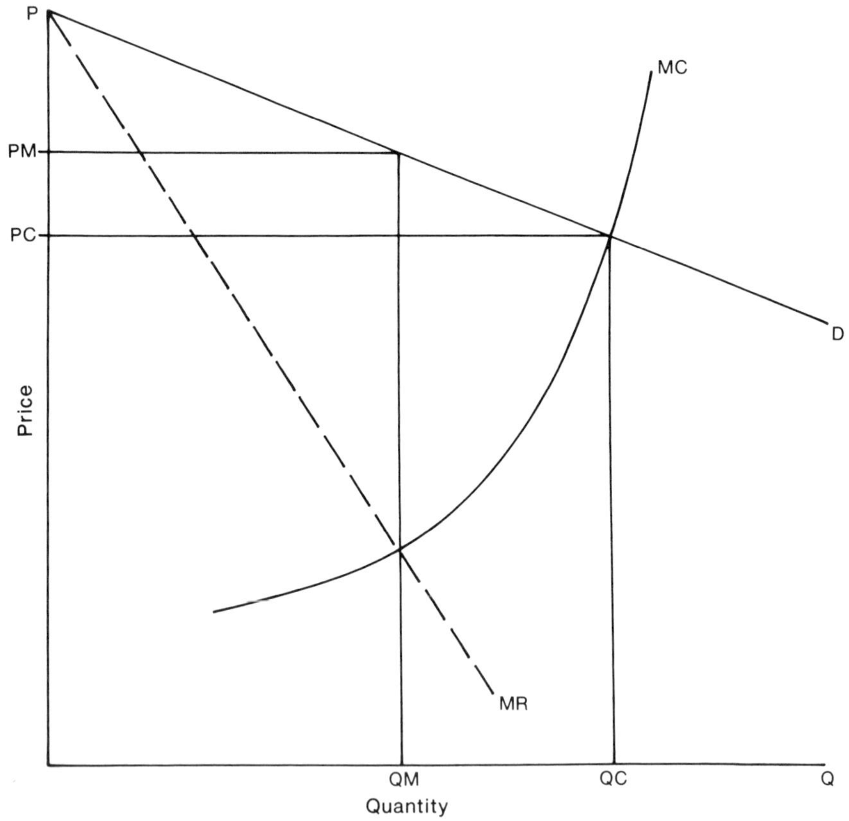

FIG. 12.10. MONOPOLISTIC OUTPUT (QM) COMPARED WITH SOCIALLY OPTIMAL (COMPETITIVE) OUTPUT (QC)

charged is $\bar{P}$ which exceeds both marginal revenue and marginal cost. No supply curve can be obtained for a monopolist, since price is an endogenous (determined by the decision) rather than an exogenous (predetermined) variable.

It is the excess of P over MC that occasions much of the criticism of monopoly from a social welfare standpoint. Price (indicated by the demand curve) reflects society's valuation of an extra unit of output. MC reflects the cost to society of producing it. Since marginal value to society is greater than marginal cost to society, society would benefit by production of more of the good (to the point where D = MC) which would then be sold at a lower price per unit (Fig. 12.10). From society's viewpoint, monopoly results in higher prices and lower output than desired, and thus a less than optimal allocation of society's resources.

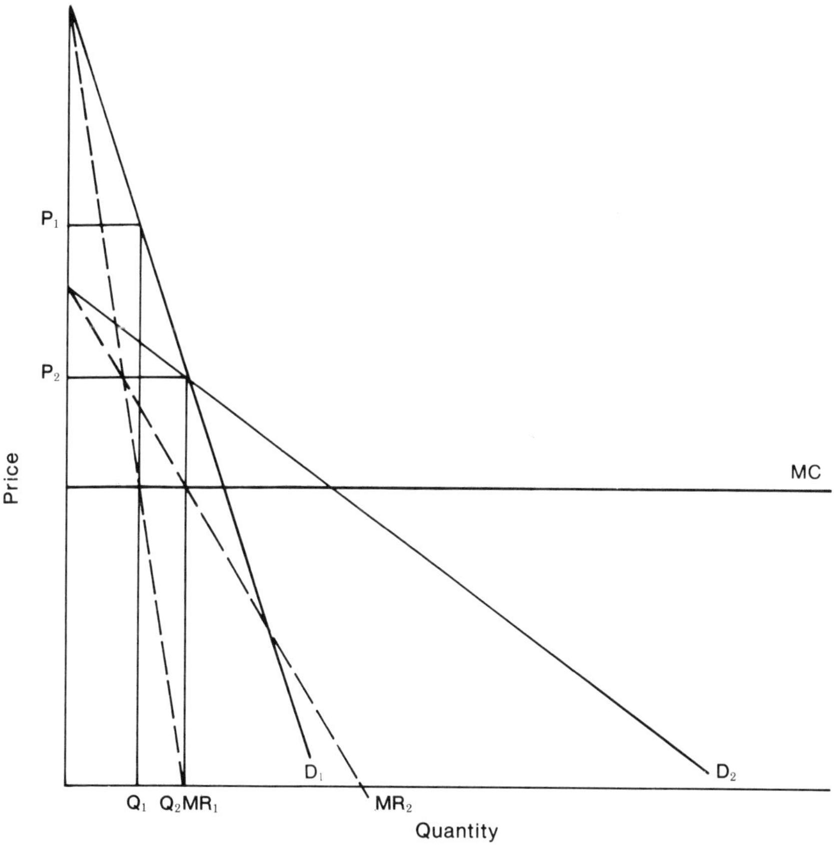

FIG. 12.11. PRICE DISCRIMINATION BETWEEN TWO SUBMARKETS

The long-run monopoly situation is basically no different from that of the short run. The monopolist operates where long-run marginal cost equals marginal revenue. There is no tendency toward zero profits, since there is no competition. However, a monopolist will not earn a pure loss in the long run, since more profitable alternatives would be available and the monopolist would exit this industry and enter another.

As the monopolist has full control over the market, several options in strategy are available which would not be available to the perfect competitor. A major one is price discrimination. This can profitably be practiced if:

(1) the monopolist can completely segregate two or more submarkets. Complete segregation is necessary to prevent arbitrage, or buying in one submarket for resale in the next, which could defeat the purpose of discrimination.
(2) Also, the price elasticities of demand must be different for the different submarkets. Otherwise, as will be seen, the same price would be charged in each submarket, and there would be no point in segregating them.

As before, marginal cost equals marginal revenue. Here, however, marginal revenue *in each submarket* equals marginal cost (Fig. 12.11). If the elasticities of demand are different, this will result in different prices in each submarket. The monopolist acts to equalize the marginal revenue of the last unit sold in each market, and allocates quantity (and charges prices) accordingly.

The more inelastic submarket will be charged the higher price. If there are two submarkets, e = elasticity of demand and $MR = P\left(1 - \frac{1}{e}\right)$ (from Chapter 8), if $MR_1 = MR_2$ then $P_1\left(1 - \frac{1}{e_1}\right) = P_2\left(1 - \frac{1}{e_2}\right)$. If $e_1 < e_2$, then $P_1 > P_2$ for the equality to hold. Thus, a submarket which is more dependent on a product will be forced to pay more for it than would a less dependent submarket. In the absence of substitutes, this must mean that the product is a less essential part of the life-style in one submarket than in another.

Monopoly may exist on the buyer's side of the market as well as the seller's. (In the buyer's case, it is called monopsony.) Corresponding to the marginal revenue curve for the demand curve is the marginal expense of selling curve for the supply curve. The reasoning is exactly analogous. Assuming that for this case a perfectly competitive selling market exists, the supply curve is the marginal cost curve. While a monopolistic seller would operate where a marginal revenue curve intersected a marginal cost curve and read the price off the demand curve, here a marginal

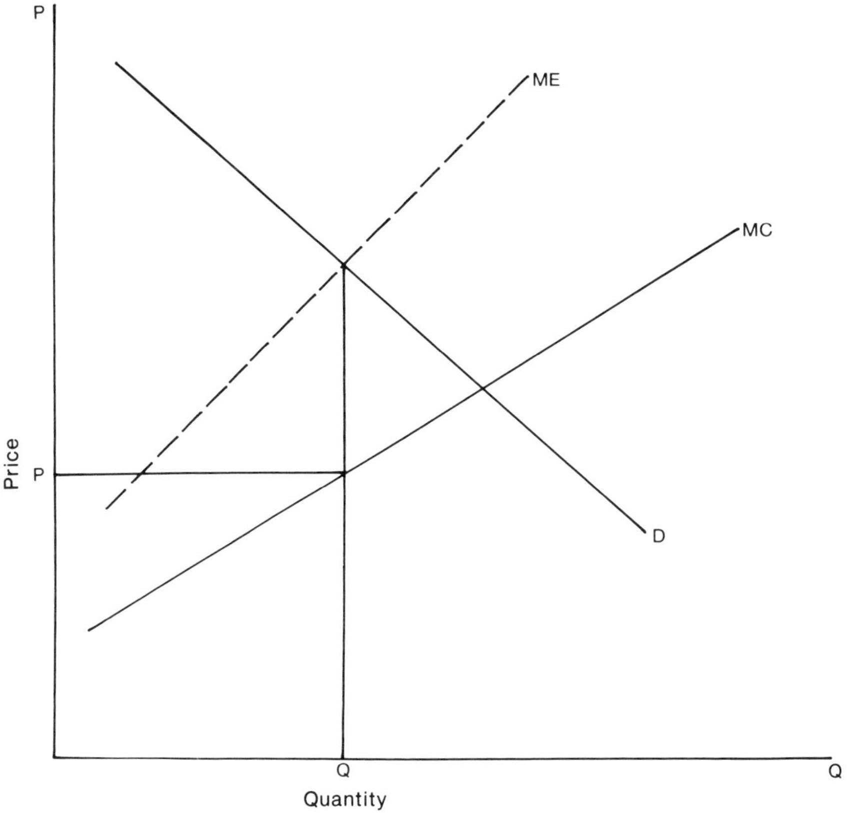

FIG. 12.12. PRICE AND OUTPUT DETERMINATION FOR A MONOPSONIST

expense of selling curve intersects a demand curve and the price is read off the supply curve (Fig. 12.12).

If bilateral monopoly exists, with a monopoly meeting a monopsony, the result is indeterminant (Fig. 12.13). Where in this region the sale will occur depends on the relative bargaining skill and power of the two parties. This will be more fully explored in the next chapter.

CHAPTER 12: REVIEW QUESTIONS

(1) Why has the bulk of analytic literature on price-output determination traditionally been devoted to the case of perfect competition?

(2) What do economists imply about (1) the amount of "abnormal profit," (2) the amount of "normal profit," and (3) the degree of product and factor market competition when they conclude: In the

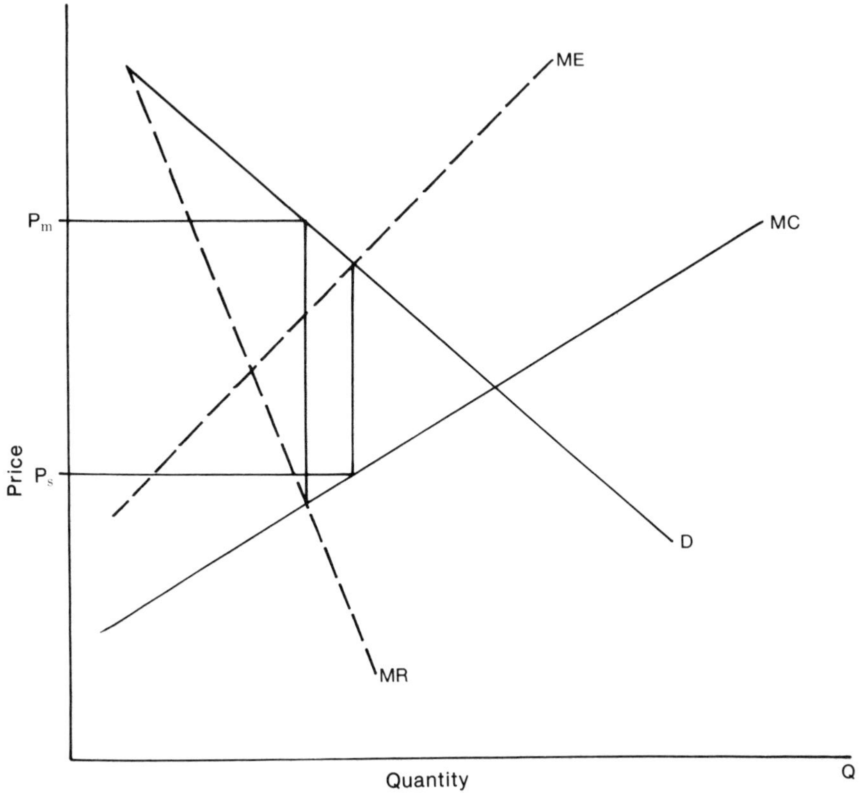

FIG. 12.13. BARGAINING REGION UNDER BILATERAL MONOPOLY

long run the firm will achieve equilibrium by producing an output where average total cost equals average total revenue?

(3) Explain why in the competitive equilibrium of the firm the marginal value product is equal to the factor price and indicate the implications for marginal cost and price.

(4) Show how price regulation of a monopoly, if accurately done, can bring about price and output determination comparable to that of a perfectly competitive firm.

(5) It is generally considered socially desirable to regulate monopolies. This can be done through taxation and/or price regulation. Discuss and illustrate the effect of

(a) an *ad valorem* tax,
(b) a percentage of profits tax, and
(c) a lump sum tax on pricing and output decisions.

Can these taxes or any part of them be shifted to the consumer?

(6) Explain (use graphs) how a firm may increase profits through price discrimination. When is such discrimination possible?

(7) A two-price plan to reduce the surplus and balance the supply and demand for dairy products is proposed. The plan would fix individual producer quotas which, aggregated, are equal to demands for Class I (bottled products). A relatively favorable price would be established for this quota. All other milk would sell at competitive prices and/or at a price no greater than 60% of parity. Assuming the Class I market is less than unit elasticity, and that the manufacturing alternative products have elasticities greater than one: Analyze this proposal from the standpoint of

(1) economic theory involved
(2) its impact on individual producers of Class I and manufacturing milk
(3) the impacts on all producers taken collectively

Suppose a referendum vote was 45% opposed. From your knowledge of the issues give the situation and reasons that might cause different individuals to favor or oppose the plan. Present both sets of arguments.

(8) Discuss and illustrate the social cost imposed by shifting from perfect competition to monopoly. Discuss who bears the cost due to monopoly and how much, if any, is a net loss.

13

Market Structure: Major Dimensions

The locus of an industry between perfect competition and monopoly is traditionally indicated by some measure utilizing market shares of firms. The larger the market share of individual firms, the further from perfect competition and the closer to monopoly is the industry. As firms are generally unequal in size, averaging measures such as the four-firm or eight-firm concentration ratio have arisen. The four-firm ratio, the most widely used, represents the percentage of industry sales accounted for by the four largest firms in the industry. This percentage, and thus the ratio, rises as the industry approaches monopoly. (A four-firm ratio obviously could not adequately indicate a case of pure monopoly.) However, the concentration ratio is only one indicator of market structure. Other dimensions may prove at least as fruitful for analysis.

PRICE ELASTICITY OF DEMAND

Effects

A major dimension of market organization is the price elasticity of demand for the product. This affects market structure, conduct and performance. As indicated previously, greater incentive exists to raise price and lower quantity with a lower price elasticity of demand. In terms of market conduct, the argument has been made that a highly elastic demand promotes price cutting among competitors, both because of the resulting increased revenue and because such firms are less likely to recognize their interdependence and it might be harder to detect cheating on a price-fixing agreement. However, both these effects are influenced by market structure.

Johnson and Helmberger (1967) argue (on a theoretical level) that the impact of output change on price varies directly with market share, inversely with market elasticity, and not at all with the level of output change.[1] If the market share of a given firm equals one, a pure monopoly exists and the effect of output change on price is inversely related to elasticity. If the market share approaches zero, the market approaches perfect competition and changes in the firm's output have no effect on price. The effect of market share on price is inversely related to market elasticity[2]; if elasticity is high (as would occur as one approached perfect competition), changes in a firm's share of the market have little effect on price, but if elasticity is low, then market share can have much more impact on price. Further, the effect of changes in elasticity on price is very sensitive (in an inverse relationship) to the degree of elasticity, and is also directly related to market share.[3] With a higher elasticity, the effect of changes in it on price is less; this effect is also less the lower the market share (which tends to correlate inversely with elasticity, as the limiting cases of monopoly and perfect competition demonstrate). In addition, the effects of changes in output and market share on price decrease at an increasing rate with increases in the magnitude of the elasticity.[4] Johnson and Helmberger illustrate this with an example of a firm with a 20% share of the market where E = – 0.3, which would have the same effect on market price as a firm with a 60% market share where E = –1.2. They conclude that price elasticity of demand has a highly significant impact on market performance.

Product Differentiation

Given that price elasticity of demand greatly affects market pricing behavior and results, the next question concerns its determinants and relationship to market structure.

The major determinants of price elasticity for a given firm are the number and closeness of available substitutes. With few close substitutes for a product, the buyer is relatively dependent on a given seller and will not decrease quantity demanded in response to a price increase as much

---

[1] Let Q = industry output, X_i = output of ith firm, cX_i = change in firm i's output, $-E = \frac{dQ}{dP} \cdot \frac{P}{Q}$, S_i = market share of ith firm $= \frac{X_i}{Q}$, $K = \frac{dP}{P}$.

Then $dQ = cX_i$, $K = \frac{dP}{P} = -\frac{cS_i}{E}$, $\frac{\delta K}{\delta c} = \frac{-S_i}{E}$.

[2] $\frac{\delta K}{\delta S_i} = \frac{-c}{E}$.

[3] $\frac{\delta K}{\delta E} = \frac{cS_i}{E^2}$.

[4] $\frac{\delta^2 K}{\delta c \delta E} = \frac{S_i}{E^2}$; $\frac{\delta^2 K}{\delta S_i \delta E} = \frac{c}{E^2}$.

as he or she would if more alternatives were available. Thus, the mere number of sellers in an industry may affect the price elasticity facing each seller as well as the average location from the origin of a firm's demand curve.

The closeness of available substitutes refers to product differentiation. In general, an industry is defined as a group of firms whose products are close substitutes (not necessarily perfect substitutes) for each other, but poor substitutes for products of all firms outside this group. The closeness of substitutes should be measurable by the cross price elasticity of demand between the outputs, which should be relatively large within the industry but approach zero between industries.

Although physical sources of product differentiation exist, such as differences in product design and quality, much of it is a psychological effect. Sales promotion serves to promote perception of real or imagined product differences, especially of quality. Brand names and company reputations contribute to perception of quality differences, and in some cases of physical product differences (such as in the case of soft drink manufacturers). The service a seller offers in connection with a product, and the convenience of location of a seller, become part of the overall package a seller offers; thus, differences in these serve to differentiate products in the buyer's eyes even if the physical product is identical. These sources of product differentiation are reflected in the forms which nonprice competition may take.

The more highly differentiated a product is from others, the fewer close substitutes are perceived for it, and the more dependent a buyer with a preference for its particular characteristics is on that seller. The seller then develops a degree of monopoly power for that product. This monopoly power will increase as the degree of product differentiation increases. In the limit, it will approach pure monopoly where there are no substitutes and the firm's elasticity of demand will approach (from above) the market elasticity. In the other direction, as product differences fade and a given product has more close substitutes, monopoly power would decrease, approaching the limit of perfect competition and the firm's elasticity of demand would approach infinity. Price elasticity of demand, along with the related concepts of market power, number of sellers and product differentiation, becomes a major dimension of the continuum along which one measures market structure.

As sales promotion is a major source of product differentiation, selling costs should also vary with market structure. However, these will not form a linear relationship, since for neither perfect competition nor for monopoly should selling expenses increase the market share of the individual firm. Therefore, selling expenses should be greatest for firms in the intermediate range. At present, one cannot predict *a priori* the exact relationship; empirical work suggests that selling expenses are greatest in industries with only a few sellers and where price competition is limited.

Selling expenses add to the costs of a firm and their presence may change the optimal level of output for a firm. If, for example, a competitive industry adds selling expenses to its costs (assume for simplicity that in equilibrium it would in both cases produce the quantity corresponding to the minimum total average cost curve) and selling costs carried economies of scale of their own (as they frequently do), the firm would find it more efficient to operate at the larger output Q^1 (Fig. 13.1). If the market has not also expanded, this creates a tendency toward fewer firms and larger market shares per firm. (It can also be seen from the preceding that the greater the economies of scale of production, the greater the tendency toward monopoly. This may constitute still another dimension of market analysis.)

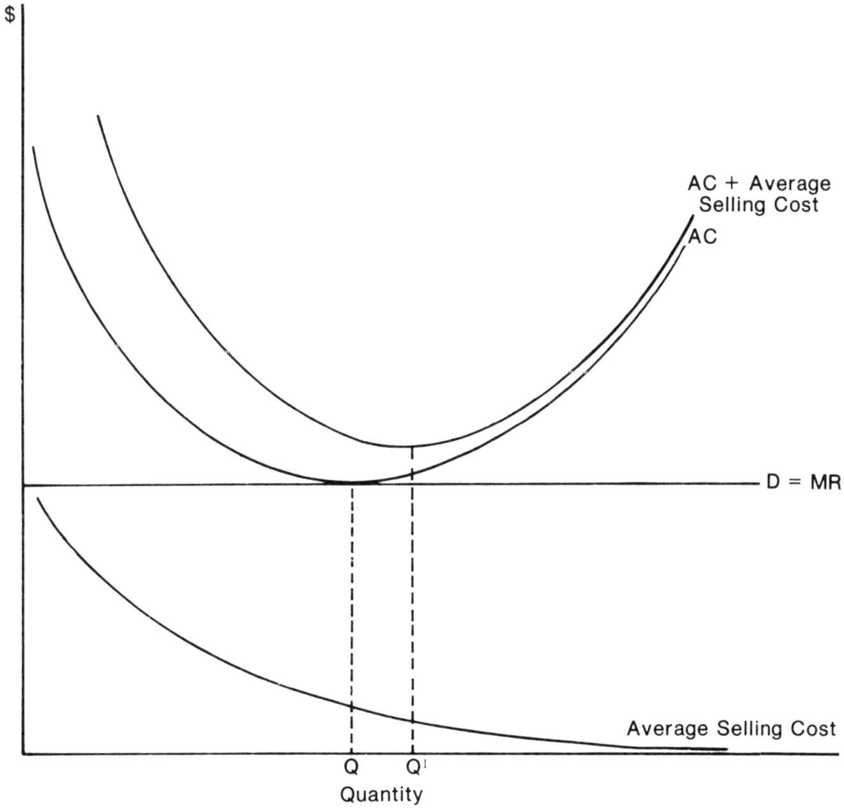

FIG. 13.1. EFFECT OF ECONOMIES OF SCALE OF SELLING COSTS ON A COMPETITIVE FIRM'S OUTPUT

OTHER DIMENSIONS

The quality of competition also changes as market structure changes. Except for a discontinuity when one reaches pure monopoly (where there is no competition), competition becomes increasingly personal as one's rivals become fewer, better known and more interdependent. There is also a tendency toward nonprice rather than price competition as interdependence increases, as the mechanics of second-guessing one's competitor's responses to price changes become complicated.

Other relevant dimensions include ease of entry and exit into and from the industry, and the amount of information market participants possess. Ease of entry and exit progressively decreases as one moves from perfect competition to monopoly, reaching the condition of being completely barred in pure monopoly. The amount of information buyers and sellers possess also declines with the movement toward monopoly. This absence of information reveals itself in the presence of industrial espionage undertaken to obtain it.

MARKET POWER

A major theme running through this discussion of dimensions of market analysis has been dependency and (consequent) power. (Even economies of production carry power connotations, since the larger firms which result will generally carry more market power.) One can turn to exchange theory, in both economics and social psychology, as a means of analysis of relative strength in the market. Buyers trade money for goods and sellers exchange goods for money. The prices, or terms of trade, are determined in the process. Economic exchange theory sets up the framework and indicates solutions for special cases (such as those corresponding to pure monopoly and perfect competition) and social psychological research helps fill the gap between these special cases.

Exchange Theory

The economic theory of exchange depends upon the notions of the indifference curve and utility maximization. Indifference curves and their assumptions have been described in Chapter 6. For present purposes, the total stock of commodities between traders is assumed fixed, so they cannot trade in other markets or alter production. Assume a two-person trading situation; each person has an indifference map as in Chapter 6, and their maps may be superimposed on each other, with one person's rotated 180° (Fig. 13.2). The total stock available here is b° of good b plus a° of good a; in the initial allocation each person may bring part of the total, as for person 1, $b^1 + a^1$; for person 2, $b^2 + a^2$; $b^1 + b^2 = b^\circ$; $a^1 + a^2 = a^\circ$.

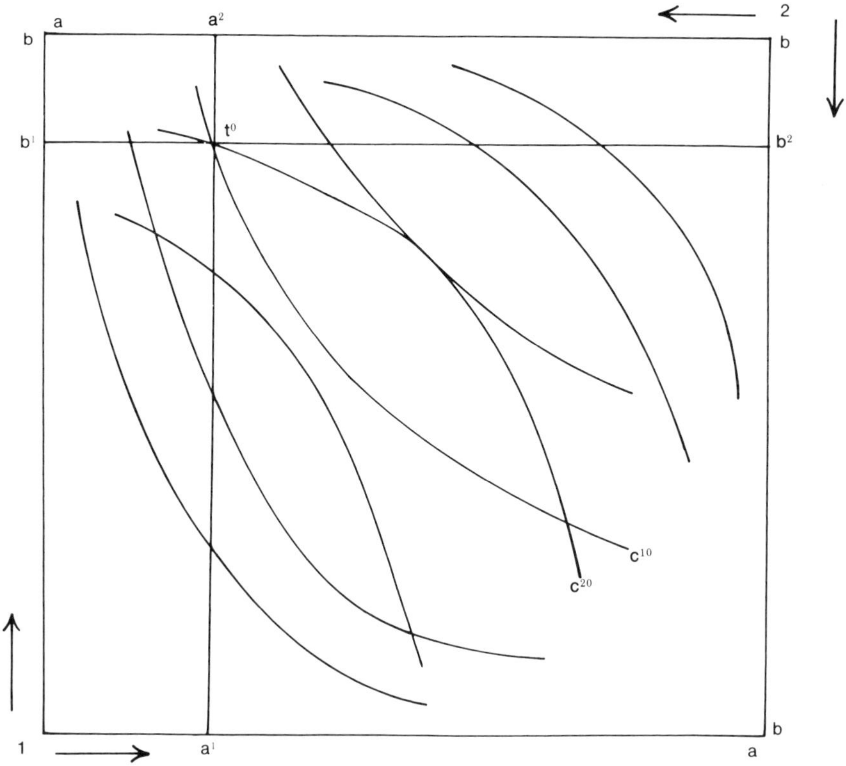

FIG. 13.2. ROTATION AND SUPERIMPOSITION OF PERSON 2'S INDIFFERENCE MAP ONTO PERSON 1'S INDIFFERENCE MAP; AT INITIAL ALLOCATION t°, PERSON 1 HAS a^1 AND b^1, WHILE PERSON 2 HAS a^2 AND b^2

Working from the initial allocation t° (Fig. 13.3) and the corresponding indifference curves $C^{1\circ}$ and $C^{2\circ}$ through that point, the set of points better than t° for person 1 is the area northeast of $C^{1\circ}$; for person 2, the area southwest of $C^{2\circ}$. The trading set determined by t° is the intersection of these areas; only here can trading take place (and only if t° is not the only point in the set), for otherwise one party will refuse to accept a lower indifference curve through trading. Where curves cut, there is always a nontrivial trading set; where they only touch (Fig. 13.4) there is not. If initial endowments change, the whole diagram will change.

The two parties will work toward an efficient trade. A trade t^1 is efficient if there is no trade which dominates it. A trade dominates another if at least one person is better off and no one is worse off by it. The dominating trade will be the preferred one. The effect is that if there is any nontrivial set determined by the proposed trade (i.e., if the

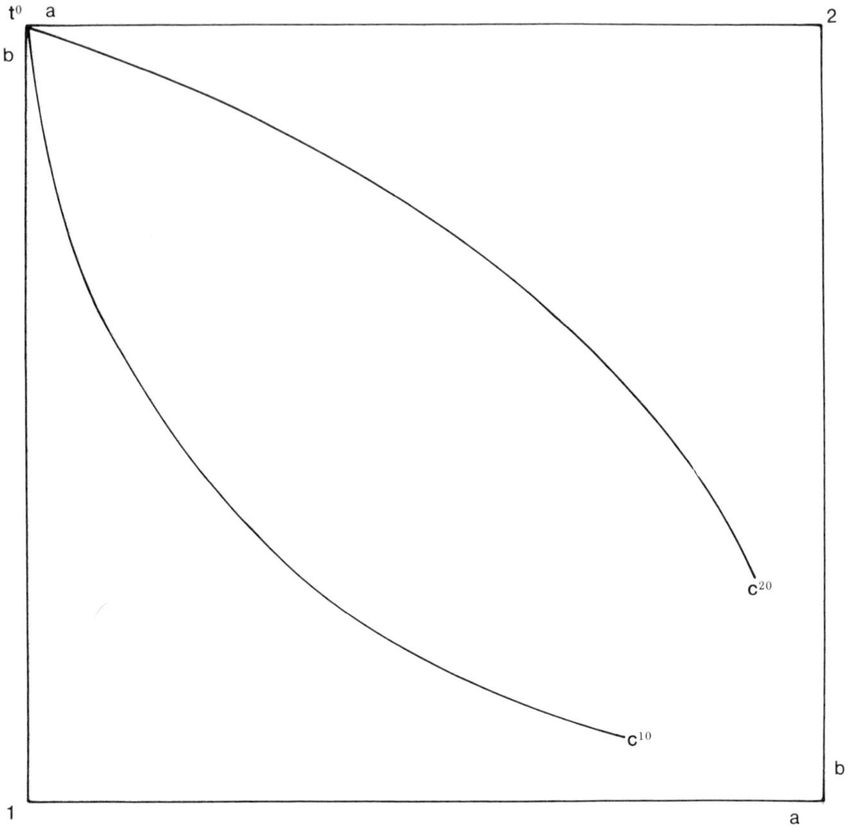

FIG. 13.3. PORTION OF FIG. 13.2.; RELEVANT TRADING SPACE DEFINED BY INITIAL ALLOCATION t° OF GOODS a AND b

indifference curves will intersect), the trade is not efficient, and if efficient there is no nontrivial set (i.e., the indifference curves will be tangent), so a necessary and sufficient condition for efficiency is that the trading set be composed of only one point where the indifference curves are tangent. This condition can be expressed as the equality of the MRS of person 1 and 2.

The efficiency locus is defined as the locus of such equalities, or tangencies of indifference curves (Fig. 13.5). The complete set is seldom used, as an initial allocation is essential and defines only a part of it (Fig. 13.6). No point on this efficiency locus dominates another, so thus far there is no basis for determining which point is chosen; further, a chosen point R can only be said to dominate the shaded area and no other. Given the initial allocation t°, this "contract curve" is the set of all efficient points

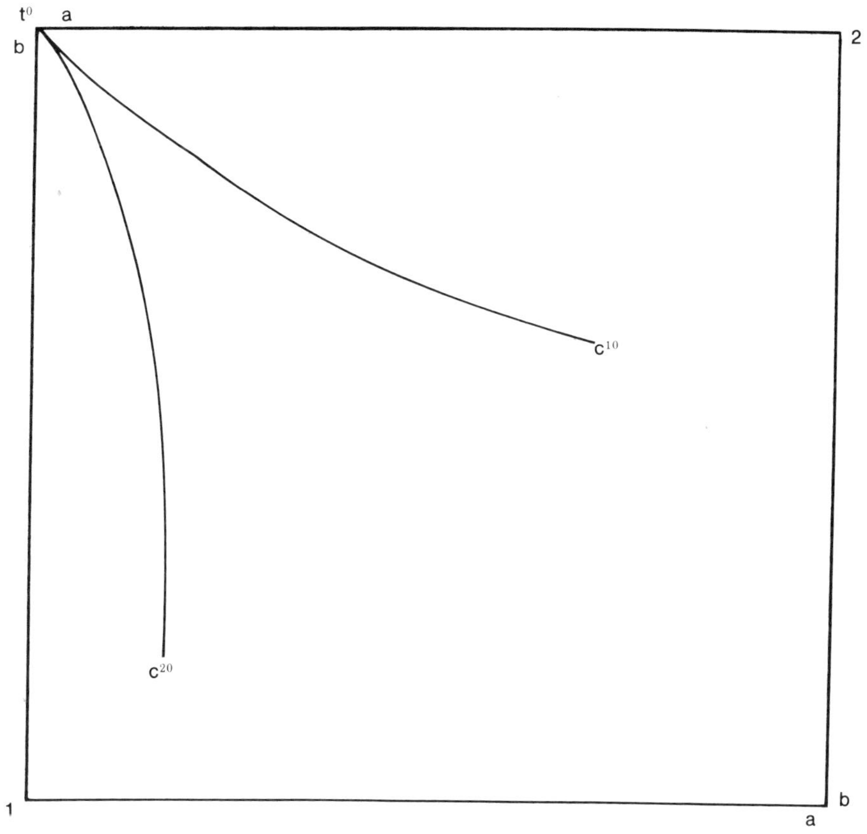

FIG. 13.4. NO POSSIBILITY OF FURTHER TRADE FROM t°

which are acceptable to both parties; it has been named the "conflict curve" because where on the curve (and to whose greater advantage) they end up depends on their relative bargaining strengths.

The preceding indeterminacy applies in a barter situation. If prices are introduced and the parties are price takers (that is, their actions have no effect on prices), it can disappear.

If prices are in existence (no matter how; assume for the moment arbitrarily), the price exchange ratio is presented by a straight line through t°, and indicates the attainable set for the person(s) affected (Fig. 13.7). Person 1, for example, is no longer bound by $C^{2°}$ but by this exchange ratio. This person will move to point A, where the "budget line" is tangent to an indifference curve, the highest possible (thus maximizing utility). The optimality condition is the equality of the slope of the

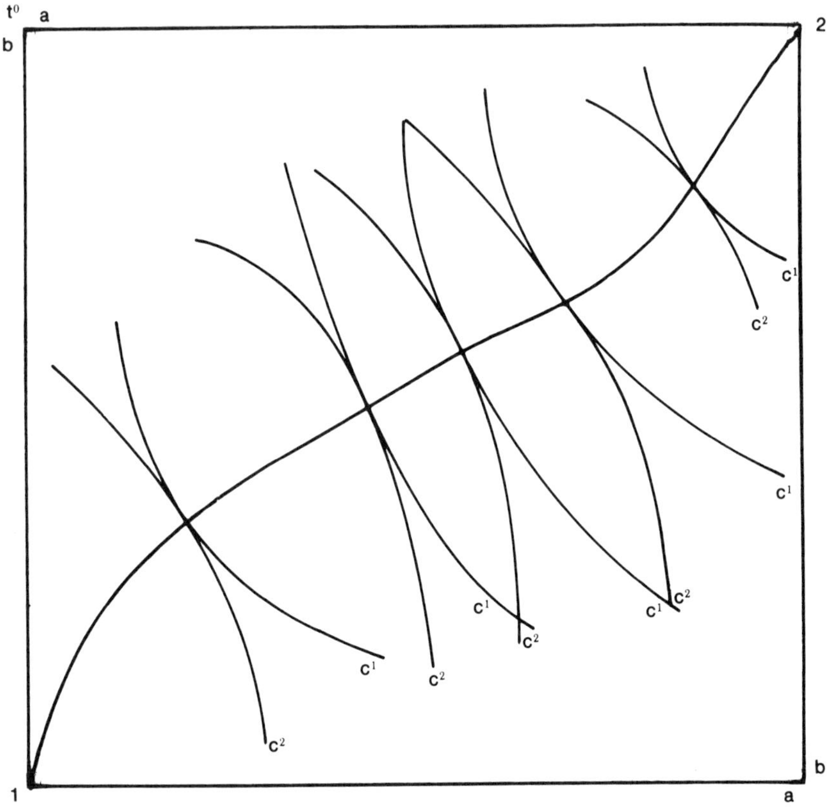

FIG. 13.5. THE COMPLETE "CONTRACT CURVE" FOR PERSONS 1 AND 2

exchange ratio line to the slope of the indifference curve at the optimal point A. The exchange ratio is thus equal to the person's MRS.

The same holds for person 2. Both parties will reach optimum positions where their MRSs are equal to each other and to the exchange ratio. This does not guarantee an efficient trade or even a trade, as a situation like Fig. 13.8 could arise where offers are incompatible.

It can be proved (Newman 1965) that there is a (at least one) point P* on the contract curve such that a line from P* to t° will also be the common tangent to the two indifference curves; or, given t°, there is an exchange ratio (an "efficient" exchange ratio) which will lead the parties from t° to an efficient trade P* (Fig. 13.9).

So, an efficient exchange ratio

(1) leads to optimal positions which constitute a feasible trade (no excess demand for either good exists), and
(2) leads to an efficient trade (on contract curve).

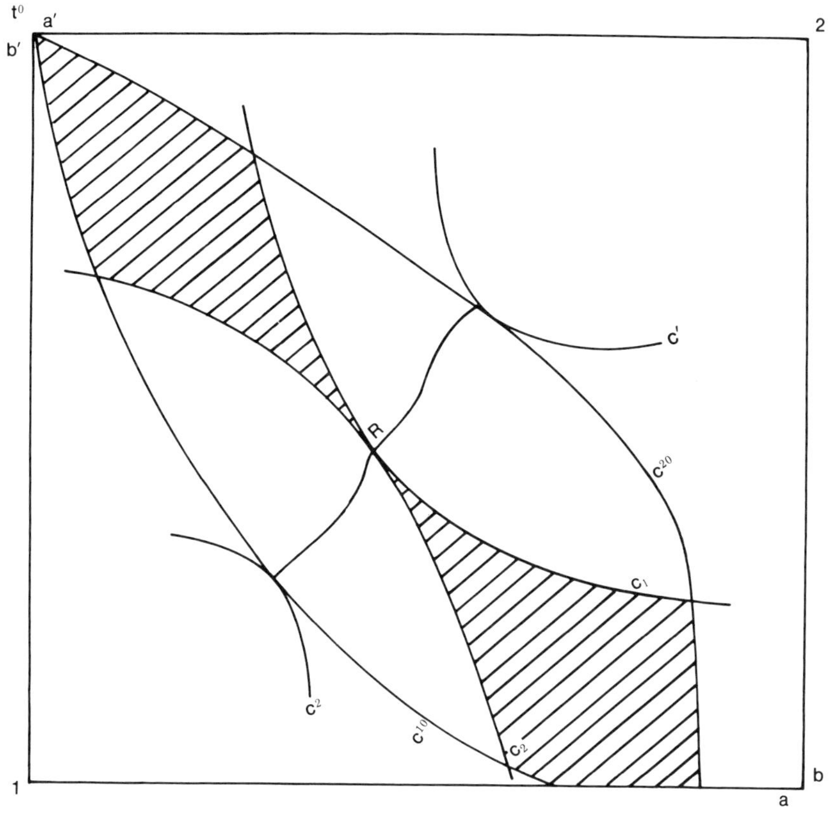

FIG. 13.6. CONTRACT CURVE FOR PERSONS 1 AND 2, GIVEN t°

If each individual's income is $(p_a a^1 + p_b b^1)$ and $(p_a a^2 + p_b b^2)$ and they adjust, given prices, to (a^{11}, b^{11}) and (a^{21}, b^{21}), then $p_a a^{11} + p_b b^{11} = p_a a^1 + p_b b^1$, $p_a a^{21} + p_b b^{21} = p_a a^2 + p_b b^2$; adding, $p_a(a^{11} + a^{21}) + p_b (b^{11} + b^{21}) = p_a(a^1 + a^2) + p_b(b^1 + b^2)$ (Walrasian Law). By definition of feasible trade, $a^{11} + a^{21} = a^1 + a^2 = a^0$ and similarly for good b, so this identity should hold for any set of prices. Criterion 1 of an efficient ratio means the prices and efficient allocation satisfy this equation; criterion 2 means the MRSs will equal each other and the exchange ratio. Equilibrium price ratios are "efficient" marginal rates of substitution (Newman 1965).

This situation can be redrawn slightly to show the adjustment mechanism and its convergence. Recontracting is assumed possible; none of the offers made out of equilibrium are binding on the participants. The traders thus experiment with different exchange ratios.

At $t^\circ t^1$ (Fig. 13.10), person 1 would be well off but person 2 would refuse to trade, since person 2 would be below the indifference curve of the

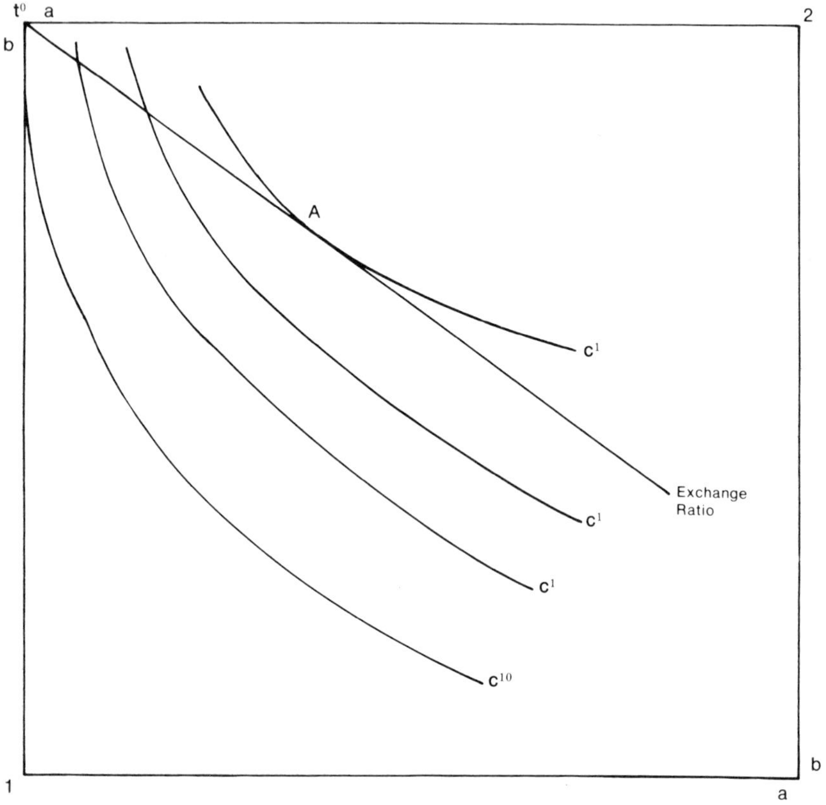

FIG. 13.7. PERSON 1'S CHOICE WHEN PRICES EXIST

initial allocation. At $t^\circ t^5$, the reverse holds, with person 1 refusing to trade. At $t^\circ t^2$ and $t^\circ t^4$ (and ratios in between, as these bound the contract curve), one or both could gain from trade, but the trade is not necessarily feasible (compare points E and C, A and F). Only at $t^\circ t^3$ is there a feasible efficient trade.

However, this diagram could also be expressed as two demand-and-supply curves, or "offer curves." At each price shown, each person will offer a certain amount and demand a certain amount, represented by the coordinates of the point of tangency of the exchange ratio line and highest indifference curve. The dotted offer curves result. Rotating the diagram, it appears as Fig. 13.11. The equilibrium is at the intersection of the offer curves. (There may be multiple equilibria, as the curves could cross more than once.) No exchange line can cut an offer curve more than once, because of the convexity of indifference curves which also implies the relative curvatures of the offer curves. The recontracting option and

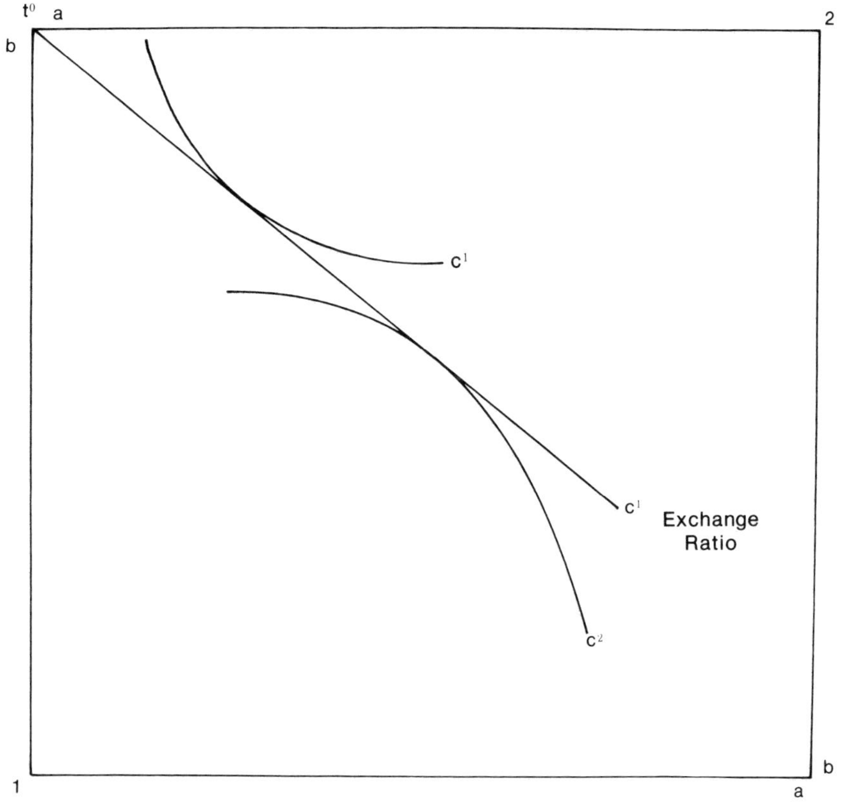

FIG. 13.8. A CASE WHERE PRICES EXIST YET NO TRADE IS POSSIBLE

the resulting exchange of information should lead the parties to the intersection of their offer curves, or to the equilibrium point (Newman 1965).

While the offer curve situation does yield a determinate solution, it requires that both parties be price takers, uninfluenced by power considerations. This situation is not very realistic, except possibly in agriculture and in international trade where offer curves are used extensively (Kindleberger 1968). There would be no bargaining, only a mutual exchange of information to determine the point.

If one of the parties has market power over the other (realizes his or her ability to influence the terms of trade), the indeterminacy of the barter situation is reduced but not eliminated. If the other party is a price taker, he or she will operate along his or her offer curve. The powerful party (1) will be able to choose the price so party 2's offer curve is tangent to the highest possible indifference curve of party 1 (so party 1 is maximizing

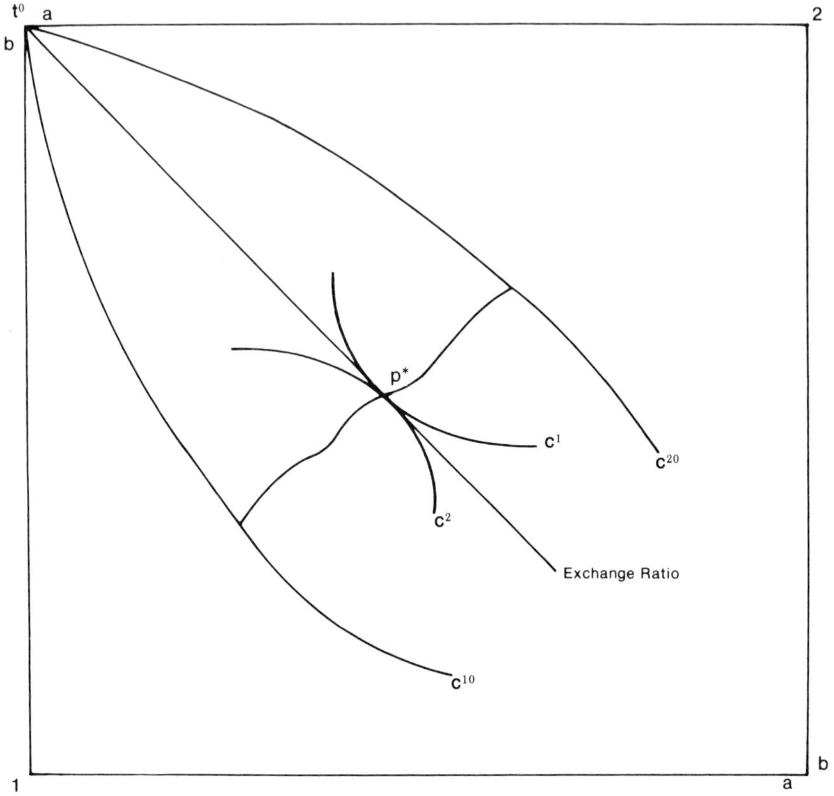

FIG. 13.9. DETERMINATION OF EFFICIENT TRADE, GIVEN PRICES

his/her utility subject to party 2's operations) (Baldwin 1948). (Fig. 13.12).

This point will not be on the contract curve; it is not efficient, so there is further incentive to trade and another indeterminate segment of the contract curve which, however, is smaller than the original indeterminate region. The parties then begin all over again in their preference structure and negotiations, unless recontracting is assumed continued. The person with the greater power is thus able to push the other toward his/her original C° and corresponding end of the contract curve. If party 2 never reacts to the power situation by abandoning his/her offer curve, the process converges to a point on the contract curve very much in favor of party 1, as possibly in a monopoly situation. The minute the assumption on party 2 is relaxed, however slightly, the whole equilibrium set becomes indeterminate again.

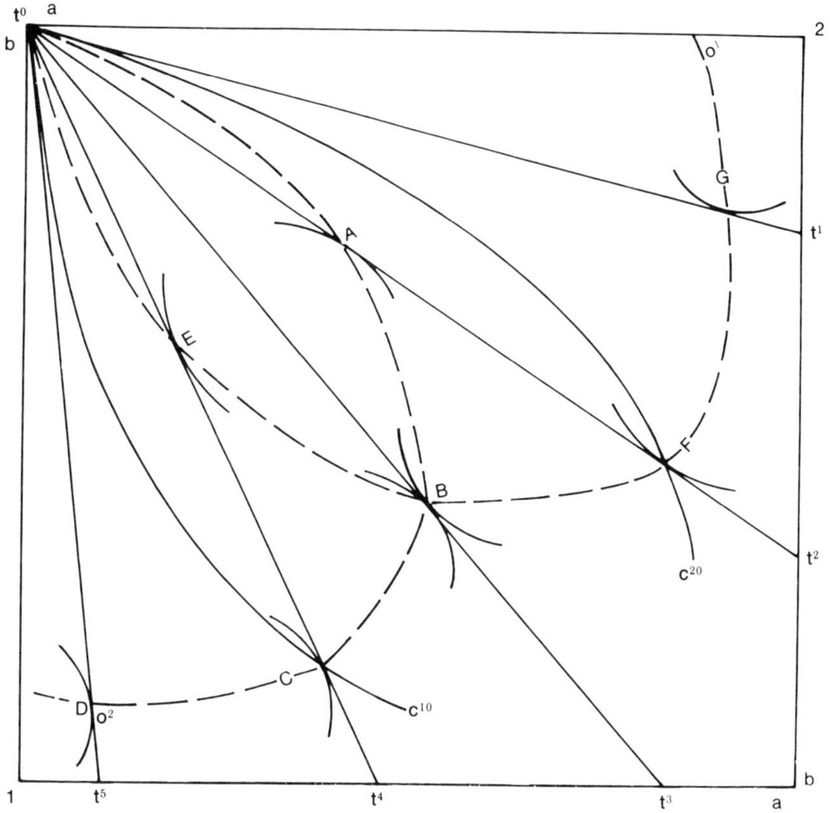

FIG. 13.10. OFFER CURVE; ILLUSTRATION OF WHY POINT B REPRESENTS THE ONLY FEASIBLE EFFICIENT TRADE

Another way market power can be shown is through the number of people aligned on each side. Whether all these people actually bargain or not is immaterial, as long as their existence is known to the bargainers. By the concept of the core solution, the contract curve shrinks as the number of bargainers is increased, because it will have to consist of the points which would still be undominated if coalitions formed (Newman 1965). In the limit, it would converge to a single point, the competitive equilibrium.

If (for an extreme example) there remained only one of party 1 and there were many of party 2, the contract curve would shrink but only on one end, as from XY to ZY in Fig. 13.13. This arrangement would clearly benefit party 1 at the expense of party 2 and resembles a monopoly situation, where party 1 has many fewer numbers and relatively more market power.

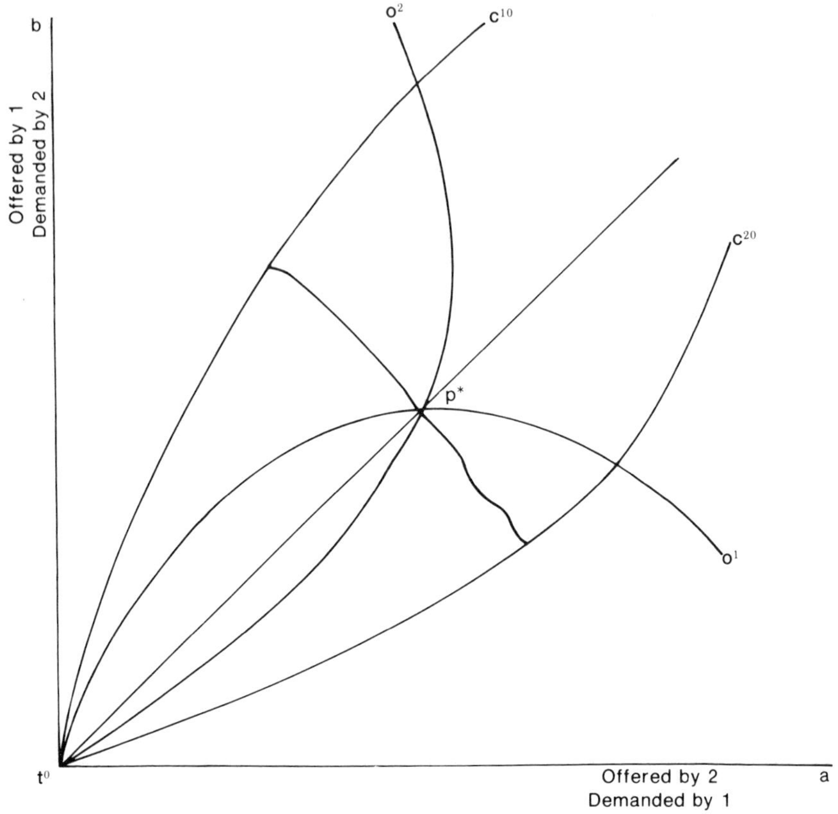

FIG. 13.11. OFFER CURVES OF PERSON 1 (O¹) AND PERSON 2 (O²) AND THE TRADING RESULT P*

Factors Influencing Bargaining Strength

So far it has been shown that there is a large region in which the conclusion of exchange is indeterminate, at least given the tools of economic theory. The relative power of the two parties, though, and the factors which affect it, can be further explored through a review of the social psychological literature.

Thibaut and Kelley (1959) listed possible strategies for a person A to increase his or her power over person B in the dyadic situation:

(1) develop better alternatives for A (such as more promising outlets for A's product), thus raising A's minimum acceptable satisfaction level from trading with any partner, so B's performance would keep the trade with B barely above it

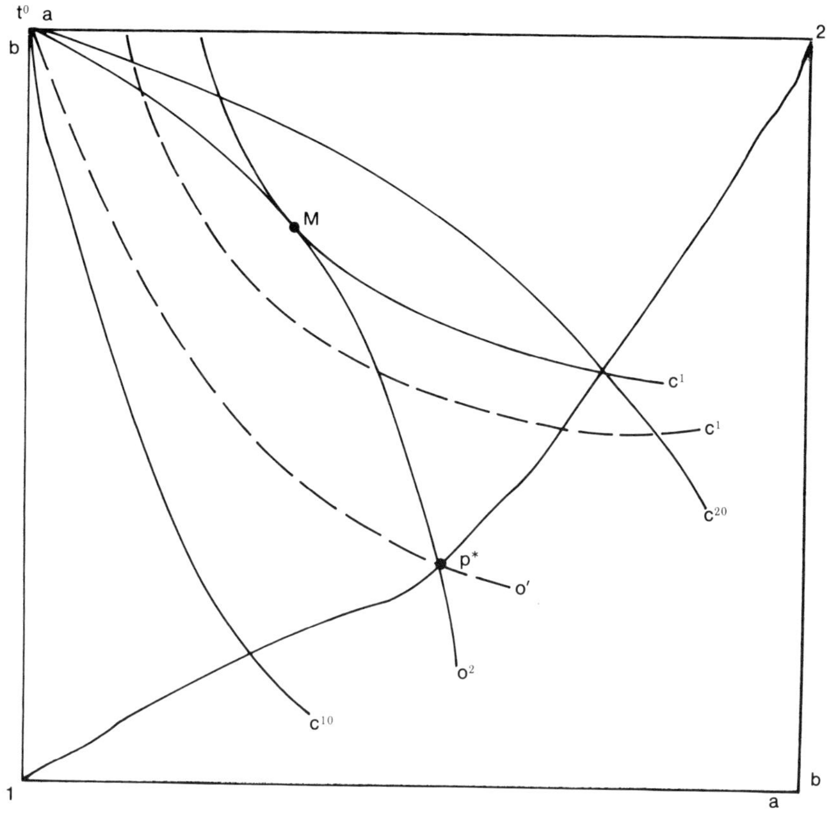

FIG. 13.12. PARTY 1 EXERCISING MARKET POWER OVER PARTY 2; RESULT IS AT M RATHER THAN P*

(2) reduce B's alternatives, through arrangements like tying contracts or illegal blacklisting, or vertical integration of a manufacturing firm A with raw material firms or retail outlets
(3) improve A's ability to reward B
(4) reduce B's skills
(5) build up the value of A's product
(6) devalue B's product (as in times of inflation)
(7) lengthen A's time perspective (defer rewards to future, lowering A's dependence on B)

These could be reflected in the situations described above.

Blau (1969) deals with four requirements of power: the person must

(1) remain indifferent to benefits others can offer in exchange for his or hers

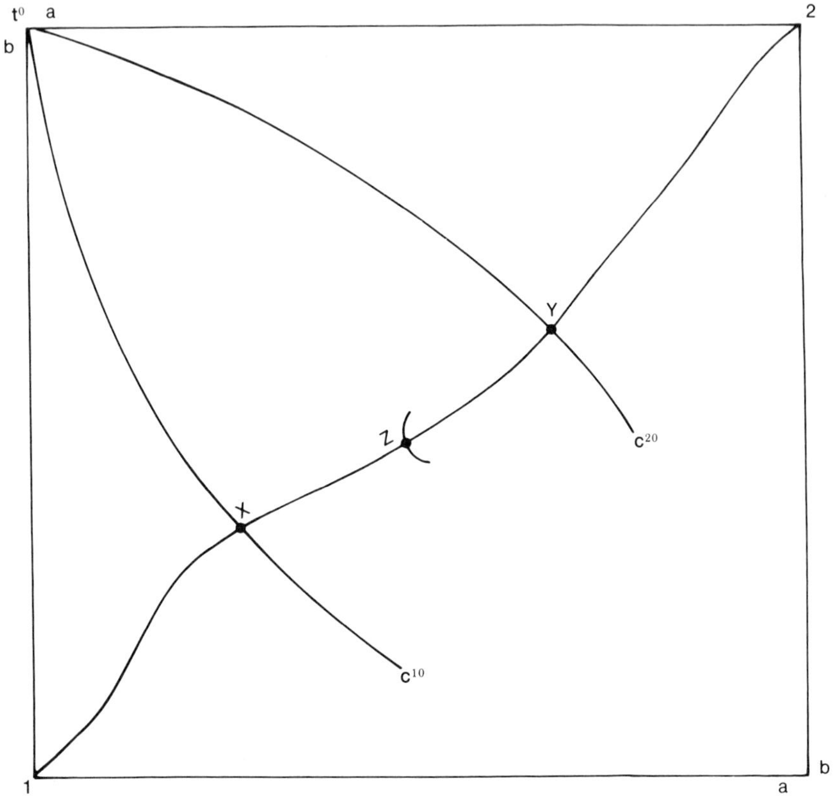

FIG. 13.13. SHRINKAGE OF CONTRACT CURVE FROM XY TO ZY AS THE NUMBERS IN PARTY 2 INCREASE

(2) bar access to alternative supplies of services person has
(3) prevent others from using coercive force (as in coalitions) to effect their demands
(4) maintain others' needs for person's services

These are similar to but not identical with Thibaut and Kelley's list.

A person is a tougher bargainer the less the person values the reward from the other. This can be reflected in the indifference curves in the exchange analysis presented above; in Fig. 13.14, the person values a good a more than in Fig. 13.15, as in Fig. 13.14 it requires more b to reconcile the person with a unit loss of a than it does in Fig. 13.15. This affects the shape of the initial indifference curves (Fig. 13.16), thus altering the bargaining region in person 1's favor when person 1 values the other's good less; in the case of offer curves it (through shifting

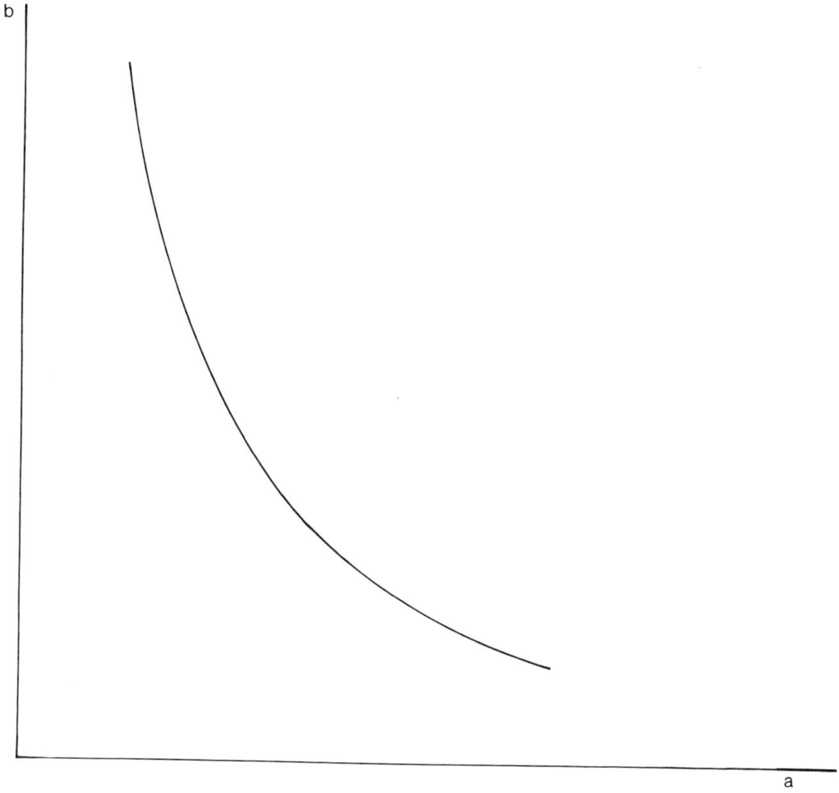

FIG. 13.14. PERSON VALUES GOOD a RATHER HIGHLY RELATIVE TO GOOD b

indifference curve) shifts the offer curve (Fig. 13.17), altering the terms of trade thus determined.

Information is a key element in bargaining (Bartos 1970). The negotiation and the give and take of offers and counteroffers in bargaining will not occur unless each participant is at least partially ignorant of the opponent's true interests; otherwise, they could reach an agreement immediately. Control of a situation through control of information is both more advantageous and more predominant than through actual control of the outcome (Kelley and Thibaut 1969). In other words, a monopolistic party 1 would operate along party 2's offer curve by leading party 2 to believe that party 1 was also a competitive price taker rather than by forcing the power structure and outcome on party 2.

The less information relevant to the task the bargainers possess, the tougher will be the bargaining because both sides will be uncertain as to what is reasonable to expect and toughness is the safer approach. It also

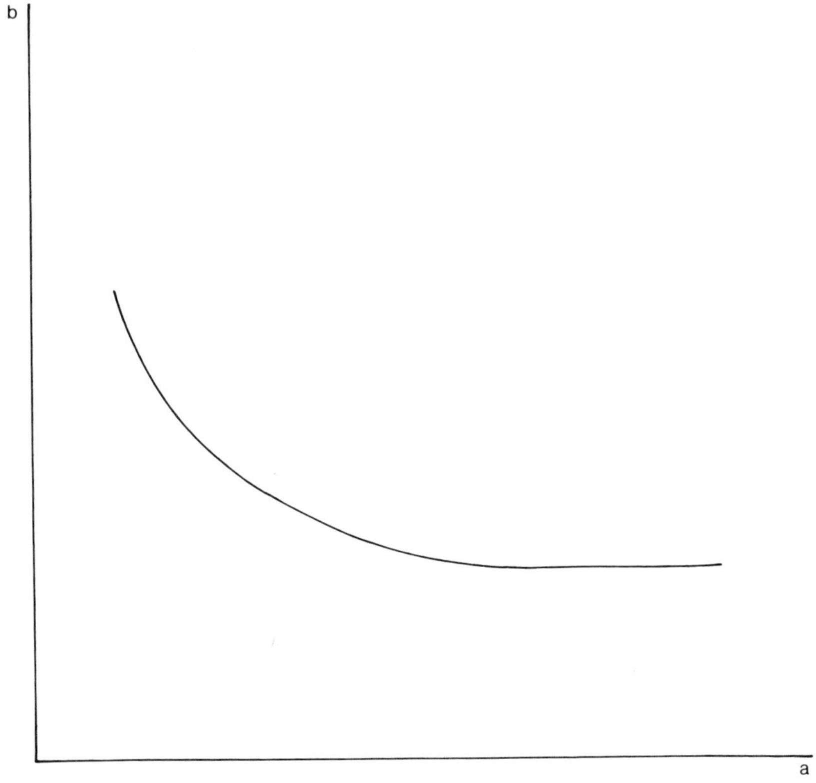

FIG. 13.15. PERSON VALUES GOOD a LESS HIGHLY RELATIVE TO GOOD b, COMPARED WITH FIG. 13.14

has the greater potential for gathering information about the opposing position (Kahn and Kohls 1972).

If one's perceptions of opponents are fairly accurate, insistence on more than one's fair share is more likely to break off negotiations than if perceptions are inaccurate. In general, the uninformed use their opponents' bids to set their own goals, while the informed use them to assess the reasonableness of their opponents' goals (Liebert *et al.* 1968). A buyer who doesn't know the market well may, when confronted with an exorbitant price, assume that it is the normal market price for the good. A buyer who has done extensive comparative shopping, on the other hand, may in the same situation conclude that this seller is a scoundrel and refuse to consider trading there.

Although bidding reflects the bargainer's goal, most bargainers initially bid above their goals because they realize a compromise will be needed

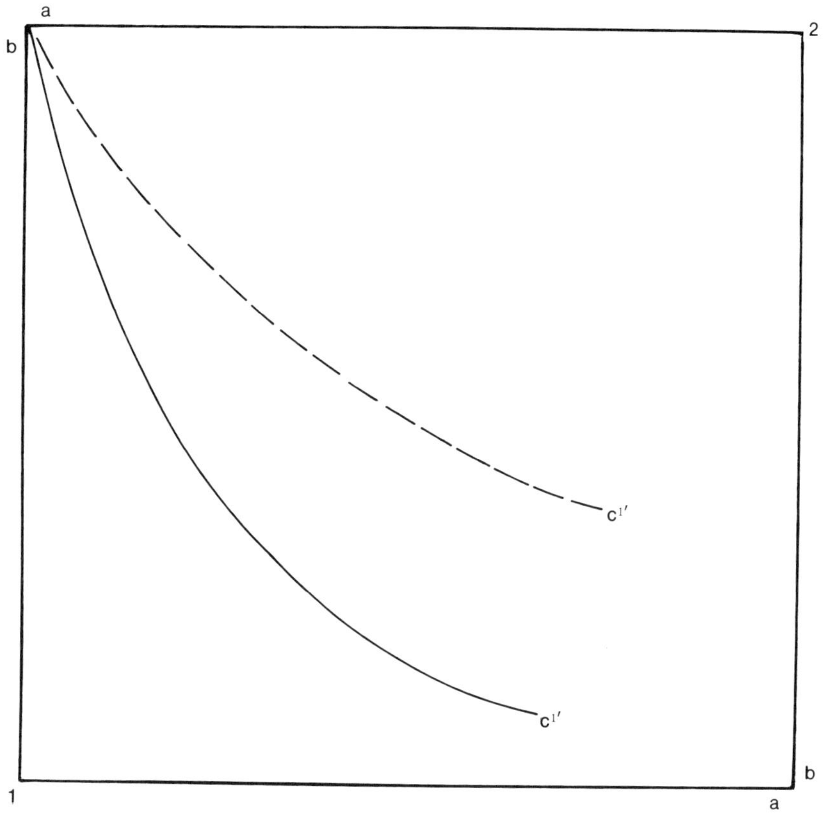

FIG. 13.16. EFFECT ON PERSON 1'S INITIAL ALLOCATION INDIFFERENCE CURVE OF PERSON 1'S LESS FAVORABLE VALUATION OF PERSON 2'S GOOD a

and they want to force a lowering of their opponent's goals (Kelley 1966). This creates several dilemmas: uncertainty on how high a level of outcome one should expect or insist on from the relationship, how much and when to trust the other's assertions, and how much and when to be open and honest oneself. Any decision can be wrong and disrupt the bargaining process. Open communication is a means by which goals can be reached, but expectations which are too high lead to communication which is not open, honest or trusted.

A prebargaining atmosphere which leads to consideration of the negotiations as collaborative problem solving in which neither side is committed to a unilateral position facilitates conflict resolution (Druckman 1968). Here, bilateral open discussion occurs before either side has a chance to develop a rationale for its own position. The personalities of

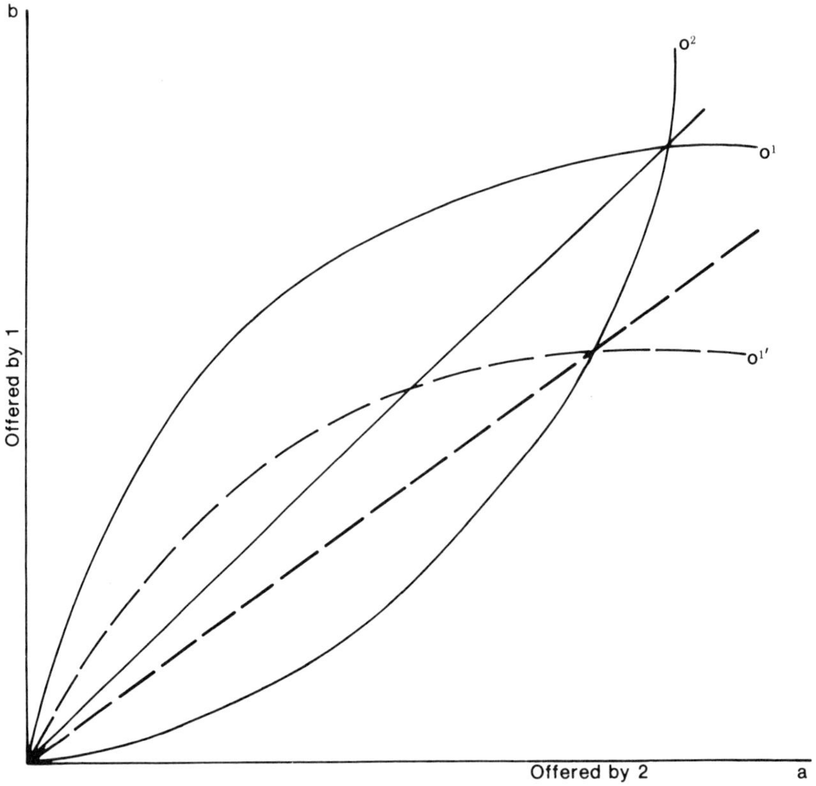

FIG. 13.17. EFFECT OF CHANGE IN PREFERENCE IN FIG. 13.16 ON PERSON 1'S OFFER CURVE AND RESULTING TERMS OF TRADE

the individuals also have an effect; specifically, the more dogmatic are the more resistant to compromise (Druckman 1967). A person will also be more resistant to making further concessions in bargaining as the person is pushed back toward the minimum requirement level which that person has for the trade. The higher the resistance, the longer time is required for further concessions to come forth and the more likely that person is to quit negotiations. The person with the lowest resistance will make the next concession (Kelley *et al.* 1967).

Another relevant form of information is the bargainer's perception of his or her own toughness (Kahn and Kohls 1972). Toughness apparently carries social prestige, and each bargainer thinks he or she is tough. In a group formed before negotiations, the bargainer finds that since others are also tough he or she must become tougher to keep this self-image. In this way, toughness is very similar to risk-taking; a group will often take a more risky position than will any individual in the group.

The two parties' attitudes toward risk-taking are important in determining the position of the agreement point on the contract curve (Harsanyi 1956). A bargaining party will reach better terms for him or herself the greater his/her risk preference and the smaller the risk preference of the opponent. The party that least wants to risk losing a sale will make the most concessions in order to complete it. Risk-taking thus appears to be closely related to toughness, and may be a significant part of toughness.

The key factor in determining bargaining strength, and as a result the position on the contract curve, thus seems to be relative dependence. The party more dependent on the other is at a disadvantage, while the less dependent party has more alternatives and has less need to bow to the wishes of any given opponent. Ways of decreasing dependence and increasing power have been given. Information is a major factor in the power situation and in the smoothness of negotiations. Exchange theory appears to be particularly relevant to buyer/seller negotiations and to cases of interdependence among few buyers and/or few sellers.

REFERENCES

BALDWIN, R. 1948. Equilibrium in international trade. Q. J. Econ. *62*, 748–762.

BARTOS, O.J. 1970. Determinants and consequences of toughness. *In* The Structure of Conflict. P. Swingle (Editor). Academic Press, New York.

BLAU, P.M. 1969. Exchange and Power in Social Life. John Wiley & Sons, New York.

DRUCKMAN, D. 1967. Dogmatism, prenegotiation experience, and simulated group representation as determinants of dyadic behavior in a bargaining situation. J. Pers. Soc. Psych. *6*, 279–290.

DRUCKMAN, D. 1968. Prenegotiation experience and dyadic conflict resolution in a bargaining situation. J. Exp. Soc. Psych. *4*, 367–383.

HARSANYI, J.C. 1956. Approaches to the bargaining problem before and after the theory of games: A critical discussion of Zeuthen's, Hicks', and Nash's theories. Econometrica *24*, 144–157.

KAHN, A.S. and KOHLS, J.W. 1972. Determinants of toughness in dyadic bargaining. Sociometry *35* (2) 305–315.

KELLEY, H.H. 1966. A classroom study of the dilemmas in interpersonal negotiations. *In* Strategic Interaction and Conflict. K. Archibald (Editor). Inst. Int. Stud., Berkeley.

KELLEY, H.H., BECKMAN, L.L. and FISHER, C.S. 1967. Negotiating the division of a reward under incomplete information. J. Exp. Soc. Psych. *3*, 361–398.

KELLEY, H.H. and THIBAUT, J.W. 1969 Group problem solving. *In* Handbook of Social Psychology. G. Lindzey and E. Aronson (Editors). Addison-Wesley, Reading, Mass.

JOHNSON, A.C. and HELMBERGER, P. 1967. Price elasticity of demand as an element of market structure. Am. Econ. Rev. *December*, 1218–1221.

KINDLEBERGER, C.P. 1968. International Economics. Richard D. Irwin, Homewood, Ill.

LIEBERT, R.M., SMITH, W.P., KEIFFER, M. and HILL, J.H. 1968. The effects of information and the magnitude of the initial offer on interpersonal negotiation. J. Exp. Soc. Psych., 431–441.

NEWMAN, P. 1965. The Theory of Exchange. Prentice-Hall, Englewood Cliffs, N.J.

THIBAUT, J.W. and KELLEY, H.H. 1959. The Social Psychology of Groups. John Wiley & Sons, New York.

CHAPTER 13: REVIEW QUESTIONS

(1) Economists in academic and business circles make frequent use of the term "competition," yet they are not always specific regarding its definition. Give an economic definition of competition, giving due regard:

(a) to the various dimensions of competition
(b) to the factors influencing competition in the long run and short run, and
(c) to the measures employed internally and externally (and their legitimacy) to the market to "regulate" or "control" competition

(2) Explain how each of the following factors may be important in explaining market structure and performance.

(a) Barriers to entry in the industry
(b) Product differentiation
(c) Vertical integration
(d) Economies of scale
(e) Demand growth of the industry

(3) Briefly explain the concepts of the contract curve and the Walrasian system.

(4) In the past, the farmer has been at a competitive disadvantage in the marketplace because of individual inability to influence prices received for the product. However, the recent growth and expansion of producer cooperative associations has changed this to some

extent. Cooperative organizations are beginning to exercise some power in bargaining for prices of agricultural products. Thus, the competitive situation in the marketplace has changed to that of bigness *vs* bigness. With this type of market structure, a bilateral oligopoly model becomes a relevant tool for explaining or illustrating the determination of price of agricultural products.

Using any example you wish:

(a) Discuss the adequacy of a bilateral monopoly model for explaining price determination for agricultural products.
(b) Show the limits of the price bargaining range.
(c) Discuss and/or illustrate price level determination within the price bargaining range.

(5) The wave of merger activity in the late 1960s raised concern among a number of economists regarding the long-run implications of the growth of the merging firms on firm size, industry concentration and ultimately market competition. Other economists, however, expressed the view that the trend in firm growth and size was a natural phenomenon of our economic system, and that the resultant firm organization was economically justified and desirable.

How would you go about determining whether or not this recent large growth by merger on the part of some firms was (or is) economically justified and whether or not economic forces would, of themselves, maintain "optimal" levels of market performance in the face of these large firms? Be specific regarding the type of analysis you would employ and the types of economic information you would need.

(6) "A major determinant of the efficiency in the marketing system is the degree of competition that exists. However, a continual trend toward increasing the size of firm through vertical integration and, therefore, reducing competition, has occurred over the last two decades. Clearly, the future efficiency of the markets for farm products and the welfare of farm people in the future will depend upon a much more aggressive enforcement of the Sherman Antitrust Act to restore competition in the industries which have experienced vertical integration."

Critically evaluate this statement showing clearly the reasons for either agreeing or disagreeing with conclusions or assumptions upon which they are based.

Paper Four: A Case Study of Food Retailing

Thomas N. Barclay

Food retailing is one of the most basic industries of our nation. United States consumers spend about one-fifth of their total consumption expenditures on food, and food stores account for about 17% of all U.S. retailing establishments (USDA 1972).[1] The price elasticity of demand for food retailing services has been estimated as 0.76, and the income elasticity as 0.70 (Waldorf 1966); this compares with a price elasticity of 0.26 and an income elasticity of 0.08 for food products per se.

In the last half century there have been some very significant changes in the structure of food retailing, which have brought about fewer retailing establishments and increased concentration and sales. This has been shown in the growth of the food chain, which is defined as a firm operating 11 or more stores (Hammond 1967). The sheer size of these firms leads to questions about their market power and performance. Some major characteristics of food distribution which need to be considered include: the concentration of firms, economies of scale, the barriers to entry faced by new firms, product differentiation, pricing policies and profit rates.

CONCENTRATION

Market concentration refers to the proportion of sales that is directly distributed by a particular firm or group of firms. In food retailing, concentration increased through the rise of food chains, but also with this rise single store independent numbers have correspondingly dropped. The chains operate a disproportionately large share of the big firms. About 50% of the supermarkets are owned by chains; however, 97% of the small stores are independent (Anon. 1978).

A four firm concentration ratio of Standard Metropolitan Statistical Area food retailers of 1954 and 1972 shows markets with concentration ratios above 60% increased from 5.1% in 1954 to 24.7% in 1972. Furthermore, those markets with ratios less than 40% dropped from 13.8% in 1954 to 10.9% in 1972. During this period the average four-firm concentration ratio increased 7.1 points to 52.1% in 1972 (Cotterill 1978). These statistics would indicate that a larger proportion of consumers is buying food from relatively fewer firms that have larger market shares.

The food retailing industry has been vertically integrated for many years. The degree of integration depends upon the particular product. The larger food chains have integrated to such an extent that in 1963, 11 of the largest chain manufacturers were included in the nation's top 200 food manufacturers with two of these in the top 50 (Natl. Comm. Food Mktg. 1966).

Concentration in food retailing is clearly evident. But why do firms strive to grow? What factors cause the increased concentration seen in today's food distribution? Some of the major factors that must be dealt with are mergers, economies of scale, product differentiation and entry barriers. These factors are not exclusive but represent some important cause and effect relationships.

A good part of the rise in national and local concentration in the retail food industry may be attributed to chain store mergers. Of the seven largest firms, those which have been active in mergers through the years have retained or improved their rank whereas those which have not merged as readily have declined in importance. Most acquired firms have gone through a rapid growth period prior to their merger, which leads to the conjecture that the larger acquiring firms were looking for aggressive companies with which to merge (Natl. Comm. Food Mktg. 1966).

Diversification through expansion into new geographical areas adds to market power. This expansion is achieved usually through funds made available by the larger chain stores. The firm often feels that bigness is something to be desired in order to keep its name before the consumer; this may explain the oversaturation of supermarkets that takes place when a chain opens a store close to competitors. However, it is much quicker and easier for a firm to merge than to build new stores and fight to enter a new market area. With a merger, there is a ready-made and usually successful operation to take over.

ECONOMIES OF SCALE

The size of a firm will directly affect a firm's degree of efficiency (Bain 1968). Economies of scale can more clearly be analyzed by separating stores and firms. At the store level, the Food Commission of 1966 found that increased volume has little effect on per unit cost. The efficiency of food stores was primarily influenced by the size of the store and utilization. Utilization, which is sales per ft^2 (0.09 m^2), was affected by store size; in other words, larger stores do not tend to have higher sales per ft^2 (0.09 m^2) (Natl. Comm. Food Mktg. 1966). It would seem simple, then, to raise the utilization rate and increase efficiency. But this type of action has certain limits which depend on how much inconvenience a consumer is willing to experience in order to realize lower per unit costs. For example, shoppers generally purchase during 2 to 3 days of the week and do so after 10 a.m. but before 8 p.m. (Natl. Comm. Food Mktg. 1966). A given store thus has considerable excess capacity, but within this time period its capacity must be such that consumers are not significantly inconvenienced.

The firm level efficiencies or economies of scale are not what one would expect. If one determines optimum size with respect to account purchases, marketing and administrative efficiency, there should be a negative relationship between firm size and the number of inputs per unit output. This relationship has not been reliably shown for the food retailing industry (Natl. Comm. Food. Mktg. 1966). Although the relationship does not hold for the industry, scale economies do hold for particular products. The products with significant economies relating to size are those that require longer time intervals for volume such as peanut butter and spices. For products such as milk and bread, the time-volume relationship is decreased so that smaller firms may be able to enjoy the same scale economies as larger firms (Natl. Comm. Food Mktg. 1966).

There are some advantages of absolute size, two of which are buying and advertising. It has been contended that large firms can organize buying teams and thus bypass middlemen. However, maintaining this team carries a cost which may not be low. The advertising of products has some significant economies of size that are taken advantage of by large firms. Large firms can and do use large, expensive newspaper ads which small independents can't afford. According to one estimate, food chains account for about 63% of newspaper advertising expenditures (Food Mktg. Inst. 1977).

PRODUCT DIFFERENTIATION

Another way retail firms protect and expand markets is through product differentiation of retailing services. Service differentiation is not easy in an industry where, except with respect to location, most products are standardized and where it is not difficult to maintain cleanliness and cheerfulness. Reliance must be placed on devices such as an unusual firm name or the provision of novel promotions not entirely connected with food products (games and stamps), but these moves can be easily countered. Alert management attempts to differentiate the products, for example, by improving the quality of meat and taking care of the vegetables and fruits properly.

Supermarkets have greatly expanded the number of nonfood items they carry; the typical supermarket today carries well over 1400 nonfood items that accounted for 6.3% of total sales in 1977 (Anon. 1978). Efforts to link discount supermarkets physically with discount department stores can be explained in part by a desire to differentiate the food retailing service, but this is a joint differentiation.

BARRIERS TO ENTRY

Barriers to entry for the food retailing industry could be defined as the economic advantages that a firm already established in a market has over a potential entrant. These advantages can be measured by the cost new firms must incur to enter the market. Construction costs have increased substantially over the years; this can be attributed to store size increases and inflation. The average total capital investment for a new store in 1976 was $997,000 (Food Mktg. Inst. 1977). This indicates the amount that is necessary to enter the industry with one store, aside from the promotion costs. The capital required in relative terms, however, is less than that for manufacturing (Natl. Comm. Food Mktg. 1966).

The barriers are there; they range from being known by consumers to store labels, and except where a merger is a tool they are almost impossible to overcome if one considers chain entry. For the local level, entry is fairly easy. The local store can contract with wholesalers and rent store space without major difficulties.

PRICING STRATEGY

The price margin in food retailing is the difference between what the retailer pays the wholesaler and what the consumer pays the retailer for the same items. Put more simply, it is the cost the consumer incurs for the retailing service. The retailer covers all his/her costs from the margins included in the price. A large part of these costs of providing the service are fixed and cannot be traced to any single product or even group of products.

The food retailer is a multiproduct firm; the shopper's demand is seldom for only one type of retailing service. A once-a-week shopper may purchase a $20 or $25 composite. The margin may vary widely from item to item without discouraging purchases (Food Mktg. Inst. 1977). In the first place, the shopper is unlikely to substitute one commodity for another in order to reduce his/her expenditures on retailing services. There is little cross elasticity of demand between beer and ground beef.

Second, once in the store, the customer is unlikely to consider immediately shifting part of his/her purchases to a different retailer unless he/she becomes aware of a wide difference in the selling price of an important product. This means that with respect to the customer on a weekly visit, the retailer is a monopolist.

Wide variations exist on margins among groups of items and products. The retailer discriminates among products, selling some at margins very slightly above (sometimes below) invoice cost and pricing others at substantial amounts above cost. Discrimination that is optimal from the point of view of profit maximization should equate marginal cost with the marginal revenue associated with each segment of demand (Fuchs 1968). The demand for canned pears, for instance, may be less elastic than the demand for beef; the price of the retailing service associated with pears should therefore be higher. However, there is little evidence to show that retailers actually follow such discriminatory practices. Because of interrelated demand among their products, they may accept a low price and margin on an advertised item in order to bring shoppers into the store, on the assumption that they can sell as part of the market basket a substantial amount of other items. Total sales and profits may rise because of the pattern of purchases and the price structure on other items. There may be several combinations of margins that will result in the same profit, depending upon the number of shoppers attracted (Holdren 1960).

Despite a locally oligopolistic market structure, food retailers do not appear to collude on prices. There are several reasons for independent pricing policies. First, entry is relatively easy, even for nonoptimal size firms. Second, the complementarity of demands makes individual price cuts attractive. Because of the variety of competitive responses and ignorance of consumers, there is a long lag between the initiation of action and the time when competitors feel the results, so competitors are never sure what caused the changes in sales. Finally, differences in product lines among stores and differences in location make it very difficult for retailers to agree on price levels and structures that would satisfy each seller, even if there were no differences in personalities and skills of entrepreneurs (Holdren 1960).

PROFITS

Profits of a firm that are consistently above a competitive level are important but not conclusive evidence that market power is being exploited. If excess capacity is found associated with normal profits, there is a strong indication that the consumer is paying for the maintenance of too many stores. Prevalence of less than optimum size stores might suggest that the industry could give equal service with the use of fewer resources (Bain 1968).

The retail food industry's profit rates give no indications that consumers are being exploited by the large chains. Returns on net worth for food retailers are not out of line with those for other industries such as manufacturing, transportation or financial investments (such as bonds) (USDA 1977). Retail food distributors' profit rates (as a percentage of net worth) generally are in the 11–13% range. For example, in 1975, returns on net worth for the industry were 10.7% and in 1976 they rose to 12.8% (Food Mktg. Inst. 1977).

During the years 1956–1962, consumer demand shifted to the larger supermarkets. Until the number of supermarkets increased to respond to the demand, the existing ones may have earned a "quasi-rent" (Henderson and Quandt 1971). This may have been reflected in the earnings of the larger chains, which had a noticeably higher return on net worth from 1956 to 1962 than in the following years (Natl. Comm. Food Mktg. 1966).

The returns of the large chains dropped as more supermarkets were constructed. The very largest chains are not necessarily the most profitable. A study by the Federal Trade Commission showed that for 1964 there was no difference between the returns on net worth among three size groups of chains. Each group averaged approximately 11.0%, and all showed a declining trend, dropping approximately 25% from 1948 to 1964 (Natl. Comm. Food Mktg. 1966).

CONCLUSION

The food distribution industry has performed relatively well in the opinion of most economists. Most of the inefficiencies and inequities that persist today can be traced to the general rise in concentration which, however, antitrust legislation has helped restrain. Local oligopoly seems inevitable because of the relationship between the most efficient size of store and the territory from which it can draw customers, but the ease of entry at the local level hinders consumer exploitation. Food distribution performance could be improved even more if consumers were better educated and informed so that they could make purchase decisions which would more adequately answer their desires and at lower cost.

REFERENCES

ANON. 1978. Forty-fifth annual report of the grocery industry. Progr. Grocer *47* (119) 107.

BAIN, J.S. 1968. Industrial Organization. John Wiley & Sons, New York.

COTTERILL, R. 1978. Declining competition in food retailing. Mich. State Univ., Agric. Econ. Rep. *348*.

FOOD MKTG. INST. 1977. The Food Marketing Industry Speaks. Food Mktg. Inst., Washington, D.C.

FUCHS, V.R. 1968. The Service Economy. Natl. Bur. Econ. Res., Cambridge, Mass.

HAMMOND, L.H. 1967. Competition in Food Marketing. Paper presented at Agric. Policy Inst. Conf., Raleigh, N.C.

HENDERSON, J.M. and QUANDT, R.E. 1971. Microeconomic Theory. McGraw-Hill, New York.

HOLDREN, B. 1960. The Structure of a Retail Market and the Market Behavior of Retail Units. Prentice-Hall, Englewood Cliffs, N.J.

NATL. COMM. FOOD MKTG. 1966. Organization and Competition in Food Retailing. Natl. Comm. Food Mktg. Tech. Study No. *7*. U.S. Govt. Printing Off., Washington, D.C.

USDA. 1972. Market Structure of the Food Industries. USDA Econ. Res. Serv. *971*. U.S. Govt. Printing Off., Washington, D.C.

USDA. 1977. Market Performance in the Food Sector. Kenneth R. Farrell (Editor). USDA Econ. Res. Serv. *653*. U.S. Govt. Printing Off., Washington, D.C.

WALDORF, W.H. 1966. The demand for and supply of food marketing sources: An aggregate view. J. Farm Econ. *48*, 42–60.

14

General Equilibrium

EXCHANGE IN PRODUCTION

The same exchange analysis described in Chapter 13 can also be applied to production theory (Fig. 14.1). Isoquants take the place of the indifference curves in the Chapter 13 presentation, and the items on the axes now are inputs instead of goods. As described in Chapter 3, isoquants exist which reflect the technological possibilities of production of each good using various combinations of inputs. Assume for simplicity a two-good economy. There exists a fixed stock of labor and a fixed stock of capital, both of which must be allocated between the two goods in production. Suppose, for example, that 10 cooks and 30 pots exist for the preparation of food for 2 banquets. A given cook could use between 1 and, for example, 4 pots simultaneously depending on the amount of close attention each dish required. A dish that simply cooks for 1 hr as is requires much less attention than one to which something must be added or stirred every 5 min. Isoquants will exist describing the production of each banquet (assuming fixed menus, variable size of banquet) in terms of alternative cook/pot combinations. In Fig. 14.1, these isoquants are superimposed on each other as were the indifference curves in Fig. 13.2. The tangencies of the isoquants represent the equalities of marginal rates of substitution (given relative prices of cooks and pots) described in Chapter 3. The movement along the contract curve can be represented by a product transformation curve (Fig. 14.2); as more is produced of one good, less must be produced of another.

THE GENERAL EQUILIBRIUM SOLUTION

The resolutions of amounts of goods produced, factors used in their production, relative prices of goods and factors, and distribution of these goods are all interdependent. Assume that in this two-good economy society has made a choice of combination of goods it wants; in other

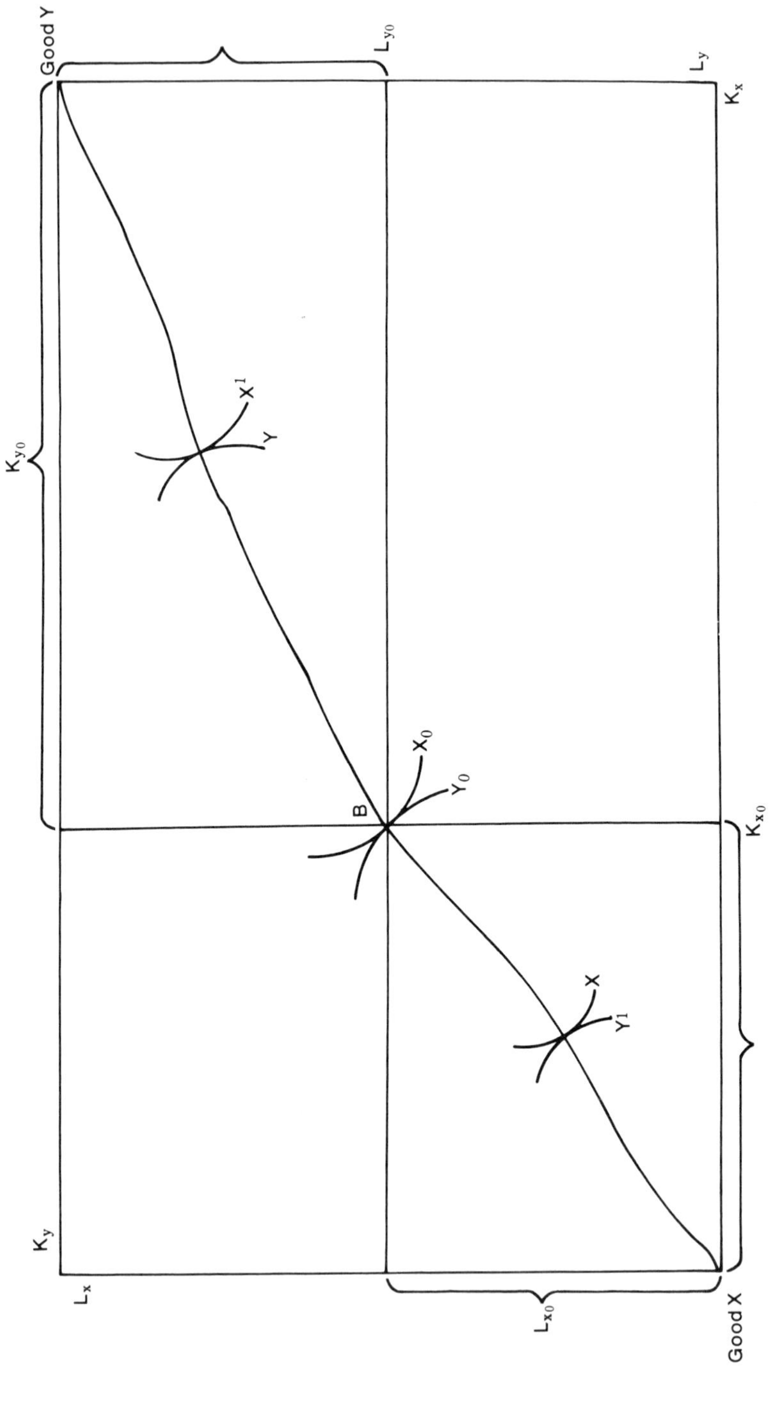

FIG. 14.1. EXCHANGE ANALYSIS IN PRODUCTION

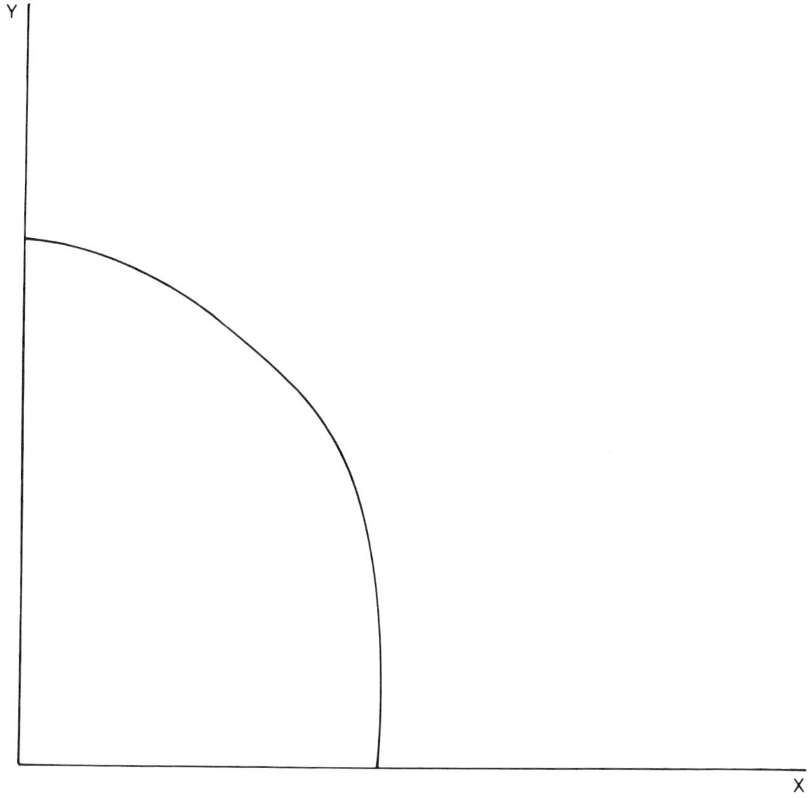

FIG. 14.2. PRODUCT TRANSFORMATION CURVE

words, the point on the product transformation curve that society thinks most desirable or gives society the greatest utility. The theoretical mechanisms of this choice have long been a subject of controversy; let it suffice for now that the choice is made. Assume this is point A (Fig. 14.3), with X_0 of X and Y_0 of Y. The choice itself, determining the relative scarcity of X and Y, will also determine their relative prices, P_x/P_y, denoted by the slope of the line passing through A.

Once X_0 and Y_0 have been determined, these quantities are the total quantities available for all consumers in the economy. Assume for graphic simplicity only two consumers exist. Then the same exchange theory as in the previous chapter applies, with X_0 the total quantity of X available between them and Y_0 the total quantity of Y. Prices this time are given from the societal choice of A and the resulting price ratio. Therefore, the allocation of goods between consumers will be denoted at that point

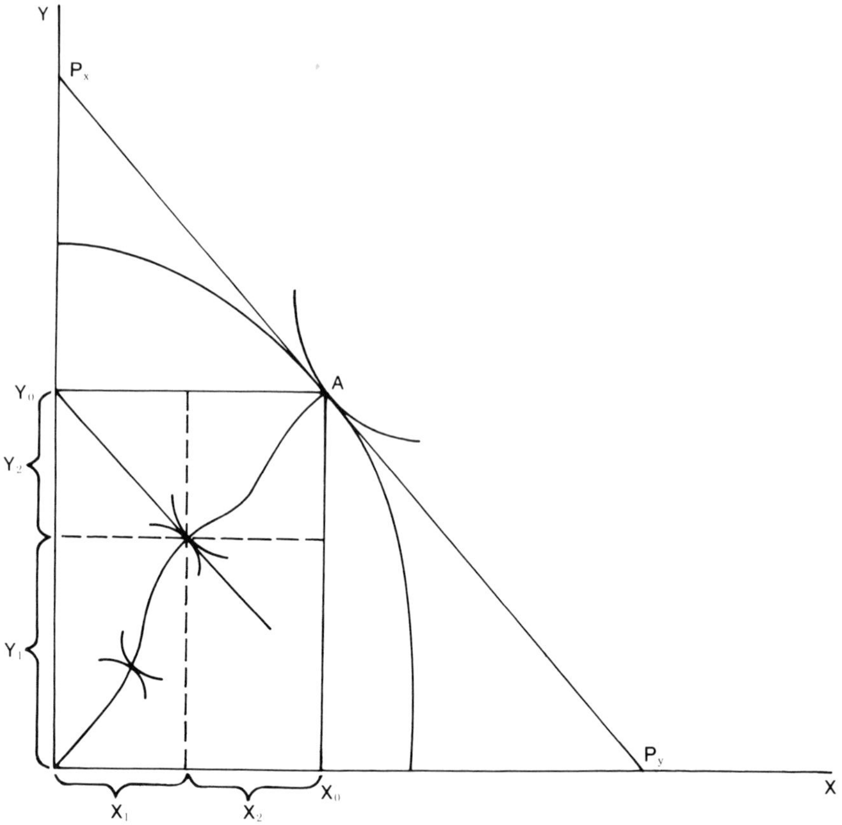

FIG. 14.3. SOCIETAL DETERMINATION OF AMOUNTS OF GOODS X AND Y TO BE PRODUCED

where their marginal rates of substitution are equal to each other (i.e., on the contract curve) *and* equal to the price ratio. A determinate point on the contract curve is thereby reached and distribution of goods is determined.

So far outputs, relative prices of goods and distribution of goods have been determined. The quantities used and prices of factors of production may also be derived from the above analysis.

As each point on the contract curve in Fig. 14.1 corresponds to a point on the product transformation curve in Fig. 14.2 and 14.3, point A in Fig. 14.3 will correspond to some point B in Fig. 14.1. The isoquants for goods X and Y in Fig. 14.1 (X_0 and Y_0) reflect the production of the quantities X_0 and Y_0 from Fig. 14.3. From point B in Fig. 14.1, one can easily determine the resources allocated to the production of each good. Further, since in equilibrium (from Chapter 3) the marginal rate of substitution must equal the ratio of input prices, the input price ratio is determined from the slope of a line tangent to both isoquants.

Assuming free markets and profit-maximizing behavior, each resource will be employed so that the value of its marginal product, equalling its marginal product times the price of the good it produces, equals its (input) price. In other words, $P_k = P_x\ MP_{k\ in\ x} = P_y\ MP_{k\ in\ y}$ and $P_L = P_x MP_{L\ in\ x} = P_y MP_{L\ in\ y}$. Since the marginal rate of (technical) substitution in production (MRTS) of each good must equal the price ratio of the inputs, $P_k = P_L$ (MRTS). Since the marginal rate of substitution in consumption (MRS) of each good must equal the price ratio of the goods produced, $P_x = P_y$ (MRS). Then, $P_L = P_y$ (MRS) ($MP_{L\ in\ x}$) and $P_k = P_y$ (MRS) ($MP_{L\ in\ x}$) (MRTS). MRS, MRTS and $MP_{L\ in\ x}$ are known. P_y/P_x is known, but the absolute levels of P_y and P_x are not. Since there are only two goods in this economy (assume a barter economy to dispense with the problem of currency), X may be taken as the unit of account and P_y may be expressed in terms of amounts of X for which Y could be exchanged. Thus, not only is P_y/P_x known, but for all practical purposes P_x may be taken to equal 1, so $P_y/P_x = P_y$ and P_L and P_k may be determined. The general equilibrium for the economy is then completely determined. However, only the ratios of prices are required for maximization of utility and output to occur. This general equilibrium may be extended to an economy with more than two goods through the use of algebra, though not through graphs. It can also be shown that the reverse process is also true; that fulfillment of these equilibrium conditions implies maximization of social welfare. The underlying principles, however, are the same.

QUALIFICATIONS

The preceding analysis indicates maximization of social welfare if and only if the market pricing system truly works. It assumes, in effect, that one gets what one pays for, no more and no less. With some types of goods, however, this is no longer true. In these cases, external economies or diseconomies may arise, or the good may be by nature a public good.

In the case of external economies, society is receiving more benefit from the production of a good than is the person who pays for the good. Social benefit exceeds private benefit. As the person who purchases the good does so on the basis of his or her private benefit from it, society would benefit from greater production of it than that which occurs. Although the preceding equilibrium conditions may be satisfied, society's welfare is not maximized. The classic example of this is enhanced honey production due to the presence of an apple orchard next door to a beekeeper. As the owner of the apple orchard does not realize personally the benefits from the honey production, apple production will likely occur at less than the socially optimal level.

With external diseconomies, cost to society exceeds cost to the individual producer. Since the individual produces only with reference to his or her private cost, production of the good will likely exceed that which is socially optimal. The traditional example here, and one which has received increased attention in recent years, is pollution of all sorts, particularly of air and water.

Public goods are those in which the consumption by one person does not decrease the consumption possible by another person. This is in contrast to private goods; normally, given production, if one person consumes more another must do with less. Examples of public goods include beautiful gardens, music and artwork. The producer of a public good will most likely produce less than the socially optimal amount, since he or she will consider only his or her private benefits from it.

All the cited cases involve divergence from marginal cost-marginal benefit equality at the social level, though not at the private level. However, even a divergence at the private level may be involved. In the case of a natural technical monopoly, average cost constantly declines (for example, in some public utilities). Society may permit the monopoly to develop. In this case, while private marginal costs and benefits are equal, social marginal benefit exceeds social marginal cost. This is the problem with any monopoly, due to inequality of price and marginal cost. But since the marginal cost curve is always below the average cost curve, at a price low enough to equal marginal cost the firm would be earning a pure loss and not voluntarily produce the socially desired output. In any case, where a natural monopoly exists, true social welfare maximization is thwarted.

The preceding has considered only allocative efficiency in the maximization of social welfare and the resulting general equilibrium solution. However, allocative efficiency constitutes only one aspect of efficiency. Dynamic efficiency, meaning conditions most conducive to economic growth, is also important. Leibenstein (1966), for example, argues that the social welfare loss due to monopoly is extremely small and one should instead primarily concern oneself with what he calls "X-efficiency," or the incentives for greater productivity of existing resources in their existing allocation. This deals in large part with organizational and motivational theories. Other theorists are primarily concerned with capital investment as a means of promoting future growth; any allocative inefficiency today, they argue, will be more than compensated by the greater quantities available of all goods tomorrow. As shown previously, dynamic and static allocative efficiency are interdependent.

It is beyond the scope of this book on (static) resource allocation and price theory to debate the relative merits of allocative *vs* dynamic efficiency if these must be incompatible, especially in the absence of much hard evidence and the abundance of value judgments required concerning the priority of present *vs* future generations' consumption, but the importance of dynamic efficiency to static resource allocation cannot be denied.

REFERENCES

LEIBENSTEIN, H. 1966. Allocative efficiency *vs* X-efficiency. Am. Econ. Rev. *June*, 392–413.

CHAPTER 14: REVIEW QUESTIONS

(1) Discuss the meaning and significance of the notion of equilibrium in economic analysis. In your discussion, point out its importance in statics, comparative statics and dynamics.

(2) Explain carefully each of the following economic concepts. Give a specific illustration or example of a type of analysis in which each might be used:
   (a) partial equilibrium analysis
   (b) general equilibrium analysis
   (c) static analysis
   (d) comparative statics
   (e) dynamic analysis
   (f) external economies and diseconomies
   (g) general Pareto optimality

(3) It can be argued that free-market forces in a private enterprise economy will lead to an "optimum allocation of resources." Explain what is meant by an optimum allocation of resources. Develop an argument in which you explain in a logical fashion how such a situation might be achieved in a free-market economy. Describe briefly the circumstances under which optimum resource allocation would not be achieved in a free-market economy.

(4) Explain the elements which will determine the amount of productive factors hired by the firm, from the standpoint of general equilibrium analysis.

(5) From society's point of view, is it ever expedient to knowingly accept inefficiencies in the marketing system? Explain.

(6) What is the importance of the marginal concept in analysis?

Index

mikroökonomi